The Quest for Security in the Caribbean

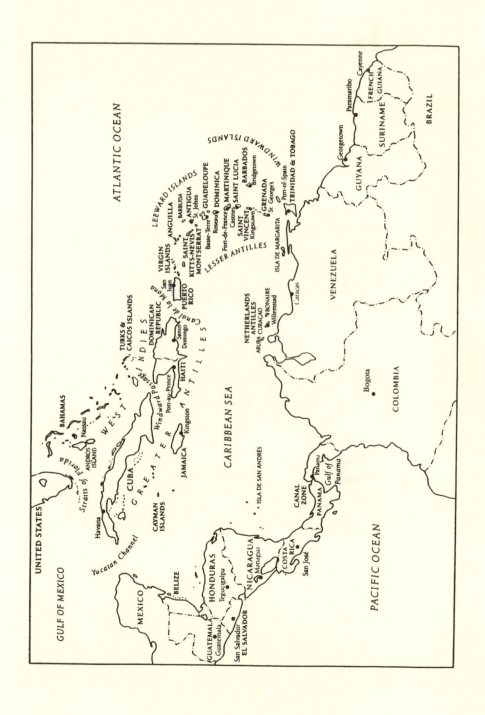

The Quest for Security in the Caribbean

Problems and Promises in Subordinate States

Ivelaw Lloyd Griffith

M. E. Sharpe
Armonk, New York
London, England

Copyright © 1993 by M. E. Sharpe, Inc.

Library of Congress Cataloging-in-Publication Data

Griffith, Ivelaw L.
The quest for security in the Caribbean:
problems and promises in subordinate states / Ivelaw L. Griffith.
p. cm.
Includes bibliographical references and index.
ISBN 1-56324-089-0
1. Caribbean Area—National security.
I. Title.
UA609.G75   1993′
355′.0330729—dc20
92-31398
CIP

Printed in the United States of America

The paper used in this publication meets the minimum requirements of
American National Standard for Information Sciences—
Permanence of Paper for Printed Library Materials,
ANSI Z39.48–1984.

MV   10   9   8   7   6   5   4   3   2   1

TO
Francille, my loving wife,
and to
Mothers who fathered me

- Sybil Griffith, my natural mother
- Lucy Roberts, my grandmother
- Waveney Felix, my foster mother
- Geraldine Thomas, my godmother

CONTENTS

TABLES and FIGURES

Tables

Figures

PREFACE AND ACKNOWLEDGEMENTS

A fall 1981 journalistic assignment took me across the equator, on a twenty-seven-hour round trip from Guyana to Melbourne, Australia, for the Commonwealth of Nations Heads of Government Meeting. My interest in small-state security problems dates from that conference, where the late Maurice Bishop of Grenada and leaders of other small states, including Fiji, Vanuatu, and the Seychelles, highlighted actual and potential threats to their countries and called for more collective safeguards.

Two years later there was the Grenada affair, a series of events involving factional disputes within the Bishop government that culminated in United States intervention. The Grenada episode dramatized the need for greater attention to the internal and external security of small states. The Commonwealth leaders met shortly after the Grenada affair in New Delhi, India. They responded to this need by issuing the *Goa Declaration on International Security*. Later, in keeping with a mandate of the New Delhi meeting, an expert group was convened to study the security problems of small states in the Commonwealth of Nations. Its report was published in 1985 as *Vulnerability: Small States in the Global Society*. Since then, several small states, both in and out of the Commonwealth, have faced either new or continuing internal and external security problems. This book examines security dilemmas facing one region of small states, the Commonwealth Caribbean.

For reasons too numerous to explain here, research on Caribbean security is a very difficult proposition. Completion of this study is, therefore, partly attributable to the assistance of several people and institutions, only some of whom can be named here. Several people provided data sources, among them: Wilfred Elrington in Belize; Compton Hendy in Barbados; Peter Laurie, Theresa Marshall, Yvette Goddard, and Philo Best of the Barbados Foreign Ministry; Patrick Lewis, Ambassador of Antigua-Barbuda to the United States and the

Organization of American States; Dion Phillips of the University of the Virgin Islands; Assistant Superintendent Stephen Roberts of the Royal Grenada Police Force; and Godfrey Springer in the Bahamas.

Thanks also to Puis Bannis of York College; Frank Campbell, former Caribbean Community and Common Market (CARICOM) Foreign Affairs Officer; Thelma Ferguson, Deputy Permanent Secretary, Bahamas Ministry of National Security; Volville Forsythe of the Caribbean Development Bank; Brigadier David Granger, former National Security Adviser to the President of Guyana; Jennifer Hackett of the CARICOM Secretariat; Hilary Harker of the Jamaican Mission to the United Nations; Sheila Hazelwood of the Guyana Mission to the United Nations; Anne Langhaug of the United States Agency for International Development (USAID); Patricia Phillips of the Trinidad and Tobago Mission to the United Nations; and Lt. Commander Peter Tomlin of the Regional Security System (RSS), who retired in 1992.

The Organization of American States (OAS) and the City University of New York (CUNY) Graduate School provided research support during 1987 and 1988. CUNY librarians Jean-Jacques Strayer, Marve Brooks, Olga Torres-Seda, and Jeanne Hodgson provided invaluable help with library material from near and far. Preparation of the manuscript was aided by a 1991 Shuster Fellowship from Lehman College and by support from the Bronx Institute and its Director, Donna Kirchheimer. Helpful comments on manuscript drafts were provided by Asher Arian, CUNY; Jacqueline Braveboy-Wagner, CUNY; Anthony Bryan, North-South Center, University of Miami; Neville Duncan, University of the West Indies, Barbados; Brigadier Granger; Howard Lentner, CUNY; Commander Tomlin; and Donald Zagoria, CUNY.

My students Erlene Ellis, Eric Holder, and Alvin Mitchell provided various forms of assistance. Wanda Hughes of Lehman College helped me prepare the Selected Bibliography. My wife, Francille, and Wanda assisted with the tables and figures. Francille also provided the kind of support and understanding during stints away from home and during the preparation of drafts without which I could never have completed this project with my sanity intact. Thanks to all of them. Shortcomings in this work are, however, entirely mine.

ILG
Far Rockaway, New York
October 1992

The Quest for
Security in
the Caribbean

1 INTRODUCTION

Small states by their nature are weak and vulnerable.... Sometimes it seems as if small states were like small boats pushed out into a turbulent sea, free in one sense to traverse it; but, without oars or provisions, without compass or sails, free also to perish. Or perhaps, to be rescued and taken on board a larger vessel.
—Sir Shridath Ramphal
Former Commonwealth Secretary-General

This book examines security problems of the English-speaking Caribbean, also known as the Commonwealth Caribbean. The area's security concerns have received little comprehensive attention in the past, with writers doing either country case studies or focusing on selected issues.[1] Otherwise, Caribbean security problems have been examined as tangents to the interests of the United States or of European powers.

The approach here is different. The interests of the United States and of European and other countries are not ignored, but I focus directly on the Caribbean. And while case studies and selected works have been invaluable and will continue to be so, there is equal value in the holistic approach adopted here. Although I deal sometimes with countries in the Caribbean littoral, my primary concern is with Antigua-Barbuda, the Bahamas, Barbados, Belize, Dominica, Grenada, Guyana, Jamaica, St. Kitts-Nevis, St. Lucia, St. Vincent and the Grenadines, and Trinidad and Tobago. These are the independent member-countries of CARICOM—the Caribbean Community and Common Market.

These countries form a region by virtue of their geographic proximity, social and cultural homogeneity, political interdependence through shared institutions, and economic interdependence. They also constitute a subordinate state system, with geographic delimitation and recognition by others as constituting a distinctive community. These states also identify themselves as a community, accept that their units of power are relatively inferior to those in the dominant state system, and realize that changes in the dominant system have greater effect on them than the reverse.[2]

The security problems of Caribbean states fit the larger portrait of small-state security dilemmas. The preeminent issue is vulnerability. Other important concerns are internal instability, intervention, and militarization. Although there are differing definitions of the security situation in the Caribbean, several issues recur in the literature and in conversations with political actors in the region.

The first is the military, political, and economic vulnerability of Caribbean states, both individually and as a subordinate state system, to the foreign policy and security actions of the United States, other important hemispheric actors such as Brazil, Cuba, and Venezuela, of other states, such as Britain, and to such international financial institutions as the International Monetary Fund (IMF).

A second issue is the need for domestic stability in the face of several episodes: invasion scares in Barbados in 1976, 1978, and 1979; rebellion in St. Vincent and the Grenadines in 1979; the overthrow of the Gairy government in Grenada in 1979; coup attempts in Dominica in 1981; factional disputes in Grenada in 1983 that precipitated United States intervention; an army mutiny in Trinidad and Tobago in 1970, and a bloody coup attempt there in July-August 1990. There is the need to protect territorial sovereignty, and to guard against the militarization manifested in a few states in the 1970s and early 1980s. Problems of economic insecurity because of economic vulnerability and economic deficiencies are also quite critical. And finally, drug problems are becoming increasingly important.

Although the exact nature of these problems might be disputed, there are undoubtedly both internal and external dimensions to the causes and consequences of the region's security problems. Responses to the region's problems have led to several initiatives. One is the Regional Security System (RSS), a security mechanism created in October 1982 through a Memorandum of Understanding (MOU). Antigua-Barbuda, Barbados, Dominica, St. Lucia, and St. Vincent and the Grenadines are the original members. St. Kitts-Nevis joined in February 1984, and Grenada followed in January 1985.

The Security of Small States

The military, political, and economic dimensions of the security of small states are the most critical ones. A variety of threats can arise in each area. In the military area there could be civil war, terrorism, foreign intervention, or war with other nations. In the political one factionalism, destabilization, protracted social conflict, and coups could present grave threats. And huge foreign debts, economic mismanagement, and famine are some of the critical economic threat areas. Some states face multiple threats in more than one dimension.[3] Overall, the main security problem areas in these three dimensions are vulnerability, internal instability, intervention, and militarization.

Vulnerability arises where geographic, political, economic, or other factors cause a nation's security to be compromised. It is not usually a function of any single factor. Those factors that combine to create it result in the removal or reduction of a state's influence or power, thereby opening it up to internal subversion or external incursion. Some writers feel that small states are "inherently vulnerable" because they can be perceived as potentially easy victims for all forms of external aggression.[4] This, however, is only part of the problem. What other states perceive is certainly important. But vulnerability relates to objective geographical, economic, political, and organizational deficiencies such as populations that are too small to meet security needs, limited ability to acquire defense-related material, and fragile economies.

One study identified six factors of vulnerability: great power rivalries; territorial claims; possession of rich resources; provision of refuge to refugees or freedom fighters; corruption; and suppression of democracy.[5] Military and political vulnerability often dominate the analysis of this dilemma, but it is increasingly recognized that economic vulnerability is significant in its own right, and affects military and political vulnerability.[6] Edward Azar and Chung-in Moon, for example, identify three kinds of threats related to economic vulnerability: systemic vulnerability threats; sensitivity dependence threats; structural dependence threats. With the first,

states are exposed to the transmission of external economic disturbances originating in the international system. The second stems from
transactions among states based on asymmetric relationships. The third
compromises economic sovereignty by the existence of distorted economic structures and production relationships.[7]

Internal political instability, protracted in some places, recurring in
others, is for many small states the most dangerous security threat.
Instability can result from political factionalism, economic deprivation,
military coups, ethnic or racial conflict, civil war, or insurgency. Sri
Lanka, Haiti, the Sudan, Liberia, Surinam, Lebanon, and El Salvador
are but a few Third World states with differing kinds of political instability during the late 1980s and early 1990s. Whatever its source or
explanation, internal political instability undermines domestic order
and sometimes external security.[8]

Political stability requires attention to at least four matters: political
authority; political equality; political participation; and political legitimacy. The first relates to a reciprocal relationship between government and people where the former manages the society and the
latter accept and consent to that rule. The second implies the possession of rights by citizens to participate actively in the political process. The third involves the ability of citizens to influence the nature
and operation of the political system through institutions such as
political parties, unions, and free media. Political legitimacy, the
fourth, requires that the governing body be appropriate, widely representative, and have the capability to govern. It is the absence of all
or some of these in small states that creates problems of internal
instability.[9]

The issue of fair political representation in any single country is a
matter of increasing concern for the international community. Gone are
the days when "internal political questions" are left solely to nationals
of a state. The link between political instability and means of acquiring
legitimacy is progressively a compelling reason for international observers to give their imprimatur to elections. Observers come from
both governmental and non-governmental bodies. As one writer observed, "From its humble beginning, observing elections has grown
into a major political industry."[10] In Latin America, for instance,
while there is a long history of observing elections, recently there
have been dramatic examples of this: in Chile and Panama in 1989,
Nicaragua and Haiti in 1990, Haiti and Surinam in 1991, and Guyana

in 1992. Indeed, there was a small army of 2,500 observers in Nicaragua for the February 1990 elections, coming from the United Nations, the OAS, the Atlanta-based Carter Center, Americas Watch, and other groups.

Intervention, the third problem area, could be defined in very broad terms. Joseph Nye, Jr., for example, argues: "Intervention is a matter of degree, with actions ranging from statements and limited economic measures at the low end of the spectrum, to full-fledged invasions at the high end."[11] Nevertheless, here intervention is defined as the forceful intrusion by a state or entities from it, such as mercenary or terrorist groups, into the territorial and political jurisdiction of another. Societies that are victims of intervention are generally politically unstable and in dispute over a central political authority. Panama in 1989, Grenada in 1983, Seychelles in 1981, Uganda in 1979, and Lebanon on several occasions since 1975 are examples of this.

States intervene in the affairs of others for a variety of reasons: to fulfill ideological commitments; to secure influence; and for strategic considerations, among other things.[12] Potential interveners must consider the degree of cohesion in the target society. They could be constrained by adversaries, their own military limitations, economic costs, and the state of international relations at the time. Changes in international politics since the Second World War have led to a climate in which the international community deprecates unilateral intervention by big powers, leading, among other things, to a decline in big power intervention. This decline has been replaced by intervention of Third World states in the affairs of others.[13] Some of the more notable cases are Vietnam in Laos and Cambodia; Indonesia in Malaysia, and in West Irian and East Timor; Jamaica, Barbados, and others (alongside the United States) in Grenada; Tanzania in Uganda; Libya in Chad.

The latest case of significance, in the Middle East, was unprecedented, both in terms of Arab-Arab relations, and in terms of collective action taken by the international community against a single state. Iraqi troops stormed into Kuwait on August 2, 1990, occupied the country, and drove the Kuwaiti leader—Sheik Jaber al-Ahmed al-Sabak—into exile. This action plunged the area into a new crisis involving confrontation with the international community, especially the United States and Egypt, when Iraq seemed poised to invade Saudi Arabia. Iraq's adamance in the face of the United Nations' insistence upon its withdrawal from Kuwait eventually led to the forty-two-day war against it by a United States-led coalition of states. The war ended with Iraqi acceptance of United Nations Security Council Resolution 687, adopted April 3, 1991. Iraq was expelled from Kuwait and made to accept all the Security Council resolutions dealing with compensation, recognition of Kuwaiti sovereignty, restitution of their government, and other issues.[14] However, as of fall 1992 some of these issues were still unresolved.

Finally, there is the problem of militarization. It involves increasing the allocation of resources for the development, purchase, and deployment of military equipment and forces. Betty Sedoc-Dahlberg identifies several indexes of this phenomenon: percentage of budget allocated for military purposes; total size of armed forces; level, number, and kind of political positions held by military officials; the status of the military in the decision-making process.[15] As used here, militarization is not necessarily a function of military intervention in politics in the sense used in *The Man on Horseback*: "The armed forces' substitution of their own policies and or their persons, for those of the recognized civilian authorities."[16] It could result from the military's control over a civilian regime, or from that model of civilian control where "civilian governors obtain loyalty and obedience by penetrating the armed forces with political ideas and political personnel."[17] In the latter case, the army practically becomes an arm of the ruling party and is compensated with accretions of money, equipment, and personnel, as happened in Guyana during the 1970s and early 1980s.

Some writers argue that militarization was an option chosen by several states because of a fear of neocolonialism. Others contend that often it was inevitable since the military was the institution to which ex-colonial powers transferred authority. But one critic maintains that:

> In most Third World states, however, the quest for arms is often unrelated to security needs; hypothetical external threats and the responsibility to preserve law and order are only convenient arguments for extravagant militarization. The desire for prestige and the determination to stay in power have been, more often than not, the true incentives of many governments to build up armed forces and acquire unnecessary sophisticated and expensive military hardware.[18]

Vulnerability, internal instability, intervention, and militarization are often interrelated, with one problem leading to another or facilitating it. I have already explained how internal instability can precipitate intervention. Militarization may be pursued as a solution to instability problems, or it can result from attempts by political elites to cushion the effects of their military vulnerability. These problem categories are not exclusive to small states. Some are problems for middle powers, big powers, and even the superpowers at various times.

Vulnerability has been a problem for China, France, Poland, and others. Rumania, the former Yugoslavia, and the now defunct USSR are among the many states that have experienced instability in recent times. There was a bloody coup attempt in Venezuela as recent as November 27, 1992. Intervention has been a concern for India, China, Germany, and others. And militarization has been a problem for Vietnam, the former USSR, Indonesia, and others. Although some of these states are in the Third World, none of them is small in terms of size, population, GNP, and military capability. It is the "soft" nature of small states, the capability limitations from which they suffer, and the extent to which they could be subordinated to others in the international community that make these problems all the more acute for them.

States encountering the gamut of problems referred to above have used several countervailing measures, with varying degrees of success. These have included unilateral action to resolve social conflict; alternative economic strategies; legitimation of regimes; and neutrality. On the collaborative side, states have pursued alliances, non-alignment, regional cooperation, or regional integration. Most states adopt complementary safeguards, from both the unilateral and the collaborative areas.

Studying Small State Security

The scholarship on small-state security has expanded over the years in several significant ways. First, the preoccupation with external security has given way to recognition that internal security questions are not only important in their own right, but they complicate (and sometimes aggravate) external problems. Moreover, the distinction between internal issues and external ones is becoming increasingly blurred.[19]

Second, the tendency to cast security analysis in military-political terms has been replaced by acceptance that security concerns go beyond these to the economic arena. Some scholars address ecological and environmental issues as well, arguing that these also qualify for substantive security treatment because of their impact on the survival of states.[20] A third change lies in the recognition of and emphasis on the link between security and development.[21] Robert Rothstein, a scholar whose work now reflects a departure from the conventional approach to which he once subscribed, describes part of the change this way: "The traditional concern with territorial integrity and political independence has had to be broadened to include a concern with domestic stability—and thus also a concern with prospects for, and means of, domestic development."[22]

Quite accurately, Barry Buzan explains:

> With the nuclear paralysis imposed on the rational use of force among the great powers, political and societal issues have come more to the foreground in their own right. As the military security agenda has become more static, those for economics and the ecology have become more dynamic and more central to day-to-day concerns. . . . The linkage of economic and environmental events throughout the [international] system is becoming increasingly visible, ranging from weather patterns and acid rain, to interest rates, currency values, and stock market prices. All these developments . . . point to the centrality of interdependence in security issues.[23]

As might be expected, this expansion and refocusing of security has been accompanied by several new conceptual approaches to the subject. For example, Azar and Moon suggest a multidimensional approach with four facets—military, political, ecological, and protracted ethnic or social conflict—and policy responses relevant to the various dimensions. They examine the security dilemmas of Lebanon and South Korea within this framework to demonstrate its utility.[24] To facilitate the appreciation of security interdependence, Barry Buzan introduced the concept of "security complex": "a group of states whose primary security concerns link together sufficiently closely that their national security concerns cannot realistically be considered apart from one another."[25]

Robert Rothstein argues for a pretheory based on the conviction that "grand generalizations miss important differences between apparently similar countries, and case studies or regional analyses provide little general guidance about either policy or theory."[26] He recognizes the existence of several problems and declares the need for a more differentiated analytic approach. Preliminary to this would be a pretheory to categorize and differentiate developing countries and to stimulate development of a conceptual framework that facilitates explanatory hypotheses. For him, the problems of most Third World countries do not arise from universal structural constraints, but from limited power capability, domestic disorder, and from threat perception by small ruling elites.

The security challenges for the small states in the Third World are considered linked with problems of development. The common features of these two relate to threat perception, resource constraints, and legitimacy. The concern of the elites is not only with external threats to national survival, but with internal challenges to their rule. Resource constraints not only narrow the range of elite choices, but incline them to increase coercion and repression. Linked to all this is legitimacy. The degree of their own legitimacy perceived by the ruling elite is likely to affect the perception of threats and the use of resources to deal with them. Rothstein emphasizes linkages among domestic security, development choices, and the provision of greater international resources. It is improbable that significant external resources will be provided. Anyhow, additional external resources do not guarantee greater spending on development and less on security. He suggests, though, that the absence of such resources almost guarantees that security will get priority attention by ruling elites.[27]

Because security is a highly contested concept with a multiplicity of definitions and usages, it is important to state the working definition of the term that guides this study. Arnold Wolfers once offered an attractive proposition: "Security, in any objective sense, measures the absence of threats to acquired values, in a subjective sense, the absence of fear that such values will be attacked."[28] However, that proposition raises so many questions that it is necessary to pursue a more explicit statement. Thus, I am drawn to the conception of security as the protection and preservation of a people's freedom from external military attack and coercion, freedom from internal subversion, and from the erosion of cherished political, economic, and social values.

This definition is multidimensional, and goes beyond the confines of the Realist "high politics" notion of security. As will become clear in this book, military power and power relations, the fundamentals of traditional Realism, are important in the Caribbean.[29] However, one needs to go beyond these to understand the problems and promises of Caribbean security. I consider perception, capability, geography, and ideology to be the factors central to understanding the security circumstances of small states in the Caribbean and elsewhere, such as the Pacific, where some or all of the problems mentioned above have been experienced.[30] These factors are interactive, each having several elements. Perception is a function of education, social class, and the international environment, among other things. Capability involves size of territory and population, strength of military, governmental organization, nature of economy, and international support relationships. Geography relates primarily to spatial location, land form and density, and climate. Ideology is shaped by several elements, including beliefs, political consciousness, and level of political activism.

Security does not relate to any single factor. The elements of these factors are dynamic. A simple way to appreciate this is to remember that although there are objective factors that affect a state's security—such as territorial claims or ethnic conflict—its security concerns are largely defined by the elites. The key here is their perception. How those elites define their security problems relates to their worldview, the strength or weakness of the state, and the location of the state. The kinds of security mechanisms that the state creates would depend on its capabilities, on the elite assessments of the need for such, and on the location of the state, among other things. And the ideological posture of a state is not only affected by its elite images; it also influences the state's international support relationships.

Each of the four factors is important. Perception is crucial to security because policy choices are based on the images of policymakers. In small states, policy-making is usually dominated by single leaders, and the narrow institutional basis for decision making magnifies the importance of the leaders' images. Moreover, the consequences of misperception may lead to conflict.[31] Capability is vital because security should depend essentially on national capacity. External threats become more credible where capability is low, and consciousness of low capability could influence the perception of threats and the intentions of others, and thereby help determine policy choices. In addition, awareness of capability limitations could trigger preemptive measures in situations of tension.[32]

The importance of geography derives from several things. Geographical factors like small size or large size and low population density create vulnerability. Furthermore, geography includes the advantages or disadvantages of being close to large and powerful states and to vital Sea Lanes of Communication (SLOCs). It is also crucial because it affects foreign and security policy since the security options of small states rarely, if ever, avoid being influenced by proximate big powers.[33] Finally, ideology helps to shape images held by the elite. Ideological differences could be the basis for conflict, both domestically and with other states. As Kalevi Holsti has remarked, "Men have frequently gone to war over [ideological] ideas."[34] Similarly, ideological consensus could be the basis for security collaboration between or among states. Moreover, ideology could be the tool for deflecting attention from domestic crisis to external issues, thereby precipitating conflict with other state or non-state actors.[35]

Conclusion

I posit that coming to terms with the security problems and prospects of Caribbean countries requires understanding the perceptions of their political elites, their security capability, the geopolitical environment in which the countries exist, and the ideological matrixes affecting them. Using these factors as a theoretical framework, I examine the security problems of the Caribbean, look at security measures adopted there, and explore some steps Caribbean states might take to safeguard their interests as we move further into the final decade of the twentieth century.

Chapter two examines the perception-security nexus by identifying the security decision makers in the Caribbean, assessing their definitions of the region's security concerns and threats, and explaining some of the implications of their perceptions. The argument is made that while perception is not the sole determinant of security policy, it has been a neglected factor in efforts to interpret security action taken by Caribbean leaders. The chapter shows that security policymaking revolves around dominant leaders who have a range of military, political, and economic security concerns.

The capabilities of Caribbean states is the subject of chapter three. The institutional, human, natural, and military resources of the region are outlined, as are its international relationships. I show that although some Caribbean states have oil and bauxite, the region is resource poor. There is heavy reliance on a few products and on foreign economic and technical assistance. I conclude that Caribbean capabilities are insufficient for security measures that could rely primarily on countries in the region.

In light of the region's capability limitations, chapters four, five, and six examine the security measures Caribbean states have adopted over the years since becoming independent. Chapters four and five look at individual country measures, and chapter six assesses collaborative measures. In looking at the latter, particular attention is paid to the RSS. I find the RSS to be a significant initiative, but it is a halfway measure that fails to redress meaningfully the virtual external security dependency of the region.

Chapter seven analyses the geography-security nexus. Attention is paid to the Caribbean's strategic character, to the geopolitical interests of the United States and of big and middle powers inside and outside the hemisphere, and to the manner in which the pursuit of these interests affect the Commonwealth Caribbean. The argument is made that the United States, Venezuela, and other states affect Caribbean security partly because they have subordinated and can continue to subordinate Commonwealth Caribbean states to their interests. The discussion suggests that historical contacts, trade patterns, transportation and communications linkages, and ideology are among the features that affect the nature of the region's geopolitics and the security measures that Caribbean states adopt.

The ideology factor comes under scrutiny in chapter eight. Ideology has been important because it has contributed to internal instability, fueled militarization, and helped to precipitate the 1983 Grenada intervention. Moreover, it once helped to undermine the regional integration movement. Ideology also has been a key to whether the United States dispensed rewards or punishments to Caribbean states. Chapter eight discusses ideological doctrines in the Caribbean and shows the decisive shift from a left-orientation to a right-orientation by Caribbean ruling parties over the last two decades. It also explains the domestic and international variables that accounted for the change.

Chapter nine is dedicated to examining drugs, the single most critical security question in the region. Narcotics production, abuse, and trafficking, and money laundering are identified as the main problems. These have presented political, military, and economic dilemmas, especially corruption, gun running, and a negative impact on tourism. Mention is also made of countermeasures adopted by states in the region, including passage of tough anti-narcotics legislation, the revocation of banking licenses, and signature of mutual assistance treaties. Finaly, chapter ten offers some safeguards that might be useful in the forthcoming decade.

Notes

1. Of course, there is nothing wrong with this. Indeed, it is necessary. I also have done it. See Ivelaw L. Griffith, ed., *Strategy and Security in the Caribbean*, New York: Praeger, 1991.

2. The regional and subordinate state system characterizations here are based on Michael Banks, "Systems Analysis and the Study of Regions," *International Studies Quarterly* 13 (December 1969): 335–60; Michael Brecher, "The Subordinate State System of Southern Asia," in James N. Rosenau, ed., *International Politics and Foreign Policy*, New York: The Free Press, 1969; and Louis Cantori and Steven Speigel, *International Politics of Regions: A Comparative Approach*, Englewood Cliffs, NJ: Prentice Hall, 1970.

3. One example of this is Lebanon, which simultaneously has faced a variety of threats: civil war, terrorism, and intervention in the military area; factionalism and destabilization in the political area; and high debt in the economic one. Other examples in the 1980s are Angola, Cambodia, Nicaragua, Somalia, and Zaire.

4. See, for example, Commonwealth Study Group (hereinafter CSG), *Vulnerability: Small States in the Global Society*, London: Commonwealth Secretariat, 1985, p. 15.

5. Sheila Harden, ed., *Small Is Dangerous: Micro-states in a Macro World*, New York: St. Martin's Press, 1985, p. 13.

6. For military and political aspects, see Robert L. Rothstein, *The Weak in the World of the Strong*, New York: Columbia University Press, 1977; David Vital, *The Inequality of States*, Oxford: Clarendon Press, 1985; Michael Handel, *Weak States in the International System*, London: Frank Cass, 1981; George Quester, "Trouble in the Islands: Defending the Micro-states," *International Security* 8 (Fall 1983): 160–75. For economic aspects, see CSG, *Vulnerability*, 1985; Edward Azar and Chung-in Moon, "Third World National Security: Toward a New Conceptual Framework," *International Interactions* 11 (No. 2, 1984): 103–135; Stephen Krasner, "Third World Vulnerability and Global Negotiations," in Robert Art and Robert Jervis, eds., *International Politics: Anarchy, Force, Political Economy, and Decision-making*, Boston: Little, Brown, 1985; and York Bradshaw and Zwelakhe Tshandu, "Foreign Capital Penetration, State Intervention and Development in Sub-Saharan Africa," *International Studies Quarterly* 34 (June 1990): 229–51.

7. Azar and Moon, "Third World National Security," 1984.

8. See Zalmay Khalilzad, "The Politics of Ethnicity in Southwest Asia: Political Development or Political Decay?" *Political Science Quarterly* 99 (Winter 1984–85): 657–79; Edward Azar and Chung-in Moon, "Managing Protracted So-

cial Conflict in the Third World: Facilitation and Development Diplomacy," *Millennium: Journal of International Studies* 15 (No. 3, 1986): 393–406; Anthony Maingot, "Haiti: Problems of a Transition to Democracy in an Authoritarian Soft State," *Journal of Interamerican Studies and World Affairs* 28 (No. 4, 1987–88): 75–102; and José Garcia, "Tragedy in El Salvador," *Current History* January 1990, pp. 9ff.

9. See Perry Mars, "The Conditions of Political Stability," *GISRA* 6 (No. 1, 1975): 1–6; Samuel Huntington, *Political Order in Changing Societies*, New Haven: Yale University Press, 1968; and Charles Andrain, *Political Change in the Third World*, Boston: Unwin Hyman, 1988.

10. William Crotty, "The Political Scientist as Comparative Election Observer," *PS: Political Science and Politics* 24 (No. 1, 1991): 64.

11. Joseph S. Nye, Jr., "What New World Order?" *Foreign Affairs* 71 (Spring 1992): 92.

12. See Neil MacFarlane, *Intervention and Regional Security*, Adelphi Papers No. 196, London: International Institute for Strategic Studies, 1985; Zalmay Khalilzad, "Intervention in Afghanistan: Implications for the Security of Southwest Asia," in William Dowdy and Russel Trood, eds., *The Indian Ocean: Perspectives on a Strategic Arena*, Durham, NC: Duke University Press, 1985; and Peter Schraeder, ed., *Intervention in the 1980s: U.S. Foreign Policy in the Third World*, Boulder, CO: Lynne Rienner, 1989.

13. See Talukder Maniruzzaman, *The Security of Small States in the Third World*, Canberra Papers on Strategy and Defense No. 25, Canberra, Australia: The Strategic and Defense Studies Center, 1982; Jagat Mehta, ed., *Third World Militarization*, Austin, TX: LBJ School of Public Affairs, 1985; and MacFarlane, *Intervention and Regional Security*, 1985.

14. See R.W. Apple, Jr., "Invading Iraqis Seize Kuwait and its Oil; U.S. Condemns Attack, Urges United Action," *New York Times*, August 3, 1990, pp. A1, A8; R.W. Apple, Jr., "Allies Destroy Iraqis' Main Force; Kuwait is Retaken after Seven Months," *New York Times*, February 28, 1991, pp. A1, A9; and Allan Crowell, "Truce Now Official," *New York Times*, April 7, 1991, pp. L1, L14. For a comprehensive analysis of the Gulf crisis and the war, see Micah L. Sifry and Christopher Cerf, eds., *The Gulf War Reader: History, Documents, Opinions*, New York: Times Books, 1991.

15. See her "Interest Groups and the Military in Surinam," in Alma H. Young and Dion E. Phillips, eds., *Militarization in the Non-Hispanic Caribbean*, Boulder, CO: Lynne Rienner, 1986.

16. S.F. Finer, *The Man on Horseback*, 2d ed., Boulder, CO: Westview Press, 1988, p. 20.

17. Eric Nordlinger, *Soldiers in Politics*. Englewood Cliffs, NJ: Prentice Hall, 1977, p. 15.

18. Mehta, *Third World Militarization*, p. 17.

19. See, for example, Kumar Rupesinghe, "The Disappearing Boundaries between Internal and External Conflicts," in Elise Boulding, ed., *New Agendas for Peace Research: Conflict and Security Reexamined*, Boulder, CO: Lynne Rienner, 1992.

20. For example, see Azar and Moon, "Third World National Security, 1984;" Jessica Tuchman Mathews, "Redefining Security," *Foreign Affairs* 68 (Spring

1989): 162–77; Patricia Mische, "Ecological Security and the Need to Reconceptualize Sovereignty," *Alternatives* 14 (No. 4, 1989): 389–427; Peter Gleick, "The Growing Links among Environment, Resources, and Security," Paper delivered at the 1991 Topical Symposium, National Defense University, Washington, D.C., November 14–15, 1991; and Lothar Brock, "Security Through Defending the Environment: An Illusion?" in Boulding, *New Agendas for Peace Research.*

21. CSG, *Vulnerability*; Colin Clarke and Tony Payne, eds., *Politics, Security, and Development in Small States*, London: Allen and Unwin, 1987; Anthony Bryan, J. E. Greene, and Timothy Shaw, eds., *Peace, Development, and Security in the Caribbean*, New York: St. Martin's Press, 1990; and Yezid Sayigh, *Confronting the 1990s: Security in the Developing Countries*, Adelphi Papers No. 251, London: International Institute for Strategic Studies, 1990.

22. Robert L. Rothstein, "The Security Dilemma and the 'Poverty Trap' in the Third World," *The Jerusalem Journal of International Relations* 8 (No. 4, 1986): 8–9.

23. Barry Buzan, *People, States, and Fear*, 2d ed., Boulder, CO: Lynne Rienner, 1991, pp. 133–34.

24. Azar and Moon, "Third World National Security."

25. Buzan, *People, States, and Fear*, p. 190. For a full discussion of security complexes see, pp. 186–229.

26. Rothstein, "The Security Dilemma," pp. 1–2.

27. For other recent conceptual approaches see Abdul-Monem Al-Mashat, *National Security in the Third World*, Boulder, CO: Westview Press, 1985; Muthiah Alagappa, *The National Security of Developing Countries: Lessons from Thailand*, Dover, MA: Auburn House, 1987, pp. 1–31; and J. E. Greene, "External Influences and Stability in the Caribbean," in *Peace, Development, and Security in the Caribbean.*

28. Arnold Wolfers, *Discord and Collaboration*, Baltimore, MD: Johns Hopkins University Press, 1962, p. 150.

29. For a discussion of Realism, see Hans J. Morgenthau and Kenneth W. Thompson, *Politics among Nations: The Struggle for Power and Peace*, New York: Alfred Knopf, 1985; and James E. Dougherty and Robert L. Pfaltzgraff, Jr., *Contending Theories of International Relations*, 3d ed., New York: Harper and Row, 1990, pp. 81–135.

30. For Asian/Pacific-Caribbean comparisons see W. Andrew Axline, "Lessons for the Caribbean from Small States of other Regions," in Bryan et al., eds., *Peace, Development, and Security in the Caribbean*; and Ivelaw L. Griffith, "Security for Development: Caribbean—Asian-Pacific Regional Mechanisms," in Jacqueline A. Braveboy-Wagner, W. Marvin Will, Dennis Gayle and Ivelaw L. Griffith, *The Caribbean in the Pacific Century*, Boulder, CO: Lynne Rienner, 1993.

31. On the issue of perception see Robert Jervis, "Hypotheses on Misperception," in James N. Rosenau, ed., *International Politics and Foreign Policy*, New York: The Free Press, 1969; Robert Jervis, *Perception and Misperception in International Politics*, Princeton, NJ: Princeton University Press, 1976; Alexander George, "The Causal Nexus between Cognitive Beliefs and Decision-Making Behavior: The 'Operational Code' Belief System," in Lawrence Falkowski, ed., *Psychological Models in International Politics*, Boulder, CO: Westview Press, 1979; and Yaacov Vertzberger, *The World in Their Minds*, London: Oxford University Press, 1990.

32. See Vital, *The Inequality of States*; Handel, *Weak States in the International System*; CSG, *Vulnerability*; Stephanie Neuman, "Third World Industries: Capabilities and Constraints in Recent Wars," in Stephanie Neuman and Robert Harkavy, eds., *The Lessons of Recent Wars in the Third World*, Lexington, MA: Lexington Books, 1987; and William J. Perry, "Desert Storm and Deterrence," *Foreign Affairs* 70 (Fall 1991): 66–82.

33. For an examination of the importance of geography in international politics see Halford Mackinder, *Democratic Ideals and Reality*, New York: Norton, 1962; Bernard Cohen, *Geography and Politics in a World Divided*, New York: Oxford University Press, 1973; Saul Cohen, "Asymmetrical States and Global Geopolitical Equilibrium," *SAIS Review* 4 (No. 2, 1984): 193–212; and Jack Child, *Geopolitics and Conflict in South America*, New York: Praeger, 1985.

34. Kalevi J. Holsti, *Peace and War: Armed Conflicts and International Order 1648–1989*, Cambridge: Cambridge University Press, 1991, p. 311.

35. On ideology and international politics, see Walter Carlsnaes, *Ideology and Foreign Policy: Problems of Comparative Conceptualization*, New York: Basil Blackwell, 1986; Alexander George, "Ideology and International Relations: A Conceptual Analysis," *Jerusalem Journal of International Relations* 9 (No. 1, 1987): 1–21; and Yehezkel Dror, "High Intensity Aggressive Ideology as an International Threat," *Jerusalem Journal of International Relations* 9 (No. 1, 1987): 153–73. The entire issue of this journal was dedicated to ideology and international politics.

2 CARIBBEAN SECURITY PERCEPTIONS

Studies on security problems and policies in the Caribbean over the last two decades have revolved around four main themes: United States militarization of the region; drugs, political instability, and other security challenges; increased emphasis on domestic military and paramilitary institutions in parts of the region; and assessment of the Regional Security System (RSS) as a collective security mechanism. Although much of the analysis is policy oriented, very little has been written about the perceptual backdrop against which security initiatives are undertaken *by Caribbean leaders*. Some studies do comment on elite thinking, but those comments are always tangential to other concerns.[1] Partly to stress the importance of the perception factor, this study begins with an examination of the perception-security nexus in the region.

It is not suggested that the linkages among problem, policy, and implementation in the Caribbean are either solely or primarily dependent on factors indigenous to Caribbean states generally, or on the perception factor specifically. As will be seen below and elsewhere in this book, this is not the case. Because Caribbean states are small and subordinate, they and their leaders are subject to myriad environmental influences, some of which have greater effect on their policies and conduct than domestic factors. It must, however, be stressed that present Caribbean political leaders are not pliant surrogates of any state or non-state actor elsewhere. This is in spite of the pandering to the

This chapter is a revised and updated version of my "Security Perceptions of English Caribbean Elites." In Ivelaw L. Griffith, ed., *Strategy and Security in the Caribbean*, New York: Praeger, 1991. Published with permission.

United States by Dominica's Mary Eugenia Charles, by Edward Seaga while Prime Minister of Jamaica (1980–1989), and by Tom Adams while Prime Minister of Barbados (1976–1985). Thus, what Caribbean decision makers think and why they think it are important and have direct impact on policies and actions they adopt. The task here, therefore, is to determine who makes security policy in the region, assess the security matrix as the policymakers see it, and note some implications of their definition of the region's security state of affairs.

Security Policymakers

The ultimate security and foreign policy decision-making unit of a state usually follows one of three models. First, there is the Predominant Leader—a single individual with power to make the choice and to stifle opposition. The second is the Single Group—a set of interacting individuals all of whom are members of a single body, having the ability to select a course of action and secure compliance. Finally, Multiple Autonomous Groups—groups or coalitions of important actors, none of which can separately decide and force compliance on the others; or the lack of an overarching body in which all the necessary parties are members.[2]

The security and foreign policy elites of the Caribbean may be defined broadly as the political officeholders and senior appointed officials involved in the formulation, execution, and evaluation of foreign and security policy for their states. This definition suggests that the elites operate in the context of a Single Group decision unit—the Cabinet.[3] Closer scrutiny, however, reveals that the Single Group structure is more form than substance. Indeed, when the political institutions of Antigua-Barbuda were placed under scrutiny in 1990, it was found that although the Cabinet Secretariat was housed within the same building as the Prime Minister's office, conditions within the building were not condusive to the effective conduct of Cabinet government.

The Cabinet Chambers, where the sixteen-member Cabinet met weekly, was the office of the Secretariat. Therefore, the Secretariat staff had to vacate their desks on days when the Cabinet met. Even when the Cabinet did not meet, staff accommodation was inadequate. I agree with the observation that "The Cabinet system of democratic government is too important for such neglect to provide proper accommodation in which the Secretary and his staff are required to work."[4] While the Antigua-Barbuda situation does not reflect the circumstances of all Caribbean countries, it certainly reflects what is true for many of them: the relative diminution of the Cabinet in the scheme of political things. The Caribbean reality is, thus, more a situation of Predominant Leaders operating within Single Group frameworks.

Several reasons explain this. First, irrespective of leadership type (charismatic or rational-legal), or foreign policy orientation, the political culture of the Caribbean has accommodated strong and decisive, although not tyrannical, leadership. Many of these leaders—Eric Williams (Trinidad and Tobago), Norman Manley and Alexander Bustamante (Jamaica), Errol Barrow (Barbados), Forbes Burnham (Guyana), and Vere Bird, Sr. (Antigua-Barbuda) are the most noteworthy—were and are acknowledged political giants in their own societies as well as within the wider region. Their political beliefs, political styles and experiences, and the histories of their societies all combined to facilitate their exercise of predominance. This pattern persists, although the era of the charismatic leader is waning.

Second, security and foreign policy-making is the preserve of the executive branch in the Caribbean. In most societies with coequal or roughly coequal branches of government—for example the United States with the executive, the legislature, and the judiciary—meaningful foreign and security policy roles are played by at least two of the branches. Taking the United States again, while the executive branch's preeminence in security and foreign policy is established, the Congress has well-recognized roles in these areas, which it utilizes and cherishes.[5] Caribbean states have governments with multiple branches, although these operate differently than in the United States. Nevertheless, security and foreign policy-making are the sole preserve of the executive branch there. Some parliaments have committees with foreign and security policy mandates. They are, however, either emasculated by the executive branch or have abdicated such roles, all in the context of political environments where the predominance of the leader of the ruling party and head of the executive branch is the norm.

Moreover, a combination of practical circumstances (for example, small size and dearth of skills) and political expediency creates situations of multiple role performance, especially in the Eastern Caribbean. Thus, as Table 2.1 shows (see p. 24–25), many Prime Ministers are also Defense Ministers. Some also hold the foreign affairs portfolio as well as others. For instance, in the Cabinet lineup in St. Vincent and the Grenadines following the May 1989 elections, Prime Minister James Mitchell retained power over the ministries of Finance, Defense, and Foreign Affairs. He reassigned Foreign Affairs after a Cabinet reshuffle in February 1992. After the March 13, 1990, elections in Grenada, Prime Minister Nicholas Braithwaite took control of National Security, Information, and Carricou Affairs. In St. Kitts-Nevis, Prime Minister Kennedy Simmonds holds the portfolios for Defense, Finance, Home Affairs, and Foreign Affairs.

Elsewhere in the region, Belize Prime Minister George Price is responsible for Finance, Home Affairs, and Defense. In Jamaica, following his March 1992 succession of Michael Manley, Percival Patterson took control of the Information, Economic Development, and Defense portfolios. And in Guyana, President Cheddie Jagan, who was elected on October 5, 1992, continued the tradition of his predecessors—Forbes Burnham and Hugh Desmond Hoyte—in taking the Defense portfolio. Moreover, as Hoyte did between November 1990 and October 1992, Jagan also initially took control of Foreign Affairs, assigning day-to-day responsibilities to Clement Rohee as Senior Minister in the Office of the President. Later— on November 12, 1992—Rohee was made foreign minister. In addition, all the Prime Ministers—and President in Guyana's case—are leaders of their respective political parties. This fusion of power enables them to exercise clout even in cases where Single Groups seem firmly operational. As Searwar says, "the ruling group, in the case of the Caribbean, nearly always reflects the perceptions and views of a dominant leader."[6] Braveboy-Wagner is also correct: "In particular, crisis decisions tend to be personal decisions with little attention paid to opposition sentiment and not enough alternative information and opinion solicited."[7]

The Multiple Autonomous Group decision structure has not been a fixture of Caribbean political systems or decision making. But there have been structural, if not functional, approximations of it in Grenada and Guyana during the time of their socialist experiments—1979–1983 in the case of Grenada, and 1970–1985 in that of Guyana.

Revolutionary Grenada had three decision-making groups. In order of importance, these were: the Central Committee of the New Jewel Movement (NJM); the Politburo; and the Cabinet. The first, with about seventeen members at the time the revolution aborted, met monthly and gave overall policy direction. The Politburo, comprised of seven people, was the executive arm of the Central Committee. The last group, the Cabinet, was the largest. And while membership in the first two groups was restricted to full or candidate members of the NJM, the Cabinet's membership was broader. In the overall scheme the Central

Committee was supreme. Moreover, Maurice Bishop presided over all three bodies, and like him, some top leaders held positions in all three. For example, General Hudson Austin was on the Central Commitee and the Politburo. He was also in the Cabinet, with two ministries: Defense and Construction.[8]

In Guyana's case there was the Central Executive Committee of the ruling People's National Congress (PNC) with subcommittees for foreign affairs and other subjects, paralleling some of the decision structures of the executive branch of the government.[9] But then there was the doctrine of Party Paramountcy, under which the ruling party ranked supreme, above all other organizations and institutions, including the Cabinet and the Parliament. This detracted from the autonomy of multiple groups, in subordinating government bodies to party ones. Moreover, President Burnham exercised hegemony over all policy agencies in a way that permitted no real autonomy. Members of PNC subcommittees and government agencies, therefore, did little more than influence some of the decisions of the paramount leader.[10]

"Leaders' personal characteristics are more likely to influence foreign [and security] policy decisions if the leaders are predominant in their government."[11] This is certainly true of the Caribbean. One study by Basil Ince on Trinidad and Tobago showed Prime Minister Eric Williams to be the consummate decision maker; more *deus inter homines* than *primus inter pares* within the Cabinet.[12] Williams's erudition, charisma, intellect, and political style made him special. But then the Caribbean has had, and still has, other leaders who, although not fully comparable with Williams, have towered over their societies intellectually and/or politically. The late Forbes Burnham (Guyana), Robert Bradshaw (St. Kitts), and Errol Barrow (Barbados) were among them, as was Lynden Pindling (Bahamas) who held power for 25 years. In addition, there are Vere Bird, Sr. (Antigua-Barbuda), John Compton (St. Lucia), and Michael Manley of Jamaica, who demitted office on March 28, 1992, because of failing health.

The youngest leader among the independent Caribbean countries, at age forty-five, is Hubert Ingraham of the Bahamas. He defeated Lynden Pindling in elections held on August 19, 1992. The oldest leader is Vere Bird, Sr., eighty-two years of age. Cheddie Jagan of Guyana is the most junior leader in terms of tenure, having been elected on October 5, 1992, as noted above. The only leader who was not elected is Percival Patterson of Jamaica. He was appointed succes-

Table 2.1

Independent Commonwealth Caribbean Leaders, 1992

COUNTRY	LEADER	AGE	PORTFOLIO
Antigua-Barbuda	Vere C. Bird, Sr.	82	P.M.; Defense
Bahamas	Hubert A. Ingraham	45	P.M.; Finance & Planning
Barbados	Lloyd Erskine Sandiford	55	P.M.; Finance; Economic Affairs; Civil Service; Defense
Belize	George Price	73	P.M.; Finance; Home Affairs; Defense
Dominica	Mary Eugenia Charles	73	P.M.; Finance; Economic Development; Defense
Grenada	Nicholas Braithwaite	62	P.M.; National Security; Cariacou Affairs
Guyana	Cheddie B. Jagan	74	President; Defense
Jamaica	Percival J. Patterson	57	PM; Defense; Information; Economic Development
St. Kitts-Nevis	Kennedy Simmonds	56	P.M.; Home Affairs; Foreign Affairs; Defense
St.Lucia	John M. Compton	66	P.M.; Finance; Planning & Dev.; Home Affairs; Defense
St. Vincent & The Grenadines	James F. Mitchell	61	P.M.; Finance; Defense
Trinidad & Tobago	Patrick Manning	46	P.M.

Sources: Missions of the various countries to the UN; *CARICOM Perspective* (various issues); Office of the Prime Minister, Grenada; *Guyana Chronicle* (1992).

[ ]— Includes total number of years served in the role of head of government: Prime Minister; President; Premier; Chief Minister.
PM: Prime Minister
LL.B.: Bachelor of Laws
M.B.B.S.: Bachelor of Medicine Bachelor of Surgery

YEARS IN POWER		HIGHEST EDUCATION	PREVIOUS OCCUPATION
11	[32]	High School	Trade Unionist
1a	[1]	Legal Education	Legal Counsel
5	[5]	M.A.	Educator
3	[23]	College	Trade Unionist
12	[12]	LL.B.	Lawyer
2	[2]	B.A.	Educator
1b	[8]	D.D.S.	Dentist
1c	[1]	LL.B.	Lawyer
9	[12]	M.B.B.S.	Doctor
10	[25]	LL.B.	Lawyer
8	[10]	Diploma Tropical Agriculture	Agronomist
2d	[2]	B. Sc.	Geologist

a Elected August 19, 1992
b Elected October 5, 1992
c Appointed March 28, 1992
d Elected December 16, 1991

sor to Michael Manley following his election as leader of the ruling People's National Party (PNP) at a party special convention held on March 28, 1992. Under the Jamaican constitution, the leader of the party that controls the Parliament becomes Prime Minister.[13]

As is evident from Table 2.1, these leaders generally hold power for long periods. The "Elder Statesman" in this regard is Vere Bird, Sr., who has been in power for thirty-two years. John Compton has been at his nation's helm for a quarter-century, and George Price for twenty-three years, although not continuously. Compton's mandate to rule was renewed for another five years on April 27, 1992, when he and his party won the general elections in St. Lucia. It is remarkable that except for Forbes Burnham (1964–1985), Maurice Bishop (1979–1983), Eric Gairy (most years between 1951 and 1979), and Hugh Desmond Hoyte (1985–1992), Caribbean leaders have all won and held power without electoral fraud or military rule.

The predominance of these leaders in security, foreign policy, and, indeed, all other matters makes the consequences of their perceptions and subsequent actions loom larger in relative terms compared with states where other models prevail. This is partly because the institutional context in which decisions are presented magnifies the images of the leaders. The consequences of misperception or inexpedience could, therefore, be severe. As one international politics specialist points out:

> The failings and errors of leaders of great powers can be disguised and compensated for by the organizational and material resources they can bring to bear. Even the awe in which they tend to be held may suffice. *But the errors of the leaders of a minor power [small state] have immediate and unmistakable consequences and are only too often beyond repair; and there is no disguising them.*[14]

The existence of the Predominant Leader model in the Caribbean, however, accommodates the involvement of other entities and individuals in decision making, primarily as decision influencers. Some leaders give credence to the principles of Cabinet government and consult their Cabinets before making most decisions. Others use their Cabinets to give official imprimatur to essentially personal decisions, if only because under the terms of their constitutions and in the context of parliamentary government, the Cabinet is a key institution.

Bureaucratic elites also influence some security decisions. This group includes the Permanent Secretaries, Chairmen of constitutional agencies like the Public Service Commissions, the Police Service Commissions, and the Judicial Service Commissions, and the heads of public corporations in places like Guyana, Jamaica, and Trinidad and Tobago, which have large public sectors. One such influencer has observed, though, that "A well-trained political directorate, exuding greater self-confidence, feels less dependent on its civil service advisers, relegating them to sorting out the nuts and bolts."[15] In some cases, decision influencers are also to be found among the business elite, labor and religious leaders, and in the foreign diplomatic corps where one or two diplomats "have the ear" of the Prime Minister or the President. Of course the extent to which such individuals are influential depends on their access to leaders and the leaders' willingness or obligation to act on their advice.

The security policy elites of the Caribbean are, therefore, the sum of the President (of Guyana), Prime Ministers, Foreign Ministers, and Defense Ministers of the various states. A few states have different portfolios and individuals for external security (Defense) and internal security (Home Affairs/National Security). Two such states are Guyana, with Home Affairs Minister Feroze Mohamed, and Jamaica with National Security Minister K. D. Knight. Guyana's Defense Minister is President Cheddie Jagan. Jamaica's is Prime Minister Patterson. These leaders operate ostensibly within Cabinet decision structures with supporting bureaucratic mechanisms, but the reality is less one of Single Group and more one of a Predominant Leader situation. This is especially so when one individual controls the powerful positions of Prime Minister, Defense Minister, and Foreign Minister.

Security Perceptions

Although some Caribbean leaders are inclined to view security in traditional military terms, most subscribe to the view that the protection of their nations requires a broad definition of the term to account for the dimensions from which the most critical threats emerge—the economic and the political. Thus, in the Caribbean, security is defined to encompass military, political, and economic dimensions. Predictably, for some leaders there is greater emphasis on some dimension(s) than on others. For example, Trinidad and Tobago, Dominica, and Barbados have experienced mercenary and coup attempts at undermining the stability of their polities. The leaders in these countries are, therefore, very sensitive to actual or potential threats coming from those directions.[16]

The Military Dimension

While many Caribbean elites are sensitive to potential military threats, overt military threats are the least of their concerns. Terrorism as experienced in Europe and the Middle East is not a matter of great import. However, the potential for narcoterrorism is a matter of grave concern. Guyana and Trinidad and Tobago are the states with the greatest racial pluralism and both have experienced racial strife. In the late 1950s and early 1960s Guyana's racial conflict developed to dangerous proportions. Both Guyana and Trinidad and Tobago have come a long way in terms of racial harmony. The race issue has largely shifted from politically centered struggles for poltical empowerment to more economically centered struggles for survival. Nevertheless, ethnic political polarization still exists.[17] However, ethnically based civil war is not likely in Guyana, Trinidad and Tobago, or elsewhere in the Caribbean.

There is some concern about United States military operations in the region, given the U.S. record of military interventions in the area—Guatemala in 1954; Dominican Republic in 1965; and several times in Haiti and Nicaragua earlier on. The 1983 Grenada invasion was the first in the English Caribbean. It is etched indelibly in the memories of West Indians, both those who supported it and those who opposed it. However, the latest intervention episode was not Grenada, but Panama in December 1989. The United States justified its actions on four grounds: the need to protect American lives; to help restore democracy; to preserve the integrity of the Panama Canal Treaty; and to bring General Manuel Noriega to justice for drug trafficking, among other things.[18] Noriega was ultimately convicted on eight counts of drug trafficking, money laundering, and racketeering, and was sentenced to 40 years in prison on July 10, 1992.

Thus, even for those states that defended the United States action in Grenada and in Panama as being beneficial to the Caribbean, the prospect of intervention, whether solely for United States interests or in pursuit of American-Caribbean interests, is not entirely dismissed. The Grenada action signaled the low tolerance of the United States for Marxist pursuits in the area. This has contributed to an eclipse of radical politics in the region. At the moment, there are no "Grenadas" in the Caribbean to occasion similar American action (although a "Grenada" is not the only possible basis for intervention); nor are any on the horizon.

Concerns about the United States also derive from another factor. As America's strategic rear and a key element in the Western defense mechanism, the Caribbean Basin has a considerable American military presence. As we will see in chapter seven, the principal force concentrations are in Puerto Rico, at the Atlantic threshold of the Caribbean; in Panama, at the southern rim of the Caribbean Basin; and in Cuba— at Guantánamo—on the northern perimeter. The United States also has military installations, facilities, and personnel in the Bahamas, Bermuda, and the United States Virgin Islands, as well as military advisory groups and attachés in various other parts of the region. This military network is designed to secure the region from external and internal threats to American security interests. As such, a threat to the United States becomes, by extension, a potential threat to the Caribbean. The concern of Caribbean elites about the possibility of the region's becoming embroiled in conflicts of an East-West nature because of its linkages to the Western defense was, thus, well founded. However, it has become a matter of diminishing concern in light of the end of Cold War tensions.

Cuba has significant military capability. In 1988 its per capita defense spending was U.S. $125, the highest in Latin America. In 1991 its active military numbered 180,500, with reserves of 135,000 and a sophisticated weapons inventory, including surface-to-air missiles, submarines, frigates, MiG fighters, tanks, and attack helicopters.[19] Cuba once actively pursued relations with English Caribbean states as will be seen in chapter seven. These matters are of interest to Caribbean leaders. But they have been of comparatively greater concern to Americans. Some Caribbean leaders have been known for their strident anti-Communist enunciations and their distaste for Castro's political overtures. Among them are Mary Eugenia Charles of Dominica and John Compton of St. Lucia. Former Prime Minister of Jamaica Edward Seaga and the late Herbert Blaize of Grenada were also in this group. However, the kinds of concerns voiced in the United States about probable military adventures by Cuba in the Caribbean are not paralleled within the Caribbean. As one example, much more fuss is made about the MIGs and the surface-to-air missiles in Cuba and to their potential threat to the area by North American statesmen and scholars than by those in the Caribbean.

Until recently, a realistic, although latent, concern based on East-West politics existed. Any armed conflict between the two superpowers would most likely have drawn Cuba into the picture, either initially by the Soviets, or by American preemptive action. Caribbean leaders worried about the inevitability of military spillovers into the area in such scenarios. Moreover, some felt—and some still do feel—that because the United States perceives Cuba as a threat, Cuba becomes an indirect threat to the Caribbean. The cases of Guyana (under Burnham), Jamaica (under Manley, 1972–1980), and Grenada (under Bishop) show how close contacts with Cuba can result in the kind of economic ostracism, diplomatic hostility, and military intervention from which the entire region can suffer.

Another source of regional military tension has been Venezuela's territorial claims against several states, among them Dominica, Guyana, and Trinidad and Tobago. The dispute with Trinidad and Tobago was settled by treaty in April 1990, as will be seen in chapter seven. The claim against Guyana has been the largest and most significant—for five-eighths of its territory. And in pursuit of that claim, Venezuela has used aggression (in 1966) as well as political and economic intimidation.[20] Fears of military intervention up to the early 1980s were not unfounded, and they can never be entirely dismissed.

Since 1985, however, relations between Guyana and Venezuela have been improving, with heads of state visits, economic and technical assistance by Venezuela, and Venezuelan investment in Guyanese mining and oil exploration ventures.[21] For instance, Guyana, which had successfully lobbied to deny Venezuela full membership in the Non-Aligned Movement in the early 1980s, was Venezuela's main sponsor for membership in the Movement, granted at the 1989 Summit in Yugoslavia. The following year, December of 1990, Venezuela reciprocated and sponsored Guyana's membership in the Organization of American States (OAS). Guyana was admitted to the OAS at a special sesssion of its General Assembly on January 8, 1991, along with Belize. Thus, even though military intervention cannot be ruled out, it is doubtful that Venezuela would use such methods to settle its claims.

The experiences of some states in the region cause them to be sensitive to military-political threats stemming from mercenary adventures or coup attempts. In 1970, Trinidad and Tobago was the scene of a military uprising. In October 1976, a conspiracy to topple the Tom

Adams government in Barbados was exposed. There were also mercenary threats in 1978 and 1979. In March 1979, Eric Gairy was removed by force in Grenada by the New Jewel Movement (NJM). In 1980, Jamaica Defense Force (JDF) officers were implicated in a coup plot against Michael Manley. In April 1981, there were two unsuccessful attempts to oust Mary Eugenia Charles in Dominica.

The six-day bloody coup attempt in Trinidad and Tobago in July-August 1990 is the region's latest internal military-political crisis. The grim drama began on July 27 when Abu Bakr, a black Muslim leader and 113 members of his Jamaat al-Muslimeen (Group of Muslims), took control of the Parliament building and held Prime Minister A.N.R. Robinson and fifteen other government officials hostage. The police headquarters in Port of Spain were fire-bombed, and the headquarters of Trinidad and Tobago Television was occupied, with twenty-five hostages taken there. Massive looting, arson, and vandalism left thirty-one people dead, 693 wounded, about 4,000 people unemployed, and property damage estimated at TT $500 million.

Abu Bakr explained that the action was intended to replace the government with a different regime. He blamed the Robinson government for Trinidad's continuous economic decline and for the country's corruption and mismanagement. During the seizure, Bakr secured an amnesty from Acting President Joseph Carter and an agreement from Robinson to vacate office, have Deputy Prime Minister Winston Dookeram serve as interim ruler, and prepare elections within three months. The government later repudiated that agreement. Bakr and his rebels surrendered on August 1. Treason and other charges were filed against all 114 of the participants in the affair. Bakr himself was charged with fifteen offenses, including treason, nine counts of murder, firearm possession, and hostage taking.[22] The following year both the Trinidad and Tobago Defense Force (TTDF) and the Trinidad and Tobago Police Service (TTPS) received the country's highest award for their roles in "the preservation of democracy and constitutional government" during the crisis. The award, *The Trinity Cross*, was granted on the occasion of the country's twenty-ninth independence anniversary on August 31, 1991.[23]

Speaking about the incident almost a year later, Prime Minister Robinson made a very prescient observation about the intent of the coup-makers in the context of the international winds of change:

One of the supreme ironies of the attempt last July to overthrow our democratically elected government is that it should come at a time when people the world over are moving in the opposite direction and demanding that their authoritarian governments follow the democratic path.

Democracy is by its very nature a complicated business. . . . Despite its shortcomings and its pitfalls it has proven itself vastly superior to authoritarian government, whether it be theocratic, messianic, military or other. This is one of the major lessons of history as the 20th century draws to a close.[24]

One month before the second anniversary of the coup attempt, Justice Clebert Brooks of the Trinidad and Tobago High Court made an unprecedented judicial decision in ordering the release of all 114 insurrectionists. Justice Brooks ruled on June 30, 1992 that the Carter amnesty was valid since, among other things, the acting President did not act under duress when he signed it. The judge reasoned that in spite of the crisis, Carter was not obligated to grant the pardon since there were several options available to him. In addition, Justice Brooks ordered that the insurrectionists be awarded damages and that their legal costs be borne by the state. Attorneys for the Muslimeen estimated that, when combined, damages to their property, loss of earnings, and "loss of family life" amounted to TT $50 million. Meanwhile, Trinidad and Tobago government officials figured that legal cost to the state for prosecuting the Muslimeen amounted to TT $4 million. As might be expected, the state began preparing to appeal the Brooks decision. The Brooks decision came after nearly two years of legal wrangling, including a stalled preliminary inquiry in a specially built court, and decisions by the British Privy Council, Trinidad and Tobago's highest court.[25]

Especially in the Eastern Caribbean, leaders perceive their security problems primarily in terms of drugs and of thwarting potential subversion from within. They consider American support to be an ultimate resource for meeting security threats. Speaking in Washington at the James Monroe Memorial Foundation in April 1987, Dominica's Mary Charles argued that the Monroe Doctrine was an appropriate framework for Caribbean countries to seek United States security assistance. She contended: "I have no doubt that the Monroe Doctrine was applied fittingly in this [the 1983 Grenada intervention] case. . . . We in the

Caribbean who see ourselves as allies of the Americas wish to maintain that tradition and uphold the Monroe Doctrine as it has developed over the ages."[26]

Other leaders are less specific in naming potential invitees. Barbadian Prime Minister Erskine Sandiford went to New York in August 1990 shortly after the Trinidad coup attempt, and in a speech at the Fifth Anniversary Breakfast of the Caribbean-American Chamber of Commerce and Industry, he was frank about the willingness of Barbados to invite outside assistance if a crisis similar to Trinidad's developed. Without naming countries, he declared: "If there were a threat or an attempt to overthrow a government of Barbados, a democratically elected government of Barbados by force, I would have no hesitation in seeking support from friendly government in the region or outside the region."[27]

The Political Dimension

Political factionalism has been a prominent feature in the political histories of Caribbean states. Jamaica, Trinidad and Tobago, Dominica, Grenada, Antigua, the Bahamas, and St. Kitts have all known the kind of factional politics and elite in-fighting that can rupture the fabric of a society. Factionalism has arisen from conflicts among strong-willed leaders, and it has also correlated with race. It is, therefore, a matter to which leaders are very sensitive.

In addition to factionalism, outsiders have sought to change either the regional balance of power or, relatedly, the ideological posture of particular states through destabilization. There have been destabilization efforts by at least one Caribbean Basin state: Venezuela against Guyana in 1968, and during 1980–1982. But destabilization attempts have generally been made by the United States. America's geopolitical interests in the region, coupled with its record of interventions, make the prospect of U.S. destabilization a political reality that the Caribbean must live with. American destabilization has been both overt and covert. It is usually the result of a perception by the U.S. of actual or potential threats to its national interests by Cuba, Cuban surrogates, or from Cuban-Soviet pursuits in the region.

Caribbean states have responded differently to destabilization. Grenada under Maurice Bishop adopted the Popular Mobilization approach in which the ruling New Jewel Movement conducted political education campaigns on the nature and objectives of its political changes and emphasized antipathy toward the changes by the United States and some states in the region. Extensive use was made of groups of workers, professionals, and others to help persuade Grenadians to prepare to "defend the revolution" politically and physically.

The Defensive/Reactive Diplomacy approach was used by Guyana under Forbes Burnham and by Jamaica under Michael Manley (1972–1980).[28] These nations used their diplomats to alert the international community to threats to their sovereignty, and to garner international support and sympathy. They operated particularly within the Non-Aligned Movement, the United Nations, G–77, and CARICOM. Perry Mars concluded that the response of Caribbean states to the problem of external destabilization has generally been piecemeal. He argues that where there is consensus, the response is nevertheless inadequate to meet challenges by the most powerful international actors. And he has suggested that "perhaps the most significant problem undermining effective responses to external destabilization is the tendency toward political disunity or ideological fragmentation of the region."[29]

Some Caribbean leaders have harbored muted suspicions about Venezuelan pursuits in the region. It is felt though, that judging from the nature of its present conduct, any ulterior motives of Venezuela would be more economic in nature than anything else. Cuba's achievements and its firm position in "standing up" to the United States are popularly admired in parts of the Caribbean. But many leaders, especially in the Eastern Caribbean, are wary of Cuba and the likelihood of their being victims of Cuban destabilization. Former Barbadian diplomat Charles Skeete presents what is perhaps a sentiment of most Caribbean leaders: "While we believe that Castroism may be good for Cuba, we have our reservations as to whether Castro is entitled to spread his ideology to our region."[30] This is despite Cuba's new rapprochement with the Commonwealth Caribbean, which led, for example, to the restoration of diplomatic relations with Jamaica in July 1990 after nearly a decade of mutual hostility following Edward Seaga's victory in 1980, and to Cuba's admission to the Caribbean Tourism Organization in 1992.

Drugs present perhaps the single most critical security challenge to the region. Prime Minister Sandiford of Barbados has called the drugs issue "perhaps the most serious problem for the region in the next decade."[31] The problems relate mainly to drug production, abuse, trafficking, and money laundering. The drug trade itself is a billion-dollar international business, valued at about U.S. $500 billion, and Caribbean countries are being drawn into it. Drugs are no longer a problem for a handful of countries. All Caribbean nations are implicated in some way, some more than others.

Because of the gravity of the drug problems, an entire chapter—chapter nine—is dedicated to examining the question of drugs and security. Nevertheless, it deserves to be stated here that the drug problems have political, military, and socioeconomic dimensions. Among other things, drug money has been used to finance criminal activities as well as the operations of political parties. Gun running has also developed as an ancilliary industry. The effects of drugs on the values of Caribbean societies is a major cause for alarm, especially given the growing level of tolerance for drug corruption in some places. Moreover, the efforts to deal with the various problems are taking a heavy economic toll on Caribbean countries.

The Economic Dimension

The aspect of the region's security about which there is the greatest agreement among elites is the economic. For most Caribbean leaders, the economic problems gripping their societies present the greatest cluster of security threats. The economic security dimension has both manifest and latent elements. Economic problems are seen as likely precipitants of political and military challenges. Many leaders would endorse the position of the Prime Minister of St. Vincent and the Grenadines, James Mitchell:

> Fundamentally, in my view, the sores of poverty in our region cannot be cured by military therapy. I lead a popular government and I need to deliver the goods. Opportunities for subversion will emerge when the people are frustrated again. It is the collapse of social institutions that creates avenues for international intrigues. If the people's expectations are not fulfilled through the channels that people like me create, we will, in due course, be inviting the colonels or the commissars. And the more arms we have available in the country, the greater will be the temptation to solve our problem with a coup.[32]

Economic vulnerability is a critical security dilemma for most small states.[33] The economic vulnerability of the Caribbean is an increasingly burning issue.[34] It is not merely a functional vulnerability, but also a structural one where Caribbean economies suffer from, among other things, heavy reliance on foreign trade, limited production and export diversification, low savings, heavy reliance on foreign capital, and a dearth of capable economic and commercial management skills.

Caribbean economists are almost universally in agreement that the economies of Caribbean countries suffer from what William Demas has called *dependent underdevelopment*.[35] And the Caribbean Community and Common Market (CARICOM), on which many hopes lay to mitigate the situation, has not fulfilled expectations. There are several reasons for this. First, the expansion of CARICOM trade has been frustrated by import restrictions, especially by the larger states, a situation occasioned by their adverse balance-of-payments situations. Moreover, CARICOM states have failed to agree on industrial allocation policies. This has stymied efforts at industrialization and economic diversification.

In addition, regional trade expansion has been unable to generate the foreign exchange required for imports from hard currency areas. Further, the limited regional labor mobility will continue to affect the region adversely until the full implementation of the Grande Anse Declaration signed at the 1989 CARICOM Summit in Grenada. In this declaration, Caribbean leaders agreed to remove progressively barriers to intra-regional movement of workers by January 1991. Project AF-FIRM (Arrangements For Freer Intra-Regional Movement) was based on this decision. It calls for the phased waiver of passports for CAR-ICOM nationals beginning with sports, cultural, and media personnel, and for professional, skilled, and contract workers. However, at the spring 1991 meeting of attorneys-general and immigration ministers, it was agreed to defer commencement of the program until mid-1993. Nevertheless, Grenada took the lead in January 1992 by introducing "hassle-free travel," where passports are no longer required for Caribbean citizens traveling to Grenada. Grenada had been assigned responsibility by CARICOM leaders, at their 1991 summit, to develop the travel initiative. Guyana, Jamaica, St. Kitts, and St. Lucia followed Grenada's lead in Spring 1992.[36]

A major problem is the high indebtedness of Caribbean countries. According to the Caribbean Development Bank (CDB), Commonwealth Caribbean countries had a total 1990 debt of U.S. $10.2 billion.

As Table 3.1 shows (see chapter three), Jamaica's debt was U.S. $4,386 million, Trinidad and Tobago had U.S. $2,508 million, and Guyana, U.S. $1,840 million. Among the independent countries, St. Kitts had the smallest figure—U.S. $35 million. The CARICOM debt problem dates to the 1970s when the region, and indeed the entire world, was faced with dramatic oil price increases. This was compounded over the years by reduced demand for Caribbean exports, especially bauxite, and natural disasters in several places which, adversely affected production.[37] Poor economic management in places like Guyana, Jamaica, and Trinidad and Tobago was also a contributor.

Most of the debt in the Caribbean is owed not to commercial banks, but to bilateral official creditors and multilateral institutions like the International Monetary Fund (IMF), the World Bank, and the Inter-American Development Bank (IADB). The debt from the latter sources was accumulated in pursuit of economic development through capital projects and economic stabilization. However, because of the factors mentioned above, what was pursued as part of the solution to the region's economic problems has now become part of its problem. Servicing the debts is a major headache because debt ratios run very high. In 1989, for instance, the ratio of Jamaica's debt service to exports was a dramatic 36 percent; in 1990 it was 31 percent. In explaining the debt burden facing Guyana, whose 1988 debt was U.S. $1.6 billion, one diplomat-economist observed:

> In Guyana, the [1988] debt/GDP ratio is 522 percent, which means that the debt outstanding is 5 and 1/4 times larger than the economy's total output of goods and services or, put another way, it would take 5 and 1/4 years to pay off if the output of all economic activity was devoted exclusively to this purpose.[38]

In his 1992 Budget Speech, Guyana's Finance Minister reported on the country's critical debt situation: "Scheduled external debt service payments by the public sector range from 50 to 70 percent of merchandise exports in 1991–93, and are projected to be above one third of exports in the rest of the decade."[39]

The debts are not only a great economic burden, but in attempting to manage them, states run the risk of jeopardizing their internal security because of popular, labor, business, or other reaction. Both Guyana and Trinidad and Tobago found themselves in this situation in 1988 and 1989 with riots, strikes, public demonstrations, and arson and vandalism of public property costing millions of dollars.[40] A similar fate befell Barbados in fall 1991. It followed Parliament's September approval of a supplementary budget providing for an 8 percent public sector salary cut, retrenchment of some 2,000 government employees, tax increases, and termination of certain duty-free exemptions. The measures, part of an eighteen-month economic recovery program designed to attract U.S. $58.1 million from the IMF, evoked opposition from labor unions, manufacturers, and other segments of the society. There was even opposition within the ruling Democratic Labor Party (DLP), manifested through no-confidence motions by branches of the party against its leader, Prime Minister Sandiford.[41]

Edward Seaga, former Prime Minister of Jamaica, has argued that the ability of the developing world to meet necessary welfare considerations while servicing external debts requires real economic growth. Quite rightly, he feels that the priority should be to achieve sustainable economic growth in the medium term.[42] One can hardly challenge this proposition. But there seems to be a chicken and egg dilemma: can such countries strive for growth before seeking debt solutions, or should efforts be concentrated on debt crisis solutions at the expense of real growth? Both approaches have serious implications for economic and political stability. Firm decisions on these issues are difficult. Most leaders—especially those of Guyana, Jamaica, and Trinidad and Tobago—are working on half-measures or on coping strategies in collaboration with regional and international bodies.[43]

Economic security issues have been progressively pushed to the top of the agendas of Caribbean leaders over the last few years. In November 1986, at the direction of Caribbean leaders, the CARICOM Secretariat, in association with the London-based Commonwealth Secretariat, commissioned a study of medium- to long-term economic development performance and prospects of the region. The study, *Development Performance and Prospects in the Caribbean Community to the Year 2000*, was completed in 1988. Called "the Bourne Report" after the Guyanese-born University of the West Indies (UWI) economics professor, Compton Bourne, who led the study team, the report gave technical and policy recommendations to bolster economic stability and add economic security safeguards in the region. It cautioned that there are no magical solutions to the immense development problems of Commonwealth Caribbean economies. The report also suggested that long-run development will depend more on the sustained hard work, ingenuity, productivity, and thrift of individuals and business enterprises with government support and accommodation than on any grandiose schemes or projects.[44]

Publication of the Bourne Report and the existence of economic deprivation in most of the region led to calls for further policy focus on economic security issues. Thus, at the suggestion of Prime Minister A.N.R. Robinson of Trinidad and Tobago, the 1989 CARICOM Summit in Grenada agreed to convene a tripartite regional economic conference—with participation by governments, the private sector, and labor groups—to examine further the range of issues raised in the Bourne Report and to chart a common action program based on it. This conference, originally planned for November 1990, was held from February 27 to March 1, 1991, in Port of Spain. Two hundred delegates from the Dutch, English, French, and Spanish-speaking Caribbean attended.[45]

The conference statement, *The Port of Spain Consensus*, recognized four mutually reinforcing strategies incorporating the efficient use and management of human and material resources as necessary for the region's economic growth and survival in the twenty-first century and beyond. Calling for a "sustainable development model in which human, social, economic, and environmental considerations are integrated," the document identified the strategies as:

- assignment of the highest priority to human resource development;
- preservation and enhancement of the democratic traditions and processes, especially through the consultative involvement of all the social partners in policy formulation and implementation;
- pursuit of outward-looking development strategies with measures to enhance the internal sources of growth;
- expansion of regional cooperation, with strong outreach to the wider Caribbean, Latin America, and the hemisphere as a whole.[46]

It should be noted that while the above assessment presents the most prominent security concerns, these are not the only ones. In the context of a wider redefinition of the concept of security mentioned in chapter one, there is also some concern about the environment.[47]

Influences and Implications

Like leaders elsewhere, Caribbean political elites formulate and execute policies partly in response to their perception of issues and problems. Kenneth Boulding's assertion more than two decades ago still holds true today:

> we must recognize that the people whose decisions determine the policies and actions of nations do not respond to the "objective" facts of the situation, whatever that may mean, but to their "image" of the situation. It is what we think the world is like, and not what it is really like, that determines our behavior.[48]

Barry Buzan explains, "perception affects both what things are seen as facts and what significance these 'facts' carry in security analysis. . . . Perceptions vary according to where the observer is located in relation to the thing viewed, and according to the internal constitution of the viewer."[49] Elite perception is a function of several factors, some within a society and others in the political environment in which it exists. The educational levels of leaders, their previous political and professional experiences, their social class, their interpretation of history, and their beliefs about their nations and about their roles in them are all among the internal factors.[50]

With few exceptions, Caribbean leaders have all had tertiary-level education. The exceptions are Vere Bird, Sr., of Antigua, and George Price of Belize. Bird was unable to go beyond high school. Price was forced by family exigencies to end his religious training at St. Augustine Seminary in Mississippi prematurely. Most leaders had their higher education in British or North American universities. The exceptions are Dr. Kennedy Simmonds of St. Kitts-Nevis, who received his medical degree from the University of the West Indies (UWI), Nicholas Braithwaite, who received his B.A. in education from UWI, and Patrick Manning of Trinidad and Tobago whose Bachelor of Science in geology was from UWI (Mona). Some leaders have studied at both regional and foreign institutions. Sandiford of Barbados, for example, got his B.A. in english from UWI and his M.A. in Economics from Manchester University in England. Patterson of Jamaica secured a B.A. in English from UWI before proceeding to the London School of Economics to study law.

Caribbean leaders generally make a career of politics and act as though they are indispensable to the political survival of their nations. As such, some of them tend to see little distinction between the security of their regimes and that of the nation. Hence, in a few places—notably Grenada, under Eric Gairy, and Guyana, under Forbes Burnham and Hugh Desmond Hoyte—leaders have sought to entrench themselves in power through intimidation and fraud.[51] Nevertheless, it is evident from Table 2.1 that before entering politics most of the current leaders had reputable professions to which they can return if ousted from office, or when they retire from politics, although their egos may prevent this. Even if these leaders decline to return to their professions, they at least have the credentials and basis for gainful employment outside of politics.

Apart from Vere Bird, Sr., and George Price, Caribbean leaders have middle class origins. But some of them, notably Maurice Bishop, Forbes Burnham, Cheddi Jagan, and Michael Manley, developed working-class affinities and advocacy over the course of their political lives. They have been more inclined than the others to interpret local and international issues through Marxist or democratic socialist conceptual lenses. Caribbean leaders are now essentially capitalist in ideological orientation and pragmatic in political strategies, a marked contrast to ten to fifteen years ago. They espouse social democratic principles and place a premium on civil and political rights, such as freedoms of speech and association, and free and fair elections. They endorse free enterprise and actively seek foreign investment.[52]

As we will come to appreciate in the discussion on geopolitics in chapter seven, Caribbean states exist in a geopolitical milieu that makes them subordinate to the interests of more powerful states, such as the United States and Venezuela in the hemisphere, and others elsewhere. They accept that their "power" is inferior to that within the dominant state system, and they realize that changes in the dominant system have greater effect on them than the reverse. As such, the international political environment has considerable impact on how leaders in the region define and interpret issues.

Much of the interplay between elites in subordinate and dominant states described by Paul Johnson is true for the Caribbean. Johnson talks about "ideological, cultural, and other normative mechanisms of manipulation," explaining:

Essentially I am referring to those recurrent social processes whereby decision-making elites in subordinate states come to share the values, beliefs and attitudes of the elites in the hegemonic power, and hence are spontaneously disposed to identifying their own and their country's interests with those of the hegemon and to devise their own policies accordingly. These elites of subordinate states may be educated abroad, rely on foreign technical experts, read mass media dominated by imported wire service reports, attend movies imported from the hegemonic country, travel extensively there, associate with the foreign diplomatic community, adapt a foreign life-style, and so on.[53]

Caribbean security decision makers, therefore, operate within frameworks that oblige them to be mindful of internal and external considerations. Their decisions and initiatives hinge on several factors, the most important of which are:

- assumptions about the Caribbean, the hemisphere, and the international milieu;
- the way they define threats to the regime, the society, or to both;
- the response to threats, and opportunities for the threat or use of force, or other measures;
- the human, material, and other capabilities required to respond to internal and external security needs;
- public opinion and political support for regime and national objectives and policies;
- the creation of incentives and controls to ensure the support of objectives by security agencies.

It was suggested in chapter one that vulnerability, internal instability, intervention, and militarization are the four major security problem areas confronting small states. It is clear from the above that all of these problem areas have featured in the perceptual lenses of Caribbean leaders. Vulnerability, the first of the four, is not merely the most critical for small states generally; it is so for the entire Caribbean. One Caribbean leader defined it this way: "Our vulnerability is manifold. Physically, we are subject to hurricanes and earthquakes; economically, to market decisions taken elsewhere; socially, to cultural penetration; and now politically, to the machinations of terrorists, mercenaries, and criminals."[54]

The perception profile presented here suggests that there is both image convergence and divergence in the Caribbean. This reflects similarities and differences among Caribbean elites as to the nature and intensity of threats. The greatest convergence lies in the economic area; the divergence lies in the military and political ones. Political histories, present political and economic circumstances, and the nature of Caribbean leadership do not permit the definition of a single set of security perceptions.

Although Caribbean nations share several common historical, political, and other features, there are still strong definitions of national and subregional interests that often conflict with what seem to be manifestly regional ones. Thus, for example, there is common recognition of military, political, and economic vulnerability, but there is divergence in perceptions regarding the source and intensity of threats. As one leader remarked, "On the question of regional security, it is essential that [there be] a much clearer definition of and a more proactive approach to the problems that the region faces and the kind of cooperation mechanism that could be established."[55]

The greatest concentration of common problems exists in the Eastern Caribbean. Members of the Organization of Eastern Caribbean States (OECS) place premiums on drugs and potential threats from internal subversion and on mercenary action. And they seem more disposed than the others to invite the United States to deal with actual and potential threats to their security. Jamaica worries justifiably about political violence and, along with the Bahamas, Belize, and most other states, it is finding the drug problem to be intractable. Guyana and Belize, the mainland states, still worry about potential political, and possibly military, problems stemming from Venezuelan and Guatemalan territorial claims, despite improved relations between the respective parties. (In the Belize-Guatemala case, there was official recognition of Belizian sovereignty by Guatemala in August 1991. Diplomatic relations were established between the two countries one month later, on September 10, 1991.[56])

Three related implications flow from this profile. First, while the disparities are not critical in all areas, they could necessitate the use of precious time and already scarce resources in attempting to narrow the range of differences. Second, because external security measures by these states individually hold few prospects for success, collaboration is vital. But collaboration needs consensus, if not unanimity, to be credible and successful. Divergences of the kind noted above can present obstacles to this. Third, Caribbean states stand to create greater scope for others, such as the United States, Venezuela, and Cuba, to determine fully the nature and direction of events in the region. In such circumstances, they stand to lose initiative and act by default, progressively being carried by the turn of events and the interests of other states, rather than by their own volition and in pursuit of their own interests. Events related to the October 1983 Grenada intervention dramatize this last point. The failure of CARICOM leaders to adopt a decisive position at the emergency summit in Trinidad, coupled with the inclination of some leaders to facilitate extraregional initiatives, helped accommodate the pursuit of American interests.

The differences among the elites, however, are not conflicting enough to prevent initiatives at both the individual and collective levels. Some of the security policies and initiatives over the last few decades have derived partly from these perceptions. Among initiatives at the individual level were: strengthening of military and paramilitary establishments in Grenada and Guyana over several years; repression of leftist parties and interest groups in Grenada, Dominica, and St. Lucia, particularly after 1983; deemphasis of the military in Barbados following the Democratic Labor Party's return to power there in 1986; and strengthening of security around Parliament buildings in Barbados, Jamaica, and elsewhere in the region following the 1990 coup attempt in Trinidad and Tobago. At the collective level, the Regional Security System (RSS) was created in 1982; Jamaica and Eastern Caribbean countries secured increased military purchases, aid, and training from the United States following the Grenada intervention. Moreover, the Caribbean Democratic Union was formed as a conservative ideological coalition in 1986; and after the 1990 Trinidad crisis calls were renewed for the expansion of the RSS. These policies and initiatives will be discussed later.

Notes

1. As far as I know, the only other work where perception is the central and not a peripheral concern is by Anthony P. Maingot. See his *Security Perspectives of Governing Elites in the English-speaking Caribbean*, Essays on Strategy and Diplomacy No. 4, Claremont, CA: The Keck Center for International Strategic Studies, 1985.

2. See Margaret Hermann, Charles Hermann, and Joe Hagan, "How Decision

Units Shape Foreign Policy Behavior," in Charles Hermann et al., eds., *New Directions in the Study of Foreign Policy*, Boston: Allen and Unwin, 1987, esp. pp. 311–18. Also, see Margaret Hermann and Charles Hermann, "Who Makes Foreign Policy Decisions and How: An Empirical Enquiry," *International Studies Quarterly* 33 (December 1989): 361–87.

3. For a discussion of Cabinet leadership see Stanley de Smith, *Constitutional and Administrative Law*, London: Penguin, 1977, pp. 144–75.

4. Louis Blom-Cooper, *Guns for Antigua: Report of the Commission of Inquiry into the Circumstances Surrounding the Shipment of Arms from Israel to Antigua and Transshipment on 24 April 1989 En Route to Colombia*, London: Duckworth, 1990, p. 111.

5. See Marc Smyrl, *Conflict or Codetermination: Congress, the President, and the Power to Make War*, Cambridge, MA: Ballinger, 1988; Charles Kegley and Eugene Wittkopf, eds., *The Domestic Sources of American Foreign Policy*, New York: St. Martin's Press, 1988, pp. 1–11 and chapters 8 and 11; Robert Art, "Congress and the Defense Budget: Enhancing Policy Oversight," *Political Science Quarterly* 100 (Summer 1985): 227–48; and Barry Blechman, "The Congressional Role in U.S. Military Policy," *Political Science Quarterly* 106 (Spring 1991): 17–32.

6. Lloyd Searwar, "Dominant Issues in the Role and Responses of Caribbean Small States," in Anthony T. Bryan, J. Edward Greene, and Timothy M. Shaw, eds., *Peace, Development, and Security in the Caribbean*, New York: St. Martin's Press, 1990, p. 5.

7. Jacqueline A. Braveboy-Wagner, *The Caribbean in World Affairs*. Boulder, CO: Westview Press, 1989, p. 226. She also adds a salutary note in recording her observation of a decrease in personalism and increased bureaucratic and interest group influence.

8. Mark Adkin, *Urgent Fury: The Battle for Grenada*, Lexington, MA: Lexington Books, 1989, p. 15. For more on PRG political system and decision-making see Adkin, pp. 9–23; and Tony Thorndike, "People's Power in Theory and Practice," in Jorge Heine, ed., *A Revolution Aborted: The Lessons of Grenada*, Pittsburgh: University of Pittsburgh Press, 1991, pp. 33–49.

9. For many years, the PNC Foreign Relations Subcommittee was chaired by Central Committee member Rashleigh Jackson, Foreign Minister from 1978 until November 26, 1990. Jackson resigned following the indictment of his son, Martin, on narcotics possession charges.

10. For more on Guyana see Forbes Burnham, *Toward the Socialist Revolution*, Georgetown, Guyana: People's National Congress, 1975; and Rudolph James and Harold Lutchman, *Law and the Political Environment in Guyana*, Georgetown, Guyana: University of Guyana, 1984.

11. Margaret Hermann and Charles Hermann, "A Look Inside the 'Black Box': Building on a Decade of Research," in Gerald Hopple, ed., *Biopolitics, Political Psychology, and International Politics*, New York: St. Martin's Press, 1982, p. 4.

12. Basil Ince, "Leadership and Foreign Policy Decision-making in a Small State: Trinidad and Tobago's Decision to Enter the OAS," in Basil Ince et al., eds., *Issues in Caribbean International Relations*, Lanham, MD: University Press of America, 1983.

13. See Howard W. French, "Jamaica Party Elects Successor to the Prime Minister," *New York Times*, March 29, 1992, p. L3.

14. David Vital, *The Survival of Small States*, London: Oxford University Press, 1971, p. 12. Emphasis added.

15. Gladstone E. Mills, "Politics and Administration: Outstanding Issues Related to Peace and Security," In Bryan et al., eds., *Peace, Development, and Security in the Caribbean*, p. 151. Mills, Professor Emeritus of Government of the University of the West Indies (Mona), has served as Chairman of Jamaica's Public Service Commission and of its Electoral Advisory Committee, among other posts.

16. The analysis that follows is based on focused, semi-structured interviews with people in the Caribbean who make, influence, and implement decisions, and on examination of speeches and writings of political elites.

17. See Linda Edwards-Romain, "Overt Racism in Trinidad and Tobago," *Caribbean Contact* (Barbados), October, 1987, pp. 1, 2; Lindsay Mackoon, "Trinidad and Tobago: The Fangs of Race Bared," *Caribbean Contact*, January, 1988, p. 6; Selwyn Ryan, "One Love Revisited: The Persistence of Race in the Politics of Trinidad and Tobago," *Caribbean Affairs* 1 (January-March 1988): 67–127; and Perry Mars, *Foreign Influence and Political Conflict in the Post-Colonial Caribbean*, Working Paper No. 133, New York: Center for Studies of Social Change, New School for Social Research, 1992, pp. 20–21.

18. See "A Transcript of Bush's Address on the Decision to Use Force in Panama," *New York Times*, December 21, 1989, p. A19; and Andrew Rosenthal, "U.S. Forces Gain Wide Control in Panama: New Leaders Put In But Noriega Gets Away," *New York Times*, December 21, 1989, pp. A1, A18.

19. International Institute for Strategic Studies, *The Military Balance 1991–1992*, London: International Institute for Strategic Studies, 1991; and *Latin America Weekly Report*, May 9, 1991 (WR–91–17): 8.

20. See Government of Guyana, Ministry of Foreign Affairs, *Memorandum on the Guyana/Venezuela Boundary*, Georgetown, Guyana, 1981; Ivelaw L. Griffith, *On the Western Front*, Georgetown: Ministry of Information, 1981; Jacqueline Braveboy-Wagner, *The Venezuela-Guyana Border Dispute: Britain's Colonial Legacy in Latin America*, Boulder, CO: Westview Press, 1984.

21. See Government of Guyana, *Good Neighbours*. Address of the President to the Fourth Sitting of the First Session of the Second Supreme Congress of the People, Georgetown, Guyana, April 3, 1987.

22. See "Trinidad Rebels Threaten to Kill Premier and Other Hostages," *New York Times*, July 29, 1990, pp. L1, L14; David Pitt, "Muslim Rebels in Trinidad Free All Their Hostages and Surrender," *New York Times*, August 2, 1990, pp. A1, A8; Michael Roberts, "Terror in Trinidad," *New York Carib News*, August 7, 1990, p. 3; "Over 100 Muslimeen to Be Charged with Treason," *New York Carib News*, August 21, 1990, p. 3. For a comprehensive analysis of the coup, see Selwyn Ryan, *The Muslimeen Grab for Power: Race, Religion, and Revolution in Trinidad and Tobago*, Port of Spain, Trinidad: Imprint Caribbean, 1991. The Carter amnesty is reproduced at p. 170. The data on fatalities, damages, etc., are at p. 55.

23. "Trinidad Cops, Army Get Nation's Highest Honor," *New York Carib News*, September 10, 1991, p. 17.

24. Government of Trinidad and Tobago, *Address by the Honorable A.N.R.*

Robinson, Regional Conference on Democracy, Subversion, and National Security, Port of Spain, Trinidad, May 31, 1991, pp. 17–18.

25. Carlton Khan and Kathy Ann Waterman, "Judge Frees Muslimeen: Amnesty is Valid," *Daily Express* (Trinidad and Tobago), July 1, 1992, pp. 1, 6; "$4 Million Spent on High Court Hearing," *Daily Express*, July 1, 1992, p. 6; Paul Charles, "Decision A Landmark in the Commonweath," *Daily Express*, July 2, 1992, p. 5.; and Ria Taitt, "[Attorney General] Sobion: We Have Nothing to Fear," *Daily Express* July 2, 1992, pp. 1, 4.

26. See her "Isolationism vs. One-ness: The Continuing Validity of the Monroe Doctrine," *Caribbean Affairs*, 1 (April-June 1988): 153–54. Charles was the first recipient of the James Monroe Award inaugurated by the Foundation.

27. "Barbados Would Go Outside," *New York Carib News*, August 14, 1990, p. 27. The Trinidad authorities refused to invite Caribbean or other security assistance during the actual crisis, but accepted military assistance from Caribbean countries afterward.

28. See Perry Mars, "Destabilization, Foreign Intervention, and Socialist Transformation in the Caribbean," *Transition* 7 (1983): 33–54. Using a definition of the Caribbean to include Cuba, Mars also talks about the "Belligerent Opposition" approach used by that country.

29. See Mars, "Destabilization," p. 48.

30. See U.S. Congress, House, Committee on Foreign Affairs, *The English-Speaking Caribbean: Current Conditions and Implications for U.S. Policy*, Report by the Congressional Research Service for the Subcommittee on Western Hemisphere Affairs, 99th Cong., 1st Sess., September 13, 1985, p. 96.

31. See "Sandiford Addresses Caribbean Coast Guards," *New York Carib News*, July 31, 1990, p. 36. Sandiford was at the time addressing participants of the Caribbean Maritime Training Assistance Program in Barbados in July 1990.

32. See Gary Brana-Shute, "An Eastern Caribbean Centrist: Interviewing Prime Minister James F. 'Son' Mitchell," *Caribbean Review* 14 (1985): 28.

33. See Commonwealth Study Group (hereinafter CSG), *Vulnerability: Small States in the Global Society*, London: Commonwealth Secretariat, 1985, esp. pp. 16–35, 54–90; Sheila Harden, ed., *Small is Dangerous*, New York: St. Martin's Press, 1985, pp. 7–13; Edward Azar and Chung-in Moon, "Third World National Security: Toward a New Conceptual Framework," *International Interactions* 11 (No. 2, 1984): 103–35.

34. See Compton Bourne, *Development Performance and Prospects in the Caribbean Community to the Year 2000*, Report prepared for CARICOM Secretariat, March 1988; William Demas, "Consolidating Our Independence: The Major Challenge for the West Indies," Distinguished Lecture, Institute of International Relations, St. Augustine, Trinidad, delivered June 10, 1986; Carl Stone, "The Caribbean and the World Economy: Patterns of Insertion and Contemporary Options," in Jorge Heine and Leslie Manigat, eds., *The Caribbean and World Politics*, New York: Holmes and Meier, 1988.

35. See William Demas, ibid., pp. 6–19. Demas, former Secretary-General of CARICOM and President of the Caribbean Development Bank, now heads the Central Bank of Trinidad and Tobago.

36. See "Freer Travel in CARICOM Expected by 1993," *Stabroek News* (Guyana), May 12, 1991, p. 4; and Caribbean Community Secretariat, *Communi-*

qué, *Third Intersessional Meeting of the Conference of Heads of Government of the Caribbean Community*, Caricom Press Release No. 17/1992, 26 February, 1992, p. 2.

37. Richard Bernal, "Caribbean Debt: Possible Solutions," *Caribbean Affairs* 4 (April-June 1991): 45.

38. Bernal, "Caribbean Debt," p. 47.

39. Government of Guyana, Parliament, *1992 Budget Speech: Parliamentary Sessional Paper No. 1 of 1992*, Presented 30 March, 1992 by Minister of Finance, Carl B. Greenidge, to the Fifth Parliament of Guyana, p. 44.

40. See Lindsay Mackoon, "Strike Shuts Down T&T," *Caribbean Contact*, April 1989, p. 2; Courtney Gibson, "Guyana Devalues Dollar," *New York Carib News*, April 11, 1989, p. 3; Rickey Singh, "Guyana Strike Crippling," *New York Carib News*, April 24, 1989, p. 17; Bert Wilkinson, "Protest Over Harsh Budget," *Caribbean Contact*, May 1989, p. 8.

41. See Colin King, "Shut Down Planned by Business," *New York Carib News*, October 1, 1991, p. 5; "Manufacturers Complain About Austerity Budget," *New York Carib News*, October 1, 1991, p. 35; "Barbados Wage Cut Bill Passed by One Vote Margin," *New York Carib News*, October 1, 1991, p. 35; and Canute James, "Unrest on Island of Tranquility," *Financial Times* (London), November 5, 1991, p. 8.

42. See Edward Seaga, "Toward Resolving the Debt Crisis," *Caribbean Review* 16 (Spring 1988): 3.

43. See Jerome McElroy and Klaus De Albuquerque, "Recent Debt and Adjustment Experiences in the OECS Countries of the Caribbean," *Caribbean Affairs* 3 (January-March 1990): 49–64; Roland Ely, "Guyana and the International Monetary Fund," Paper presented at the X1Vth Annual Conference of the Caribbean Studies Association, Trinidad, May 1990; and Terrence Farrell, "Structural Adjustment and Transformation in the Caribbean: Management Strategies Based on the Lessons of Experience," in Bryan, Greene, and Shaw, eds., *Peace, Development, and Security in the Caribbean*.

44. Executive Summary, *Development Performance and Prospects in the Caribbean Community to the Year 2000*, March 1988, p. 51.

45. Rickey Singh, "The Hurdles against Economic Progress," *Caribbean Contact*, March-April 1991, pp. 1, 7.

46. *Port of Spain Consensus of the Caribbean Regional Economic Conference*, Port of Spain, Trinidad and Tobago, March 1, 1991, p. 1.

47. See, for example, "Tony Best, Earl Bousquet, and Colin Hope, "Danger: Toxic Waste in the Caribbean," *Caribbean Contact*, May 1988, pp. 8–9; Desmond Hoyte, "Growth, Development, and the Environment in the Caribbean," *Caribbean Affairs* 2 (October-December 1989): 63–70; *The Port of Spain Accord on the Management and Conservation of the Caribbean Environment*, Declaration of the First CARICOM Ministerial Conference on the Environment, Port of Spain, Trinidad and Tobago, May 31-June 2, 1989; and West Indian Commission, *Time For Action: The Report of the West Indian Commission*, Back Rock, Barbados, 1992, pp. 216–33.

48. Kenneth Boulding, "National Images and International Systems," in James N. Rosenau, ed., *International Politics and Foreign Policy*, New York: The Free Press, 1969, p. 423.

49. Barry Buzan, *People, States, and Fear*, 2d ed., Boulder, CO: Lynne Rienner, 1991, p. 343.

50. See Robert Jervis, "Hypotheses on Misperception," in Rosenau, *International Politics and Foreign Policy*, pp. 239–254; and Yaacov Vertzberger, *The World in their Minds*, London: Oxford University Press, 1990, esp. chapters 3 and 4.

51. Curiously enough, though, Burnham who ruled Guyana for 21 years had been one of the country's leading lawyers.

52. For profiles of present leaders see Harold Hoyte, "Will Erskine Sandiford Find That Barrow and Tom Adams Are Tough Acts to Follow?" *Caribbean Affairs* 1 (July-September 1988): 96–104; and the relevant sections of Robert Alexander, ed., *Biographical Dictionary of Latin American and Caribbean Political Leaders*, New York: Greenwood Press, 1988. Vere Bird, Sr. is profiled in "A Man for All Seasons," *The Caribbean and West Indian Chronicle* (October-November 1981): 21ff. Cheddie Jagan, *The West on Trial: The Fight for Guyana's Freedom*, Berlin, Germany: Seven Seas, 1975 is an autobiography by the Guyanese leader. For biographies of recent leaders, see Darrell Levi, *Michael Manley: The Making of a Leader*, London: Deutsch, 1989; Raoul Pantin, "The Man from Castara, Tobago: A Moses Leading his People to the Promised Land?" *Caribbean Affairs* 1 (January-March 1988): 161–71; F.A. Hoyos, *Tom Adams: A Biography*, London: Macmillan, 1988; Ken Boodhoo, ed., *Eric Williams: The Man and the Leader*, Lanham, MD: University Press of America, 1986; "A Chronicle Tribute to Guyana's Greatest Hero," *Guyana Chronicle* (Special Supplement), August 23, 1985; and Jorge Heine, "The Hero and the Aparatchnik: Charismatic Leadership, Political Management, and Crisis in Revolutionary Grenada," in Jorge Heine, ed., *A Revolution Aborted: The Lessons of Grenada*, Pittsburgh: University of Pittsburgh Press, 1991.

53. Paul Johnson, "The Subordinate States and Their Strategies," in Jan Triska, ed., *Dominant Powers and Subordinate States: The United States in Latin American and the Soviet Union in Eastern Europe*, Durham, NC: Duke University Press, 1986, p. 297.

54. Address by L. Erskine Sandiford, Prime Minister of Barbados to 1990 CARICOM Summit in "Communiqué and Addresses—Eleventh Meeting of the Heads of Government of the Caribbean Community," *CARICOM Perspective* (Special Supplement) 49 (July-December 1990): 6. Also, see "Address by the Honorable A.N.R. Robinson;" and CSG, *Vulnerability*.

55. Mary Eugenia Charles, "Effecting a Regional Plan for Progress," *Caribbean Affairs* 4 (April-June 1991): 29.

56. Mission of Belize to the United Nations, "Press Release Issued by the Guatemalan Government on 14th August 1991," Security Council Document A/46/36/B; and Government of Belize, Ministry of Foreign Affairs, "Press Release," September 11, 1991.

3 THE CAPABILITIES OF CARIBBEAN STATES

Security analysts agree that meaningful national and regional security requires states to own or have access to appropriate security capabilities. It is important to look at both the internal and external aspects of security capability. There are five categories of internal elements: geographic; human resource; material resource; institutional; and military. External elements include membership in regional and international organizations; signature of regional and international agreements; and bilateral alliances and other bilateral relationships. The international contacts enable states to complement their internal capabilities for whatever security objectives or strategy they design.[1] One way to appreciate the link between capability and security in the Caribbean is to look first at the internal capabilities of Caribbean states. We can next examine their international support relationships and then be able to assess their prospects for providing credible protection.

Internal Capabilities

Geography

Except for mainland Belize and Guyana, Commonwealth Caribbean countries are island-states. Some, like Grenada, St. Vincent and the Grenadines, and Trinidad and Tobago, are plural island-states. The Bahamas is an archipelago of about 700 islands and hundreds of cays. Caribbean nations are all very small. Guyana, with 214,970 square kilometers, is the largest. Population densities vary from a strategically dangerous low of four persons per square kilometer in Guyana, to 597 per square kilometer in Barbados. Except for the northern Bahamas, the area lies within the tropics.

The region's climate is an asset to the agricultural production on which much of the region's economy depends, especially sugar cane and bananas. The hurricane is the most destructive natural hazard. Jamaica was severely damaged by Hurricane Gilbert in September 1988. It left forty-five people dead, 300,000 homeless, and one billion (Jamaican) dollars worth of damage. In September 1989 Hurricane Hugo left a trail of death and destruction in Antigua, Guadeloupe, the United States Virgin Islands, and Puerto Rico, among other places.[2]

The Caribbean Sea has an area of 1,049,500 square miles. Its north-south width ranges from 380 miles to about 700 miles. The greatest depth of passage connecting the Eastern Caribbean with the Atlantic Ocean is the Anegada Passage (see Table 7.3). The channel across the submarine ridge south of the Virgin Islands is more than 6,000 feet deep. The name "Caribbean" for this waterway was introduced in 1773 by Thomas Jeffreys, author of *The West Indies Atlas*. He named the sea after the Carib people, who are native to many of the islands in the area. The Caribbean Sea shares a geographic feature with the Mediterranean Sea: a series of elongate depressions separated by submarine ridges. The Mediterranean is larger, but the Caribbean is deeper, and has deeper connections with the Atlantic Ocean.[3]

Human Resources

The region's total population is a little over five and a half million. As Table 3.1 indicates, population sizes vary. Among the independent states, St. Kitts-Nevis, with 43,000 people, has the smallest population. Among the dependencies, Anguilla has the smallest number. Jamaica has the largest–2.4 million people. Population growth rates are low. For the 1987–1990 period they were highest in the Cayman Islands and the British Virgin Islands, and lowest in Guyana, Barbados, and Trinidad and Tobago. Demographers argue that while population growth rates are the result of the combined interaction of mortality, fertility, and migration, the latter two are the main determinants in the Caribbean since mortality levels have been substantially controlled.

Declining fertility, increased life-expectancy, and emigration affect the age structure of country populations. Experts estimate that the pro-

Table 3.1

Commonwealth Caribbean Socioeconomic Indicators

COUNTRY	SIZE (km^2)	POPULATION ('000, 1990)	PER CAPITA GDP (U.S.$, 1990)
Anguilla*	91	8.5	5,906
Antigua-Barbuda	440	84.0	4,985
Bahamas	13,942	253.3	10,565
Barbados	431	257.4	6,683
Belize	22,960	184.9	1,973
British Virgin Islands*	150	16.6	9,946
Cayman Islands*	260	27.3	23,320
Dominica	750	83.5	2,049
Grenada	345	100.2	2,100
Guyana	214,970	754.4	340
Jamaica	11,424	2,403.0	1,631
Montserrat*	102	12.0	6,133
St. Kitts-Nevis	269	42.9	3,359
St. Lucia	616	151.3	2,414
St. Vincent & The Grenadines	388	118.0	1,620
Trinidad & Tobago	5,128	1,234.4	4,127
Turks & Caicos*	417	12.4	5,669

Source: Caribbean Development Bank, *Annual Report 1991*, Bridgetown, Barbados, 1992.

N.A.—Not Available
* —British dependency
( )—Decline

GDP GROWTH (%, 1990)	PUBLIC DEBT (U.S.$ Million, 1990)	NATURAL RESOURCES
8.3	N.A.	none
2.8	268.3	none
N.A.	266.9	aragonite
(3.3)	466.6	oil
8.4	133.4	oil & gold (unexplored)
8.5	N.A.	none
11.2	30.8	none
6.2	77.7	none
5.2	82.1	none
(6.2)	1,839.8	bauxite, gold, diamonds, manganese; oil (under exploration)
3.8	4,386.4	bauxite
13.5	2.7	none
2.5	35.1	none
4.0	58.2	none
6.6	51.7	none
(0.4)	2,507.8	oil
1.8	N.A.	none

portion of the working-age population (ages 15–64) will increase over the next fifteen years while the under–15 group decreases. The number of senior citizens is also expected to increase steadily. Both scholars and statesmen in the region worry about the lack of adequate social security provision in the region and the fall in the real value of pensions and savings. When added to the estimates of probable decline in family-based support, the prospect of a future where aging is tied to poverty becomes both real and troubling.[4]

Caribbean emigration is not a new phenomenon. Dawn Marshall once described West Indians as having a "basic propensity to migrate." In the immediate post-World War II years and up to the late 1950s, the bulk of the outflow of people was to Britain. The major destination, however, changed in the mid-1960s to become the United States. This shift was due mainly to economic difficulties and tighter immigration regulations in Britain, and greater prospects in the United States.

Data from the United States Immigration and Naturalization Service (INS) indicate that between 1965 and 1985 there was a continuous pattern of high immigration from the Caribbean. During those two decades, 38,023 people migrated from Barbados; 306,084 from Jamaica; 101,664 from Trinidad and Tobago; and 92,515 from Guyana. Between 1985 and 1988 alone, 168,345 people from the twelve independent CARICOM states were admitted to permanent residency in the United States. Thousands of undocumented aliens also left the Caribbean during that period.[5] Studies by both American and West Indian scholars confirm that Caribbean emigrants are generally not unemployed, and are among the most highly skilled and motivated migrants. As one writer put it: "Contrary to popular belief, the United States is not receiving poor rural peasants from most Caribbean countries."[6]

Education levels in the Caribbean are fairly high, and literacy levels are very high. In 1991, Jamaica, St. Lucia, and Dominica had the lowest literacy rates in the region—74 percent, 78 percent, and 80 percent, respectively. Barbados, Trinidad and Tobago, and the Bahamas had the highest—99 percent, 98 percent, and 95 percent, respectively. Primary education is compulsory in all countries, and secondary education is mandatory in most.

The universities of the region are the University of the West Indies (UWI), the University of Guyana (UG), and the University of Belize (UB). The Bahamas also has a higher education body called the College of the Bahamas, and Trinidad and Tobago has the Eric Williams Medical Complex. These institutions offer certificates and degrees in a wide variety of disciplines. Many are undertaken on a joint basis. The Bachelor of Laws (LL.B.), for example, is offered jointly by UWI and UG, through the Council of Legal Education. Between March 1, 1970, when the Council was formed, and March 1992, 1,944 individuals have graduated from the law program. Many of them have gone on to serve in top governmental, judicial, and academic positions within the region.[7] UWI and UG also conduct joint M.Sc. and Ph.D. programs in development studies through the Consortium Graduate School of Social Sciences. And both the UWI and the College of the Bahamas have developed joint programs with the University of Miami in Florida and other American universities.

UWI awards terminal degrees, among them doctorates in law, medicine, and philosophy.[8] According to UWI Vice Chancellor Alister McIntyre, the UWI graduates some 2,600 students annually.[9] UG runs several Masters programs and a medical program, but over the years, low salaries, poor facilities, and migration of reputable faculty and staff have undermined UG's academic credibility.[10] Caribbean students also attend the University of the (U.S.) Virgin Islands, and American-run colleges in Antigua, Grenada, and Montserrat. In addition, the Cayman Islands has its own law school, established in 1982 to train Caymanians to practice law solely within the Caymans.

The 1988 Bourne Report mentioned in chaper two, however, notes that the main deficiencies of Caribbean education are at the tertiary level. It indicates that although there is a wide range of programs and institutions in the larger countries, facilities are rudimentary elsewhere. Moreover, only a very small proportion of the working-age population seems to have benefited from post-secondary education and training.[11] Vice Chancellor McIntyre has said: "In no English-speaking country other than Barbados is more than five percent of the population of tertiary age enrolled in a tertiary institution."[12] In addition, the brain drain from the region creates a significant depletion of the corps of technical, managerial, and other trained personnel. For instance, of the 2,600 annual UWI graduates mentioned above, some 1,600 emigrate, creating a critical situation considering that private and public sector demands for college graduates in the region are about 6,000 annually.

It was partly their awareness of these circumstances that led Caribbean leaders to express the following at their 1989 Summit:

[We are] *deeply conscious* of the critical importance of upgrading human resources at all levels and of enhancing the scientific and technological capacity of the Region if it is to overcome the present economic challenges and to avail itself of the opportunities unfolding in the Global Economy. . . .

[It is] *agreed* that Government should support the regional Universities in mobilizing resources—both from private sources and donor institutions and agencies—for expanding access to University education and for developing programs and activities in science, technology and related fields.[13]

Material Resources

There are some important natural resources in the area: oil, gold, diamonds, bauxite, and manganese. The problem though, is that very few countries have these or other natural resources. Bauxite is mined only in Guyana and Jamaica. Active oil exploration is underway in Guyana,[14] and geological evidence suggests that the Bahamas and Belize may have deposits in large enough quantities for commercial drilling. But currently, only Trinidad and Tobago, and Barbados, to a much lesser extent, have developed petroleum industries. Nevertheless, Antigua, the Bahamas, Jamaica, and St. Lucia do derive some economic benefit from the refining and transshipment activities that take place there. Aragonite is found in the Bahamas, but it has only decorative uses.

There are large manganese deposits in Guyana, but commercial mining ceased some years ago. Guyana also has timber, diamonds, and gold. Guyana's gold production, which had plummeted over recent years, increased to 39,000 ounces in 1990, from 17,288 ounces the previous year. Two Canadian companies, *Gold Star Resources* of Edmonton and *Cambior* of Montreal, are engaged in a U.S. $150 million gold mining investment expected to place production at 255,000 ounces from 1993 onward. Several companies are pursuing gold mining interests in the country, including England's *Consolidated Gold Fields*, Canada's *Dennison Mines*, and Brazil's *Paranapanema*. The reserves in the Omai District alone are estimated at 2.4 million ounces.[15] There is also evidence of gold in Belize.[16]

A Caribbean Stock Exchange was inaugurated on April 8, 1991, enabling investors in Barbados, Jamaica, and Trinidad and Tobago to trade in securities listed on the national stock markets of the three countries. The stock exchange, first proposed by Jamaican Prime Minister Michael Manley, is capitalized at U.S. $1.5 billion, and it lists ninety-two companies. Trading was delayed for three months because of differences over the method of settling transactions. The three governments later agreed that all settlements of cross-border trading will be completed within five days of transactions. The largest of the regional exchanges is that in Jamaica. Created in 1979, it listed forty-two companies at the beginning of April 1991, and had a capitalization of U.S.$850 million. Next is that in Trinidad and Tobago, created in 1981. It listed thirty-one firms at the creation of the regional exchange, and was capitalized at U.S. $420 million. Finally, the Barbados Stock Exchange. It was created in 1986, and was capitalized at U.S. $280 million in April 1991, with a trading list of thirteen companies. Guyana also plans to introduce a stock exchange. Finance Minister Carl Greenidge told the Guyana Parliament in March 1992 that the government had been pursuing the idea since 1987. However, there are several institutional, legal, and financial hurdles to be crossed before the exchange becomes a reality.[17]

Export income in the Caribbean comes mainly from oil, bauxite, tourism, agriculture—mainly sugar and bananas—and some light manufactures. On average, these contribute about 90 percent of the GDP of Caribbean countries. The region's economic profile is thus one of heavy reliance on foreign trade and aid, limited production and export diversification, low savings, and a dangerous dependence on foreign capital, among other things. The agricultural and public sectors are among the major employers. In both sectors productivity is low, but in the capital-intensive mining sector it is high. And, as was noted in the previous chapter, the public debt is astronomical. By CDB calculations it was U.S. $10.2 billion in 1990. Table 3.1 gives the figures for individual countries. Taxation and public spending as a percentage of GDP are also high. The state plays a major role in the economies of the region. Indeed, some analysts consider this to be essential for economic development.[18]

Several countries have had majority state participation in the agricultural and mining industries, and sometimes complete or dominant ownership and control, as in Guyana and Trinidad. However, the situation is changing, especially in Guyana and Jamaica, as governments pursue privatization and denationalization among voluntary and IMF-mandated measures to deal with their deteriorating economic circumstances.[19] In December 1990 for example, Atlantic Tele-Network of the United States Virgin Islands acquired 80 percent interest in the government-owned Guyana Telecommunications Corporation (GTC) for U.S. $16.5 million.[20] The GTC is one of eleven state agencies in the economic sector to be privatized over the next few years, part of the government's divestment program, started in 1989. Guyana's Finance Minister reported in his 1992 Budget Speech that up to the end of 1991, nine of the agencies had been privatized. As for Jamaica, up to September 1990, 263 public sector units were divested or targeted for privatization. According to Carl Stone, the World Bank ranks Jamaica first among twenty-six Third World countries in terms of the number of public sector agencies privatized or targeted for privatization.[21]

In spite of all of the negatives reflected above, what Thomas Anderson said about the Caribbean in 1984 is still largely true today:

> Compared with the Third World as a whole, the people are not as poor, ill-fed, unhealthy, or uneducated. In general there exists a substantial corps of well-educated civil servants, modern skills, and an awareness of their place in the world. Improvements are needed in all socioeconomic aspects, but . . . the Caribbean is not a backward region.[22]

Indeed, the Commonwealth Caribbean has produced two Nobel laureates—both from St. Lucia. In 1979, the late Sir Arthur Lewis was awarded the prize in Economics (with Theodore Schultz of the United States), and in 1992, the prize for Literature went to Derek Walcott.

Institutional Resources

The Caribbean is a stable region politically. No one can really challenge the assertion: "That the Caribbean is the fourth most democratically ruled region in the world—after Anglo-America, Western Europe, and Southwest Pacific—is a political reality."[23] Yet there has been a tendency in parts of the region to adopt repressive measures in the name of national security, in response to emergent militant opposition. Grenada, Guyana, Jamaica, St. Lucia, and Trinidad and Tobago have at varying times shown evidence of this.[24]

In the case of Guyana, Burnham era politics (1964–1985) saw the transformation of the country's political profile such that the regime's political security became indistinguishable from the nation's overall security. In the quest for power and the pursuit of "socialist transformation," the ruling party harassed critics, intimidated the opposition, and eliminated any serious threats. The best known case was the 1980 murder of Walter Rodney, well-known historian and leading political activist. The electoral process was subverted, freedoms of speech and assembly were curtailed, and the human rights situation deteriorated as the regime became progressively repressive.[25]

Like Australia, Canada, New Zealand, and many other members of the Commonwealth of Nations, most Caribbean nations retain the British Queen as their head of state, with resident Governors-General representing her. People in the Hispanic Caribbean find this curious since it appears to contradict the very sovereign independence for which Caribbean leaders fought.[26] In a sense it does, but it does not detract from the independent pursuit of policies. It has also facilitated some beneficial international support relations. Political systems in the region are patterned after the British model of parliamentary government, with modifications in Dominica, Guyana, and Trinidad and Tobago, which have presidential arrangements. Under this model, political parties vie for representation in Parliament, which is key to control of the government. Parties with such control form the government, either singly or in coalitions.

Dominica, Guyana, St. Kitts-Nevis, and St. Vincent and the Grenadines have unicameral legislatures; the others have bicameral ones. In the bicameral legislature, the Senate, the second chamber, is an appointed body and not an elected one. Although Dominica and St. Vincent and the Grenadines have no "upper house," some of their parliamentarians are designated as Senators. Barbados celebrated the 350th anniversary of its bicameral Parliament in June 1989,[27] making it the Commonwealth country with the second oldest Parliament after Britain, whose Parliament dates to 1275. While Guyana's president wields effective political power, presidents in Dominica and Trinidad and Tobago perform largely ceremonial duties, much like the Governors-General elsewhere. The real power in those republics and elsewhere (except Guyana) lies with the Prime Minister.[28]

Most CARICOM leaders have endorsed the proposal presented by Barbados at the 1989 Summit in Grenada to establish an Assembly of Caribbean Community Parliamentarians. The idea is to have each

CARICOM member-state select a maximum of four of their legislators to comprise a deliberative and consultative body to examine region-wide issues within the purview of the Treaty of Chaguaramas, the agreement that created CARICOM. According to the Barbados plan, the regional assembly would meet annually, rotating among member-states. It would mandate studies and reports on regional issues, hold hearings with regional officials, and adopt resolutions on region-wide matters.

Caribbean officials feel the regional Parliament would give a fillip to the integration process by allowing legislators to become more involved in regional concerns. It is also expected to be a catalyst in shaping regional public opinion. As a step toward implementing the initiative, while in Jamaica for the Intersessional CARICOM Summit on February 19, 1992, the Prime Minister of Barbados and the President of Guyana signed the Inter-Governmental Agreement establishing the Assembly. Other governments were also invited to sign it.[29]

Dominica is resolutely opposed to the Assembly. Speaking after the July 1992 regular summit in Trinidad and Tobago, Dominica's Prime Minister called the Assembly an unnecessary "Talk Shop." However, the West Indian Commission (WIC) not only applauded the Assembly initiative, but went one step further. The Commission recommended the creation of a CARICOM Assembly, where national parliaments would elect a mix of parliamentarians and non-parliamentarians. Under the Commission proposal, non-parliamentarians could come from non-governmental organizations, the private sector, the labor movement, academia and even the Caribbean diaspora, notable in Britain and North America. As an alternative, the Commission proposed that non-parliamentary observers be invited to participate in the work of the Assembly.[30]

Caribbean judiciaries are generally impartial and respected. Indeed, a dramatic tribute to this impartiality was the June 4, 1992 decision by the Trinidad and Tobago High Court to release the 114 people involved in the 1990 coup attempt, which was discussed in chapter two. Guyana has been striving for legal autochthony and has its own terminal appeals court.[31] There is a regional appeals court for the Eastern Caribbean based in St. Lucia. In 1967 the West Indies Associated States Court of Appeal was formed as successor to the British Caribbean Court of Appeal. It assumed the latter's appellate powers in relation to the then Associated States (Antigua-Barbuda, Dominica,

Grenada, St. Kitts-Nevis, St. Lucia, and St. Vincent), Montserrat, and the British Virgin Islands. The name was changed in 1982 to Eastern Caribbean Supreme Court. After Maurice Bishop assumed power in Grenada following the March 1979 coup, he withdrew Grenada from the court. However, Grenada rejoined the court on August 16, 1991.[32]

Most states, however, opt for ultimate recourse to the Judicial Committee of the British Privy Council as the final judicial arbiter. The Judicial Committee is essentially a court for the Commonwealth of Nations, with origins deep in English history. It hears appeals from the superior courts of the Channel Islands, the Isle of Man, British colonies and associated states, and independent countries in the Commonwealth of Nations that retain the system. Members of the Committee are not only British. They also come from other Commonwealth countries. Former Chief Justices Telford Georges of the Bahamas and Sir William Douglas of Barbados, and Trinidadian legal scholar and jurist Hugh Wooding are among West Indians who have served on the Judicial Committee. Moves are afoot to create a region-wide Caribbean Court of Appeals. The idea for the regional appeals court was endorsed by the WIC in its 1992 final report. The Commission even suggested that the court be designated the CARICOM Supreme Court. However, Trinidad and Tobago, which had been a leading advocate of the court (under Prime Minister A.N.R Robinson), has reversed its position (under Prime Minister Patrick Manning).[33]

Over the last few decades there have been several shades and models of conservatism and radicalism in the region. As will be seen in chapter eight, left-oriented parties controlled several governments during the 1970s, but for reasons also explained in chapter eight, a shift to the right began late in that decade. Some Caribbean societies are racially plural and have experienced racially based conflict. Guyana and Trinidad and Tobago are the primary cases. As was mentioned in chapter two and will be explained in chapter eight, political factionalism and ideological cleavages also have been part of the contemporary political histories of several Caribbean countries.

A long-time Caribbean specialist provided an excellent summary of the institutional aspects of the region:

> Throughout the Caribbean, opposition political parties win elections and take office. More significant, the courts retain their independence, the press is privately owned and relatively free, civil liberties are recog-

nized and respected, and dissent is tolerated. The military and security forces are removed from politics and as a rule do not abuse citizens. Although there are exceptions, there is an active civil society that protests, dissents, takes its cases to the courts, contests free elections and provides an effective opposition. *It is hard to find similar regimes in such numbers elsewhere in the world.*[34]

Military Resources

The security establishments in the region are uniformly minuscule, as Table 3.2 indicates (see page 64). The countries with standing armies are Antigua-Barbuda, the Bahamas, Barbados, Belize, Guyana, Jamaica, and Trinidad and Tobago. They are all poorly armed. The other states have Special Service Units (SSUs) and police forces. (See Appendix 2 for a list of military, paramilitary, and police forces.) The military arsenals of these states comprise mostly British and American weapons, some of World War II vintage. Arms and equipment include automatic rifles, mortars, artillery guns, anti-aircraft guns, observation aircraft, small troop transports, helicopters, and patrol boats. The inventories of some countries have been expanded by the United States, Britain, Canada, and other countries recently. While some countries, like Guyana, once had high military expenditures, there is neither research and development nor indigenous arms manufacture in the region.

Forbes Burnham of Guyana, and Eric Gairy and Maurice Bishop of Grenada were among the few West Indian leaders to use the military to help maintain political power, often under the guise of national security. Caribbean leaders have generally not been militarists in the sense of allowing the military to assume a high profile or become architects of state policy. Nor have they generally approached their roles with any military psyche. Perhaps the sole exception in the latter regard was Tom Adams, Prime Minister of Barbados from 1976 to 1985. Dion Phillips explains Adams's "undue emphasis on 'the security model'" as stemming partly from a psychological predisposition to martial values and life-styles. Not only did Adams increase the size of the Barbados Defense Force (BDF) from 610 in 1983 to 1,800 in 1985, but he was the first Barbadian leader to deploy the military overseas. As will be shown later, military expenditure increased considerably during his tenure and he used repressive measures to deal with dissent.[35]

Tom Adams articulated what came to be known as the "Adams

Doctrine." This was a political-military proposition relating to the security of the Eastern Caribbean. He saw the subregion's main security threat coming from internal subversion, coups, and mercenary action. Adams felt that the security of the entire region was jeopardized with such a development in any one country. Quick corrective action was needed in such an eventuality. The most expeditious action would require a speedily mobilized and deployed military force; a kind of rapid deployment force. He was thus a prime actor in the creation of the Regional Security System (RSS), a collective security arrangement that is assessed fully in chapter six.

Mention should also be made of Dominica and Guyana, where Patrick John and Forbes Burnham, respectively, took a keen interest in the military. Both leaders developed their interest as part of a strategy to use the military for political entrenchment. Especially in the case of Guyana, the political elites made no distinction between national security and regime security. Both John and Burnham donned military uniforms. John sported the uniform of the Dominica Defense Force (DDF), and gave himself the rank of Colonel. Burnham appeared at different times in uniforms from all three of the primary security agencies: the Guyana Defense Force (GDF), the Guyana National Service (GNS), and the Guyana People's Militia (GPM). Of course, his rank was the highest—that of General. Moreover, both leaders militarized their societies by increasing the size, expenditure, visibility, and political role of national security agencies.

Following the 1983 Grenada intervention, Eastern Caribbean countries developed, in conjunction with the United States, what may be termed a "Crisis Contingency Strategy." It is a strategy revolving around the SSUs, which are the equivalent of the American SWAT teams. The SSUs offer a combination of paramilitary and police skills, and are designated to deal with crises beyond the capacity of the regular police forces of which they are structurally a part. They were initially trained and armed by the United States and Britain.[36] However, both RSS and American officials in the region told me training is progressively becoming an American-British-Caribbean affair.[37] The United States commitment to training assistance was reaffirmed in February 1991 by Admiral Leon Edney, Commander-in-Chief of the United States Atlantic Command (LANTCOM) at a meeting with RSS officials in Barbados.

The idea of a subregional standing army was mooted in 1984, again by the late Tom Adams. He felt that one such army, rather than a

Table 3.2

Security Establishments in the Caribbean

COUNTRY	ARMY	COAST GUARD/NAVY
Anguilla	-----	-----
Antigua-Barbuda*	120	N.A.
Bahamas	868	868
Barbados*	800	(90)
Belize	760	(50)
British Virgin Islands	----	-----
Cayman Islands	----	-----
Dominica*	----	[20]
Grenada*	----	[25]
Guyana	5,000	(150)
Jamaica	3,350	(175)
Montserrat	----	-----
St. Kitts-Nevis*	----	[35]
St. Lucia*	----	N.A.
St. Vincent & The Grenadines*	----	N.A.
Trinidad & Tobago	2,600	(600)
Turks & Caicos	----	-----

Sources: The Military Balance 1990–91, London: International Institute for Strategic Studies, 1990; Richard Sharpe, ed., *Jane's Fighting Ships*, Surrey, UK: Jane's Information Group, 1990; Sandra W. Meditz and Dennis M. Hanratty, eds., *Islands of the Commonwealth Caribbean*, Washington D.C.: Library of Congress, 1989; Belize Police Force; Royal St. Lucia Police Force; Bahamas Ministry of National Security; Royal Cayman Islands Police, *Annual Report 1991*, George Town, January 20th, 1992; Jamaica Ministry of National Security and Justice, 1992.

* RSS member state
( ) Part of army establishment
[ ] Part of police establishment
N.A. Not available

AIR FORCE/AIR WING	POLICE	TOTAL
----	90	90
----	350	470
(40)	2,000	2,868[a]
----	1,500	2,300
(15)	640	1,400
----	110	110
----	253	253
----	370	370
----	655	655
(300)	4,800	9,800[b]
(150)	5,947	9,297[c]
----	106	106
----	415	415
----	590	590
----	570	570
(50)	4,000	6,600[d]
----	108	108

a The Bahamas "army" is really a "navy." The figures in the two categories are the same, hence this total.

b Guyana also has the GNS and the GPM.

c There are several other internal security agencies in Jamaica: ISCF; PMRB; SDC's. The Port Security Corps had a 1992 strength of 900.

d There is also a Special Reserve Force of about 1,000.

number of national armies, would provide an additional safeguard, namely protection of small governments against their own security services. Adams contemplated a 1,000-member Regional Defense Force headquartered in Barbados with smaller garrisons of fifty to ninety members on two other islands, preferably Antigua and Grenada. It was expected to cost between U.S. $60 million and $100 million with the financial support coming from the United States and Britain. Brigadier Rudyard Lewis of the BDF and the RSS presented a similar idea. His was for a five-year plan to develop a Caribbean Defense Force of 1,800. Seven hundred were to be combat infantry troops with the remainder in a Coast Guard and an air wing. He contemplated the force operating on the basis of "minimum force." Police deployment was to be the first line of operation, with the SSUs and army troops being second and third lines of action under a graduated crisis plan.[38]

Neither version of the standing army proposition survived. First, the United States, expected to be the main financial sponsor, was not keen on the idea. Not only were the anticipated costs substantial, but the United States preferred to operate bilaterally as much as possible. This permits more influence to be exerted on individual states. Moreover, the United States was not enthusiastic about creating too great a relative military independence within the Caribbean. It preferred to be the source on which Caribbean states rely for protection.

The idea also failed to pass muster with many Caribbean leaders. There were two basic reasons for this. The first was cost. Assuming equipment was secured free of charge, the annual recurrent cost of Caribbean support of the standing army was estimated at U.S. $12 million, equivalent to the annual public sector investment program of some Eastern Caribbean countries. Prime Minister James Mitchell of St. Vincent and the Grenadines declared: "My government has no intention of releasing one cent for the creation of any regional army or to waste money on security matters in preference for a basic needs program."[39] Second, some Caribbean leaders, mindful of the political implications of the plan, were not amenable to having Barbados be their *de facto* security guarantor.

External Capabilities

The paucity of the Caribbean's internal capability resources necessitates varying degrees of reliance on the support and assistance of several countries and regional and international organizations. Table 3.3

Table 3.3 **Major International Networks of Caribbean States**

COUNTRY	CARICOM	RIO PACT	OECS	COMMONWEALTH	INTERPOL	RSS	OAS	NAM	SELA	UN	ACP-EEC
Antigua-Barbuda	X		X	X	X	X	X			X	X
Bahamas	X	X[a]		X	X	X	X	X		X	X
Barbados	X			X	X	X	X	X	X	X	X
Belize	X			X	X		X	X	X	X	X
Dominica	X		X	X	X	X	X	X		X	X
Grenada	X		X	X	X	X	X	X	X	X	X
Guyana	X			X	X		X	X	X	X	X
Jamaica	X			X	X		X	X	X	X	X
St. Kitts-Nevis	X		X	X	X	X	X	X		X	X
St. Lucia	X		X	X	X	X	X	X		X	X
St. Vincent & The Grenadines	X		X	X	X	X	X			X	X
Trinidad & Tobago	X	X		X	X	X	X	X	X	X	X

Sources: Treaties and Alliances of the World, Detroit: Gale Research, 1986; *International Security Directory*, London: R. Hazel and Co., 1987; Michael Fooner, *Interpol*, New York: Plenum Press, 1989; *New York Carib News* (1991); *The World Fact Book* (1991).

[a] signed but never ratified
x— full member/subscriber
CARICOM—Caribbean Community and Common Market
RIO PACT—Inter-American Treaty of Reciprocal Assistance
OECS—Organization of Eastern Caribbean States
INTERPOL—International Criminal Police Organization
RSS—Regional Security System

OAS—Organization of American States
NAM—Non-Aligned Movement
SELA—Latin American Economic System
UN—United Nations
ACP-EEC—African, Caribbean, and Pacific States-European Economic Community

indicates the major regional and international organizations with which Caribbean countries are affiliated: the Caribbean Community and Common Market (CARICOM), the Organization of Eastern Caribbean States (OECS), the Commonwealth, the Organization of American States (OAS), the Regional Security System (RSS), the Non-Aligned Movement (NAM),[40] the United Nations (UN), the Latin American Economic System (SELA), and the ACP-EEC. Some countries are also members of other groups. For example, Barbados, Grenada, Guyana, Jamaica, and Trinidad and Tobago are part of the Latin-American Energy Organization (OLADE).

The capability support varies with the nature of the organization. It also varies in kind and among states. Some of it is bilateral; some is multilateral. For example, all states benefit from the various functional operations of the Commonwealth of Nations, especially the Commonwealth Fund for Technical Cooperation and the Commonwealth Caribbean Technical Assistance Program. That support is essentially economic and political. I noted earlier that some countries retain a constitutional link with the British monarch. The argument for this in many places, particularly in some of the very small states, is that the connection has material advantages. These nations expect, and often do get, the kind of favorable economic and political attention that they otherwise would not receive because of their small size and relatively little geopolitical importance to Britain.

States that are part of CARICOM and the OECS often take maximum advantage of the functional and political linkages of these organizations. The capability support there is essentially economic and political. For the RSS member-states, the assistance is military and political. In the case of the NAM, the support is mainly political. The Movement supported Guyana, Jamaica, and Barbados in 1976 in the face of destabilization efforts against them. It has consistently stood by Belize and Guyana in their disputes with Guatemala and Venezuela respectively. As I noted in the previous chapter, Guyana's activism within the Movement enabled it to secure the denial of membership to Venezuela in the early 1980s at a time of heightened tension between the two over the territorial claim by Venezuela.[41]

Perhaps the single most dramatic and extensive set of military relations ever involving an independent Caribbean country were those by Grenada with Cuba and the now defunct USSR during the Bishop era. Among the military agreements with Cuba was a Protocol of Military

Collaboration, signed either in 1981 or 1982, that established a twenty-seven-member Cuban military mission in the Grenada capital, St. George's. The Cuban team comprised specialists in infantry, engineering, logistics, and communications and reconnaissance. They were to be responsible for training military and civilian officials. Agreements with the Soviet Union were concluded in 1980, 1981, and 1982. One drafted before the 1983 United States intervention was never signed.

The 1980 agreement, signed in Cuba, provided for U.S. $5.8 million worth of military supplies including mortars, machine guns, carbines, trucks, anti-aircraft guns, and appropriate ammunition. That of 1981 provided for eight armored personnel carriers, 1,000 submachine guns, 1,000 grenades, 60 radios, uniforms, generators, and other equipment. The 1982 treaty provided for U.S. $13 million worth of arms and equipment that included 50 armored personnel carriers, 30 76-mm guns, 30 anti-tank guns, 50 portable missile launchers, 2,000 AK–47s, and mortars. The Bishop government also had military agreements with North Korea, Vietnam, Libya, and Czechoslovakia.[42]

There is a military relationship between Belize and Britain. Guatemala's claim to the entire territory of Belize led to serious national security threats as Belize advanced toward independence. Guatemala's invasion threats led to Belize's arranging a British security guarantee at the time of its independence in 1981. Since then the British have maintained a garrison there for "an appropriate period." The British presence is intended to defend Belize against Guatemalan aggression, assist in training the Belize army, gather intelligence on Central American developments, and help with disaster relief. Belize wants the military force to remain until a settlement is negotiated. As we will see in the next chapter, Belize does have a military establishment, but it is too small to be effective against the much better armed and trained Guatemalans.

The British detachment in Belize is designated British Forces Belize (BFB), with army, air force, and navy elements. It has its headquarters at Airport Camp, next to the Belize International Airport, and operationally it is divided into two Battle Groups. Battle Group North is based at Airport Camp with a forward base at Holdfast Camp in Cayo District, in western Belize. Battle Group South is headquartered at Rideau Camp in the Toledo District in the south of the country. There is also a detachment at Salamanca Camp near the border with Guatemala.

The main army element is an infantry battalion. Early in 1988, the Second Battalion of the Parachute Regiment led by Lt. Colonel Peter Dennison was on duty. Support was provided by an Armoured Reconnaissance Troop, an Artillery Gunnery Battery, a Field Squadron, and an Army Air Corps Flight, with ordnance, engineer, military police, and other support units. The Royal Navy component consists of a frigate or a destroyer from the West Indies Guardship, while the Royal Air Force contribution comprised Harrier ground-attack jets, Puma helicopters, and Rapier surface-to-air missiles.

The British forces are rotated every six months. In 1990, they numbered 1,500.[43] Guatemala officially recognized Belize as a sovereign state on August 14, 1991, although the territorial claim was not renounced.[44] The military tension is therefore expected to ease. Under such circumstances, the British presence will be reduced progressively. The Chief of the British Defense Staff, Field Marshall Sir Richard Vincent, has, however, expressed a strong desire to remain in Belize, partly because of the country's "superb training environment." Field Marshall Vincent paid a three-day visit to Belize during March 1992, during which he observed: "We will have to adapt our presence to move with the times, but we certainly very much want to remain."[45]

There are no other formal military alliances either within the Commonwealth Caribbean, or involving states in the region and elsewhere. But as Table 3.4 shows, Caribbean states are signatories to several multilateral security agreements. The Geneva Protocol deals with the prohibition of the use of poisonous gases and bacteriological weapons in war. The Partial Test Ban Treaty bans atmospheric and underwater nuclear testing. The Outer Space Treaty governs the activities of states in space and outer space exploration. The Treaty of Tlatelolco deals with nuclear weapons prohibition in Latin America, and the Non-Proliferation Treaty deals with nuclear proliferation globally. The Sea Bed Treaty prohibits the emplacement of nuclear weapons in sea and ocean floors. The Bacteriological Warfare Convention prohibits the development, production, and stock-piling of bacteriological and toxic weapons.[46] A few Caribbean states are also signatories to other agreements. Guyana, for example, is party to the Treaty of Amazonian Cooperation signed in July 1978 to facilitate economic cooperation in the Amazonian basin area. President Hugh Desmond Hoyte of Guyana participated in the third summit of Amazonian basin leaders, held in Brazil, February 10–12, 1992.[47]

Table 3.4 Caribbean Subscription to Multilateral Agreements

COUNTRY	GENEVA PROTOCOL	PARTIAL TEST BAN TREATY	OUTERSPACE TREATY	TREATY OF TLATELOLCO	NON-PROLIF TREATY	SEA BED TREATY	BACTERIO-LOGICAL CONVENTION
Antigua-Barbuda	.	.	.	1983[2]	1985[1]	.	.
Bahamas	.	1976[1]	1976[1]	1977[1]	1976[1]	.	1986
Barbados	1976	.	1968	1969[2]	1980	.	1973
Belize	.	.	.	.	1985[1]	.	1986
Dominica	.	.	.	1990	1984[1]	.	.
Grenada	.	.	.	1975[2]	1975[1]	.	1986
Guyana	.	.	S	.	.	.	S
Jamaica	1970[1]	S	1970	1969[2]	.	1986	1975
St. Kitts-Nevis	.	.	.	.	.	.	.
St. Lucia	.	.	.	.	1979[1]	.	.
St. Vincent & The Grenadines	.	.	.	.	1984[1]	.	.
Trinidad & Tobago	1970[1]	1964	S	1970[2]	1986	.	.

Sources: SIPRI Yearbook 1987,. New York, Oxford University Press, 1987; New York Carib News, (1990).

S—signature without further action
1 Notification of succession.
2 In force due to declaration which waived the requirements for the entry into force of the Treaty.

There is a certain artificiality about the signature by Caribbean countries of most of these agreements. These countries have neither the military and technological capability nor the "political weight" to enable them to contribute substantively to the subjects of those agreements. Nor is there concern by the international community about any serious consequence of their breach of these agreements. Moreover, financial constraints prevent some states from participating meaningfully in initiatives sponsored under some of them. Grenada, for instance, tried in 1988 to withdraw from OPANAL, the Mexico-based secretariat established by the Treaty of Tlatelelco, on grounds of financial incapacity.

The involvement of Caribbean countries in international organizations places severe financial burdens on several of them. One gets a sense of this burden by noting that in 1988, payments to the United Nations by the OECS (Antigua-Barbuda, Dominica, Grenada, St. Kitts-Nevis, St. Lucia, and St. Vincent and the Grenadines) amounted to U.S. $735,720. However, their arrears were U.S. $576,893, much of it accumulated over several years. Debts to the regular United Nations budget for 1991 by CARICOM countries amounted to some U.S. $988,173. In addition, they owed almost U.S. $200,000 for peacekeeping operations. In 1991, Guyana owed the United Nations U.S. $223,000 in arrears, but Jamaica, with an annual assessment of U.S. $92,131, paid nothing. Moreover, in spring 1991 Grenada's voting rights in the United Nations, the Pan American Health Organization (PAHO), and the African, Caribbean, and Pacific (ACP) Group were jeopardized due to payment defaults. Grenada's arrears to the United Nations amounted to U.S. $571,000. Those to PAHO totaled just over U.S. $125,000.[48]

Nevertheless, the signatures of the Caribbean states indicate to the international community a certain commitment to the issues in question. They also reflect endorsement of certain principles regarding the use of force, instruments of destruction, and the peaceful approach to the settlement of disputes. Further, such signatures offer Caribbean states a measure of political respect which they may use, and often have used, to their advantage in pursuing their own limited security interests.

Much of the external capability support comes through bilateral relationships. Most of this aid comes from the United States, Britain, and Canada in the form of security assistance, development aid, and

Table 3.5

U.S. Military and Economic Assistance to the Caribbean
(U.S. $ in millions)

COUNTRY	1962-86	1987	1988	1989	1990	1962-90
Bahamas	0.1	0.1	0.1	*	1.6	1.9
Barbados	4.1	----	*	0.4	*	4.6
Belize	73.5	16.3	10.8	11.0	8.5	120.0
Grenada	59.8	0.1	0.1	0.2	*	60.3
Guyana	142.9	6.5	7.0	7.1	8.8	172.2
Jamaica	930.6	93.2	80.9	119.7	74.5	1,299.2
Trinidad & Tobago	36.0	0.1	0.1	2.3	0.9	39.3
Other Eastern Caribbean Countries a	535.6	64.3	41.3	36.5	35.4	713.0

Source: USAID, *U.S. Overseas Loan and Grants and Assistance from International Organizations July 1, 1945-September 30, 1990, Washington, D.C. 1991.*

* Less than $50,000.
a Includes British Dependencies in the Caribbean.

technical assistance. Aid from these countries, illustrated in Tables 3.5–3.8, is always a mere fraction of their total foreign aid packages. Nevertheless, it is considered essential by people in the region. Over the years, Caribbean countries also have received economic and military assistance from the former USSR, China, Cuba, Germany, North Korea, South Korea, Venezuela, and Brazil, among other countries. Multilateral support comes from the European Economic Community (EEC), the Inter-American Development Bank, and other agencies.[49]

Apart from the British security guarantee to Belize, there are no security patron-client relationships in the area. The closest to this recently have been the relations developed between the United States and a few Caribbean countries. The 1980 victory of Edward Seaga in Jamaica witnessed the blossoming of a special United States-Jamaica relationship between 1980 and Seaga's departure in February 1989. This was intended primarily to reverse relations developed with

Table 3.6

IMET Assistance to Caribbean Countries
(U.S. $ in thousands and students)

COUNTRY	FY 1980	FY 1981	FY 1982	FY 1983	FY 1984
Antigua-Barbuda	---- [----]	---- [----]	---- [----]	14 [9]	30 [9]
Bahamas	---- [----]	---- [----]	---- [----]	---- [----]	---- [----]
Barbados	36 [14]	17 [12]	56 [10]	52 [22]	70 [22]
Belize	---- [----]	---- [----]	20 [16]	48 [19]	50 [23]
Dominica	---- [----]	8 [7]	4 [1]	11 [6]	43 [16]
Grenada	---- [----]	---- [----]	---- [----]	---- [----]	60 [----]
Guyana	---- [----]	---- [11]	14 [22]	25 [10]	---- [----]
Jamaica	13 [11]	49 [8]	73 [20]	168 [73]	201 [60]
St. Kitts-Nevis	---- [----]	---- [----]	---- [----]	---- [----]	32 [10]
St. Lucia	---- [----]	2 [2]	8 [3]	14 [6]	42 [15]
St. Vincent & The Grenadines	---- [----]	---- [1]	---- [----]	31 [8]	44 [12]
Trinidad & Tobago	---- [----]	---- [----]	---- [----]	---- [----]	---- [----]

Source: U.S. Defense Security Assistance Agency, *Foreign Military Sales, Foreign Military Construction Sales, and Military Assistance Facts as of September 30, 1990,* Washington, D.C. 1991.

[ ] Number of students.

FY 1985	FY 1986	FY 1987	FY 1988	FY 1989	FY 1990
45 [11]	42 [10]	40 [7]	46 [10]	3 [----]	22 [----]
44 [24]	42 [26]	55 [17]	70 [18]	37 [19]	51 [19]
69 [18]	69 [14]	71 [14]	88 [12]	2 [----]	53 [13]
98 [79]	72 [23]	95 [21]	64 [18]	107 [19]	106 [19]
44 [8]	46 [10]	53 [11]	44 [7]	45 [9]	22 [4]
63 [18]	75 [18]	78 [18]	71 [13]	71 [15]	66 [12]
---- [----]	---- [----]	---- [----]	---- [----]	---- [----]	---- [----]
278 [72]	284 [57]	317 [63]	298 [60]	613 [53]	301 [55]
26 [7]	32 [8]	54 [10]	64 [13]	44 [8]	65 [14]
48 [12]	48 [13]	36 [8]	21 [4]	45 [9]	47 [12]
51 [13]	51 [13]	50 [10]	48 [8]	47 [8]	43 [9]
39 [11]	50 [10]	65 [16]	60 [13]	10 [6]	43 [4]

Table 3.7

British Aid to the Caribbean, 1985–1990 (£ in thousands)

COUNTRY	1985	1986	1987	1988	1989	1990	TOTALS
Antigua-Barbuda	544	767	955	1,171	757	998	5,192
Bahamas	8	7	15	11	30	81	152
Barbados	298	442	542	524	285	4,394	6,485
Belize	5,706	3,179	2,120	3,072	3,786	5,461	23,324
Dominica	1,600	2,337	854	1,976	2,493	1,331	10,591
Grenada	1,450	776	739	1,230	1,352	1,110	6,657
Guyana	354	487	635	647	6,561	15,303	23,987
Jamaica	7,986	3,777	13,493	20,014	20,304	14,778	80,352
St. Kitts-Nevis	918	954	1,432	2,096	711	934	7,045
St. Lucia	530	1,018	3,174	2,852	8,872	2,373	18,819
St. Vincent & The Grenadines	1,250	857	1,093	898	1,091	1,337	6,526
Trinidad & Tobago	136	61	1,874	262	640	732	3,705
TOTALS	20,780	14,662	26,926	34,753	46,882	48,832	192,835

Source: Overseas Development Administration, *British Aid Statistics 1985–1989,* London, 1990; Overseas Development Administration; *British Overseas Aid: 1991 Annual Review,* London, 1991.

Table 3.8

**Canadian Assistance to the Caribbean, 1987–1990
(Canadian $ in millions)**

COUNTRY	1987-88	1988-89	1989-90	TOTAL
Antigua-Barbuda	0.73	1.72	0.59	3.04
Barbados	4.81	−0.35	−0.27	4.19
Belize	5.10	1.06	0.68	6.84
Dominica	1.46	5.61	4.72	11.79
Grenada	6.09	3.65	0.70	10.44
Guyana	2.61	2.76	17.45	22.82
Jamaica	31.11	41.16	33.34	105.61
St. Kitts-Nevis	1.23	2.12	0.60	3.95
St. Lucia	2.37	1.32	1.66	5.35
St. Vincent & The Grenadines	2.10	0.50	0.94	3.63
Trinidad & Tobago	−0.12	1.71	2.43	4.02
TOTAL	**57.58**	**61.26**	**62.84**	**181.68**

Source: Canadian International Development Agency, *CIDA Annual Report 1989–90*, Ottawa, 1990.

These figures represent government-to-government assistance only. Negative figures represent differences between grant disbursements and loan payments.

Cuba by Michael Manley between 1972 and 1980. It was also designed to show Jamaica as a model of conservative politics in the Caribbean. Moreover, Jamaica was to serve as a surrogate in the region. (This is explained more fully in chapter five.) Close relationships with the United States also developed in Grenada and Dominica after the 1983 intervention in Grenada. They developed to the point where Prime Minister Mary Eugenia Charles of Dominica felt confident to declare: "We in the Caribbean, who see ourselves as allies of the Americans, wish to maintain that tradition and uphold the Monroe Doctrine, as it has developed through the ages."[50]

Some countries have had bilateral security agreements with the United States pertaining to territory leased for military installations. The use of Caribbean states for this purpose dates to World War II when territory in Antigua-Barbuda, the Bahamas, Guyana, Jamaica, St. Lucia, and Trinidad and Tobago was granted by Britain, then the region's major colonizer, under ninety-nine-years' lend-lease agreements. Changes in American defense planning, technological innovations in the defense industry, and nationalism within the region have since then drastically reduced the use of Caribbean states for this purpose.

Recently, only Antigua-Barbuda and the Bahamas have had such relationships. An eleven-year agreement signed between Antigua-Barbuda and the United States in 1977 gave that Eastern Caribbean country an annual rent of U.S. $1.2 million. In 1980, U.S. $20,000 was added annually for the Voice of America transmitter established there. In 1984, the Bahamas secured an agreement to lease facilities for U.S. $100 million over ten years. In August 1992, the Bahamas and the United States signed an agreement extending the 1984 agreement for an additional five years. The 1992 agreement provides for continued operation of the Atlantic Underwater Test Evaluation Center (AUTEC), the United States Navy anti-submarine warfare facility at Andros Island. It also covered the lease of three additional sites on Eleuthera Island—totalling 40 acres—to support AUTEC.[51] As will be seen in chapter seven, the United States also has military installations, facilities, and personnel in Bermuda, the U.S. Virgin Islands, Cuba, Puerto Rico, Panama, and elsewhere.

Conclusion

In sum, Caribbean countries are not only small in size with small populations, but most of them have no strategic resources. Oil, bauxite, gold, and other natural resources exist in the region, but few countries have them. While political systems are stable and there are good educational and other institutions, emigration contributes to a significant brain drain. All of this helps explain the dependency of Caribbean countries on a few products and on foreign aid and technical assistance.

The military establishments of the six countries with armies are both small and poorly equipped. Belize, one of the six, consequently had to obtain a security umbrella from Britain in the face of major threats from neighboring Guatemala in 1981. Most states are signatories to international treaties dealing with weapons of mass destruction and the peaceful settlement of disputes. A few of them have military installation agreements with the United States, and in the early 1980s there were dramatic deals between Grenada and some communist countries. But apart from Tom Adams of Barbados and the use of the military for political expediency by leaders in Grenada and Guyana, Caribbean leaders have not been militarists.

The combined effects of poor internal capability and the extensive reliance on external sources produce vulnerability within the Caribbean. Caribbean countries are not only vulnerable to fluctuations in world market price for commodities like sugar, bauxite, and oil, but also to natural hazards such as hurricanes, which often create havoc in both the banana and tourist industries. External aid and development financing are also subject to political and economic vicissitudes outside the control of the region. Moreover, with the Cold War now ended, many Caribbean and other developing countries fear that the democratizing states of Eastern Europe will be perceived as having more attractive investment prospects, and greater need for scarce aid resources.[52] Indeed, during spring 1990, Mark Edelman, Deputy Administrator of USAID, admitted that the United States had slashed U.S. $20 million from Jamaica's 1990 aid package and had given it to Poland. According to Edelman, Jamaica's case was not singular.[53]

In addition, during late spring 1991, it was learned that Canadian aid to the region was being cut. Canadian aid is managed through the Canadian International Development Agency (CIDA). According to one report, a primary reason for the cuts pertains to CIDA's own effort to help the government of Prime Minister Brian Mulroney build a special fund of Can. $135 million dollars to support economic recovery programs in post-communist Eastern Europe, post-war rebuilding in the Persian Gulf, and specific environmental projects.[54] Given this, it was reassuring to hear from Lynda Chalker, Britain's Minister of State for Foreign and Commonwealth Affairs, that Britain's increased Middle East aid will not result in reductions to the Caribbean.[55]

In the final analysis, the capabilities of Caribbean nations are considerably limited. While this by itself does not militate against the development of regional security measures, Caribbean capabilities are insufficient for security measures that could rely primarily on countries in the region. Moreover, they do not enhance the credibility of present measures to reduce vulnerability, or to deal with the drug or other problems that the political elites deem critical. In light of this reality, it is important to see in the next three chapters what security initiatives Caribbean states have undertaken over the years since independence.

Notes

1. See David Vital, *The Inequality of States*, London: Clarendon Press, 1967; Michael Handel, *Weak States in the International System*, London: Frank Cass, 1981; Edward Kolodziej and Robert Harkavy, "Developing States and the International Security System," in John Stremlau, ed., *The Foreign Policy Priorities of Third World States*, Boulder, CO: Westview Press, 1982; Stephanie Neuman, "Third World Industries: Capabilities and Constraints in Recent Wars," in Stephanie Neuman and Robert Harkavy, eds., *The Lessons of Recent Wars in the Third World*, Lexington, MA: Lexington Books, 1987; and William J. Perry, "Desert Storm and Deterrence," *Foreign Affairs* 70 (Fall 1991): 66–82.

2. Conrad Mason, "Devastation," *Caribbean Contact* (Barbados), October 1988, pp. 1, 2; "Devastation," *Caribbean Contact*, October 1989, pp. 1, 7; and June Degia, "Life after Hurricane Hugo," *Caribbean Contact*, November 1989, pp. 8–9.

3. *Encyclopedia Britannica*, volume 4, London: Encyclopedia Britannica Inc., 1971, p. 902; and Thomas D. Anderson, *Geopolitics of the Caribbean*, New York: Praeger, 1984, pp. 15–16.

4. See Patricia Anderson, "The Demographic Basis of Social Instability in the Caribbean of the Eighties," in Anthony T. Bryan, J. Edward Greene, and Timothy M. Shaw, eds., *Peace, Development, and Security in the Caribbean*, New York: St. Martin's Press, 1990.

5. Dennis Conway, "Emigration to North America: The Continuating Option for the Caribbean," *Caribbean Affairs* 3 (April-June 1990): 109–19.

6. See Robert Pastor, "Caribbean Immigration and U.S. Immigration Policy," in Jorge Heine and Leslie Manigat, eds., *The Caribbean and World Politics*, New York: Holmes and Meier, 1988. Also see Dawn Marshall, "Toward an Understanding of Caribbean Migration," in Mary Kritz, ed., *Immigration and Refugee Policy: Global and Domestic Issues*, Lexington, MA: D.C. Heath, 1983.

7. See Oscar Ramjeet, "Law School Churning Out Graduates, But Miss Charles Questions Quality," *Stabroek News* (Guyana), April 25, 1992, p. 9.

8. The 1990–1991 academic year saw the phased introduction of the semester system at UWI. Before then, like UG, UWI worked according to the British system, with year-long courses. See "UWI Introduces Two Semester System," *CARICOM Perspective* 49 (July-December 1990): 64.

9. "More University Graduates Needed," *Stabroek News*, May 16, 1991, p. 2.

10. See, for example, "UG Dean Warns of Academic Isolation Threat," *Stabroek News*, February 19, 1992, p. 12.

11. Compton Bourne, *Development Performance and Prospects in the Caribbean Community to the Year 2000*, Report prepared for the CARICOM Secretar-

iat, Georgetown, Guyana, March 1988. Also, see Errol Miller, "The Legacy of Post-Emancipation Education: Whose Interests Does it Serve?" *Caribbean Affairs* 2 (July-September 1989): 125–42; Alister McIntyre, "The West Indian University Revisited: Sixth Eric Williams Memorial Lecture, Central Bank of Trinidad and Tobago, June 10, 1988," *Bulletin of Eastern Caribbean Affairs* 14 (Nos. 5 and 6, 1988): 1–11; Gerald Lalor, " Education and Training in the Caribbean," *Courier* 123 (September-October 1990): 68–70; and Shridath Ramphal, "The University in the 1990s: Finding Ways to Reduce the Knowledge Gap," *Caribbean Affairs* 3 (July-September 1990): 109–14. Ramphal, former Guyana Foreign Minister and Commonwealth Secretary-General, is at present Chancellor of UWI.

12. "More University Graduates Needed" (see note 9).

13. *Grand Anse Declaration*, Annex 1, *Resolution on Human Resource Development and the University of the West Indies*, Grand Anse, Grenada, July 1989.

14. See "Oil Exploration is a Top Priority," *Stabroek News*, March 21, 1991, pp. 6–7.

15. See Canute James, "Guyanese Gold Comeback Planned," *Financial Times* (London), January 23, 1991; and "Guyana Gold Rush," *Latin Finance* 25 (1991): 7.

16. See Jean Cornec, "Gold Potential of the Maya Mountains of Belize," *Belizean Studies* 18 (1990): 2–10.

17. See *Caribbean Update* 17 (May 1991): 1; and Government of Guyana, Parliament, *1992 Budget Speech: Parliamentary Sessional Paper No. 1 of 1992*, Presented 30 March 1992 by Minister of Finance Carl B. Greenidge to the Fifth Parliament of Guyana, pp. 38–41.

18. See, for example, Clifford E. Griffin, "Postinvasion Political Security in the Eastern Caribbean," in Ivelaw L. Griffith, ed., *Strategy and Security in the Caribbean*, New York: Praeger, 1991, pp. 83–91.

19. See Clive Thomas, *The Poor and the Powerless*, New York: Monthly Review Press, 1988, esp. chs. 9, and 11.; Linden Lewis, "Privatization in the Caribbean: A Response to Global Restructuring," Paper presented at the XVth Annual Conference of the Caribbean Studies Association, Trinidad, May 1990; and Ronald Kempe Hope, Sr., "Privatization and Economic Renewal in Developing Countries with Special Reference to Guyana," Paper presented at the 1990 Conference of the Caribbean Studies Association.

20. "Guyana Gov. Rights to Only 20% of Telephone Co," *New York Carib News*, February 12, 1991, p. 37.

21. See Carl Stone, "Putting Enterprise to Work: The Jamaican Divestment Experience," *Caribbean Affairs* 5 (January-March 1992): 12–23.

22. Anderson, *Geopolitics of the Caribbean*, p. 41. For analysis of the region's economic situation see Thomas, *The Poor and the Powerless*; Bourne, *Development Performance and Prospects*; Caribbean Development Bank, *Annual Report 1991*, Bridgetown, Barbados, 1992; Terrence Farrell, "Structural Adjustment and Transformation in the Caribbean: Management Strategies Based on the Lessons of Experience," in Bryan et al., *Peace, Development, and Security in the Caribbean*; and West Indian Commission, *Time For Action: The Report of the West Indian Commission*, Black Rock, Barbados, 1992, esp. chapters 4, 5, and 6.

23. Anderson, *Geopolitics of the Caribbean*, p. 6. The fact that Anderson defines the Caribbean in "Caribbean Basin" terms does not change the reality.

24. See Dion E. Phillips, "Caribbean Militarization: A Response to the Cri-

sis," *Contemporary Marxism* 10 (1985): 92–109; Mark Adkin, *Urgent Fury: The Battle for Grenada*, Lexington, MA: Lexington Books, 1989, Chs. 1–3; and Neville Duncan, "Political Violence in the Caribbean," in Griffith, *Strategy and Security in the Caribbean*.

25. For more on this see Ivelaw L. Griffith, "The Military and the Politics of Change in Guyana," *Journal of Interamerican Studies and World Affairs* 33 (Summer 1991): 143–48.

26. For example, see Andrés Serbín, "Race and Politics: Relations Between the English-speaking Caribbean and Latin America," *Caribbean Affairs* 2 (April-June 1989): 146–71.

27. Mark Lee, "Colorful Ceremony Marks 350th Annivesary of Bajan Parliament," *New York Carib News*, July 4, 1989, p. 4.

28. Guyana also has a number of constitutional "houses"—the Supreme Congress of the People, the National Congress of Local Democratic Organs, and so forth. These are not legislative, but deliberative. See Ivelaw L. Griffith, "New Approaches to Political Change and Development in the Third World: An Assessment of Guyana's System of Local Democracy," Unpublished paper, 1982; Francis Alexis, *Changing Caribbean Constitutions*, Brigetown, Barbados: Antilles Publishers, 1983, pp. 140–59; and Fred Phillips, *West Indian Constitutions: Post Independence Reforms*, New York: Oceana Publishers, 1985, ch. 2. Also see Arend Lijphart, "Size, Pluralism, and the Westminster Model of Democracy: Implications for the Eastern Caribbean," in Jorge Heine, ed., *A Revolution Aborted: The Lessons of Grenada*, Pittsburgh: University of Pittsburgh Press, 1991; and Donald C. Peters, *The Democratic System in the Eastern Caribbean*, Westport, CT: Greenwood Press, 1992.

29. See Caribbean Community Secretariat, *Proposal for the Establishment of an Assembly of Caribbean Community Parliamentarians*, Document HGC 89/10/3, May 31, 1989; and Caribbean Community Secretariat, *Communiqué, Third Intersessional Meeting of the Conference of Heads of Government of the Caribbean Community*, CARICOM Press Release No. 17/1992, 26 February 1992, p. 2.

30. Sandra Baptiste, "Dominica Remains Opposed to CARICOM Assembly of Parliamentarians," *Stabroek News*, July 3, 1992, p. 16; and *Time For Action*, pp. 485–90.

31. See Rudolph James and Harold Lutchman, *Law and the Political Environment in Guyana*, Georgetown, Guyana: Institute of Development Studies, University of Guyana, 1984, chapters 1 and 3.

32. See "Grenada Rejoins OECS Court," *New York Carib News*, August 27, 1991, p. 4.

33. Rickey Singh, "Caribbean Leaders Say 'Yes' to Court of Appeal," *Daily Nation* (Barbados), July 7, 1988, p. 12; "Manning Says 'No'," *New York Carib News*, July 7, 1992, p. 6; and *Time For Action*, pp. 497–510. Isaac Hyatali, a former Chief Justice of Trinidad, lauds the work of the Privy Council, but presents eight compelling reasons for a Caribbean Court of Appeal. See his "Towards a West Indian Jurisprudence," *Caribbean Affairs* 1 (July-September 1988): 41–56. For an examination of Caribbean legal systems see Velma Norton, *Commonwealth Caribbean Legal Systems: A Study of Small Jurisdictions*, Holmes Beach, FL: Wm. W. Gaunt and Sons, 1989.

34. Aaron Segal, "The Caribbean: Small is Scary," *Current History* 90 (March 1991): 107. Emphasis added.

35. See Dion E. Phillips, "Change and Continuity in Barbados Defense Policy," in Griffith, *Strategy and Security in the Caribbean.*

36. See Bernard Diederich, "The End of West Indian Innocence: Arming the Police," *Caribbean Review* 13 (Spring 1984): 10–12; Frank Prail, "U.S. Teaching Defense in the Caribbean," *New York Times*, February 19, 1984, p. 3; Andrew Walker, "Security of the Eastern Caribbean," *Jane's Defense Weekly* January 17, 1987, p. 61; and Humberto García Muñiz, *Boots, Boots, Boots: Intervention, Regional Security, and Militarization in the Caribbean 1979–1986,* Río Piedras, Puerto Rico: Caribbean Project for Justice and Peace, 1986, pp. 11–15.

37. Interviews with Commander Dean Schopp, Chief, United States Military Liaison Office in the Eastern Caribbean, Bridgetown, Barbados, August 12, 1987; and with Lt. Commander Peter Tomlin, Staff Officer, RSS, Hastings, Barbados, July 21, 1988.

38. For more on this, see U.S. Congress, House, Committee on Armed Services, *Report on the Delegation to the Eastern Caribbean and South American Countries,* 98th Cong., February, 1984, pp. 24–43.

39. Rickey Singh, "Policy Turnabout," *Caribbean Contact*, September 1984, p. 1.

40. In February 1989, Grenadian Foreign Minister Ben Jones announced that Grenadian membership in the Non-Aligned Movement would be reactivated later that year. It had been deactivated in 1984 following the crisis in Grenada that precipitated the October 1983 intervention by the United States.

41. See Rashleigh Jackson, *Safeguarding the Security of Small States,* Georgetown, Guyana: Ministry of Foreign Affairs, 1982; Perry Mars, "Destabilization, Foreign Intervention, and Socialist Transformation in the Caribbean," *Transition* 7 (1983): 33–54; Lloyd Searwar, "The Security of Small States," *CARICOM Bulletin* 6 (1988): 1–11; and J. Braveboy-Wagner, *The Caribbean in World Affairs*, Boulder, CO: Westview Press, 1989, ch. 3.

42. For more on this, see *Grenada Documents: An Overview and Selection,* Washington: Departments of State and Defense, 1984, esp. documents 13–20; and Adkin, *Urgent Fury,* pp. 21–26. For a discussion of Grenada's foreign policy during the Bishop years, see Henry Gill, "The Foreign Policy of the Grenada Revolution," *Bulletin of Eastern Caribbean Affairs* 3 (1981): 1–5; Gregory Sandiford, *The New Jewel Movement: Grenada's Revolution, 1979–1983,* Washington, D.C., U.S. Dept of State, Foreign Policy Institute, 1985, pp. 111–41; and Anthony Payne, "The Foreign Policy of the PRG," in Heine, *A Revolution Aborted.*

43. Major-General Edward Fursdon, "Belize," *The Army Quarterly and Defense Journal* 118 (January 1988): 39–41; International Institute for Strategic Studies, *The Military Balance 1990–1991,* London: International Institute for Strategic Studies, 1990, p. 186; and Alma H. Young, "The Territorial Dimension of Caribbean Security: The Case of Belize," in Griffith, *Strategy and Security in the Caribbean,* pp. 136–37.

44. Mission of Belize to the United Nations, "Press Release by the Guatemalan Government on 14th August 1991," Security Council Document A/46/36/B. Diplomatic relations between the two countries were established a month later, on September 10, 1991.

45. "Troops Want to Remain in Belize," *New York Carib News*, March 17, 1992, p. 32.

46. For more explanation of these treaties and agreements, see *SIPRI Yearbook*, New York: Oxford University Press, 1987, pp. 457–59.

47. George Baird, "Amazon Summit Opens on Optimistic Note," *Guyana Chronicle*, February 11, 1992, p. 1.

48. See "OECS States among UN Deadbeats," *New York Carib News*, February 7, 1989; "Grenada May Lose Voting Rights," *Jamaican Weekly Gleaner*, May 6, 1991, p. 9; and "Caribbean Nations in Arrears on UN Dues," *New York Carib News*, January 4, 1992, p. 10.

49. On the question of aid, see William Demas, "Notes on Aid Programs and Systems and the CARICOM Integration Process"; and Edwin Carrington, "The Record of CARICOM /ACP-EEC Relations," both in *Ten Years of CARICOM*, Washington: Inter-American Development Bank, 1984.

50. Mary Eugenia Charles, "Isolation vs. One-ness: The Continuing Validity of the Monroe Doctrine," *Caribbean Affairs* 1 (April-June 1988): 154.

51. "U.S. Expands its Military Bases in the Bahamas," *Stabroek News* August 22, 1992, p. 11.

52. For a useful discussion of this, see Yezid Sayigh, *Confronting the 1990s: Security in the Developing Countries*, Adelphi Papers No. 251, London: International Institute for Strategic Studies, 1990.

53. Tony Best, "Manley Got Screwed," *New York Carib News*, April 24, 1990, p. 3.

54. Rickey Singh, "Reduced Aid for CARICOM," *New York Carib News*, June 26, 1991, p. 5.

55. "Caribbean Will Still Get British Aid," *Jamaican Weekly Gleaner*, March 18, 1991, p 4. The British Minister made the commitment while in Grenada as part of a visit to the Eastern Caribbean during March 1991. She held talks with officials in Barbados, Dominica, Grenada, St. Kitts-Nevis, and St. Vincent and the Grenadines.

4 INDIVIDUAL SECURITY MEASURES: THE LARGER STATES

Decolonization reached the Caribbean in the 1960s. Jamaica and Trinidad and Tobago secured their independence first, in 1962. Barbados and Guyana won theirs in 1966. The other countries became independent in the 1970s and 1980s as folllows: the Bahamas, 1973; Grenada, 1974; Dominica, 1978; St. Lucia, and St. Vincent and the Grenadines, 1979; Antigua-Barbuda, and Belize, 1981; St. Kitts-Nevis, 1983.

Among other things, sovereign statehood by these nations meant that the responsibility for security passed from Britain to them. In the case of Jamaica and Trinidad and Tobago, Britain even made the establishment of a defense force a precondition to granting independence. The only case where Britain retained a clear security mandate after independence was in Belize because, as we saw in the previous chapter, there was a real possibility of Guatemalan aggression. In Guyana's case, while Britain retained no military defense responsibility, it helped to shoulder the initial burden of protecting against Venezuelan aggression by being party to two measures aimed at peacefully resolving the territorial dispute: the 1966 Geneva Agreement, and the 1970 Protocol of Port of Spain.[1]

In pursuit of their security responsibilities several countries tried individually to develop and maintain security mechanisms. Armies were created by Antigua-Barbuda, the Bahamas, Barbados, Belize, Dominica, Guyana, Jamaica, St. Kitts-Nevis, and Trinidad and Tobago. Not all countries considered such mechanisms either politically expedient or economically feasible. Some, like Barbados and the Bahamas, created armies years after independence. Others—Dominica and St. Kitts-Nevis—have since disbanded theirs. The task in this and the following chapter, therefore, is to examine the security policies and actions of Caribbean states since independence, as they grappled with vulnerability, internal instability, and other problems. This chapter looks at the Bahamas, mainland Belize and Guyana, and Trinidad and Tobago. Jamaica, one of the large countries, is discussed in the next chapter for reasons explained there.

The Bahamas

Although the Bahamas secured independence from Britain in 1973, the Royal Bahamas Defense Force (RBDF) was not legally formed until 1980, nearly three years after the creation of a Ministry of National Security on January 1, 1977. Although the RBDF was legally born on March 30, 1980, when the Bahamas Defense Act took effect, the *de facto* birthdate was September 29, 1979, when Princess Anne of Britain launched the army at a ceremony in Coral Harbor. Plans for a defense force were first announced in Parliament on October 6, 1976. The British played a key role in the planning. They provided loan officers for technical advice, training, and administration. The first such officer was Commander William Swinley of the Royal Navy. Upon his arrival in the Bahamas in September 1976, he was appointed Commander-Designate of the defense force. He returned to Britain on December 13, 1981.[2]

The second commander of the RBDF was also British—Commodore Christopher Belton. He served from November 27, 1981, until October 2, 1983. The first Bahamian officers were selected in January 1977. Kenneth Gorden Turnquest and Peter David Drudge, Jr., undertook the year-long International Midshipman's course at the Britannia Royal Naval College in Devon, England. The present RBDF Commander, Commodore Leon Smith, is the first Bahamian head of the army. He succeeded Commander Belton on September 30, 1983. At the time, he held the rank of Captain (navy). Because of the maritime orientation of the RBDF, these ranks are all naval ones, with army equivalents, of course. Under the British tradition, the rank of Commodore, for example, equals that of Brigadier in the army, and a naval Captain is equivalent to an army Colonel.

The Minister of National Security has direct political charge over the army as well as the police. But under the Defense Act, overall policy responsibility for RBDF command, discipline, and administration falls to the National Security Council, with operational control left to the Commander as the top military officer.[3] Section 9 of the defense law provides for the National Security Council to be headed by the Prime Minister, and to include the National Security Minister and "such other Ministers as may be appointed by the Prime Minister." The law also provides for a three-member Commissions Board to advise the Governor-General on the appointment of military commissions.

The mission of the defense force is defined by Section 4 of the defense act:

- Defense of the Bahamas
- Protection of the country's territorial integrity
- Disaster relief support
- Assisting with domestic law enforcement.

The RBDF has three other significant objectives:

- Prevention of drug trafficking and arms smuggling
- Protection of fishing rights
- Prevention of illegal immigration.[4]

To execute its mandates, the RBDF has several patrol vessels of varying sizes with different weapons capabilities. In 1986, three high-speed 33-meter vessels were commissioned. They were fitted with modern electronic surveillance and navigational equipment to combat drug smuggling and illegal immigration, and to protect the marine resources of the Bahamas. During 1989, six 95-foot patrol craft were acquired from the United States: the *Fenrick Sturrup*, ex-*Cape Shoalwater*; the *David Tucker*, ex-*Cape Upright*; the *Edward Williams*, ex-*Cape Current*; the *Austin Smith*, ex-*Cape York*; the *Cape Fox*; and the ex-*Cape Morgan*. The first five were transferred on June 30, 1989, and the last one on October 20 of the same year.[5]

At present, the main preoccupation of the RBDF is with the last three objectives, especially those related to drugs and immigration. As will be seen in chapter nine, the nature of Bahamian geography, as a bridge between North America and South America, facilitates its use for the transshipment of drugs. The 1984 Commission of Inquiry that probed the drug trafficking concluded that "the Defense Force cannot carry out its [drug combating] tasks effectively with the resources at its disposal."[6] There have been plans to develop and expand the RBDF between 1988 and 1995 to deal with drugs and other problems. The expansion is to involve recruitment of an additional 500 members, and modernization of naval and air facilities, including the provision of more powerful naval and air craft for surveillance and interdiction.[7] The 1989 acquisitions mentioned above were part of this process. They also reflect efforts by the United States to assist the Bahamas in dealing with the drug problems that affect both nations.

The RBDF is essentially a maritime defense force, with a small air unit (see Figure 4.1). The air wing itself was not started until November 28, 1981. Structurally, there are five major departments: Administration; Operations; Supplies; Technical; and the Military Operations Platoon. Each of these has sub-departments. The RBDF has its headquarters at Coral Harbor, in the south of New Providence Island, where the country's capital, Nassau, is also located. There are several "forward operating bases," staffed entirely by RBDF marines. One is at Gun Cay, a small island in the Bimini chain in the northwestern part of the archipelago. Another is at Cal Sal, thirty miles north of Cuba, where allegedly there are a considerable number of unauthorized military overflights by Cuba. Others are at Gorda Cay, West End, Grand Bahama, and Lerner Marina, Bimini.

Recruitment for the RBDF began in 1976, but the entry of women was only allowed in 1985. The RBDF has grown considerably over the years, from a complement of 68 in 1980 to 868 in 1991. The RBDF inventory includes twenty-seven vessels, nine of which are 60 feet and above in length. There are also two Cessna aircraft. The United States, Britain, and Canada are the chief sources of weapons, equipment, and training. Between 1977 and 1990, 354 members of the RBDF benefitted from overseas training in seventy-four different subjects. Bahamian defense personnel also went for training in Barbados in 1990 for the first time.[8]

Internal security in the Bahamas is provided by the Royal Bahamas Police Force (RBPF). It is headed by a Commissioner of Police (COP) and had a complement of 2,000 officers in 1991.[9] The Commission of Inquiry mentioned above found considerable police corruption. According to the Commission's report, "Evidence emanating from known drug traffickers and the testimony of corrupt police officers who have been dismissed from the service leads to the conclusion that there is an

Figure 4.1 **RDBF Organizational Chart**

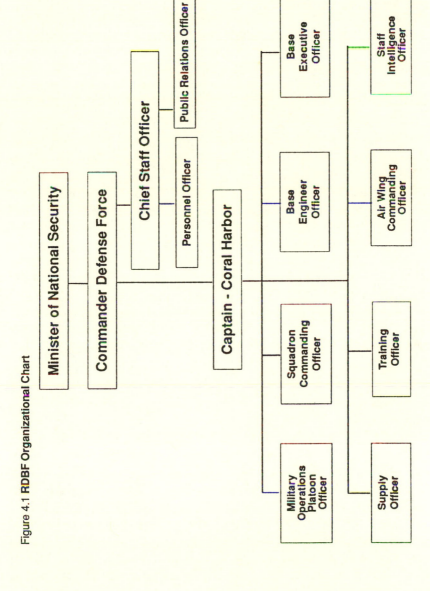

unacceptable level of corruption within the police force."[10] Although the investigators felt that "the lack of integrity is more likely to be found in the junior ranks," it found one top official, Assistant COP Howard Smith, guilty of taking monthly bribes of U.S. $10,000 for information on police operations. Consequently, reorganization of the RBPF was planned at the end of the 1980s. The reorganization was expected to concentrate on general administration, training, and investigation procedures. Both the size and the facilities of the force were expected to increase.[11]

Belize

Unlike some Caribbean armies that were formed years after independence, such as those in the Bahamas and in Barbados, the Belize Defense Force (BDF) was formed before independence, on January 1, 1978. Its nucleus came from the British Honduras Volunteer Guard and the elite Belize Police Special Unit, both of which were disbanded at the time of the army's creation.

The British Honduras Volunteer Guard had a history dating to the early nineteenth century. According to Edward Fursdon, a retired British officer, in 1814 a volunteer force was organized to defend the then British colony of Honduras from the Spanish. Called the Prince Regent's Royal Honduras Militia, in 1824 it comprised three artillery companies, one light infantry and one grenadiers company, and eight "Companies of the Infantry Line." The name of the outfit was changed subsequently and it was known at various times as the British Honduras Territorial Force, the British Honduras Defense Force, the Belize Volunteer Force, the Belize Volunteer Corps, and the Belize Light Infantry Volunteer Force.[12]

In 1942, Britain formed the British Honduras Battalion of the North Caribbean Force. Active able-bodied men were transferred into it while the others formed the core of the newly created British Honduras Home Guard. The Home Guard was redesignated the British Honduras Volunteer Guard in 1943. When Britain created the British Regiment a year later for active duty in World War II, there was a detachment from the British Honduras Battalion. Like troops from elsewhere in the then "British Caribbean," troops from Belize served in Egypt, Palestine, and Mesopotamia (now Iraq) during the World War I, and in Italy, Egypt, and elsewhere in World War II. The British Honduras

Volunteer Guard was maintained after the end of World War II and, as noted above, became the core of Belize's standing army.[13]

The BDF is essentially a ground force with small maritime and air units. Like all Caribbean armies, it is patterned on the British Army, with "regular" and reserve elements. The total army consists of one infantry battalion, three regular and three reserve rifle companies, and administration and support companies. The reserve element is based on the British Territorial Army system with sub-units located in various towns around the country. Of the three reserve companies, one is stationed at Corizal in the north of Belize, another is based at Belize City with a platoon at Cayo, in the west, and the bulk of the third company is located at Stann Creek in the south of the country with a platoon at Punta Gorda.[14]

According to the London-based International Institute for Strategic Studies, in 1990 the army in Belize had an active complement of 760 regulars and 500 reserves. However, there are plans to increase the army progressively to about 3,000 regulars and reserves combined. The main military base is at Price Barracks, ten kilometers outside of the capital, Belize City. A ground force base is also maintained at Belizario Camp, near San Ignacio on the Guatemalan border. The BDF is equipped primarily with British arms, including SLR (Self-Loading Rifles), "Sterling" submachine guns, "Bren" light machine guns, and 81 mm. mortars. Weapons also have been provided by the United States.

The United States recognizes the limitations of Belize and its army:

> Belize's 220,000 people do not provide a tax base sufficient to meet its defense requirements. In June 1990, native Belizeans took over full command of the BDF from British loan officers. The new command gave the BDF an enhanced and aggressive role in counter-narcotics operations. However, without adequate U.S. assistance, Belize's ability to support counter-narcotics programs will be severely undercut. Previous cutbacks in U.S. assistance seriously damaged BDF morale, effectiveness, and vitality.
>
> ... The proposed FY 92 FMF [Foreign Military Financing] program will provide personal equipment, communications gear, ammunition, medical supplies and vehicle spare parts to maintain the BDF capability to engage in counter-narcotics operations. IMET will provide professional military and technical training.[15]

Jungle training is done in Belize by local instructors trained in Brunei and Panama under British and American sponsorship, respectively. Foreign training assistance is provided mainly by Britain, Canada, and the United States, but other countries also assist. Barbados, Guyana, Jamaica, and Mexico are among them. The officer corps is trained in Britain at the Royal Military Academy, Sandhurst, the School of Infantry, the Commando Training Center, and at the Command and Staff College. Some of the officers are also trained in the United States, at Fort Benning, Georgia, at the Coast Guard College, and at West Point in New York.[16] In addition, BDF pilots are trained in Canada.

Defense matters are handled by the Prime Minister, who now also has the ministerial portfolio for defense. Operational control of the BDF fell to British Officers at the time of its formation, until June 1, 1990, when Governor-General Dame Minita Gordon approved the first Belizean appointments, the first step toward giving command and control of the BDF to Belizeans. The position of Chief of Staff was created and Lt. Colonel Earl E. Arthurs was named to it. Lt. Colonel Allen J. Usher was appointed simultaneously as the first Belizean Commandant.

The government of Prime Minister George Price took another significant security initiative in 1990. It disbanded the Security Intelligence Service (SIS), created in 1987 by the government of Manuel Esquivel. The mission of the SIS had been to deal with internal and external espionage, sabotage, and terrorism, with both the identity and the specific duties of SIS personnel kept secret. George Price had been a strong critic of the SIS while in opposition. He feared that the SIS would be used by the government to carry out political vendettas. Thus, two months after his election on September 4, 1989, following a five-year absence, he acted to repeal the legislation that had created the SIS. During 1990, the five SIS vehicles were distributed among other ministries and their office space was given to the ministries of Defense and Home Affairs. SIS agents were sent to the Belize Police Force (BPF), which assumed the duties previously performed by the SIS.[17]

The Belize Police Force (BPF) handles domestic law enforcement. It has several departments in addition to the main command headquarters: Training School; Dog Section; Police Band; Special Branch; and Serious Crimes Squad. In 1990 it had a staff of 640, assigned as shown in Table 4.1 (see p. 94).

Guyana

Like Belize, Guyana had territorial claims pressed against it even before independence on May 26, 1966. There is a claim by Venezuela for five-eighths of Guyana's 214,970 square kilometers, the entire mineral-rich Essequibo area. There is also a dispute with Surinam over 15,000 square kilometers of territory in the New River Triangle in eastern Guyana.[18] Guyana, therefore, found it necessary to establish a standing army when the military defense mandate of the British ended at independence.

That standing army is the Guyana Defense Force (GDF). It was created by passage of the 1966 Defense Act just four days before independence. Simultaneously, its precursors, the British Guiana Special Service Unit (BGSSU) and the British Guiana Volunteer Force (BGVF), were abolished. Although the legal birthdate of the GDF is May 22, 1966, its operational birthday on November 1, 1965 is the one traditionally observed. The GDF, therefore, celebrated its silver anniversary in 1990 with a week-long program of events, including military displays, cultural presentations, and fireworks.[19] The military in colonial Guyana had a history traceable to 1778, when the first militia was created. Also, as was the case with other West Indians, Guyanese were drafted into the British imperial army. For example, the British Guiana Militia, later designated the British Guiana Regiment, was part of Britain's South Caribbean Force during World War II. The British Guiana Regiment was partly disbanded in 1947 with three of the original seven companies reconstituted as the core of the British Guiana Volunteer Force (BGVF), created on June 14, 1948.

Essentially a part-time army, the BGVF was patterned on the British Territorial Battalion with a Battalion Headquarters and four rifle companies. The BGVF was managed by a small permanent staff headed by an adjutant. Most of their duties were ceremonial, but they were called upon to perform internal security duties during the mid-1950s and early 1960s, when Guyana experienced serious political and racial conflict. It was the protracted social conflict itself that gave rise to the formation of the BGSSU. Because of the limitations of the BGVF and the police force in dealing with the domestic conflict, the British Guiana Special Service Unit Order was approved on February 26, 1964, creating the force. The BGSSU was a fully armed elite police force whose members had Justice of the Peace authority in addition to police arrest powers.[20]

Thus, as independence drew close and plans for the standing army developed, the BGVF and the BGSSU were natural and appropriate

Table 4.1

Belize Police Force Personnel Establishment

DIVISION	RANK	NUMBER
Police Main Force	Commissioner	1
	Deputy Commissioner	1
	Assistant Commissioner	1
	Senior Superintendent	1
	Superintendent of Police	4
	Civil Secretary	1
	Assistant Superintendent	9
	Inspector	9
	Police Officer (Cadet)	3
	Assistant Inspector	9
	Sergeant	32
	Corporal	68
	Senior Radio Technician	1
	Signal Workshop Mechanic	1
	------- Workshop Mechanic	8
	Constable	369
		Total: 518
Police Training School	Superintendent	1
	Assistant Inspector	1
	Sergeant	5
	Corporal	2
		Total: 9
Police Dog Section	Corporal	1
	Constable	4
		Total: 5

Police Band

Assistant Inspector	1
Sergeant	1
Corporal	2
Constable	26
Total:	**30**

Police Special Branch

Assistant Director	1
Superintendent	1
Assistant Superintendent	1
Inspector	3
Assistant Inspector	3
Sergeant	11
Corporal	14
Constable	18
Total:	**52**

Police Serious Crimes Squad

Superintendent	1
Assistant Superintendent	1
Inspector	1
Sergeant	4
Corporal	7
Constable	12
Total:	**26**

Grand Total:	**640**

Source: Belize Police Force

sources from which to draw officers and regular ranks for the new security outfit. Personnel were selected from those forces for training at the Mons Officer Cadet School and elsewhere in England. Local training was provided at Atkinson Field Base (now Camp Stephenson) near the country's main international airport, and at the Tacama Training Camp, in the Berbice region. The GDF headquarters were established in Thomas Lands, in the northern part of the capital, Georgetown. It is now called Camp Ayanganna.

Section 5, Chapter 15:01 of the Defense Act of 1966—the army's enabling legislation—gives the GDF a rather broad mandate, with scope for elaboration by the relevant political elites: "The Force shall be charged with the defense of and maintenance of order in Guyana *and with such duties as may from time to time be defined by the Defense Board"* (emphasis added). Using the broad legal authority, the political elites identified several specific roles for the GDF:

- to maintain the integrity of the borders of Guyana and defend against aggression;
- to assist in the maintenance of law and order when required to do so;
- to contribute to the life of the country by organizing voluntary service, engaging in engineering and other projects and providing a labor/rescue organization in an emergency.

Forbes Burnham, Guyana's dominant leader from 1964 until 1985, was unambiguous about the kind of the army he desired. In an address to officers and new recruits on October 26, 1970, he declared,

> I do not share the British concept that the Army is separate and distinct from everything else and loyal to the Government of the day. As Prime Minister, I expect you to be loyal to this Government. If there is any other Government, it is a matter for you to decide about that, but so far as I am concerned I don't want any abstract loyalty. It must be a straightforward loyalty from the top down, and it must also be based on an appreciation of the philosophy of this Government.[21]

David Granger credits Burnham with creating a security strategy called "Defense in Depth." Burnham's conception of security is said to have been a multidimensional one, with military, political, economic, and psychological facets.

In other words, "defense in depth" was a form of total defense consisting of four parts:

* Military defense. This would be provided by the three
  defense forces and the ordinary citizens, organized,
  armed and trained for territorial defense.
* Civil Defense. This dealt with the protection of the
  people and their property.
* Economic Defense. The safeguarding of supplies of
  goods, fuel, and other commodities needed for survival.
* Psychological Defense. This meant maintaining the
  morale of the population and neutralizing the efforts
  of enemy propaganda and misinformation.[22]

Politically, the GDF falls under the portfolio of the Minister of Defense, a position traditionally held by the President. Before the constitutional amendment of 1980, which created an executive presidency, the position was held by the Prime Minister. (It is important to note that although Guyana had adopted a republican constitution in 1970, the President had no real political power under that constitution. Power fell to the Prime Minister, who continued to control the defense portfolio.) Nevertheless, the Defense Act vests policy responsibility in a Defense Board. Under sections 9–12 of the Defense Act, the Board is responsible for policy relating to the army's command, administration, and discipline. The six-member board is headed by the President, who is also Commander-in-Chief. It includes the Minister of Home Affairs, who is responsible for the Police and the Prisons, among other things, and the GDF Chief of Staff.

As Figure 4.2 suggests (see page 99), Guyana has a multidimensional national security establishment. Between 1990 and 1992, the policy-making framework was expanded with the creation of the position of National Security Adviser to the President. Former GDF Force Commander David Granger, a highly respected officer, was appointed to the position. Granger was among the first Guyanese trained at Britain's Mons Officer Cadet School, graduating in May 1966 as a Second Lieutenant. As National Security Adviser, Granger had no operational powers over military agencies. His role was purely policy-oriented and advisory. He chaired the Central Intelligence Committee, which included the GDF Chief of Staff and the Police Commissioner. He also sat on several security bodies, among them the Defense Board and the Committee on Narcotics Control. The office of National Security Adviser was vacated from September 1991 when Brigadier Granger left to pursue diplomatic training at UWI's Institute of International Relations. The willingness or ability of President Hugh Desmond Hoyte to vacate a position that is ostensibly vital to national security decision-making raises questions about the need for the position and about possible motives behind Granger's appointment. The position of National Security Adviser to the President was abolished by President Cheddie Jagan following his election in October 1992.

Operationally, the GDF is headed by a Chief of Staff. Expectedly, the first Chief of Staff, Colonel Ronald Pope, was British. He served from 1966 to 1969 and was succeeded by Brigadier Clarence Price who served until 1979 when Norman McLean took command. With the retirement of Major General McLean in February 1990, Brigadier Joseph Singh, GNS Director-General for eight years, became acting Chief of Staff. Singh was confirmed as Chief of Staff on December 31, 1990, retroactive to December 1 of the same year.[23] He is the first professional head of the armed forces of Indian descent.

Singh's early officer training was done at the Mons Officer Cadet School in England, where he graduated in May 1966 as a Second Lieutenant. Subsequent training was undertaken at Britain's School of Infantry in Warminister, the Army School of Education in Beaconsfield, the Army Free Fall Parachute School in Netheravon, the Staff College in Camberly, and at the University of Guyana, where he graduated with the Diploma in Public Administration in 1976. Singh holds several military medals and decorations, including the Guyana Independence Medal, the Military Efficiency Medal, the Military Service Star, the Venezuelan Army Cross (Honorary), and the Cuban XXXth Anniversary Granma Landing Medal.[24]

The Chief of Staff has overall command responsibility for the armed forces. But for fifteen years, day-to-day administrative and logistical matters were under the charge of the Force Commander, the number two official in the GDF hierarchy. The roles of Chief of Staff and Force Commander had been merged until 1972 when they were separated as the GDF expanded. The first Commander was Colonel Ulric Pilgrim. However, there was a reorganization of the military services in 1987 in which the two roles were again combined. As part of that reorganization, the former Defense Secretariat, the office of the Chief of Staff, was merged with the Force Headquarters, office of the Force Commander.[25]

Figure 4.2 National Security Establishment of Guyana

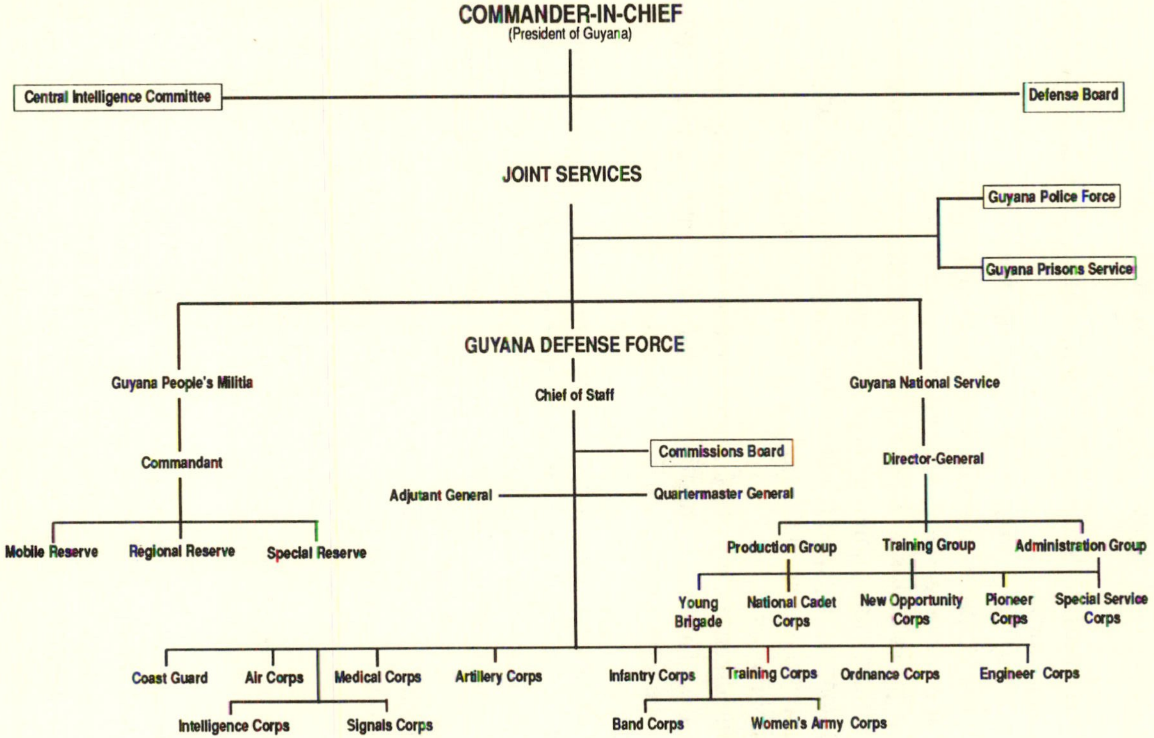

COMMANDER-IN-CHIEF
(President of Guyana)

Central Intelligence Committee

Defense Board

JOINT SERVICES

Guyana Police Force

Guyana Prisons Service

Guyana National Service

Director-General

GUYANA DEFENSE FORCE

Chief of Staff

Commissions Board

Quartermaster General

Adjutant General

Production Group

Training Group

Administration Group

Young Brigade

National Cadet Corps

New Opportunity Corps

Pioneer Corps

Special Service Corps

Ordnance Corps

Engineer Corps

Infantry Corps

Training Corps

Band Corps

Women's Army Corps

Artillery Corps

Medical Corps

Signals Corps

Air Corps

Coast Guard

Intelligence Corps

Guyana People's Militia

Commandant

Regional Reserve

Special Reserve

Mobile Reserve

The GDF was originally a one-battalion force with 750 members. Over the years it grew (and contracted) and is now basically a ground army with air and maritime units, totaling about 5,000 in 1990.[26] Structurally, as Figure 4.2 shows, there are twelve Corps:

- Air Corps, with transport, reconnaissance, and disaster-preparedness capabilities.
- Artillery Corps, started initially as the Mortar Platoon.
- Band Corps, with military and steel and "string" band components for ceremonial duties and cultural performances.
- Engineer Corps, which engages in construction and maintenance of military and community equipment and facilities.
- Infantry Corps, which is the largest element of the army, with rifle battalions, a service battalion, a weapons support battalion, and Special Forces.
- Intelligence Corps for intelligence and counter-intelligence.
- Coast Guard for maritime surveillance, antismuggling operations, fishery protection, and SAR operations.
- Medical Corps to provide medical attention.
- Ordnance Corps—traditionally considered the "Quartermaster" of the GDF. This corps undertakes procurement, storage, and maintenance of weapons, rations, and equipment.
- Signal Corps, responsible for the installation, maintenance, and repair of communications equipment.
- Training Corps to coordinate local education and training programs.
- Women's Army Corps, comprising women of varying ranks from several sections of the army.[27]

Military training is done both in Guyana and abroad. Local training is provided at five institutions: the Colonel John Clark Military School; the Colonel Ulric Pilgrim Officer Cadet School; the School of Infantry Training; the Army NCO School; and the Army Command and Staff School. Military officials from the Caribbean and elsewhere are also trained there. Foreign training has been provided by military institutions in Britain, where most of the present officer corps was trained, in the United States, Cuba, and Commonwealth countries such as Canada and India. After more than a decade's break in military exchanges between the GDF and the British Army, joint military training was planned to resume in 1991. In November 1990, Rear Admiral Peter

Abbott and Major-General Jeremy Ross were in Guyana planning for the resumption of joint training. In addition, a Royal Navy vessel visited in fall 1991. The HMS *Leeds Castle* was in Guyana from September 27 through September 30, displaying its 30 mm. guns, Avon Searider aircraft, satellite communications equipment, and its missile decoy system.[28]

There is no military research and development in Guyana. Nor are arms manufactured indigenously. The GDF's inventory of weapons is not sophisticated. Weapons come from several sources. Much of it was originally provided by the British and the Americans, but over the years, as Guyana adopted socialist and non-aligned postures, weapons and equipment were also secured from Cuba, East Germany, Commonwealth countries, and elsewhere. According to the 1990–1991 edition of *The Military Balance*, the GDF inventory includes anti-aircraft guns, automatic rifles, machine guns, artillery guns, helicopters, small troop transports, mortar throwers, and naval patrol vessels.

By Caribbean standards, Guyana was militarized between 1970 and 1987. The indexes of the militarization are the number and size of the military and paramilitary agencies, the overt and unapologetic use of military agencies for political purposes, and progressive increases in military expenditure until recently.[29] Economic difficulties have forced reductions in military spending and in the size of some military agencies since 1987. Yet one study since then was able to show that Guyana has one of Latin America's highest defense burdens. In a list of twenty-five of the largest defense spenders in the region, Guyana's military spending as a percentage of GNP for 1988 was 14.6 percent, second only to Nicaragua with 17.2 percent. While Guyana was close to the bottom of the list in absolute spending, its GNP percentage ranked above Cuba, Brazil, Venezuela, Panama, and Jamaica. The data also ranked Guyana fifth in the list of countries with the largest per capita defense spending—U.S. $57.50. Cuba ranked first with U.S. $125.[30]

Guyana's socialist experiments between 1970 and 1985 resulted in minimal contact between the GDF and the U.S. military during that period. There were no military sales to Guyana between 1982 and 1987. Between 1984 and 1988 there was no assistance to Guyana under the IMET (International Military Education and Training) program. The last time before 1989 that Guyana received IMET awards was in 1983— ten places. That same year, other Caribbean countries received the following allocation: twenty-two for Barbados; nineteen for Belize; seventy-three for Jamaica; and twenty for the Organization of Eastern Caribbean States (OECS). However, in the context of the changed foreign policy agenda, the GDF has been collaborating with military bodies elsewhere. For example, in March 1991 Brigadier Joseph Singh led a military delegation for a five-day visit to Martinique and French Guyana at the invitation of Brigadier-General Jean Yves Tête, Commandant of the French Defense Forces of the Antilles-Guyane. And in June 1991, Guyana participated for the first time in military maneuvers with RSS, United States, and British forces.[31] This collaboration has also involved visits to Guyana by top U.S. military officials.

The rapprochement between Guyana and the United States has led to renewed military assistance, primarily through the Economic Support Fund (ESF) and IMET. Guyana was even one of the countries to benefit from the distribution of extra rations from Operation Desert Storm. The rations, enough to provide 160,000 meals, were shipped to Guyana in July 1991. In the larger context of renewed United States-Guyana relations, there have been Peace Corps operations, debt rescheduling, and a U.S. $112.8 million debt cancellation in September 1991.[32] Nevertheless, the ESF program was suspended in 1990 pending the holding of free and fair elections. This suspension, however, did not prevent other forms of assistance, as in July 1992 when 17 finger-printing kits, valued at U.S. $17,000, were donated to the Guyana police. The elections were held on October 5, 1992, and ESF assistance has resumed.

As regards IMET, United States officials explained:

> The proposed IMET program would enable us to improve GOG's [Government of Guyana's] understanding of U.S. foreign and economic policy, and to encourage it to engage the Guyana Defense Force (GDF) more fully in counter-narcotics operations, which the GDF has already begun to undertake. The GDF however, is poorly equipped and has few trained technicians. The IMET program would provide military and technical training to upgrade the GDF's transportation and communications capabilities, thus enhancing its narcotics interdiction capability. IMET also promotes professionalism, and exposes trainees to U.S. traditions of democracy, human rights, and civilian control of the military.[33]

While the GDF is Guyana's premier security agency, there are several others, as is evident from Figure 4.2. The other important ones are the Guyana Police Force (GPF), the Guyana National Service (GNS), and the Guyana People's Militia (GPM). These are part of an umbrella agency called the Disciplined Services of Guyana. It also includes the Guyana Prisons Service. Until recently, the National Guard Service (NGS) was also part of the group. The NGS was created in 1980 to protect state property against theft, vandalism, and sabotage. However, on August 2, 1991, its 1,000 members were absorbed into the GPF, becoming part of its Special Constabulary. The occasion was markeded by a special ceremony at the Tactical Service Unit compound at Eve Leary, the police headquarters. Only the GNS and the GPM are discussed here.[34]

The GNS was formed in 1973 with defense and development objectives. These were to be accomplished through several corps. The first, the Young Brigade, involves children between ages eight and fourteen in the formal school system who are exposed to agriculture, creative arts, and physical education on weekends and during long school holidays. The National Cadet Corps involves twelve- to eighteen-year-olds in secondary, technical, and vocational schools who are given training similar to that of the National Cadets, but at a higher level. The third entity, the New Opportunity Corps, was designed for children in reform schools. The fourth, the Pioneer Corps, deemed "the most important branch of GNS," allows citizens between eighteen and twenty-five to secure one year of paramilitary, agriculture, and creative arts training. While participation in the Pioneer Corps is generally voluntary, it is a condition of admission to the University of Guyana and to specialized schools such as the Guyana School of Agriculture, where education is free.[35]

The Special Service Corps was intended to allow professionals and people with special skills to undertake one-to-two-month assignments at other agencies of the GNS, with full pay by their regular public or private sector employers. A National Reserve Corps was also contemplated. As the Parliamentary Paper on the subject explained, "This will be the last Corps to come into operation. It is envisaged that all groups of the Pioneer Corps will be given an opportunity to sign up as reservists to be on call for work in any area vital to the stability, security or productivity of the country."[36] The military defense role of the GNS was, therefore, intended to revolve primarily around the Pioneer Corps and the National Reserve Corps, but the Reserve Corps was never really formed.

The GPM was established on December 1, 1976, as part of a popular mobilization strategy in the face of destabilization by the United States and intimidation by Venezuela. It was given the more politically expedient than logistically feasible mission of making "every citizen a soldier." Specifically, the GPM was intended to:

- provide a framework for mass preparation for emergencies;
- support the GDF in all of its functions when required;
- provide a reservoir of trained recruits for the GDF.

This "people's army" has two components: a permanent staff, and a reserve staff. The former, full-time soldiers, are the core of the militia's command system. They provide administrative, training, and logistical services. Initially, the second component was divided into two groups: Group A, comprising able-bodied citizens under forty-five years; and Group B, comprising specialists in civil and military defense. Under a 1982 reorganization, however, Group A was redesignated the Mobile Reserve and mandated to provide mobile support for the GDF. The Mobile Reserve was formed into battalions drawn from contiguous reginal areas as follows:

- Regions 1 and 2—23rd Battalion
- Regions 3 and 4—22nd Battalion
- Regions 5 and 6—21st Battalion
- Regions 7 and 8—26th Battalion
- Region 9—25th Battalion.

Group B was further divided. Women and men over age forty were placed in the Regional Reserve, which was organized into lettered companies based on districts. There was also the Specialist Corps, organized by specialist areas, to reinforce the GDF. Moreover, in 1982–1983 the Region 10 Mobile Reserve was given anti-aircraft weapons training and reclassified the 23rd Air Defense Company.[37]

GPM recruitment is voluntary and is open to citizens between ages 16 and sixty-five. There was a record membership of 7,000 in 1977. But over the years it was progressively reduced as the country's economic difficulties increased, and as relations with both Venezuela and the United States improved and the imminence of the danger that precipitated the GPM's formation receded. In 1991, the GPM personnel establishment was a mere 500. The militia has its own central training base, Camp Seweyo, along the highway between the capital, Georgetown, and Linden, the country's main bauxite mining city. There are also training centers in different parts of the country. Nevertheless, the GPM does not have now a presence in each of the country's ten administrative regions as it did before. The GPM celebrated its fifteenth anniversary in December 1991 under a new status, as part of the GDF. But the GDF Chief of Staff stressed that "the GPM must not be seen as a poor cousin of the GDF, but rather as reservist-pillars of support, both in peace time and war."[38] It was perhaps to demonstrate this importance that GPM Commandant, Colonel Goodwin McPherson, was named in 1991 as the GDF second in command.[39]

During the tenure of President Hugh Desmond Hoyte (1985–1992), the military had an additional role: that of diplomatic security. This new role was suggested by the consistency with which detachments from the GDF and the Guyana Police Force were used in the foreign policy arena. A contingent of thirty soldiers with special skills along with aircraft and supplies were sent to Jamaica in September 1988 in the wake of Hurricane Gilbert; a joint-services detachment, with GDF, GPM, and GNS personnel, was sent to the Eastern Caribbean in 1989 following the destructive trail of Hurricane Hugo; and a detachment of thirty members of the GPF were in Namibia from June 1989 to April 1990, as part of the United Nations Special Monitoring Force.

A thirty-one member Joint Services Relief Task Force composed of servicemen from the GDF, the GPM, and the GNS was also in Montserrat from February to April 1990. They built thirty-two houses and repaired a school as a follow-up to a similar mission in 1989. And in August 1990, a forty-member contingent from the GDF's First Infantry Battalion led by Captain Andrew Pompey spent two weeks in Trinidad in the wake of the July-August coup attempt there. The GDF officers joined security detachments from Jamaica and member countries of the Regional Security System (RSS) in helping to provide internal security in Trinidad. Moreover, in March 1992, a Guyana Police Force contingent left for El Salvador to spend a year as part of a United Nations Observer Mission. Also suggestive of the diplomatic security role was the placement of military officials in the diplomatic establishment. In April 1990, GPM Commandant, Colonel Carl Morgan, was named Ambassador to Surinam. The following month, Police Commissioner Balram Raghubir was named High Commissioner to India, effective July 1990.[40]

Trinidad and Tobago

The responsibility for national security in the twin-island Republic of Trinidad and Tobago falls primarily to the Trinidad and Tobago Defense Force (TTDF) and the Trinidad and Tobago Police Service (TTPS), both of which come under the jurisdiction of the Minister of National Security.

As will be seen in chapter five, both Barbados and Jamaica had continuous military traditions in the colonial era, having maintained the Barbados Regiment and the Jamaica Regiment, respectively. However, Trinidad and Tobago disbanded its Regiment in 1947, laying up the Regiment's colors in Trinity Cathedral in the capital, Port of Spain. According to someone who was part of the region's military tradition, "It [the military tradition of Trinidad] had died out except in the hearts of men, aged by 1962, in the region of forty years, none of whom had soldiered since 1947. ..."[41]

Nevertheless, with the demise of the West Indian Federation signaled by Jamaica's withdrawal referendum of September 19, 1961, and with the August 31, 1962, independence date fast approaching, Trinidadian leaders were forced to consider formation of a standing army. As Stewart Edwards explained:

> [P]lans for a regiment began to take shape after a visit from Admiral Lord Louis Mountbatten, who as [British] Chief of Staff, had made it clear that unless a nation had an adequate defense force, it would not qualify for Commonwealth defense aid in the event of an attack. It was also necessary in order to obtain the benefits of the United Nations.[42]

In conjunction with British advisers, Trinidadian leaders decided to have an army with the smallest possible operational unit which, following the British Army model, is the battalion. The TTDF was, thus, created primarily from the 2nd Battalion of the West Indies Regiment (WIR).[43] Economic considerations influenced the decision to have the Lieutenant Colonel commanding the battalion also be the commander of the entire defense force. The planners did not contemplate ever having the defense establishment expand to the point where it would become necessary to have Regiment and Coast Guard commanders separate and distinct from the commander of the force. The first TTDF Commander was Lt. Colonel Peter Pearce Gould. He was succeeded by Lt. Colonel Joffre Serrette who retired in February 1968.

The legal birthdate of the TTDF is June 1, 1962, when the Trinidad and Tobago Defense Act took effect. This legislation, Act No. 7 of 1962, was passed in the House of Assembly on July 27, and in the Senate on August 7. The Governor's assent was given on August 22, 1962. However, it was made retroactive to June 1.[44] This law also repealed several pieces of colonial security-related legislation: the Local Forces Ordinance; the Volunteer Reserve Ordinance; the Naval Volunteer Ordinance; the Naval Volunteer and Defense Ordinance; and the Compulsory Training Service Ordinance.

The army was formed with a set of modest objectives:

- to perform ceremonial functions;
- to aid in providing internal security; and
- to provide for a token show of force in the event of an external attack.

Trinidad did have a legitimate reason to fear an external security threat, no matter how attenuated. The basis of that fear lay in the dispute with Venezuela over the Gulf of Paria.[45] Nevertheless, it was readily appreciated that the army could not provide any credible defense against any serious external attack. Hemispheric and international networks were considered vital to the country's defense. This view was later articulated by a government-appointed study group:

> Accordingly, the external defense needs of this country, whatever these might be, must be regarded as being adequately met by (i) membership in the Organization of American States; (ii) geographic placement under the military umbrella of the states comprising the North Atlantic Treaty Organization; and (iii) membership in the United Nations.[46]

The security services were reorganized after the 1970 army mutiny, discussed below. Several laws were passed in the 1970s modifying the 1962 Defense Act. One significant one was the Defense (Amendment) Act of 1979. It created the position of Chief of Staff with responsibility for both the ground force and the Coast Guard. It also established a five-member Defense Council headed by the National Security Minister and including the TTDF Chief of Staff, the Attorney General, and the Permanent Secretary of the Ministry of National Security.

According to section 5 of the 1979 law, the Defense Council "Shall be responsible under the general authority of the Minister [of National Security] for the command, administration, and discipline of and all matters relating to the Force," except that "the responsibility of the Council shall not extend to the operational use of the Force for which responsibility shall vest in the Chief of Defense Staff subject to the general or special direction of the Minister." That 1979 amendment also created a Commissions Board to advise the President, through the National Security Minister, on appointments to commissions and promotions up to the rank of Major/Lt. Commander.

The Commissions Board comprises the chairman of the Public Service Commission as head, a member of the Judicial and Legal Service Commission, a member of the public, and the commanders of the TTDF's ground and maritime forces.[47] The 1962 Defense Act had made no provision for community service activities. Consequently, the army had a limited role in national life and in fact had very few contacts with the populace prior to the 1970 mutiny. The post-mutiny changes introduced community service projects. The army was even used to deliver fuel oil, sugar, and other supplies during major strikes in the oil and sugar industries in 1975.[48]

As is evident from Figure 4.3, the TTDF, still popularly called the Trinidad Regiment, is a defense force with ground, air, and maritime units. Presently it has one infantry battalion, one support battalion, and one reserve battalion. However, according to Caribbean military sources, there were plans in 1992 to enlarge the TTDF. Those plans envisage reducing the five-company 1st Battalion to a battalion of three companies, and using the remaining two companies as the nucleus of a second battalion, to be built up over eighteen months. The Trinidad and Tobago Coast Guard, the TTDF's maritime component, has been described as "Militarily its most important element," and as "the principal regional maritime force conducting extensive narcotics interdiction."[49] Based on *The Military Balance 1990–1991*, in 1990 the TTDF had an active strength of 2,650 men amd women, 600 of whom were in the Coast Guard, and fifty in the air wing. There is a modest weapons inventory, including SLRs, "Sterling" submachine guns, "Bren" machine guns, GPMGs (General Purpose Machine Guns), 81 mm. mortars, Swedish, British, and American patrol vessels, Cessna 402 and 301 transport planes, and Sikorsky S–76 and Aerospatiale Gazelle helicopters.[50]

Figure 4.3 **Trinidad and Tobago Defense Force Organizational Chart**

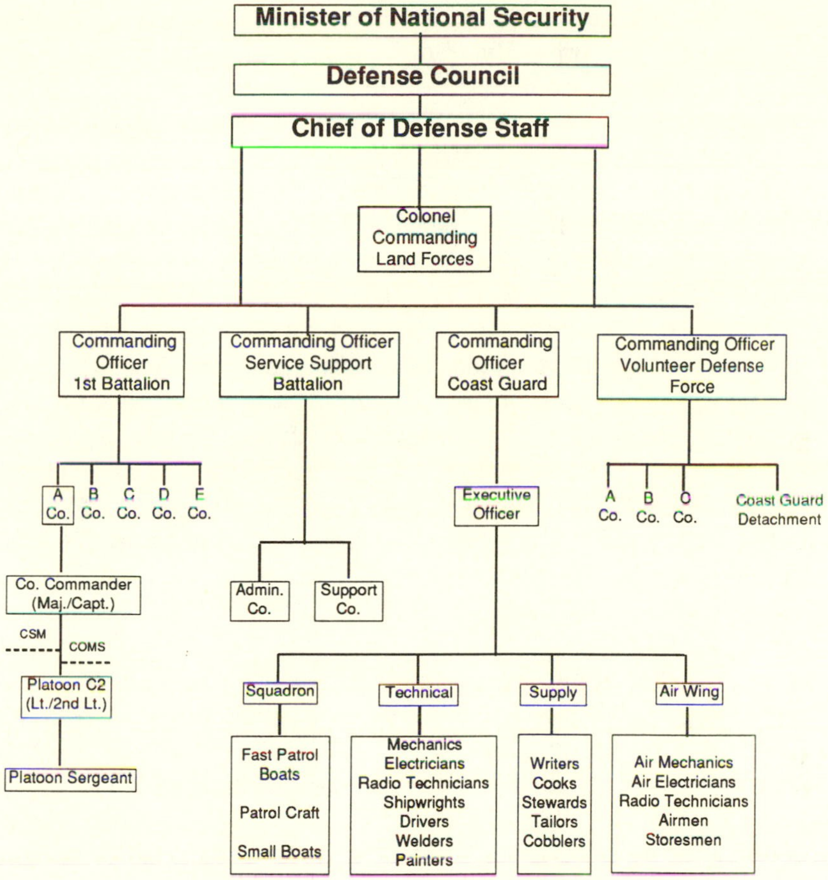

```
                    ┌─────────────────────────────────┐
                    │  Minister of National Security  │
                    └─────────────────────────────────┘
                    ┌─────────────────────────────────┐
                    │        Defense Council          │
                    └─────────────────────────────────┘
                    ┌─────────────────────────────────┐
                    │     Chief of Defense Staff      │
                    └─────────────────────────────────┘

                              ┌──────────────┐
                              │   Colonel    │
                              │  Commanding  │
                              │  Land Forces │
                              └──────────────┘

 ┌───────────────┐  ┌───────────────────┐  ┌───────────────┐  ┌───────────────────┐
 │  Commanding   │  │ Commanding Officer│  │  Commanding   │  │ Commanding Officer│
 │   Officer     │  │  Service Support  │  │   Officer     │  │ Volunteer Defense │
 │  1st Battalion│  │     Battalion     │  │  Coast Guard  │  │      Force        │
 └───────────────┘  └───────────────────┘  └───────────────┘  └───────────────────┘
```

| A Co. | B Co. | C Co. | D Co. | E Co. |

```
                                            ┌───────────┐      A    B    C   Coast Guard
                                            │ Executive │     Co.  Co.  Co.  Detachment
                                            │  Officer  │
                                            └───────────┘
```

| Co. Commander (Maj./Capt.) | | Admin. Co. | Support Co. |

CSM
- - - - - - COMS

| Platoon C2 (Lt./2nd Lt.) |

| Squadron | Technical | Supply | Air Wing |

| Platoon Sergeant |

| Fast Patrol Boats | Mechanics Electricians | Writers | Air Mechanics |

| | Radio Technicians | Cooks | Air Electricians |

| Patrol Craft | Shipwrights | Stewards | Radio Technicians |

| | Drivers | Tailors | Airmen |

| Small Boats | Welders | Cobblers | Storesmen |

| | Painters | | |

Co   Company

The air wing operates out of bases at the Piarco International Airport in Trinidad, and the Crown Point Airport in Tobago, while the Coast Guard has its headquarters at Staubles Bay, Trinidad. The TTDF has extended training assistance to other Caribbean countries, especially in coast guard operations. It was once noted that "As the senior naval unit in CARICOM, the Trinidad and Tobago Coast Guard has helped train officers for similar units in Jamaica, Barbados, and [at the moment,] Antigua. Training, both in Trinidad and in the nations concerned, has also been provided for the regiments in Barbados and Antigua."[51]

As might be expected, Trinidad and its army have received foreign military assistance, primarily from Britain, but also from the United States, Canada, and even from a country about which Trinidad has been deeply suspicious, Venezuela.[52] United States assistance has been both late and limited. For example, as Table 3.6 shows, there was no IMET assistance until 1985, and then only small awards. One reason for this relates to the "healthy distance" Trinidad kept from the United States during the rule of Eric Williams, which ended when he died on March 29, 1981. Another pertains to the country's "economic health."

In spite of its economic problems, Trinidad has a comparatively better economic profile than most Caribbean countries. This has made it ineligible for certain forms of United States military assistance. As one United States government source explained: "Despite a decade-long recession which forced it to adopt austerity measures to secure an IMF standby loan, T&T was again subject to 'high income' restrictions on IMET funds in FY 90. . . . We continue to recommend that T&T be removed from the 'high income' list."[53] The proposed United States military assistance for fiscal year 1992 is U.S. $595,000, comprising FMF and IMET outlays.

I noted in chapter three that several Caribbean countries have served as locations for United States military installations and facilities under a British-American lend-lease deal dating to World War II. The largest base was in Trinidad, at Chaguaramas. It was a naval base. There was also an army base at Waller Field, in central Trinidad. García Muñiz explained: "Chaguaramas was dismantled in 1967, but a small facility, which turned out to be a VLF Omega station for the navigation and positioning of nuclear submarines to aid their precise targeting, remained until the late 1970s when it was quietly phased out."[54]

Trinidad has the dubious distinction of being the first English-speaking Caribbean country where the army challenged the legitimate political rulers, almost succeeding in overthrowing them. The April 1970 mutiny occurred in the context of social unrest beginning the previous February 26. The unrest involved student protests and black power activism precipitated by a sense of frustration caused by increased economic deprivation, among other things.[55] On April 21, 1970, two Sandhurst graduates, lieutenants Raffique Shah and Rex Lasalle, turned their weapons against Lt. Colonel Henry Christopher

and Captain Julian Spencer, the ranking TTDF officers at the army
base at Chaguaramas. Other officers helped subdue the mutineers, but
in the process Shah's rifle fired a shot. That shot was interpreted by
others in the plan as a signal to act. Subsequently, the ammunition
bunker was occupied and Shah and Lasalle were released.[56]

Developments at Chaguaramas were reported to the Coast Guard headquarters at Staubles Bay by Captain Spencer. As one observer recounted:

> When word of the mutiny flashed from Stauble's Bay to Police Head-
> quarters in Port of Spain, there was a rush of near panic. The fear was
> that the army, which outgunned and outmanned the police, would storm
> the city in support of the Black Power activists. Within hours this fear
> appeared well founded as a convoy of army vehicles, manned by rebel
> soldiers headed by Lasalle and Shah, began winding down the single,
> narrow road that leads from Teteron to Port of Spain. At nearby
> Stauble's Bay, then Coast Guard Commander, British-born David
> Bloom, gave the order to evacuate. One Coast Guard Fast Patrol Boat
> (FPB), the "Courland Bay," had already left to deliver the detainees to
> Nelson Island. Another FPB, the "Trinity," was sent roaring towards
> Teteron. The "Trinity" decided to try to block the convoy's passage by
> shelling the hillside overhead. As the "Trinity's" Swedish-made Bofor
> 40 mm shells tore into the hillside above the convoy, the procession
> halted and then responded with a hail of machine-gun fire.[57]

Spencer and a group of loyal soldiers later established a defensive
perimeter outside Chaguaramas. This led to a standoff between the
loyalists and the rebels. Meanwhile, Venezuelan forces had been planning to intervene. Laurence Goldstraw, Commander of the "Courland
Bay," was given telephone instructions by Prime Minister Eric Williams himself to "go and stop those [Venezuelan] ships from coming
in." The Trinidadian and Venezuelan ships met in the Gulf of Paria.
According to Raoul Pantin, then editor of Trinidad's newspaper *Daily
Express*, "aboard those Venezuelan vessels, the decks were crammed
with soldiers in full battle gear, helmets affixed, their guns glinting in
the brilliant sunshine."[58] The United States also sent the USS
Guadacanal steaming from Puerto Rico, but as in the case with Venezuela, the United States was encouraged not to intervene.

Subsequent negotiations between the rebels and the government resulted in their surrender on May 1. There was a lengthy trial by a
military tribunal composed of military officials from Ghana, Nigeria,

Singapore, Uganda, and Guyana. Shah was sentenced to 20 years in prison on mutiny and treason convictions. Lasalle was give 15 years, and 30 of the 85 other soldiers involved were given lesser terms. Shah and Lasalle were freed later after their convictions were overturned by the Trinidad and Tobago Court of Appeals on legal technicalities. The other mutineers were also released.[59]

According to Steward Edwards, Shah had been convicted of a felony in 1968 and should have been forced to resign his commission as is traditional in Commonwealth armies. However, Home Affairs Minister Gerard Montano and TTDF Commander Stanley Johnson considered it politically inexpedient to force the resignation of the only officer of Indian descent. Lasalle had been court-martialed in 1969 on insubordination and other charges. He should have been cashiered, but instead was reprimanded and lost seniority. Edwards makes an interesting observation: "Thus did politics and appeasement bring Trinidad almost to the point of disaster."[60]

Prior to the 1970 disturbances, public order and national security were the responsibility of the Minister of Home Affairs. After the April 21, 1970, state of emergency, several changes were made. The Ministry of Home Affairs was abolished and reorganized as the Ministry of National Security. The new ministry was given jurisdiction over the immigration services, the fire service, the prison service, the police, the army, and the National Emergency Relief Organization. The government also took several steps to control "dissident groups" in the society, including passage of the Sedition (Amendment) Act of 1971 and the Summary Offenses (Amendment) Act of 1972. These placed restrictions on freedoms of speech, movement, and assembly.[61]

As elsewhere in the Caribbean, internal security is the main mission of the police force. Trinidad's police force was once called the Trinidad and Tobago Constabulary Force, and from 1938 to 1965 it was known as the Trinidad and Tobago Police Force. With passage of the Police Service Act in 1965, it was redesignated the Trinidad and Tobago Police Service (TTPS). There is also a reserve police force, the Special Reserve Force (SRF), organized in 1938. About 1,000 strong in 1989, its members are attached to the TTPS divisions throughout the islands. The SRP is under the jurisdiction of the country's COP, head of the TTPS.

Under the 1965 Police Service Act, there are two kinds of police officers. First are the commissioned officers: commissioner of police, deputy commissioners, assistant commissioners, senior superintendents, and assistant superintendents. Second are the non-commissioned officers—inspectors, sergeants, corporals, and constables. Constables constitute about 70 percent of the force at any one time. While the TTPS falls under the portfolio of the Minister of National Security, the commissioner and deputy commissioners are appointed by the President on the advice of the Prime Minister, who himself is advised by the Police Service Commission.

One deputy commissioner is responsible for the Special Branch which is concerned with intelligence matters. Another oversees administration, supervising the finance, personnel, training, and telecommunications units, and the mounted police. The third deputy commissioner heads the Operations Branch, which includes the law enforcement duties of the various operational divisions. The country is divided into nine operational divisions under two branches: a northern branch, operating from TTPS headquarters in Port of Spain; and a southern branch, headquartered in San Fernando.

The TTPS has several special units, among them the Larceny Mobile Patrol, to deal with theft from landed estates; and the Antisquatting Brigade, assigned to prevent illegal occupancy of private lands. The TTPS training school is at St. James Barracks in Trinidad, site of the former headquarters of British troops in the island.[62] Police officers are also trained abroad. Indeed, in July 1991 Justice and National Security Minister Joseph Toney announced that officers will be sent for foreign training to deal with kidnapping. Trinidad and Tobago had experienced nine kidnapping cases in as many months, only one of which was solved.[63]

Notes

1. See Government of Guyana, Ministry of Foreign Affairs, *Documents on the Territorial Integrity of Guyana*, Georgetown, Guyana: Ministry of Foreign Affairs, 1981; and Jacqueline Braveboy-Wagner, *The Guyana-Venezuela Border Dispute: Britain's Colonial Legacy in Latin America*. Boulder, CO: Westview Press, 1984, pp. 324–29.

2. Ena Mae Rolle, "The Royal Bahamas Defense Force: The Formative Years," *Royal Bahamas Defense Force Magazine* (Tenth Anniversary Special Issue, 1990): 14.

3. I am grateful to Thelma Ferguson, Deputy Permanent Secretary of the Bahamas Ministry of National Security, for providing the Defense Act and other valuable material.

4. Lt. Commander A. Allens, "The Role of the Defense Force," *Royal Bahamas Defense Force Magazine* 1 (No. 1, 1987): 13.

5. Robert L. Scheima, "Latin American Navies," *Proceedings of the U.S. Naval Institute* 116 (March 1990): 112. The first four vessels were named after Bahamian marines who died in 1980 following attacks by a Cuban aircraft. See Rolle, p. 23.

6. Government of the Bahamas, *Report of Commission of Inquiry Appointed to Inquire into the Illegal Use of the Bahamas for the Transshipment of Dangerous Drugs Destined for the United States of America*, November 1983-December 1984, Nassau, the Bahamas, 1984, p. 237.

7. Government of the Bahamas, Ministry of National Security, *The Royal Bahamas Defense Force* (Fact Sheet), September 1987, p. 2; and the *Royal Bahamas Defense Force Magazine* (1990): 31.

8. See Allens, "The Role of the Defense Force," and Senior Lt. St. James Wallace, "The Administration Department," *Royal Bahamas Defense Force Magazine* 1 (No. 1, 1987): 18; Government of the Bahamas, Royal Bahamas Defense Force, *Introducing the Royal Bahamas Defense Force* (Fact Sheet), 1991; and Rolle, p. 20.

9. Communication from Thelma Ferguson, Deputy Permanent Secretary of the Bahamian Ministry of National Security, July 31, 1991.

10. *Report of Commission*, p. 233.

11. See Mark P. Sullivan, "The Bahamas," in Sandra W. Meditz and Dennis M. Hanratty, eds., *Islands of the Commonwealth Caribbean*, Washington: Library of Congress, 1989, p. 558.

12. Major-General Edward Fursdon, "Belize," *Army Quarterly and Defense Journal* 118 (January 1988): 34.

13. Fursdon, "Belize."

14. Adrian English, *Regional Defense Profile No. 1: Latin America*, London: Jane's Publishing Co., 1988, pp. 338–39; and Belize Defense Force, "Belize Military Forces: Fact Sheet," 1991.

15. U.S. Department of State and Defense Security Assistance Agency, *Congressional Presentation for Security Assistance Fiscal Year 1992*, Washington D.C., 1991, p. 94.

16. "Belize Military Forces: Fact Sheet."

17. Alma H. Young, "Belize," in James Malloy and Eduardo Gamarra, eds., *Latin American and Caribbean Contemporary Record 1988–1989*, New York: Holmes and Meier, forthcoming; and Alma H. Young, "The Territorial Dimension of Caribbean Security: The Case of Belize," in Ivelaw L. Griffith, ed., *Strategy and Security in the Caribbean*, New York: Praeger, 1991, p. 143.

18. For examination of these disputes, see Government of Guyana, Ministry of External Affairs, *Friendship with Integrity*, Georgetown, Guyana: Ministry of External Affairs, 1969; Duke Pollard, "The Guyana-Surinam Boundary Dispute in International Law," in Leslie Manigat, ed., *The Caribbean Yearbook of International Relations 1976*, St. Augustine, Trinidad: Institute of International Relations, 1977; Ivelaw L. Griffith, *On the Western Front*, Georgetown, Guyana: Ministry of Information, 1981; and Braveboy-Wagner, *The Venezuela-Guyana Border Dispute*.

19. See *Guyana Chronicle* (Special Supplement), October 28, 1990; and

Green Beret 6 (November/December 1990-January 1991).

20. David A. Granger, *The New Road: A Short History of the Guyana Defense Force*, Georgetown, Guyana: Guyana Defense Force, 1975, pp. 17–19; and David A. Granger, *Defend and Develop: A Short History of the Defense Forces of Guyana*, Georgetown, Guyana: Guyana Defense Force, 1985, pp. 5–6.

21. "Guyana Defense Force—The People's Army," *Scarlet Beret* 1 (May 1971): 54.

22. Granger, *Defend and Develop*, p. 56.

23. "Chief of Staff, Police Chief, and Auditor General Sworn In," *Guyana Chronicle*, January 4, 1991, p. 1.

24. I am grateful to Dion Phillips of the University of the Virgin Islands, who provided a copy of the resume of Brigadier Singh from which this data is extracted.

25. Private communication from Brigadier David Granger, National Security Adviser, Guyana, July 12, 1991.

26. Ivelaw L. Griffith, "The Military and the Politics of Change in Guyana," *Journal of Interamerican Studies and World Affairs* 33 (Summer 1991): 156–57.

27. Granger, *Defend and Develop*, pp. 33–34; and personal communication from Granger.

28. See "U.S. Team Arrives Tommorow," *Guyana Chronicle*, March 3, 1988, p. 1; "U.S. Army Arrives for Exercise in Guyana," *New York Carib News*, January 24, 1989, p. 3; "Joint Guyana-UK Military Training Resumes This Year," *Green Beret* 6 (November/December 1990-January 1991): 2; and "The Royal Navy Cometh," *Stabroek News* (Guyana), September 26, 1991, p. 12.

29. See George Danns, "Militarization and Development: An Experiment in Nation-Building," *Transition* 1 (No. 1, 1978): 23–41; George Danns, *Domination and Power in Guyana*. New Brunswick, NJ: Transaction Books, 1982; and J.E. Greene, "Cooperativism, Militarism, Party Politics, and Democracy in Guyana," in Paget Henry and Carl Stone, eds., *The Newer Caribbean*, Philadelphia, PA: Institute for the Study of Human Issues, 1983.

30. "Focus on the Big Defense Spenders," *Latin American Weekly Report*, May 9, 1991 (WR–91–17): 8.

31. See "Chief of Staff on Overseas Visit," *New Nation* (Guyana), March 17, 1991, p. 4; and "War Games," *Sunday Advocate* (Barbados), June 23, 1991, p. 3.

32. Indranie Deolall, "U.S. Quite Confident Elections Will Be Free and Fair—[New Ambassador] Hays," *Guyana Chronicle*, October 1, 1991, pp. 1, 8–9.

33. *Congressional Presentation for Security Assistance Fiscal Year 1992*, p. 165. The proposed IMET award for fiscal 1992 is four, the same as awarded in 1991. The total 1992 assistance package is U.S. $7.69 million.

34. For examination of the Guyana Police Force see Danns, *Domination and Power in Guyana*, pp. 29–142; and John Campbell, *History of Policing in Guyana*, Georgetown, Guyana: Guyana Police Force, 1987. For more on the National Guard Service, see George K. Danns, "The Role of the Military in the National Security of Guyana," in Alma H. Young and Dion E. Phillips, eds., *Militarization in the Non-Hispanic Caribbean*, Boulder, CO: Lynne Rienner, 1986, pp. 19–20.

35. University of Guyana degree students were required to do a one-year stint in the GNS, but in 1991 it was reduced to a mandatory two-months service for graduating seniors. GNS officials deemed this "a temporary arrangement" caused

by contractions in the budget and the size of the agency. See Shaun Samaroo, "National Service Cutting Back to Fit Shrinking Budget," *Stabroek News*, June 20, 1991, p. 6.

36. Government of Guyana, Parliament, *State Paper on National Service of the Cooperative Republic of Guyana*, Parliamentary Sessional Paper No. 3, Third Parliament of Guyana, Presented December 20, 1973 by Prime Minister Linden Forbes Sampson Burnham, p. 11.

37. Granger, *Defend and Develop*, p. 44.

38. See "Fifteenth Anniversary of the Guyana People's Militia," *Sunday Chronicle*, December 1, 1991, p. 6.

39 For more on the GPM, see Government of Guyana, *People's Militia: What it Does*, Georgetown, Guyana, 1976; Bhola Ram, "The Guyanese Mode of Self-Defense: The Concept of a 'People's Militia' for Guyana," *Roraima* 2 (1976): 5–13; Danns, "The Role of the Military;" and Mahadeo Panchu, "People's Militia Makes a Tangible Contribution—Col. McPherson," *Stabroek News*, November 28, 1991, p. 16.

40. See Griffith, "The Military," pp. 161–66; and "Guyana Cops for El Salvador Peace-Keeping Mission," *Stabroek News*, March 22, 1992, p. 1.

41. Stewart Hylton Edwards, *Lengthening Shadows: Birth and Revolt of the Trinidad Army*, Port of Spain, Trinidad: Imprint Caribbean, 1982, p. 23.

42. Edwards, *Lengthening Shadows*, p. 27.

43. English, *Regional Defense Profile*, p. 260.

44. I am grateful to Trinidad and Tobago Attorney-General Anthony Smart for providing copies of this Act and subsequent amendments to it.

45. For examination of this dispute see Henry Gill, "Conflict in Trinidad and Tobago's Relations with Venezuela," in Leslie Manigat, ed., *The Caribbean Yearbook of International Relations*, St. Augustine, Trinidad: Institute of International Relations, 1976, esp. pp. 466–74, 481–85; and Anselm Francis, "The Gulf of Paria: Area of Conflict," *Caribbean Affairs* 3 (January-March 1990): 26–37.

46. Government of Trinidad and Tobago, *Report on the Caribbean Task Force*, Port of Spain, Trinidad, February, 1974, p. 105.

47. Government of Trinidad and Tobago, Parliament, *Trinidad and Tobago Defense (Amendment) Act, No. 32 of 1979*. Also see "A Peace Time Force," *Caribbean and West Indian Chronicle* (December 1981-January 1982): 13.

48. Jan Kippers Black et al., *Area Handbook for Trinidad and Tobago*, Washington, D.C.: American University, 1976, p. 244.

49. See English, *Regional Defense Profile*, p. 260; and *Congressional Presentation for Security Assistance Programs Fiscal Year 1992*, p. 288.

50. English, pp. 260–61; and Beatrice B. Meyer, Daniel J. Seyler, and John F. Hornbeck, "Trinidad," in *Islands of the Commonwealth Caribbean*, pp. 250–51.

51. "A Peace Time Force," p. 33.

52. On the link with Venezuela, see Jacqueline A. Braveboy-Wagner, *The Caribbean in World Affairs*, Boulder, CO: Westview Press, 1989, p. 45.

53. *Congressional Presentation for Security Assistance Programs Fiscal Year 1992*, p. 288.

54. Humberto García Muñiz, "Decolonization, Demilitarization, and Denuclearization in the Caribbean," *Strategy and Security in the Caribbean*, p. 32.

55. For examination of Trinidad's sociopolitical landscape at the time, see

Lloyd Best, "The February Revolution," in David Lowenthal and Lambros Comitas, eds., *The Aftermath of Sovereignty*, Garden City, NY: Anchor Books, 1973; and Susan Craig, "Background to the 1970 Confrontation in Trinidad and Tobago," in Susan Craig, ed., *Contemporary Caribbean: A Sociological Reader*, volume Two, Maracas, Trinidad: The College Press, 1982.

56. Raoul Pantin, "Black Power on the Road: Portrait of a Revolution," *Caribbean Affairs* 3 (January-March 1990): 183.

57. Pantin, pp. 183–84.

58. Pantin, p. 184.

59. See Edwards, *Lengthening Shadows*, pp. 124–49. For the text of Shah's address to the Military Tribunal see Lt. Rafique Shah, "The Military Crisis in Trinidad and Tobago During 1970," in Trevor Munroe and Rupert Lewis, eds., *Readings in Government and Politics in the West Indies*, Kingston, Jamaica: University of the West Indies, 1971, pp. 215–21.

60. Edwards, *Lengthening Shadows*, p. 121.

61. Black et al., *Area Handbook*, p. 244.

62. George Thomas Kurian, *World Encyclopedia of Police Forces and Penal Systems*, New York: Facts on File, 1989, pp. 378–79; and Meyer, Seyler, and Hornbeck, "Trinidad," p. 251.

63. "Police for Kidnap School," *Sunday Guardian* (Trinidad and Tobago) July 7, 1991, p. 1.

5 INDIVIDUAL SECURITY MEASURES IN THE EASTERN CARIBBEAN AND JAMAICA

This chapter examines security policies and initiatives in Barbados, the OECS (except Montserrat, which is still a British dependency), and Jamaica. These countries have more in common with each other than with those surveyed in the previous chapter. For one thing, they all endorsed and participated in the 1983 Grenada intervention; the countries examined in chapter four did not. In addition, as noted in chapter two, Eastern Caribbean states have faced similar security challenges. They also have a greater degree of capability deficiency compared with the rest of the region. Moreover, the leaders in these countries have demonstrated considerable convergence in their definition of the area's security situation. Finally, it was they who, in 1982, took the initiative to form a collective security mechanism, the Regional Security System (RSS).

Barbados

Like the Bahamas, Barbados did not create a standing army at the time of independence, but thirteen years afterward. No standing army was deemed necessary before 1979. The Royal Barbados Police Force (RBPF) was considered adequate for internal security, then the only security focus. One writer explained, "during the first thirteen years of its [Barbados's] existence, the police force was the factorum and security mainstay of the nation-state."[1]

The evolution of military policy in Barbados has witnessed both change and continuity, influenced by domestic as well as regional and hemispheric political changes. During the first ten years of independence when the country was led by Errol Barrow, little emphasis was placed on military matters. There was, of course, the police force, and a Coast Guard was started in 1974 to police Barbadian territorial waters, and conduct SAR and antismuggling missions. There was also the Barbados Regiment, which was used primarily for ceremonial purposes, but was deployed for other purposes on at least two occasions. One was in 1955, following Hurricane Janet, to protect the distribution of food and supplies. A second time was during the November 1966 independence celebrations, when the regular police were unable to control the unruly crowds.

Barrow and his Democratic Labor Party (DLP) lost power in September 1976 to the Barbados Labor Party (BLP) headed by Tom Adams. The BLP held power until 1986, although Adams died in March 1985. Adams's successor was Bernard St. John. Initially, Adams stayed the "low emphasis" course set by the previous government. Several developments, however, precipitated rapid departure from that position. In October 1976 an overseas-based Barbadian, Sidney Burnett-Alleyne, was intercepted off Martinique attempting to invade Barbados to overthrow the government. That same month, on October 6, a Cubana Airlines flight was destroyed in Barbadian airspace. The commercial airliner, which had originated in Guyana and was bound for Cuba, exploded shortly after departing from the international airport in Barbados. Seventy-three people were killed, including eleven Guyanese.[2] In April 1979, shortly after the successful March 13 coup in Grenada had brought Maurice Bishop and the New Jewel Movement (NJM) to power, Adams signed a joint security memorandum with Eric Williams, Prime Minister of Trinidad and Tobago. The agreement called for security cooperation given what the two leaders defined as "the growing complexity of the security problem of the Caribbean region." For them this complexity involved terrorism, piracy, the use of mercenaries, and subversion. This concern seemed justified, for, among other things, there were more invasion scares and mercenary threats from Alleyne in 1978 and 1979.

To all these developments and Adams's own fascination with military matters, as noted in the previous chapter, should be added the ominous climate in parts of the hemisphere. This included Guatemala's threats to absorb Belize, the Somoza-Sandinista battles in Nicaragua, and United States destabilization measures against Guyana and Jamaica. Together, these set the stage for Adams's creation of a standing army, the Barbados Defense Force (BDF), in 1979. But perhaps the most dramatic and significant policy initiative of the Adams government was the signature of the 1982 *Memorandum of Understanding Relating to Security and Military Cooperation* (see Appendix 1). That memorandum, a collective security agreement among Eastern Caribbean states, established the RSS, which is examined in the next chapter.

It was during Adams's tenure that Barbados began receiving military assistance from the United States. As we saw in chapter three, Adams also articulated a sub-regional defense policy called the "Adams Doctrine." The first-ever BDF overseas deployment was under Adams. Troops were sent to St. Vincent in December 1979 to help quell a rebellion; then in March 1981 and later that December they were sent to Dominica to help suppress coup attempts; next in May 1982 to St. Lucia during its elections. The most controversial deployment was in October 1983, when the BDF joined contingents from other RSS countries and Jamaica in the Grenada intervention.[3]

The increased attention of the Adams government to security matters was reflected in increased defense expenditure. For example, defense expenditure for 1978 was BDS $1.8 million; in 1979, BDS $2.4 million; in 1980, BDS $3.5 million; in 1981, BDS $8.4 million; in 1982, BDS $10.5 million; in 1983, BDS $13.3 million; in 1984, BDS $15.8 million; in 1985, BDS $19.9 million.[4] Defense expenditure, therefore, increased 90.6 percent over the eight years from 1978 to 1985. The heightened security consciousness was also demonstrated in reprisals against individuals who had become "security risks" for their criticism of the government's foreign policy and security conduct. Among the people affected was Ralph Gonsalves of the University of the West Indies (Cave Hill). His work permit was revoked in 1978. Rickey Singh, then editor of *Caribbean Contact*, a regional newspaper published by the Caribbean Conference of Churches, was put under surveillance, allegedly for associating with Cuban intelligence agents in Barbados. Later, his work permit was suspended after he condemned Barbados's complicity in the United States intervention in Grenada.[5] Singh's work permit was reissued in January 1987 by the successor government.

The DLP won the May 1986 elections and formed a successor government. The Prime Minister was, once again, Errol Barrow. Contrary to campaign pledges, Barrow did not dissolve the BDF and withdraw from the RSS. His change of heart was caused by both economic and political realities. These included a 19 percent unemployment rate at the time of the 1986 elections, the pivotal and prestigious role Barbados had played as the key element of the RSS, and the July 1987 invasion scare by Sidney Burnett-Allyene. The DLP government, however, did deemphasize the military by closing the air wing of the BDF and freezing defense expenditure.[6] Barrow also refused to endorse the plan to upgrade the 1982 Memorandum of Understanding to a full treaty, for reasons explored later.

Unfortunately, Barrow died of a heart attack on June 1, 1987. He was succeeded by Lloyd Erskine Sandiford, his deputy. Sandiford received his own popular mandate at elections held on January 22, 1991, when his party won 18 of the 28 seats in the House of Assembly.[7] The BDF has been deployed overseas twice under Sandiford. First to Jamaica in September 1988 following Hurricane Gilbert's destructive trail. Then again to Trinidad, in August 1990, following the coup attempt there. Indeed, as will be seen in chapter six, the Trinidad coup attempt saw Sandiford become a leading advocate for a strengthened RSS, even calling for a security system to encompass all CARICOM member-countries. This was a marked change from the position adopted in 1986.

As mentioned above, the BDF is key to the RSS. The BDF itself was created on August 9, 1979, out of the Barbados Regiment. However, the history of military outfits in Barbados goes back to 1649, when militia units were first created for internal security. Over the years since then there was the Barbados Volunteers, formed in 1902. It was subsumed under the Barbados Battalion in 1941. The Battalion was replaced by the Barbados Regiment in 1957.[8] The BDF is basically a ground force headed by a Chief of Staff, at present Brigadier Rudyard Lewis. The Chief of Staff is appointed by and subject to the direction of the Governor-General, but policy direction is the prerogative of the Prime Minister, who has also long held the defense portfolio. The Prime Minister's policy direction is guided by the Barbados Defense Board. According to BDF sources, in 1992 the BDF was comprised of an Infantry Army, a Commando Squadron, the Barbados Regiment, a Cadet Corps, an Administrative and Support Unit, and the Coast Guard, which, although relatively autonomous, is still an integral part of the BDF as its naval wing. The Coast Guard has vessels of varying sizes and capabilities and is primarily responsible for maritime surveillance, SAR, narcotics control, and disaster preparedness. There was also a small air wing, but, as noted above, it was closed in 1986.

The BDF receives assistance mainly from Britain, Canada, and the United States. Military assistance from the United States increased dramatically after 1983, in recognition of Barbados's supportive role in the Grenada intervention. For instance, Barbados received 158 placement awards under the IMET (International Military Education and Training) program between 1983 and 1991. Fifty-seven percent of those places were awarded between 1983 and 1987, during most of which time (except one-and-a-half years) the country was run by the government that endorsed the intervention.[9] While the three main foreign assistance providers offer training, both the training and operational structure of the BDF follow British Army lines. The establishment of the RSS in 1982 saw the expansion of the BDF's role. The BDF Chief of Staff doubles as RSS Coordinator, and the headquarters and facilities of the BDF serve as the operational nucleus of the RSS.

Internal security in Barbados is primarily the responsibility of the Royal Barbados Police Force (RBPF). Nevertheless, sharp increases in crime over the years led Barbados leaders to emulate Jamaica with joint police-army internal security operations. The operations began in December 1991 but have been sharply criticized by police union officials. However, they have been credited with curbing crime, especially in tourist areas. One dramatic success in the joint operations was the arrest in January 1992 of six men, including two policemen, in a drug raid where 400 pounds of marijuana were seized.[10]

The police force was originally established under colonial rule in 1835 and is credited with being one of the most professional of Caribbean police forces. Like all other Caribbean police forces, it is commanded by a Commissioner of Police (COP) appointed by the Governor-General on the recommendation of the Police Service Commission. Most police training is conducted at the Regional Police Training Center. It is located in Barbados, funded partly by the British, and provides training for police officials throughout the Caribbean, complementing training offered by individual law enforcement agencies.

Organization of Eastern Caribbean States (OECS)

Generally, capability limitations by OECS members and the absence of major external threats against them (the claim by Venezuela against

Dominica for Bird Island notwithstanding) have precluded the creation of standing armies in the area. The exceptions have been Antigua-Barbuda, Dominica, and St. Kitts-Nevis.

Antigua-Barbuda

The Antigua-Barbuda Defense Force (ABDF) was created on September 1, 1981, by the Antigua-Barbuda Defense Act.[11] Part II of the Act established a National Security Council (NSC) responsible for the "direction, control, and administration of the Force," and for "all other matters in relation to the Force." The NSC was designed to function subject to the powers and duties of the Defense Minister, a position always held by the Prime Minister.

The NSC comprises the Prime Minister as chairman, the Defense Minister, if that position is not held by the Prime Minister, and a maximum of five other people. However, a 1990 arms-drugs investigation, the "Guns for Antigua" affair, (which is examined fully in chapter nine), revealed that "nothing had been done by the Government to implement Part II of the Defense Act of 1981. So far as the National Security Council is concerned, the Act has been a dead letter from the day of its enactment." One of the several recommendations made by the investigator dealt directly with the NSC. Commissioner Blom-Cooper suggested amendment of Section 8(i)(c) of the National Security Act to allow for appointment to the NSC of people other than government ministers. Moreover, Blom-Cooper felt that in order to avoid politicization, appointments should be made by the Governor-General *after consultation with* the Prime Minister, not *on the advice of* the Prime Minister, the current arrangement that allows the Prime Minister to determine effectively the composition of the NSC.[12]

The ABDF has no air unit and no maritime component since the Coast Guard falls under the jurisdiction of the police force. It has a personnel establishment of 120 and is a member of the RSS. It has participated in all RSS military exercises, including the Caribbean Peacekeeping Force (CPF) in the 1983 Grenada intervention. Antigua's police force, the 350-member Royal Antigua and Barbuda Police Force (RABPF), is also a member of the RSS. It too has participated in RSS maneuvers and in the CPF.[13]

In November 1990, the ABDF Commander, Lieutenant Colonel Clyde Stevenson Walker, was dismissed on the recommendation of

Blom-Cooper. Walker, a former police officer, had headed the ABDF since 1982, first in the rank of Major. He was promoted on November 1, 1988, to Lieutenant Colonel. Walker was succeeded by Major Trevor Alistaire Thomas, Deputy Commander since 1984.[14] The "Guns for Antigua" affair involved several people, including Public Works Minister Vere Bird, Jr., son of Prime Minister Vere Bird, Sr., customs officers, and Israeli, Panamanian, Dutch, and Colombian nationals. Vere Bird, Jr., was not only removed as minister, but was also banned from holding any public office.

Dominica

The social unrest of the 1970s, precipitated by increasing economic deprivation and political discontent, led to the creation of the Dominica Volunteer Force in 1974. In November of the following year, the volunteer force was replaced by a full-time army, the Dominica Defense Force (DDF). Patrick John, Prime Minister and Minister of Defense, took more than a policy interest in the army. He even designated himself a Colonel. The DDF was reputed to be elitist, and there were serious tensions with the police—the Commonwealth of Dominica Police Force (CDPF). One contention was over the DDF's increasingly strong relations with the Guyana Defense Force (GDF). The police preferred to retain strong links with the security establishments in Barbados and Britain.[15]

Following a series of political crises in 1978 and 1979, Patrick John lost power to Mary Eugenia Charles at general elections held on July 20, 1980. On March 7, 1981, Prime Minister Charles announced the discovery of a plot to overthrow the government planned for March 14. The collaborators included ex-Prime Minister Patrick John, Major Frederick Newton and Corporal Howell Piper of the DDF, local recruits, and American and Canadian mercenaries. Among the Americans were members of the Klu Klux Klan and neo-Nazi groups. One of them, David Duke, was elected in 1989 to the Louisiana legislature and failed in a bid to become Louisiana's governor in 1991.[16] Duke's efforts to secure the Republican Party nomination for the 1992 presidential elections were also futile.

The United States collaborators in the plot were led by Michael Perdue. He later disclosed that the plan, code-named "Operation Red Dog," was to remove Prime Minister Charles and install Patrick John.

John was expected to place some of the mercenaries in key government positions. The operation, which had been delayed, was leaked to Canadian police. They in turn informed security officials in Dominica and the United States, and security agencies in the three countries organized countermeasures.

On April 27, United States Federal agents arrested two Canadians and eight Americans near New Orleans as they prepared to sail for Dominica with arms, ammunition, and supplies. The group had been infiltrated by federal agents. At the final pre-launch meeting in Louisiana, the agents convinced them to organize the convoy in a way that facilitated its capture later. Meanwhile, the Dominican authorities rounded up the local accomplices, including Mary Ann McGuire, a Canadian. She was arrested after a cable clerk became suspicious over the text of a cable sent to Canada: "Alexander is Dead." Patrick John was among nine Dominicans charged with treason and other offenses. At the October 1981 hearing, John and three other defendants were remanded to custody, but the five others were released due to insufficient evidence.[17]

The DDF had displayed its animosity toward Prime Minister Charles ever since she assumed power on July 23, 1980. This was despite her fence-mending visit to army headquarters the day after taking office. Several measures by Charles antagonized the DDF. She had voiced concern over political partisanship, and some officers were sent on early retirement. She also had ordered the inventorizing of DDF weapons and ammunition after allegations that arms were being traded for drugs. For Charles, the DDF's involvement in the coup plot was the ultimate act of disloyalty. She therefore had legislation passed disbanding the DDF in April 1981.

The Charles government later faced another coup attempt. On December 19, 1981, former DDF officer, Major Newton, led a group of armed masked men in simultaneous assaults against the prison and police headquarters. The aim was to release Patrick John and his codefendants, then awaiting trial in January 1982. Among the people killed in the incident were one police and two ex-army officers. COP Oliver Phillip was among those injured.[18] Six of the seven December coup planners were hanged for murder and treason. Meanwhile, John was released after the prosecution failed to present a credible case against him. But on appeal, he was imprisoned for twelve years. Although there is no parole in Dominica, John was given an early release in 1990.

Grenada

Grenada has been one of two Caribbean countries (the other being Guyana) where militarization was a major concern for a long time to people both inside and outside the country. The increased emphasis on the military, and on the use of legal instruments of coercion, became dramatic under Eric Gairy, the eccentric leader of Grenada from 1951 to 1962, and then again from 1967 to 1979 (as Prime Minister from 1974, when the country became independent.)

One study of militarization in Grenada noted:

> Gairy's security forces were organized into three separate branches: the army, the Mongoose Gang, and the police. After the nurses' strike, Gairy established two additional security arms: a "night ambush squad" and a "special secret police force." Once his security forces consolidated, Gairy turned to the legislature to legitimize his repressive actions. After his overwhelming victory against the GNP in the 1972 elections Gairy increased his personal stranglehold over the society through the passage of several legislative acts.
>
> In quick succession, the Explosives Amendment Act (No. 4 of 1972), the Prevention of Crime and Offensive Weapons Act (No. 38 of 1972), and the Public Order Amendment Act (No. 43 of 1972) were approved in the legislature. Each of these pieces of legislation sought to restrict the freedom of the individual, give the police the right to enter and search a private home without first obtaining a warrant, and ultimately suppress the developing popular democratic movement.[19]

The creation of the New Jewel Movement (NJM) in 1973 was largely a function of Gairy's politics of exclusion and repression and the country's economic difficulties. His March 13, 1979, ouster by the NJM led to the establishment of a People's Revolutionary Government (PRG). However, domestic and international factors, including United States destabilization measures, also led to militarization under the PRG. In a plan adopted in July 1982, the PRG contemplated a three-year expansion of its security forces, beginning in 1983. The first phase of the program anticipated Soviet assistance in establishing and training a permanent infantry battalion and five militia battalions. Three additional regular and nine more reserve battalions were to be formed. To facilitate and support the expansion, the PRG negotiated several agreements with the USSR, Cuba, North

Korea, and other socialist countries, as we saw in chapter three.

By 1983, the year the revolution aborted, there was a complex security establishment involving the People's Revolutionary Army (PRA), the People's Revolutionary Militia (PRM), the Grenada Police Service, and youth cadets. Prime Minister Maurice Bishop was Commander-in-Chief. General Hudson Austin was Minister of Defense and Interior, and of Construction. He also was Commander of the People's Revolutionary Armed Forces (PRAF), the umbrella security agency. All senior PRAF officers held military rank, even if their agency was not actually part of the standing army. Thus, COP Ian St. Bernard held the rank of Major. So did Keith Roberts, head of PRAF counterintelligence. Similarly, Justin Roberts, superintendent of the Richmond Hill Prison, was a Lieutenant. Cletus St. Paul, head of Bishop's personal security staff, was also a Second Lieutenant.[20]

An extensive system of command and control was designed for the country. PRAF headquarters were at Butler House and the PRA was controlled from Fort Rupert. The country was divided into four military regions, each with its own headquarters and regular military staff. Each region was responsible for administering, training, and mobilizing militia units, which Bishop is reputed to have favored over the standing army. The naval side of the PRAF was somewhat neglected, though. In October 1983, there were only four small patrol boats. However, the agreements with the USSR and North Korea anticipated delivery of four modern boats by the former and two by the latter between 1983 and 1986.[21]

Mark Adkin provides one of the clearest summaries of the PRG's security profile:

> Bishop and the Defense Ministry's plans for the PRAF were staggering. If all had gone well and the Soviets, Czechs, and North Koreans had fulfilled their agreements, by 1986 the PRAF would have had 4 regular infantry battalions, over 60 APCs, 108 ZU–23 AA guns, 50 GRAD P launchers, 160 military vehicles, 7 aircraft, 6 new patrol vessels, a workshop repair facility, a large new training base, a school for training Grenadian commanding officers and specialists, together with thousands of tons of equipment, stores, and ammunition. The militia would have grown to no fewer than 14 battalions.[22]

The PRG's security mechanism was abolished after the intervention. Between October 1983 and June 1985 internal security was han-

Figure 5.1 Royal Grenada Police Force

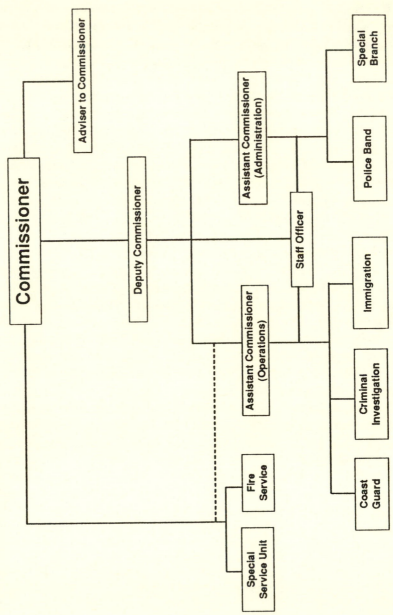

dled by the CPF as the Royal Grenada Police Force (RGPF) was reconstituted, retrained, and re-equipped. In 1986 there were reports of plans to establish a reserve force of volunteers to aid regular policemen with disaster preparedness and with any mass unrest. A key component of the police force is the SSU, discussed in chapter three. The RGPF joined the RSS in January 1985.

Figure 5.1 is an organizational chart of the RGPF, which largely reflects the police forces of Eastern Caribbean countries. There are operational departments responsible for immigration, Coast Guard operations, airport security, and ceremonial functions, as well as domestic law enforcement. These are generally headed by Superintendents, all of whom report to the Assistant Commissioner, Operations. The heads of the fire department and the SSU report directly to the COP, although they also relate to the Assistant Commissioner, Operations. The RGPF now has 600 members.[23]

St. Kitts-Nevis

Secession became a "clear and present danger" in the Caribbean when Anguilla seceded from the Associated State of St. Kitts-Nevis-Anguilla in the late 1960s. The separatist action of May 30, 1967, involved ejection of the country's police from Anguilla. British troops were subsequently dispatched to the area, and there was a flurry of diplomatic activity in the region. The net result was an overwhelming vote for secession at referendums held in July 1967 and February 1969. After the British Parliament passed the Anguilla Act of 1980, in December of that year, Anguilla reverted to full British control. St. Kitts-Nevis proceeded to independence on September 19, 1983.[24]

The separatist action by Anguilla led Premier Robert Bradshaw to create a standing army on January 22, 1968, out of the preexisting St. Kitts-Nevis-Anguilla Volunteer Force. The army, the St. Kitts-Nevis Defense Force (SKNDF), had three elements: a regular corps of about 100; a reserve corps; and a cadet corps of between 65 and 75 youths.[25] Initial training was done locally by Geoffrey Ellis, a retired British Army captain. Later, training was provided in Britain, Guyana, Jamaica, and Trinidad and Tobago. One GDF official, Captain Oscar Pollard, was said to be a major influence on the force, practically creating its code of conduct: to maintain internal security; stand beside the people if choosing sides becomes necessary; and preserve the government in power.

On the last point, there is a remarkable similarity between Guyana and St. Kitts-Nevis. As we saw in the discussion on Guyana, loyalty of the military to Burnham and his party was key to his empowerment. And as regards St. Kitts-Nevis, Whitman Browne makes this point: "Any leadership in the police or military demands loyalty to the political party, not competence or loyalty to the country."[26] Indeed, as Browne points out, with the passage of power to Premier Kennedy Simmonds in 1980, both the army head, Captain Errol Maynard, and COP Joseph Francis went to Simmonds and pledged their loyalty to him.

As time passed and the apprehension over secession abated, it became increasingly difficult to justify the maintenance of the SKNDF. Moreover, the new government distrusted the heads of the army and the police, considered loyalists to the vanquished party. All this, and developments in Dominica in early 1981, explained above, led Simmonds to disband the SKNDF in September 1981. Some former army personnel were absorbed into the police force, the Royal St. Kitts-Nevis Police Force (RSKNPF). Weapons and equipment were transferred to the police, with semiautomatic weapons reserved for the force's Tactical Unit, and later the SSU. The 300-member RSKNPF is a member of the RSS, and has duties similar to the forces in Grenada and elsewhere in the region.[27]

St. Lucia

Like most other Eastern Caribbean countries, St. Lucia has only a police force, the Royal St. Lucia Police Force (RSLPF). It has a structure and duties similar to the other police forces in the area. The RSLPF is part of the RSS and has participated in RSS operations, including the CPF in Grenada. Mismanagement and drug-related corruption in the force led to several official investigations in the 1980s, the last of which was done in 1988 by Karl Hudson-Phillips, Attorney-General of Trinidad and Tobago from 1969 to 1973.

Following submission of the Hudson-Phillips report, COP Cuthbert Phillips was dismissed. Phillips's problems were later compounded by a manslaughter conviction for the death of twenty-one-year-old Nevian Hippolyte during an altercation on a beach north of the capital, Castries. In 1990, Phillips was sentenced to five years imprisonment, but the term was reduced to three years on appeal. However, following a meeting of the country's Mercy Committee chaired by Prime Minister John Compton early September 1991, the former COP was granted an early release later that month.[28] After the dismissal of Phillips in 1988, Clive Sealy was named temporary head of the force, on loan from Trinidad. A lengthy search was conducted for a new COP, following which Algernon Hemmingway was appointed Police Commissioner, effective January 1, 1991. Hemmingway is a retired officer from London's Metropolitan Police who had served in police forces in Anguilla, Australia, and the Mediterranean. A top priority of the new commissioner is implementation of the reforms recommended by Karl Hudson-Phillips.[29]

St. Vincent and the Grenadines

There has never been a standing army in this country despite the internal security apprehensions caused by the 1979 Union Island uprising. All security matters are handled by the Royal St. Vincent and the Grenadines Police Force (RSVGPF). The country's Coast Guard, which became operational in 1981, is also under the police commissioner.

While St. Vincent is a party to the 1982 Memorandum of Understanding that created the RSS, as we will see in the discussion on the RSS, Prime Minister James Mitchell has been reluctant to facilitate "excessive militarization" in the area. Like most of the other RSS member-states—the exceptions are Antigua-Barbuda and Barbados—St. Vincent has a SSU. However, Mitchell was so worried with the potential for SSU elitism that he took the unit out of the official camouflage military uniforms and made SSU members wear local police uniforms. Mitchell recognizes the need for the RSS, but is often uncomfortable with the high profile of the Barbados Defense Force (BDF) in the collective security arrangement.[30]

In 1989 a Vincentian police official created a crisis in the subregion when he fatally shot several people in Grenada. On June 29, Assistant COP Grafton Bascombe, on loan to the RGPF, murdered Grenada's COP Cosmos Raymond, and United States Political Attaché to Grenada John Butler. He also wounded RGPF Deputy COP, Collis Barrow, and RGPF Assistant Superintendent, Daniel Searles. Bascombe, fifty years old, was later found dead in a police cell, reportedly beaten to death by irate policemen. The Grenada government's official statement, however, attributed his death to a heart attack.

Bascombe had been under investigation for fraud. He reportedly received full salaries from the governments of St. Vincent and Grenada simultaneously. He also allegedly engaged in financial irregularities as the Grenada coordinator of the 1989 RSS-United States military exercise, "Trade Winds 89." The incident created a climate of disbelief and anger in Grenada. In addition to wiping out the RGPF top brass, it also threatened to sour the atmosphere of the 1989 CARICOM Summit, then scheduled for early July in Grenada.[31]

Little more than a year later, in August 1991, the Grenada police authorities were embarassed when an ex-prisoner from St. Vincent impersonated a sergeant from St. Vincent and gained admittance to the RGPF. The sham cop, whose name was not disclosed, posed as a "Sergeant George" and secured the full cooperation of the RGPF top brass for almost a month, including provision of room and board, as he worked his way into the police force. The fraud was uncovered when a legitimate RSVGPF police officer went to Grenada for SSU training.[32]

The head of the RSVPF, COP Randolph Toussaint, was himself suspended indefinitely in August 1991, following a successful campaign for his removal. The campaign had been waged by the National Council in Defense of Law and Order, a grouping of opposition political parties, trade unions, and civic and human rights groups. The Council had been presenting several allegations about Toussaint's illegal conduct, including the giving of sensitive national security and police documents in exchange for a waiver of gambling debts. Toussaint, who was known for his gambling, even declared in a BBC radio interview: "Everybody knows I go to the casino." Prime Minister James Mitchell appointed a distinguished Guyanese jurist, Rex McKay, as a one-man commission to investigate the charges. The inquiry began on September 23, 1991 and ended three months later. Toussaint was cleared of all charges and reinstated as COP on December 23, 1991.[33]

Jamaica

Like Guyana, Jamaica has a multidimensional security establishment. The Jamaica Defense Force (JDF) and the Jamaica Constabulary Force

(JCF) are the primary agencies. Although the others are not discussed here, it is useful to note them: the Island Special Constabulary Force (ISCF); the Police Mobile Reserve Division (PMRD); the Special District Constables (SDCs); and the Port Security Corps (PSC). (National Security Minister K.D. Knight told Parliament on June 10, 1992 that the government planned absorbing the ISCF into the JCF.) There are also Authorized Persons, individuals granted limited police powers exercisable in cases such as predial larceny. As we will see below, between 1974 and 1981 there was another agency, the Home Guards.

The JDF became operational in July 1962, just weeks before Jamaica's independence from Britain on August 6, 1962. Its core element was the Jamaica Regiment, a key component of the West Indies Regiment (WIR), the defense mechanism of the ill-fated West Indies Federation (1958–1962). The 1st Battalion of the WIR was based in Jamaica. In 1960 it was organized into four companies, with about 500 men, half of whom were Jamaican. The Jamaica Territorial Regiment was set up alongside the 1st Battalion WIR in February 1961 and was redesignated the Jamaican National Reserve (JNR) a year later.[34]

The JDF was conceived as an integrated army, with a Coast Guard and an air wing, although the latter was not created until 1963. Headquarters were established at Up Park Camp, Kingston, with companies based in Kingston, Montego Bay, Mandeville, and May Pen. The JDF came under the portfolio of the Ministry of Defense with its operational head as the Chief of Staff. Naturally, the first Chief of Staff, Brigadier Paul Crook, was British. So was most of the officer corps. Indeed, although a naturalized Jamaican was named Chief of Staff in April 1965, the first Jamaican-born head of the army was not appointed until 1968. He was Lt. Colonel R.H. Green.[35] The present Chief of Staff is Commodore Peter Brady. On August 1, 1990, he succeeded Major-General Robert Neish, who had commanded the JDF for eleven years.[36]

Although the JDF had been designed for external security, the absence of any "clear and present" external danger coupled with the rise in domestic violence led to a metamorphosis in the army's security orientation. As Terry Lacey explains, "Partly for political reasons . . . and partly because it was apparently decided to bring the army in to support the police in routine operations, the JDF began to be used extensively, by the beginning of 1969, in effect as a second-line, regular police force."[37]

Britain, the United States, and Canada played critical roles in the creation and development of Jamaica's security establishment. The British provided a command structure, training, army officers on loan, and some weapons. The first Chief of Staff, Brigadier Crook, for example, came on loan from the British War Office. Upon completion of his tour as Chief of Staff in 1965, he became head of the British Joint Services Team in Jamaica. Twenty-one other officers on loan joined the team at the same time. The geopolitics of the region, combined with Britain's declining ability to retain its global stature, however, soon resulted in a decline of Britain's influence and an increase in that of the United States and Canada. Indeed, Prime Minister Sir Alexander Bustamante had declared in 1964 that "Jamaica's destiny is along with Canada and the United States of America although England has always been very kind to us."[38]

The first military assistance package from the United States was granted in 1963, primarily for the Coast Guard and the JDF's air wing: twelve trailer trucks with machine guns mounted; three AN-GRC base radio stations with supporting equipment; three sixty-three foot patrol boats with mounted machine guns; and four Cessna 185 aircraft. Up to 1977, Jamaica was the only Commonwealth Caribbean country to get military assistance under the IMET Program. The U.S. $1.053 million in military assistance given to Jamaica up to the same year also represented the greatest amount given to any English-speaking country in the region.[39]

The collaboration between the United States and Jamaica also involved exchanges between military officials. For instance, visits were made to Jamaica in 1962 by the Commander of the Guantánamo base in Cuba. The commanding officer of United States Forces Caribbean visited in 1963. So did the Commander of the then United States Armed Forces Canal Zone. In 1963, Lt. Colonel David Smith of Jamaica toured several military facilities in the United States. Operational contacts between the Jamaican and American military establishments included use of Palisadoes airport as part of "Operation Springboard," a series of military exercises held between January and March 1963, and involving more than 40,000 men, 110 ships, and some 100 aircraft.[40]

Canadian involvement in Jamaica's military began with technical advice and training assistance by the Royal Canadian Mounted Police (RCMP) at their training center in Regina, Saskatchewan. Expansion of contacts witnessed the establishment of a military cadet scheme and visits by top Canadian and Jamaican officials to each other's countries. Brigadier Crook, Jamaica's Chief of Staff, went to Ottawa in March 1963, and Canada's Brigadier E. Danby, Army Commander of British Colombia, went to Jamaica the following September. Canada was instrumental in the creation of the JDF's air wing in 1963, and with provision of technical assistance and training. Contacts with Canada later went beyond training and technical assistance. In 1969, major operational contacts were developed, among them military exercises code-named "Nimrod Caper" and "Nimrod Leap," held in March and November 1969, respectively.[41]

Thus, at the end of the 1960s, Jamaica's security profile was one focused on internal security, with British, United States, and Canadian collaboration to develop and professionalize the army. This profile began to change with the advent, on March 1, 1972, of the People's National Party (PNP) government led by Michael Manley. Prime Minister Manley advocated a "politics of change" predicated on the philosophy of democratic socialism. This resulted in dramatic foreign policy shifts, and new domestic political and socioeconomic initiatives.[42]

One such initiative was the creation of the Home Guards (HG) in 1974. The HG was intended to complement the policing functions of the JCF. Members wore no uniform, but carried badges, had powers of arrest, and were sometimes issued with handguns, which they returned to the appropriate police station at the end of their patrol. The police provided training in firearms use, first aid, and law enforcement. The JCF had operational control over the HG, and except in emergencies (and there were many in the 1970s), police officers accompanied HG members on patrol.

The high incidence of crime and violence made the HG quite popular, its numbers soaring to over 9,000 in 1980. Even Prime Minister Manley joined in 1976 to boost public confidence in it. There was considerable controversy over the HG, though. The opposition Jamaica Labor Party (JLP) charged that the ruling PNP had ulterior motives in creating the HG: laying the basis for a communist-styled people's militia. Nevertheless, the JLP encouraged some of its members to join because of the crime problem. The severity of crime, coupled with hostility to the HG by many security officials, made it largely ineffective. These factors, when added to the original antipathy by the JLP, made the prospects for its survival very unlikely. Quite predictably, when the PNP lost power to the JLP in October 1980, a high priority of the new Edward Seaga government was the disbanding of the HG. This was done in 1981.[43]

A second initiative by the Manley government was to alter some of the country's military collaboration. Military relations continued with Britain and Canada, although somewhat attenuated in the case of Britain, but those with United States deteriorated to the point of virtual suspension. For example, there was no United States military assistance to Jamaica during the Manley years (1972–1980). Even the Economic Support Fund and the PL–480 disbursements were reduced, such that in 1976 the total assistance package to Jamaica was a mere U.S. $2.2 million. Military assistance resumed when Edward Seaga assumed power in late 1980. In 1981 military assistance was U.S. $1.66 million, part of a U.S. $75.15 million package for 1981, a massive increase from the US$14.6 million package in 1980, Manley's last year in power before his return in 1989.[44]

For reasons appropriately not pursued here, Jamaica experienced considerable political polarization and accompanying political violence in the late 1970s and early 1980s. The JDF, the JCF, and the other security forces were not immune from the effects of these. In 1976 JLP Senator Pearnel Charles and former JDF officer Peter Whittingham were arrested for allegedly masterminding a coup plan. Whittingham was arrested at a JLP convention in Montego Bay with a briefcase allegedly containing plans for the operation, code-named "Werewolf." However, the police lacked sufficient evidence to press charges. Both Charles and Whittingham were released. As was mentioned in chapter two, there were also coup plans involving JDF officers. On June 22, 1980, thirty-three JDF officers and several members of a small right-wing group, the Jamaica United Front Party, were arrested and charged with plotting a coup. The plan was allegedly to commandeer two armoured cars, kidnap and possibly kill the then Chief of Staff, Brigadier Robert Neish, and capture Prime Minister Manley and force his resignation on public radio.[45]

Manley later gave his assessment of the circumstances facing the military in the context of his "politics of change." He explained that the Jamaican army had always been a potential problem. While nurtured in the tradition of constitutional neutrality, it comprised individuals who were affected by the country's social moods and currents. For example, the anti-PNP forces increased the campaign among the middle classes who, angered by the shortages and frightened by anti-communist propaganda, became increasingly hostile to the PNP government. A similar mood was reflected in the officer corps, and even among the lower ranks. Moreover, the opposition's constant assertion that the government intended to "bring in the whole Cuban army to take over the country" maintained the tense mood. According to Manley, the entire traditional system of military training is designed around the concept of an enemy, with officers exposed to "a world configuration in which the enemy is seen trough the eyes of [the] M1 5." Hence, "for people of this kind of class background, early cultural experience and training, it is extremely difficult to accept that a foreign communist—and perhaps even a local socialist—is not an enemy. Their unconscious assumption leads them into a precarious contradiction."[46]

The American defense establishment has acknowledged the importance of Jamaica to United States security, noting that "Jamaica is important to the U.S. because of its location along vital sea lanes, the ability of its government to influence opinion in the English Caribbean, and its role as a major source of bauxite and marijuana."[47] The victory by Edward Seaga at the October 30, 1980, polls was, therefore, a great boon to the United States government. Seaga was politically conservative, and he advocated socioeconomic prescriptions beneficial to big business, both in Jamaica and in the United States. He saw through conceptual lenses similar to those of President Ronald Reagan. One analyst noted: "Two of the most explicit areas of the new [Seaga] regime's foreign policies are the Cuban disconnection and the revival of the American connection."[48] In this, Seaga and Reagan stood on common ground. Indeed, Seaga had the distinction of being the first foreign leader received by Reagan, in January 1981. It was, therefore, easy for Seaga to become a surrogate of the United States in the region.

The Pentagon gave the following rationale for security assistance to Jamaica:

> Security assistance can contribute towards achieving our objectives of maintaining a stable democratic government friendly to the United States, maintaining close cooperation in preserving regional stability, and furthering cooperation in marijuana eradication and narcotics interdiction.
>
> The Jamaica Defense Force (JDF), with the support of U.S. military assistance, is capable of performing its role in maintaining internal

order to protect the democratic process, and participating in narcotics interdiction and eradication efforts. *Our military assistance will also foster a continued close relationship between the JDF and the U.S. military, and will promote the JDF's ability and willingness to participate in joint operations with friendly forces to further regional security and support U.S. foreign policy objectives.*[49]

As we saw in Table 3.6, Jamaica received U.S. $2.28 million in IMET assistance between 1981 and 1989. As we also saw in chapter three, Jamaica had 466 students trained under the IMET program during the Seaga years, the largest award to a single Caribbean country.

Upon his return to power on February 9, 1989, Michael Manley abandoned his earlier domestic and foreign policy pursuits, adopting policies even more fiscally conservative than Seaga, and with a less strident international posture.[50] Jamaica's posture became such that officials in Washington were able to offer the following argument in support of a U.S. $73.39 million security assistance package to Jamaica for fiscal 1992:

> Since assuming office in 1989, Prime Minister Manley [has] pursued a relatively moderate foreign policy, supporting U.S. positions in international fora more frequently than before. He has, also, maintained his predecessor's commitment to the Jamaica Defense Force (JDF) to cooperate in counter-narcotics activities, although Jamaican funding shortages limit JDF ability to maintain and operate the equipment needed for these operations.[51]

As noted in chapter two, Manley demitted office on March 28, 1992, because of failing health. His successor, Percival Patterson, has pledged to "stay the course" set by Manley, of which he was a main architect.

The JDF not only receives foreign assistance; it gives as well. One recent instance was in Haiti where sea-lift operations were provided for supplies and equipment for the second run-up elections in January 1991. In December 1990 and February 1991, the JDF air wing also provided support and personnel to assist with the administration of presidential elections there. The air wing was involved in transportation, day and night patrols, and flight reconnaissance. In addition, the JDF Coast Guard helped with harbor patrol and SAR and anti-smuggling operations. Special aviation assistance was given to the GDF in

1991, and security officials from Antigua-Barbuda, Barbados, and Guyana also received JDF training during that year.[52]

There is neither military research and development nor arms production in Jamaica. However, Jamaica has one of the Caribbean's best military inventories, with SLRs (Self-Loading Rifles), "Sterling" submachine guns, GPMGs (General Purpose Machine Guns), mortar throwers, attack motor vessels, "Ferret" scout cars, United States-made Cadillac Commando APCs (Armored Personnel Carriers), and small troop transport planes. Like other Caribbean countries, Jamaica's weapons and equipment originally came mainly from Britain. But over the years as Jamaica joined the United States in efforts to combat narcotics production and transshipment, weapons and equipment have come increasingly from the United States. Canadian equipment is also used extensively, especially in the JCF.

As mentioned above, the JDF is an integrated army, with ground, air, and maritime elements. The air element, the JDF Air Wing, was created in July 1963 and has been expanded over the years with British, Canadian, and United States assistance. It is equipped for ground force liaison, SAR, and transport missions. The air wing has no combat aircraft or armed helicopters. Its 1986 inventory included mostly United States made aircraft, but also some British, Canadian, and French models. The inventory now includes five Bell 206A, three Bell 212 and two Aerospatiale Alouette 11 light helicopters, two Britten-Norman Islander light transports, one DHC–6 Beech King Air 90 light transports, and four Cessna light transports. According to the International Institute for Strategic Studies, the Air Wing's 1990 personnel establishment was 150.[53]

The JDF Coast Guard conducts SAR operations, anti-narcotics interdiction, and protects the country's marine resources. One United States Coast Guard official has spoken of the Coast Guard in laudable terms: "The JDFCG officer corps epitomizes professionalism in the Caribbean. Many of the officers were trained at the British military academy at Sandhurst, and most, after transfer from the main body of the JDF, prefer to remain in the Coast Guard. Most are skilled seamen, knowledgeable engineers, and strong leaders who seek to improve their skills and equipment."[54]

The JCF, the other leading security agency in Jamaica, was formed in 1867. It has been long plagued with poor training, low salaries, and overwork, and it has a very poor reputation regarding violation of civil and political rights. For example, one Americas Watch report documented an average of 217 police killings annually between 1979 and 1986. And according to the Jamaica Council on Human Rights, there were 289 killings by the police in 1984 alone. There has often been conflict with the political power holders. The conflict was such in the 1960s that one writer was prompted to observe: "One of the main potential threats to internal security during the 1960s was the hostility of the police force to the government."[55] Two decades later, the situation was not much changed in this respect. According to Michael Kaufman, "By 1980 a majority of the armed forces and police personnel opposed the PNP. In two separate events the police or soldiers fired on PNP members or crowds. First was the 13 October killing of Junior Minister of Security, Roy McGann. In another incident soldiers broke up the final election meeting of the PNP in Spanish Town."[56]

The JCF is subject to policy control by the Ministry of National Security, created in 1974. Operationally it is headed by a COP, like other police forces in the Caribbean. Structurally there are four main branches: Administration; Services; Security; and Special Operations. The Security branch is headed by a Deputy Commissioner while the others are headed by Assistant Commissioners. Among other things, the Special Operations branch is responsible for the security of visiting officials, the Central Investigation Department, the PMRD, the Traffic Department, and the Women's Police. A 1984 security services reorganization also gave this branch the task of dealing with criminal groups and individuals who target security agencies for terrorism.

The JCF's authorized strength in 1990 was 6,317, but the actual size was 5,998, the largest figure since 1984 when the strength of the JCF stood at 6,314.[57] As Table 5.1 indicates, the force has been suffering from a serious attrition problem over the last decade and a half. Attrition is a function of several factors, among them retirement, resignation, deaths, court convictions, and dismissals. Jamaica's National Security Minister told Parliament in 1992 that the dismissal rate increased from 12 percent in 1990–91 to 20.5 percent in 1991–92. Table 5.1 shows that only twice between 1985 and 1990 have there been net gains in the force. The dramatic end in 1989 of the personnel hemorrhage and the even more dramatic improvement in 1990 offer hope for greater amelioration in the future. The 1990 net gain of 501 is remarkable. In 1990 there was the largest graduation class in the history of the JCF, with 285 new police officers, 48 percent of whom were women.[58]

Table 5.1

JCF Recruitment and Attrition, 1985–1990

	1985	1986	1987	1988	1989	1990
Recruitment	101	138	195	248	381	811
Attrition	360	393	331	349	276	310
Net Loss	259	255	136	101	+101	+510

Source: Planning Institute of Jamaica, *Economic and Social Survey 1989,* Kingston, Jamaica, 1990; *Economic and Social Survey 1990,* Kingston, Jamaica, 1991.

It was the result of an Accelerated Promotion Program, management change within the force, and intensive recruitment.

Additional measures were also adopted to boost the size and professionalism of the JCF. These include a Graduate Entry Program, allowing college graduates with special skills to enter the JCF through a special selection and training scheme. In addition, in 1990, police stations were completed in Bethel Town and in Barrett Town, and preliminary work began for new stations in Lucea and Port Maria. Construction of a computer center, which began in November 1990, was completed in June 1991. The construction was undertaken by the engineering division of the JDF aided by members of the ISCF. Officials in the National Security Ministry were so impressed with the work of the JDF that in April 1992 they created an Engineering Regiment within the army. The J $6.5 million facility computerizes JCF work in the areas of criminal records, narcotics control, traffic control, and immigration. A J $25 million contract was also signed with Motorola USA for a 800 megahertz island-wide trunked radio system. The system is intended to enhance JCF ability to deal with crime and narcotics control. In 1990 the JCF acquired an additional 140 motorcycles and 263 motor vehicles for its fleet, at a total cost of J $35.2 million. Added to all this, in 1991 a guidance counselor and a chaplain/psychologist were appointed to the force. Four assistant chaplain/psychologists were also appointed later.[59]

In the area of education, the Constabulary Staff College continues to be the center for local police management training. According to National Security Minister K.D. Knight, the college, which was established in 1984 with British assistance, has trained over 800 JCF officers. Some 142 officers from elsewhere in the Caribbean have also been trained there. There are plans to upgrade the college to an accredited tertiary institution able to award its own certificates and degrees. National Security Minister Knight told Parliament in July 1991 that in 1990 government officials began exploring the college's affiliation with the University Council of Jamaica and the UWI.

The JDF and the JCF have a long history of joint operations, dating to July 1962. However, passage of the Suppression of Crime (Special Provisions) Act in 1974 gave the JDF-JCF collaboration a new dimension. The JDF was permitted to cordon off any area of the island while the JCF conducted house-to-house searches. A study by Hudson and Seyler indicates that the police forces relied on that act extensively, and detention of persons "reasonably" suspected of having committed a crime occurred regularly without a warrant, particularly in poor neighborhoods. Almost all detainees were released eventually without being charged. To the delight of many Jamaican and Caribbean human rights observers, in July 1992 Prime Minister Percival Patterson indicated that the 1974 law was being reexamined with a view to its repeal.

Conclusion

The involvement of the countries discussed here in the Grenada intervention, and the heightened security consciousness in the area since 1983, has led to significant foreign military assistance to the security establishments. In many ways, the Grenada crisis and its aftermath marked a real end of West Indian innocence. In chapter three we saw the dramatic increase in IMET assistance after 1983. In the Eastern Caribbean, SSUs were created and trained by the United States and Britain, and Coast Guard facilities and equipment were upgraded and provided as a matter of urgency.

In 1988, for example, a noted defense information source reported that six separate Coast Guards took major steps forward. New Coast Guard bases were officially opened on June 14, 1988, in Antigua-Barbuda, St. Kitts-Nevis, and Dominica. Work progressed on new bases in Grenada, St. Lucia, and St. Vincent and the Grenadines. Each $3 million base was built with British aid, with every country receiving vessels from the United States. Each Coast Guard base was constructed with full machine shop facilities. The joint British-American program gave each country a base, vessels, follow-up training, and on-site technical assistance. In the case of Dominica, two Royal Navy officers—one engineer and one operations officer—were to be assigned for some years to assist the Coast Guard. Dominica, Antigua, and St. Kitts each received a principal patrol boat, about seventy feet in length and armed, plus two *Boston Whalers* for high-speed inshore work. Grenada secured the biggest vessel: a 120-foot ex-U.S. patrol boat. In addition, Dominica had a three-year-old vessel undergoing a $300,000 modernization program.[60]

In sum, this chapter and the previous one suggest that individual efforts by Caribbean states to deal with security concerns reflect perceptions and interests of ruling elites, which are shaped by regional and hemispheric developments, and influenced by the capabilities of the various states. While there is variation in the size and professionalism of Caribbean security agencies, armies are uniformly small, with limited armaments, no force projection capability, and heavy reliance on extra-regional support. Although all Caribbean states were obliged to seek external assistance for the development and maintenance of their military establishments, shifts in domestic and foreign policy often led some countries away from Britain, the once dominant colonizer, and from the United States, the proximate superpower. All Caribbean nations, even Guyana and Jamaica with relatively large establishments, have recognized that individual efforts are insufficient to meet their security needs. It remains to be seen in the next chapter how they have pursued their collective security agenda.

Notes

1. Dion E. Phillips, "The Creation, Structure, and Training of the Barbados Defense Force," *Caribbean Studies* 21 (January-June 1988): 128.

2. For more on this incident see "Cuban Jetliner Crashes after Bombing," *Facts on File* October 23, 1976, pp. 779–80; and Dion E. Phillips, "Terrorism and Security in the Caribbean: The 1976 Cubana Disaster off Barbados," *Terrorism* 14 (No. 4, 1991): 209–19.

3. See Mark Adkin, *Urgent Fury: The Battle for Grenada*, Lexington, MA: Lexington Books, 1989; Mohamed Shahabuddeen, *The Conquest of Grenada: Sovereignty in the Periphery*, Georgetown: University of Guyana, 1986; and Vaughan A. Lewis, "Small States, Eastern Caribbean Security, and the Grenada Intervention," in Jorge Heine, ed., *A Revolution Aborted: The Lessons of Grenada*, Pittsburgh: University of Pittsburgh Press, 1991.

4. Phillips, "The Creation," p. 142.

5. See Allan Kirton, "End of a Decade—End of an Era," *Caribbean Contact* (Barbados), December 1983, p. 1; and "Rickey Singh's Work Permit and Departure: Lamming's Challenge to Barbadians," *Caribbean Contact*, December 1983, pp. 9, 12.

6. See "Barrow to Freeze Defense Force," *New York Carib News*, March 31, 1987, p. 3.

7. See Ikael Tafari, "Sandiford Wins Decisively," *Caribbean Contact*, January/February, 1991, pp. 1–2.

8. For a discussion of the history of the military in Barbados see Frances Kay Brinkley, *The Military Tradition of Barbados*, Bridgetown, Barbados: Barbados Museum and Historical Society, 1982; Government of Barbados, *The Barbados Defense Force: Securing Your Tomorrow*, Bridgetown, Barbados: Barbados Government Printery, n.d.; and Phillips, "The Creation," pp. 124–27.

9. See U.S. Department of Defense and Defense Security Assistance Agency, *Congressional Presentation for Security Assistance Program, Fiscal Year(s) 1983–1991*. Note: the figure for fiscal 1991 (28) is a proposed one.

10. "Police Step Up Criticising of Joint Police/Army Patrols," *Stabroek News* (Guyana), January 11, 1992, p. 6; and "Two Cops Detained Following Ganja Bust," *Guyana Chronicle*, January 21, 1992, p. 7.

11. Telephone interview with Dr. Patrick Lewis, Ambassador of Antigua-Barbuda to the United States and the OAS, August 26, 1991.

12. Louis Blom-Cooper, *Guns for Antigua: Report of the Commission of Inquiry into the Circumstances Surrounding the Shipment of Arms from Israel to Antigua and Transshipment on 24 April 1989 En Route to Colombia*, London: Duckworth, 1990, pp. 99, 100.

13. Karen Sturges-Vera, "Antigua and Barbuda," in Sandra W. Meditz and Dennis M. Hanratty, eds., *Islands of the Commonwealth Caribbean*, Washington, D.C.: Library of Congress, 1989, pp. 542–53.

14. Blom-Cooper, *Guns for Antigua*, p. 7; and interview with Dr. Lewis.

15. Atherton Martin, "Dominica," in *Islands of the Commonwealth Caribbean*, pp. 287–89.

16. See Peter Applebome, "Duke: Ex-Nazi Who Would Become Governor," *New York Times*, November 10, 1991, pp. L1, L26; and Peter Applebome, "Fearing Duke, Voters in Louisiana Hand Democrat Fourth Term," *New York Times*, November 18, 1991, pp. A1, B6.

17. Lennox Honychurch, *The Dominica Story*, 2d ed., Roseau, Dominica: The Dominica Institute, 1984, p. 218.

18. Honychurch, *The Dominica Story*, pp. 215, 217, 219; and Martin, "Dominica."

19. Ken I. Boodhoo, "Violence and Militarization in the Eastern Caribbean: The Case of Grenada," in Alma H. Young and Dion E. Phillips, eds., *Militarization in the Non-Hispanic Caribbean*, Boulder, CO: Lynne Rienner, 1986, pp. 69–70.

20. Adkin, *Urgent Fury*, pp. 147–48.

21. Ibid., pp. 147–52.

22. Ibid., pp. 152–53.

23. Richard A. Haggerty and John F. Hornbeck, "Grenada," in *Islands in the*

Commonwealth Caribbean, pp. 380–82. For a discussion of the security situation since 1983 see Clifford E. Griffin, "Postinvasion Political Security in the Eastern Caribbean," in Griffith, *Strategy and Security in the Caribbean*, esp. pp 84–95.

24. For more on the secession see Colville Petty, *Anguilla: Where There Is a Will There Is a Way*, Anguilla: Colville Petty, 1983; and Francis Alexis, "British Intervention in St. Kitts," *New York University Journal of International Law and Politics* 16 (Spring 1984): 581–600. Also see Iyahnya Christian, "Anguilla's Revolt—21 Years After," *Caribbean Contact*, January 1989, p. 6.

25. Whitman Browne, "Overt Militarism and Covert Politics in St. Kitts-Nevis," Paper Presented at Conference on Peace and Development in the Caribbean, Kingston, Jamaica, May 16–18, 1988, p. 16. This paper appears as chapter seven of the conference volume, *Conflict, Peace, and Development in the Caribbean*, edited by Jorge Rodríguez Beruff, J. Peter Figueroa, and J. Edward Greene. London: Macmillan, 1991.

26. Browne, "Overt Militarism," p. 20.

27. See Richard A. Haggerty and John F. Hornbeck, "St. Christopher and Nevis," in *Islands of the Commonwealth Caribbean*, pp. 483–85.

28. "Ex-commissioner Released from Prison," *New York Carib News*, September 17, 1991, p. 34.

29. "St. Lucia Gets British Police Chief," *New York Carib News*, January 8, 1991, p. 33. For a brief discussion on national security in St. Lucia see John F. Hornbeck, "St. Lucia," in *Islands in the Commonwealth Caribbean*, pp. 316–17.

30. Mary Jo Cosover, "St. Vincent and the Grenadines," in *Islands of the Commonwealth Caribbean*, pp. 340–43.

31. See Michael Roberts, "Grenada's Commissioner of Police Assassinated," *New York Carib News*, July 11, 1989, p. 3; and Sandra Baptiste, "Mitchell Explains Why He Asked for Killer Cop's Return," *New York Carib News*, July 18, 1989, p. 4.

32. "Grenada Police Tricked," *New York Carib News*, September 10, 1991, p. 5.

33. See "Council Continues Opposition to Police Commissioner," *New York Carib News*, September 10, 1991, p. 5; "Police Under Probe," *New York Carib News*, September 17, 1991, p. 35; "Probe of Vincentian Police Chief Resumes," *Jamaican Weekly Gleaner*, October 14, 1991, p. 12; and "St. Vincent Police Chief Resumes Duties after Probe," *Barbados Advocate*, December 24, 1991, p. 10.

34. Terry Lacey, *Violence and Politics in Jamaica: 1960–1970*, London: Frank Cass, 1977, p. 107.

35. The naturalized Jamaican, of Bahamian birth, was Brigadier David Smith. See Humberto García Muñiz, "Defense Policy and Planning in the Caribbean: An Assessment of the Case of Jamaica on its 25th Independence Anniversary," *Caribbean Studies* 21 (January-June 1988): 72.

36. "Neish Hands Over JDF Command," *Jamaican Weekly Gleaner*, August 13, 1990, p. 2.

37. Lacey, *Violence and Politics in Jamaica*, pp. 115–116.

38. Cited in ibid., p. 144.

39. Ibid., p. 153; and U.S. Defense Security Agency, *Foreign Military Sales, Foreign Military Construction Sales and Military Assistance Facts as of September 30, 1987*, Washington, D.C., 1988, pp. 54, 88–90.

40. Lacey, *Violence and Politics in Jamaica*, p. 154.

41. Ibid., p. 157.

42. See Perry Mars, "Destabilization, Foreign Intervention, and Socialist Transformation in the Caribbean," *Transition* 7 (1983): 33–54; and Anthony J. Payne, *Politics in Jamaica*, New York: St. Martin's Press, 1988, pp. 50–59. For a discusion of democratic socialism, see Michael Manley, *The Politics of Change: A Jamaican Testament*, London: Andre Deutsch, 1974; and Michael Kaufman, *Jamaica under Manley*, London: Zed Books, 1985.

43. Kaufman, *Jamaica under Manley*, pp. 116–17; 178–79.

44. Congressional Research Service, *Inter-American Relations: A Collection of Documents, Legislation, Description of Inter-American Organizations, and Other Materials Pertaining to Inter-American Affairs*, Washington, D.C., December 1988, p. 988.

45. Kaufman, *Jamaica Under Manley*, pp. 117, 188–89.

46. Michael Manley, *Jamaica: Struggle in the Periphery*, London: Third World Media, 1982, p. 201.

47. U.S. Department of State and Defense Security Assistance Agency, *Congressional Presentation for Security Assistance Programs Fiscal Year 1989*, Washington, D.C., 1988, p. 200.

48. Paul Ashley, "Jamaica's Foreign Policy in Transition: From Manley to Seaga," in Jorge Heine and Leslie Manigat, eds., *The Caribbean and World Politics*, New York: Holmes and Meier, 1988, p. 153.

49. *Congressional Presentation for Security Assistance Programs Fiscal Year 1989*, p. 200. Emphasis added. This was Seaga's last year in power.

50. See Wenty Bowen, "Manley Goes Back to the Future," *Caribbean Contact*, September/October 1990, pp. 1–2; and Wenty Bowen, "Jamaica—Redefining the Role of Government," *Caribbean Contact*, January/February 1991, p. 7.

51. *Congressional Presentation for Security Assistance Programs Fiscal Year 1992*, p. 186.

52. Government of Jamaica, Parliament, *Presentation by the Honorable K.D. Knight, Minister of National Security, Parliamentary Sectoral Debate*, July 3, 1991, pp. 5–6; Government of Jamaica, Parliament, *Presentation by the Honorable K.D. Knight, Minister of National Security and Justice, Parliamentary Sectoral Debate*, June 10, 1992, pp. 23–24.

53. See García Muñiz, "Defense Policy and Planning," pp. 116–17; 122; Edward Fursdon, "The British, the Caribbean, and Belize," *Journal of Defense and Diplomacy* 39 (No. 6, 1988): 40; Adrian English, *Regional Defense Profile No. 1: Latin America*, London: Jane's Publishing Group, 188, p. 188; Rex Hudson and Daniel J. Seyler, "Jamaica," in *Islands of the Commonwealth Caribbean*, pp. 144–45; and *The Military Balance 1990–1991*, p. 198.

54. Commander Michael A. Adams, "In Our Nations' Interests," *Proceedings of the U.S. Naval Institute* 116 (March 1990): 104.

55. See Hudson and Seyler, "Jamaica," p. 146; and Lacey, *Violence and Politics in Jamaica*, p. 117. For a full treatment of relations between the police and the power brokers, see Lacey, pp. 116–43.

56. Kaufman, *Jamaica under Manley*, p. 189.

57. Planning Institute of Jamaica, *Economic and Social Survey 1990*, Kingston, Jamaica, 1991, p. 21.3; and *Presentation*, 1992, p. 35.

58. *Economic and Social Survey 1990*, p. 21.2.

59. *Economic and Social Survey 1990*, p. 21.2; *Presentation*, 1991, pp. 42–44; and *Presentation*, 1992, pp. 32–33, 43.. For explanation of the Accelerated Promotion Program see *Presentation*, 1991, pp. 36–41.

60. "New Navies of the Caribbean," *Defense and Foreign Affairs Weekly* 14 (May 30–June 5 1990): 1.

6 COLLECTIVE SECURITY MEASURES

> Obviously, it would be foolhardy to depend entirely upon moral
> suasion and so the protective services, police and military, play a
> critical role in ensuring and preserving the physical security of the
> state and of its citizens.
>
> However, it is becoming increasingly apparent that no single
> state, large or small, can in isolation ensure its own security from
> subversion or external threat. In this era of the interdependence of
> states, and the globalization of activities relating to almost every
> sphere of life—economic, cultural, and criminal to name but a
> few—the preservation of national security can no longer be seen
> in purely national terms.
>
> —A.N.R. Robinson
> Trinidad and Tobago Prime Minister, 1986–1991

Individual Caribbean countries, like small, subordinate states elsewhere, are unable to rely only on themselves for national and regional
security. Their leaders have long recognized the need to collaborate, in
spite of individual efforts examined in the two previous chapters. Perhaps the clearest expressions of the need for collective security recently were made at the August 1990 CARICOM Summit in Jamaica,
two weeks after the coup attempt in Trinidad. One eloquent statement
made at the opening session of the Summit was delivered by Lloyd
Erskine Sandiford, Prime Minister of Barbados:

> The preservation of law and order, and national security contribute
> uniquely to growth and development through the promotion of stability.
> We must, therefore, expand our integration efforts to include the area of

regional security; and we must seek further cooperation with friendly governments in our Region and beyond. *One thing is sure. No single territory can do it alone. We have to work together if we are to ensure that the Caribbean remains a zone of peace, prosperity, and democracy.*[1]

The collective initiatives examined here are the proposal for a Zone of Peace Treaty and the Regional Security System (RSS). These are not the only existing collective initiatives. There is considerable cooperation in the area of military and police training. Among other things, there is the Regional Police Training Center in Barbados that serves the entire region. There also is the OECS/Caribbean Cadet Camp, inaugurated in 1989 as an extension of the OECS Cadet Camp, created in 1985. In August 1991, 232 Cadet Officers were graduated from the Camp.[2] Nevertheless, the initiatives discussed here are the major efforts in the military-political area. Analysis of Caribbean security measures, however, should go beyond detailing security initiatives, and evaluate the credibility of present security measures. This is done in the final section.

Zone of Peace Treaty Proposal

In October 1979, at the OAS General Assembly meeting in La Paz, Bolivia, Grenada sponsored a resolution calling for a Caribbean Zone of Peace. The resolution was adopted on October 31 by the Twelfth Plenary Session of the General Assembly. It stated:

THE GENERAL ASSEMBLY

NOTING the recent increase in military activities in the Caribbean subregion, which activities have produced tension in this area;

BEARING IN MIND that the Caribbean is an area of peace and stability, and that not only is maintenance of these conditions necessary for the progress and economic and social development of its people, but is also an indispensable element in the progress and development of the region as a whole;

RECOGNIZING that it is within the exclusive competence of sovereign states to decide upon the path to be taken for the attainment of the goals of democracy, social justice and integral development for their peoples; and

FURTHER RECOGNIZING that, while the states in the Caribbean

subregion have an urgent and pressing need for external economic assistance to achieve these goals, the principles of international social justice require that such assistance be given in consultation with, and with the fullest respect for, the sovereign wishes of the recipient countries,

RESOLVES:

1. To express its deep concern over the heightening of tension in the subregion resulting from the recent increases in military activity in the Caribbean area.

2. To repudiate the concept of the region, or any of its subregions, as a sphere of influence for any power.

3. To stress its support for the principles of ideological pluralism and peaceful coexistence, which are essential to the peace, stability and development of the region.

4. To call upon all states to recognize the region as a Zone of Peace, and to devote all their efforts, in appropriate regional and international forums, to the advancement of this concept.[3]

In the English-speaking Caribbean, the Zone of Peace proposal was first raised at the Sixth Meeting of the Standing Committee of Ministers of Foreign Affairs (SCMFA), held in Grenada from June 30 to July 1, 1981. The 1979 resolution and the 1981 discussion were held against the background of crises elsewhere in the hemisphere. These included the 1980 coup in Surinam, the conflict in Central America, the coup attempt in Dominica in March 1981, subversion attempts against the government in Barbados, and United States destabilization measures against Jamaica, Grenada, and Guyana.[4]

At the Grenada meeting, the ministers formed a working group to examine the OAS resolution in a CARICOM context. That group met in Belize in March of the following year, but failed to decide on anything substantive because of differences in the perceptions of security threats and needs.[5] Nevertheless, in keeping with the letter and spirit of the OAS resolution, CARICOM governments promoted the Zone of Peace concept, both within the hemisphere and at international forums such as the United Nations General Assembly, the Non-Aligned Movement, and the Commonwealth.

The Caribbean Conference of Churches (CCC) was quite correct in observing that the willingness of CARICOM governments to discuss the concept of the Zone of Peace demonstrated their recognition of the complexity and tension of international relations. The CCC argued

"Some concrete decisions to strengthen the possibility of regional peace would be an important foreign policy initiative taken, as such initiative should be, by Caribbean governments, rather that outsider powers."[6] While this was—and still is—a laudable goal, fulfillment of the terms of the Zone of Peace resolution requires action primarily by states *outside* the Caribbean. As scholars, statesmen, and the CCC itself recognized, implementation of the OAS resolution would require several initiatives, including:

- elimination of all foreign military bases;
- cessation of all foreign military maneuvers;
- adoption of military non-intervention policies by states in the hemisphere;
- establishment of a compulsory mechanism for the pacific settlement of disputes;
- adherence to the Treaty of Tlatelolco.[7]

The geopolitics of the region and developments there over the past two decades suggest that achievement of the above is not a realistic expectation. This is despite the end of U.S.-Soviet tensions and the end of the bipolar Cold War. As we will see in the next chapter, for all the changed international climate, the United States, Britain, and other countries have geopolitical interests in the area to which Zone of Peace initiatives would be inimical. Moreover, the outcome of zone of peace efforts elsewhere do not inspire much hope for the Caribbean.

The 1971 session of the United Nations General Assembly adopted a resolution declaring the Indian Ocean as a Zone of Peace. The resolution called for the great powers to consult with states in the Indian Ocean littoral about preventing further militarization of that ocean, and reducing the nuclear and other weapons of mass destruction in the area. The resolution envisaged consultation among littoral and hinterland states, the permanent members of the UN Security Council, and other maritime users of the Indian Ocean on a system of collective security. However, implementation of that resolution was frustrated by opposition from the superpowers, both of which saw it as restricting their capacity to project sea power globally. States in the Indian Ocean littoral have also been culpable. One implication of the resolution is that states there must limit the range of their security options. No state has been very willing to do that. Thus, while much lip service has been given to the aims of the resolution, little concrete action has been taken to secure them.[8]

In the Pacific area, the South Pacific Nuclear Free Zone Treaty took effect on December 12, 1986, following ratification by Australia, Fiji, Kiribati, New Zealand, Niue, Papua New Guinea, Tuvalu, and Western Samoa. Parties to the treaty undertake to follow established nuclear non-proliferation measures, not to manufacture, acquire, or have control of nuclear devices, nor to allow the stationing or testing of such devices within their territories.

Principally at the insistence of Australia, the treaty places no restriction on access to the region by nuclear-armed or nuclear-powered ships and aircraft. Nevertheless, New Zealand has prohibited this access, leading to the virtual abrogation of ANZUS, New Zealand's defense arrangement with Australia and the United States. The Protocols to the 1986 treaty require countries with dependent territories in the area to comply with the provisions of the treaty. The known nuclear powers are also asked not to violate the treaty or to threaten parties to it with nuclear weapons. China and the USSR signed the Protocols. Britain, France, and the United States refused, thereby diluting the full effect of the zone of peace initiative.[9]

Before the end of this section mention should also be made of the Mutual Assistance Scheme (MAS) proposal, a less well-known collective security initiative that predated the Zone of Peace. The genesis of the MAS dates to April 1973 when Caribbean leaders met in Guyana before the launching of CARICOM. They agreed that the SCMFA, an "institution" of the planned Community, should prepare a scheme capable of protecting the political independence and territorial integrity of member-states. Because of the vicissitudes of the integration movement, the priorities of member-states, and the geopolitics of the region, that mandate was not really pursued until the July 1981 Grenada meeting of the SCMFA.

Based on that meeting's instructions, the CARICOM Secretariat prepared a proposal that was examined at the June 1983 meeting of the SCMFA. The ministers decided to create a Working Group to recommend ways of implementing the scheme. That group met in Nassau, the Bahamas, in February 1985, but failed to agree on implementation measures. The difficulty of achieving agreement stemmed not only from differing perceptions of security needs, but from disputes over the logistics to be involved in a region-wide scheme. Although there was no explicit agreement that the matter should be abandoned, this was the unspoken understanding.[10]

Regional Security System

In looking at individual security measures in the previous chapter, I noted several actual and potential threats that confronted Eastern Caribbean states in the 1960s, 1970s, and 1980s. More than any of the countries in the region, Eastern Caribbean countries face capability constraints that compel them to combine their resources and collaborate in many areas. One collective endeavor that set the stage for the formation of the RSS was the creation of the Organization of Eastern Caribbean States (OECS). A brief discussion of the OECS here will permit appreciation of the larger institutional context in which the RSS was born (see Figure 6.1).

The OECS was established in June 1981 by treaty, as a successor to the 1966 West Indies Associated States Council of States (WISA).[11] It brought together Antigua-Barbuda, Dominica, Grenada, Montserrat, St. Kitts-Nevis, St. Lucia, and St. Vincent and the Grenadines. The aims were varied: promotion of regional and international cooperation; promotion of unity and defense of sovereignty; harmonization of foreign policy; joint diplomacy; economic integration. In pursuit of these objectives, five principal "institutions" were created: Authority of Heads of Government; Foreign Affairs Committee; Defense and Security Committee; Economic Affairs Committee; and the Central Secretariat. The chief executive officer of the organization is the Director-General, currently Dr. Vaughan Lewis, a former Director of UWI's Institute of Social and Economic Research at the Mona campus in Jamaica. The OECS headquarters are in St. Lucia.

Security matters are dealt with under Article 8 of the OECS treaty. Section 1 outlines the composition of the Defense and Security Committee, comprising "the Ministers responsible for Defense and Security or other Ministers or Plenipotentiaries designated by the Heads of Government of the Member States." Section 2 restricts the deliberations of the Committee to members "possessing the necessary competence in respect of matters under consideration from time to time." Section 3 establishes the Authority as the body to which the Defense and Security Committee will report. It also mandates the Committee to advise the Authority "on matters relating to external defense and on

154

Figure 6.1 OECS Organizational Chart

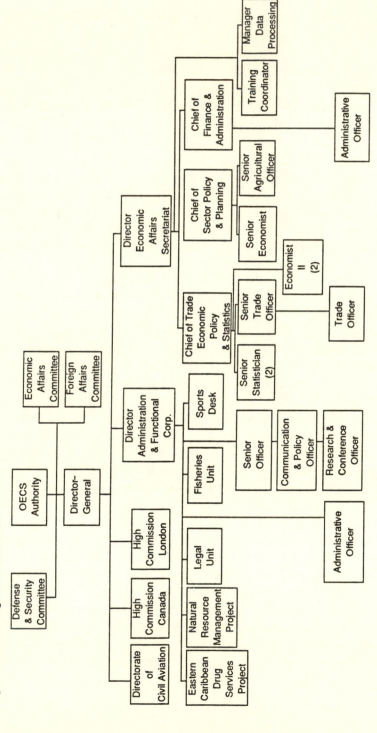

arrangements for collective security against external aggression including mercenary aggression, with or without the support of internal or national elements." According to RSS sources, the only time the Committee ever met was on October 21, 1983, in Barbados, during the Grenada crisis.

Section 4, Article 8 of the OECS treaty specifies:

> The Defence and Security Committee shall have responsibility for coordinating the efforts of Member States for collective defence and the preservation of peace and security against external aggression and for the development of close ties among Member States of the Organization in matters of external defence and security, including measures to combat the activities of mercenaries operating with or without the support of internal or national elements, in the exercise of the inherent right of individual or collective self-defense recognized by Article 51 of the Charter of the United Nations.

This provision—the subject of much controversy involving participation in the Grenada intervention[12]—is the legal and political framework for the establishment of the RSS.[13]

Structure and Operations

The RSS was created on October 29, 1982, by Antigua-Barbuda, Barbados, Dominica, St. Lucia, and St. Vincent and the Grenadines through a Memorandum of Understanding (MOU) signed originally in Roseau, Dominica. The MOU, the entire text of which can be found in Appendix 1 of this volume, was signed later by St. Lucia, on November 4, 1982. It is a forty-two-point agreement outlining a broad range of issues relating to the aims, structure, and operation of the RSS. Article 2 requires the RSS to prepare contingency plans and assist member-countries in national emergencies. The RSS mandate includes anti-smuggling operations, SAR, customs and immigration control, fishery protection, protection of offshore installations, and "natural and other disasters and threats to national security."

The RSS became operational between January and April 1983, with heads of RSS member-governments finalizing arrangements at a February 19, 1983, meeting in Castries, St. Lucia. St. Kitts-Nevis joined officially in February 1984, but it had begun involvement in the organization during the previous September. Grenada joined in January

1985 at a meeting of Eastern Caribbean leaders held in Jamaica. RSS officials are conscious of the system's limitations. They consider its greatest value to be its potential for deterrence, acknowledging that "The RSS does not pretend to have the capacity to deter or defeat any large-scale foreign aggression against any of its members. Should such an attack take place a substantial outside support would be essential."[14] They also regard the mechanism as a form of security insurance: "The RSS can be likened to an insurance policy designed to meet the more likely threat to the peace and security of the area. Without peace and security no development can take place at all, and a suitable balance must be struck between [having] nothing and having a large standing army."[15]

As is evident from Figure 6.2,[16] the structure of the RSS involves a Council of Ministers, comprised of the ministers with defense portfolios of participating states, as the central policy-making body. Operational command falls under a Central Liaison Office (CLO) headed by a Regional Security Coordinator (RSC). He is appointed by the Council of Ministers (Art. 9) and is designated "adviser to the Council of Ministers in matters relating to regional security." Figure 6.2 shows a linkage between the RSC and the United States Military Liaison Office in the Eastern Caribbean (MLO-EC) and the British High Commissions in the area (UK-HCEC) since these are the principal foreign agencies to which the RSC relates on behalf of the RSS. The CLO, the RSS headquarters, is located in Barbados, which also provides the present Coordinator, Brigadier Rudyard Lewis, head of the Barbados Defense Force (BDF). The CLO plans and coordinates in collaboration with a Joint Coordinating Committee comprising Force Commanders, defined by the MOU as the operational heads of the defense forces (of Antigua-Barbuda and Barbados) and the commissioners of police (of all participating states). Each RSS member-unit maintains a presence at the CLO in the person of a high-ranking official sent on attachment.

Financing is prescribed under Art. 12 of the MOU on the basis of 49 percent contribution by Barbados and 51 percent contribution by the other states. That formula is, however, subject to a provision: "but if circumstances change the percentage contributed by Barbados and the other participating countries shall be subject to renegotiation." Circumstances have indeed changed since 1982. The RSS is now financed on the basis of 40 percent by Barbados and 10 percent by each of the other six states. RSS funds may not be used for normal operational

157

Figure 6.2 The Regional Security System

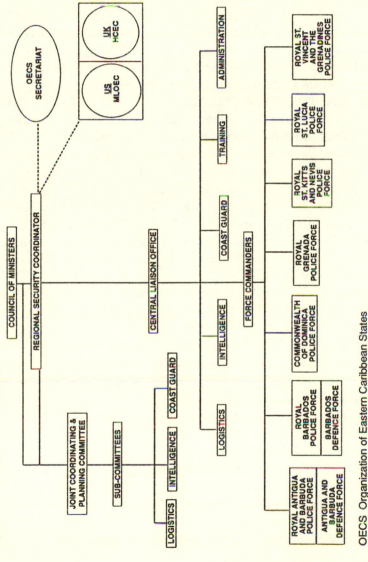

OECS   Organization of Eastern Caribbean States
MLOEC Military Liaison Office, Eastern Caribbean
HCEC High Commission, Eastern Caribbean Indirect Relations
----- Indirect Relations

purposes within participating states, but RSS supplies may be loaned to them.

Financial contributions go to a Central Fund. According to RSS officials, several states have been delinquent in contributing to the fund. Antigua once had the worst contribution record, and St. Vincent and the Grenadines the best. The capability limitations of RSS member-states make foreign support necessary. Foreign assistance is mainly bilateral, coming essentially from the United States, Britain, and Canada. As we saw in chapter three, there was a dramatic increase in United States aid to RSS countries after the 1983 Grenada intervention.

Commander Dean Schopp, head of the U.S. Military Liaison Office in the Eastern Caribbean, explained that while the United States is legally prohibited from financing the RSS as an institution, it provides training and equipment "of considerable value" to RSS member-states. Schopp and others considered this the result of national self-interest, and not altruism.[17] United States commitment was reaffirmed in February 1991 by Admiral Leon Edney, Commander-in-Chief of the United States Atlantic Command (LANTCOM). Admiral Edney visited St. Lucia and Barbados, meeting in Barbados with political and military officials from the Eastern Caribbean to discuss Caribbean-United States cooperation.[18]

Technically, the overall force level of the RSS is the sum of the security establishments of all participating states. Most states are, however, reluctant to have their entire security establishment identified for RSS purposes. They therefore designate a complement of forces for potential RSS activity. The security establishments involved are:

- Antigua and Barbuda Defense Force
- Royal Antigua and Barbuda Police Force
- Barbados Defense Force
- Royal Barbados Police Force
- Commonwealth of Dominica Police Force
- Royal Grenada Police Force
- Royal St. Kitts-Nevis Police Force
- Royal St. Lucia Police Force
- Royal St. Vincent and the Grenadines Police Force.

Eastern Caribbean Coast Guards are under the COPs, except in Barbados where the Coast Guard is under the army. As mentioned elsewhere, a key component of the police forces is the Special Service Unit (SSU)—elite police with paramilitary training and light weapons. SSUs are designated to deal with crises beyond the capacity of the regular police, or with military contingencies. The plan was for each state with a SSU to maintain at least two units of platoon strength—forty each. Antigua-Barbuda and Barbados, the states with standing armies, do not have SSUs. Their equivalents are the Task Force (Barbados) and the Special Patrol Group (Antigua-Barbuda).[19]

As can be gathered from the previous chapter, the weapons and equipment at the disposal of the RSS units are essentially light armaments (grenade launchers; automatic rifles, especially M–16s; machine guns; hand grenades), basic communications equipment, and patrol vessels. Many of the arms are old, some of World War II vintage, but since 1984 Britain and the United States have been providing more modern equipment. However, none of it is very sophisticated. There is great reliance on American, British, and Canadian assistance for training and supplies.

Security needs were once assessed by a five-member Military Advisory and Training Team drawn from American, British (police), and RSS forces. In October 1984 Baroness Young, then British Minister of State for Foreign and Commonwealth Affairs, pledged that Britain "would do everything to assist regional security operations and in particular [the establishment of] the RSS."[20] However, Britain has been reluctant to provide anything beyond police training and equipment and Coast Guard facilities. As we noted in the previous chapter, they have built port facilities in most parts of the Eastern Caribbean.

There have been several attempts to expand the RSS. In 1985 St. Lucia's Prime Minister, John Compton, proposed expansion. Not surprisingly, the Bahamas, Belize, Guyana, and Trinidad and Tobago—the countries that had condemned the Grenada intervention and criticized RSS complicity in it—balked at the idea. Jamaica, which had been part of the intervention, declined to join. At an October 20, 1985, news conference in Jamaica, Prime Minister Edward Seaga committed Jamaica to training and technical assistance, but reaffirmed his government's unwillingness to join. Some analysts speculated that Jamaica's reluctance probably stemmed from a fear that membership would saddle it with most of the system's financial burden.[21]

The second expansion initiative came the following year, when a proposal was made to upgrade the MOU to a full treaty. A draft treaty was circulated to heads of RSS member-governments and received the endorsement of most of them. There are different stories about the origin of the treaty proposal. One points to Washington, but American officials in the Caribbean denied this. Others point to Barbados and Grenada. However, Lt. Commander Peter Tomlin of the RSS explained that it was a RSS initiative that later received some United States support.[22]

The treaty was seen by RSS officials as part of the institution's evolution. It would also have given the RSS an international legal personality, simultaneously permitting direct security cooperation with the United States, France, Britain, Venezuela, and other countries. The treaty proposal encountered strong resistance from two prime ministers, both of whom held their countries' defense portfolios: James Mitchell of St. Vincent and the Grenadines; and the late Errol Barrow of Barbados. Mitchell was apprehensive about possible extra-regional interests being served with a beefed-up RSS. He later remarked: "I get a little tired of the patronizing sermons on the 'Role of Security in Small States,' and the like. We have to behave like Grenada or Fiji to get attention, and when we stop misbehaving we are left to languish in blissful 'obsecurity' (that word 'obsecurity' I got from a constituent of mine.)"[23]

In a September 2, 1986 letter to members of the RSS Council of Ministers, Barrow made his stand clear:

> The main preoccupation of this government is in the area of drug abuse control, prevention of smuggling, fishery protection and maritime training.
>
> This government, therefore, has strong reservations over the use of our resources for militaristic purposes or for the unjustifiable usurpation of the sovereignty of our country by alien influences. Consequently, the Government of Barbados is not prepared to elevate or upgrade the Memorandum to the status of a treaty and does not support the proposal that this should be done.[24]

Barbados was, and still is, the main Caribbean pillar of the RSS. Its opposition to the treaty plan, therefore, proved fatal to the initiative. This was despite Mary Eugenia Charles's strong advocacy at the October 26, 1986, meeting of the RSS Council of Ministers, where the plan was formally abandoned in favor of the status quo.[25] Barrow's reference to "alien influences" reflected his apprehension about the RSS becoming a United States surrogate outfit in the region. Moreover, as we saw in chapter five, Barbados then had a policy of deemphasizing its own military and in tempering any interest in expanding the RSS. The situation has since changed. The heightened security consciousness precipitated by the 1990 coup attempt in Trinidad has made Barbados the main protagonist of a new—third—RSS expansion effort.

In his 1990 CARICOM Summit address Prime Minister Sandiford argued:

> I think the time is now for us to look at the creation of a broader regional system of security. I should like to propose for the consideration of my fellow Heads of Government, the expansion and consolidation of the existing Regional Security System in the Eastern Caribbean to include as many Caricom states as possible. I would urge that the RSS be invested with the authority and resources to deal with all aspects of regional security including the interdiction of drug trafficking, surveillance of our coastal zones, mutual assistance in the event of natural disasters, as well as threats to constitutional democracy from criminals, terrorists, mercenaries, and other enemies of democracy.[26]

Sandiford scored an important victory in getting recognition of his proposal by the other CARICOM leaders. According to the 1990 Summit Communiqué, CARICOM leaders recognized that developments such as the 1990 Trinidad and Tobago coup attempt highlight the vulnerability of Caribbean countries to terrorist threats. They therefore "agreed on the necessity to review existing arrangements in support of regional security and decided to establish a Committee of Member States to look into the matter and report before the Twelfth Meeting of Conference."[27] Barbados was named to chair the committee which included the Bahamas, Belize, Dominica, Guyana, St. Kitts-Nevis, and Trinidad and Tobago.

Following a meeting of the committee in Barbados early June 1991, Sandiford disclosed that three studies had already been commissioned. He declined to name the subjects of the studies, but indicated that they had been undertaken by the CARICOM Secretariat, the RSS, and the Barbados government.[28] Sandiford outlined his own vision of enhanced regional security at a meeting of Caribbean Chiefs of Staff in Barbados that same June. He advocated stationing "a small core of military personnel . . . part in an Eastern Caribbean island and part in a Western Caribbean island, and paid for by the participating territories on an agreed formula."[29] In its final report, the West Indian Commission recommended the creation of a regional security service in the form of an officer corps whose members can be deployed around the region. The Commission felt this would help overcome frustrations of limited career opportunities in some places, and reduce the potential for political favoritism or victimization.[30]

There are, of course, people opposed to this latest expansion endeavor. Some are yet to be convinced of its necessity. And even among those who endorse it there is caution. One cautious supporter was then Prime Minister A.N.R. Robinson of Trinidad and Tobago. He observed quite accurately that several sensitive issues require attention in the current move, noting: "Foremost among these is the fact that a regional security system implicitly presumes the existence of a common political perception."[31] As we saw in previous chapters, while there is common acceptance of military, political, and economic vulnerability, for example, there is divergence regarding the source and intensity of threats, especially for the countries outside the Eastern Caribbean. But Robinson's concerns went beyond perception to questions about financing, structure, and deployment.

Grenada Deployment

In October 1983, the then five-country RSS had been operational for barely six months when it faced the challenge of deployment in Grenada. The idea of a mission to rescue Maurice Bishop was suggested to then Barbados Prime Minister Tom Adams by a United States Embassy official in Bridgetown on October 15. The following day, Adams gave the relevant orders to BDF Chief of Staff and RSS Coordinator, Rudyard Lewis, then a Colonel. Lewis delegated the task of formulating a plan to Staff Officer Major Mark Adkin. Adkin did so in conjunction with RSS intelligence chief, Lt. Commander Peter Tomlin.

The Adkin-Tomlin rescue plan assumed that there would be a hostile reception in Grenada. It therefore made the element of surprise a key feature. Locations targeted included Bishop's house, the Governor-General's residence, the Pearls and Salines airports, the island's radio station, and several "blocking or ambush positions" to the north and south of the island's capital. The plan contemplated the use of two battalions of troops helicoptered in, with an additional battalion flown in on D-day. It did not involve attacking People's Revolutionary Army

(PRA) positions. The planners hoped to assume strategic positions, to prevent PRA troop movement, and to let the PRA or the Cubans take the attack initiative. The rescue plan was given to Adams and was actually under discussion by the Barbados Cabinet on October 19 when Bishop was rescued by his supporters. The rapid pace of developments and United States control of initiatives thereafter caused the RSS plan to be shelved.[32]

There were also two covert missions. The first, on October 17, involved infiltrating Grenada to gather intelligence. With appropriate airline tickets and travel documents, Second Lieutenant Alvin Quintyne and Lance Corporal Marita Browne of the BDF assumed the profile of a vacationing couple from St. Vincent and the Grenadines. The agents did their surveillance and returned to Barbados on October 18. Later, Quintyne was awarded the Barbados Service Star; Browne was given the Barbados Service Medal. The second covert operation, on October 19, involved air surveillance by Lt. Commander Tomlin and Major Robin Keaney, a contract officer then recently retired from Britain's Royal Air Force.[33]

Once the United States military launched the intervention, code-named "Operation Urgent Fury," the RSS deployment became essentially a coattail exercise. There was no joint United States-Caribbean planning in "Operation Urgent Fury." As a matter of fact, the RSS head, Brigadier Lewis, was not even given advanced information about the code-name.[34] Adkin explained,

> . . . the role of the Caribbean contingents was not clear to either the U.S. or Caribbean commanders. On October 25, when Caribbean troops started landing at Salines, at least one Ranger battalion commander knew nothing of their participation in the operation at all; for a brief moment, he thought they were the PRA.[35]

Thus, when the Caribbean forces arrived in Grenada there were no ground headquarters to report to, and no tactical plan for them. Brigadier Lewis had to establish his headquarters in a building used by Cuban engineers at the Salines airport.

The Caribbean detachment, called the Caribbean Security Force, was organized on October 24 in Barbados. It was headed by Colonel Ken Barnes of the JDF, with Rudyard Lewis retaining overall control. Incidentally, Lewis was promoted to the rank of Brigadier for the operation. The detachment comprised 300 policemen and soldiers from units in all RSS member-states, plus Jamaica. Jamaica provided an infantry company; Barbados, a reinforced platoon of fifty; Antigua-Barbuda, a squad; and Dominica, St. Lucia, and St. Kitts-Nevis, units of armed policemen. The day after the landing, St. Vincent and the Grenadines sent a squad of police, and Barbados sent an additional police contingent.[36] Shortly after the landing in Grenada, the force was redesignated the Caribbean Peacekeeping Force (CPF). Later, as United States troops began withdrawing from Grenada, on December 14, 1983, the CPF was increased. At one point it was nearly 900.[37]

The Caribbean forces were not militarily critical to the United States intervention; they were politically expedient. One United States Air Force Colonel described them in a frank, yet disparaging, manner, as "a politically important, but militarily inconsequential group of policemen and soldiers from six Caribbean countries, none of whom took part in any fighting. Their role was restricted to guarding prisoners and accompanying U.S. troops on patrols."[38] Major-General George Crist of the United States Marine Corps, who had been part of "Urgent Fury," explained the role of the CPF during congressional hearings on November 2, 1983: "They are to restore civil law and order to the islands, take care of the refugees, take care of the police and the other things it needs to put a country back together again. And that they are doing right now, in fact."[39] The CPF withdrew from Grenada on September 22, 1985.[40]

RSS officials also coordinated the deployment of troops and police from several CARICOM countries in Trinidad following the aborted coup there in 1990. The two-week deployment began on August 3, 1990 and involved 150 military and police personnel, mainly from Barbados, Guyana, and Jamaica, in an operation to support the Trinidad and Tobago Defense Force (TTDF) and the Trinidad and Tobago Police Service (TTPS) with internal security. Guyana's forty-member contingent was led by Captain Andrew Pompey from the GDF's First Infantry Battalion.[41] Contrary to media reports, the Trinidad operation was not led by Colonel Errol Maynard of the Barbados Defense Force (BDF). According to RSS sources, Colonel Maynard was then acting as RSS Coordinator since Brigadier Rudyard Lewis was in Britain on official business. The CARICOM continent was led by Colonel Terrance Lewis of the Jamaica Defense Force (JDF).

Military Maneuvers

RSS units have also been deployed annually since 1985 in military exercises. These are designed to train and professionalize RSS forces and to reinforce the commitment of American and Caribbean leaders to defend democracy and the rule of law in the region.

The first exercise, "Operation Exotic Palm," was held in St. Lucia from September 11 to 15, 1985. It involved units from all RSS members except St. Vincent and the Grenadines, along with forces from Britain and the United States, totaling 600 troops. There were also observers from the JDF and the TTDF. The operation involved American C–141 and C–130 transport planes, A–10 fighter jets, one United States destroyer, one British frigate, and one support ship.[42] The war games simulated a group of revolutionaries armed and trained by Carumba and Nigarro (believed to be Cuba and Nicaragua) trying to topple the country Linus (St. Lucia.)[43] Colonel Wayne Toppin, Commander of the United States Joint Task Force 140 of Key West, Florida, indicated that the "insurgents " included twenty-five Caribbean policemen and thirteen American "Seals," members of the United States Navy Special Operations unit.

The Commander of United States Forces Caribbean explained that "Operation Exotic Palm" had three main objectives:

- to practice and refine the training and experience gained during the 1983 Grenada operations;
- to demonstrate the capability of the RSS headquarters to organize, mobilize, and deploy ground, air, and naval assets provided by the RSS governments;
- to indicate the willingness and capability of the democratic nations to respond quickly to requests for help from a neighbor in need.[44]

Moreover, the maneuvers gave the United States and Britain better overall appreciation of St. Lucian terrain, enhancing their capability for rapid troop deployment in the area.

"Exotic Palm" cost one million dollars (U.S.) and was financed entirely by the United States. The exercise amounted to a graduation ceremony for the SSUs that had been under training. Stressing the importance of the exercise, Colonel Toppin argued that it strengthened the RSS, whose greatest value is that "it creates a formal framework for a response from the United States and serves as a 'tripwire' on what the United States regards as a strategically important perimeter."[45]

The first 1986 maneuvers were called "Ocean Venture 86." They were held in April and May and involved forces from all RSS states, except Barbados, along with forces from Jamaica, Britain, and the United States. The troops from the RSS numbered 160, while those from the United States Green Berets, Marines, and 101st Air Assault Battalion totalled 700. The maneuvers involved landings on Grenada and on the Puerto Rican island of Vieques. They were designed to test the readiness of the RSS to combat external threats. In October of the same year there was another exercise, "Upward Key 86." It involved troops from the United States, Antigua-Barbuda, and St. Kitts-Nevis doing a series of land, sea, and air maneuvers.[46]

"Operation Camile," held in May 1987, was the first set of maneuvers involving units from all RSS countries. There were also troops from Britain, Jamaica, and the United States. Those maneuvers emphasized civil defense, disaster relief, and Coast Guard SAR, rather than military operations. There were also simulations of civilian evacuation during a volcanic eruption. Later that year there was a smaller exercise involving 120 RSS troops, and some from the JDF. It was held in Jamaica from September 7 to 18.[47]

Although there have been strong critics of the military exercises ever since 1985, the maneuvers have increased in political and operational value. The 1989 maneuvers, therefore, saw a larger set of players. In addition to RSS, British, and American forces, there were troops from Jamaica and, for the first time, from Trinidad and Tobago. The Caribbean forces numbered a little over 600. The exercises were code-named "Tradewinds 89" and were held between May 12 and June 24 in several phases. The first phase lasted until June 12. It focused on maritime operations: SAR, drug interdiction, damage control, target gunnery, navigation, and maritime law enforcement. Several islands were used in this phase. The second phase, from June 10 to 18, was in Camp Santiago, Puerto Rico. There, units prepared for a field training exercise that was held in Grenada from June 19 to June 24.[48]

The list of participants grew still in 1991. Guyana was included in "Tradewinds 91." This was the first time Guyana participated in any of these exercises, a reflection of recent political changes discussed in chapter four. Guyana sent a thirty member GDF contingent to spend eight days in Dominica for the exercise. Military and police units from thirteen CARICOM nations joined units from the United States and Britain for the 1991 war games. Phase one of the exercise was held in Antigua from June 3 to 8; phase two was in Puerto Rico from June 8 to 21; and phase three was in Dominica from June 22 to June 28. The maneuvers were designed to enhance mutual capabilities by providing Caribbean forces with added opportunities to use and evaluate joint and/or combined operations. During the exercise, United States units also worked on several humanitarian and civic projects in the region.[49]

"Tradewinds '92" was conducted in four phases. Phase one of the maneuvers began on April 15, 1992, and involved land and sea training of Caribbean Coast Guard units by the United States Coast Guard and the United States Navy. Training teams went to the Bahamas, Jamaica, and Trinidad and Tobago. Phase two of "Tradewinds '92" focused on disaster relief—with the simulated hurricane named Hurricane Florence—and was based in Barbados from June 8 to 14. Involved in this phase were units from Antigua-Barbuda, Dominica, St. Kitts-Nevis, Jamaica, and St. Vincent and the Grenadines. Police and army contingents from all RSS member-states and soldiers from the Bahamas, Guyana, Jamaica, and Trinidad and Tobago were part of phase three of the maneuvers, which were held from June 15 to 27 at Camp Santiago in Puerto Rico. The Puerto Rico aspect of the exercises dealt with the training of land forces by British and American teams. The final phase of "Tradewinds '92" was held in Barbados over three days, ending on July 2, 1992, with a closing parade.[50]

Security Credibility

Credible security involves adopting measures to deal meaningfully with threats to national security. The measures a state adopts depend not only on its capability, but also on the perceptions of its political leaders, and on their political will—their desire and courage to act decisively in matters of national security. Consensus and political will are critical to any credible collective effort by several states. Consensus is closely linked to the ability of the various leaders to deal with divergent security perceptions. On the other hand, political will is needed to narrow political differences, decide on common action, and then to act.

In the Caribbean, there is not so much of an absence of the will to act, but more an absence of the capacity for meaningful action. At the national level, Eric Gairy and Maurice Bishop in Grenada, Patrick John and Mary Eugenia Charles in Dominica, Forbes Burnham in Guyana, and Eric Williams and A.N.R. Robinson in Trinidad certainly demonstrated the will to act when they perceived internal security threats. In most cases, these leaders also had the capacity to deal with the threats. Generally, political will has also not been a deficiency where external threats are concerned, as the cases of Guyana, Barbados, Dominica, and Grenada have shown. Perhaps the most dramatic instance in this regard was Grenada.

Even in the context of a political crisis and clear recognition of the overwhelming superiority of the United States forces, the Revolutionary Military Council (RMC) and the PRA in Grenada did not immediately disintegrate; they demonstrated the will to act in what they considered a threat to their regime and state. Indeed, one participant in "Urgent Fury" has said: "The high command of the RMC at Fort Frederick was quick to organize two local counter-attacks early on the morning of October 25. One was a complete success, and the second caused considerable alarm on [USS] *Guam,* eventually resulting in a radical change of the U.S. plan for the whole operation."[51]

The situation has been somewhat different at the regional level, though. As we saw in chapter two and elsewhere, security perceptions diverge. Leaders define the nature and intensity of threats differently. National and subregional interests, therefore, often subordinate what appear to be manifestly regional ones, making consensus difficult and potentially fatal in times of critical danger. It was precisely this dilemma that confronted CARICOM leaders at their October 22 and 23, 1983, summit in Trinidad as they examined the crisis underway in Grenada. Yet that meeting and events before it showed that Edward Seaga of Jamaica and the Eastern Caribbean leaders had decided to act. True, they acted as supporters of United States intervention. True also, the OECS "invitation" was drafted in Washington and hand-delivered to Grenada's Governor-General, Sir Paul Scoon, who signed it after it was back-dated. The point is that Adams, Compton, and others had contemplated intervention, had recognized their limited capacity to act, and therefore, decided to facilitate United States action.

In defense of the action, the OECS Director-General argued that states in the Eastern Caribbean had little choice:

The countries were faced with an extremely difficult situation, unprecedented in the history of our part of the world. They thus felt the need to act very quickly if the situation was to be brought under some sort of control. The governments were very much aware that the RMC could only be a very, very difficult regime, given the extent of its military capabilities. . . .

This threat perception was not universally shared within CARICOM, partly a function of the differences in the strengths of the various countries. The capabilities of the Eastern Caribbean states are very limited, which differentiates them from some other countries in the Caribbean with greater forces at their disposal and greater capacity to dispose of those forces to protect themselves. Basically, the OECS found themselves in a situation of having to seek assistance from outside.[52]

Of course, the OECS "invitation" was a Washington initiative, as observed above. This fact, however, in no way detracts from the basic reality, demonstrated in 1983 in Grenada: the problem of credible security in the Caribbean is essentially one of deficient capability. We have seen the insufficiency of individual efforts to deal with actual and potential threats, making collective efforts not merely useful, but necessary. Yet, even these have weaknesses. A Zone of Peace treaty—highly improbable as was suggested above—would provide a good measure of moral deterrence, but would lack military deterrent features that could aid the region's military security. Moreover, even in its political aspect, much of the treaty's potential usefulness depends on states outside the Caribbean. The credibility of this initiative is, therefore, limited.

The RSS is an important subregional initiative. However, it operates with some dangerous ambiguities. Terms such as "national emergencies," "search and rescue," and "threats to national security" used in Article 2 of the MOU to describe RSS competence and responsibility are not defined. Such a situation has the potential for both political and operational complications in the event of a complex operational deployment *planned and executed by the RSS itself.* A security system should not operate with ambiguity about such crucial aspects of its mission. There is, therefore, need for at least a protocol to the Memorandum, or a similar instrument, to define those terms.

Article 3 of the MOU states: "[T]he interests of one participating state are the interests of the others; and accordingly the participating countries shall have the right of 'hot pursuit' within each other's territorial waters." This article seems to be stating the principle of collective defense. Under this principle, recognized by the United Nations Charter (Article 51), states agree to pool defense capabilities to deal with threats common to the security of a group of them. This is done on the conviction that creation of a military mechanism sufficient to deal with specific threats lies beyond the ability of any single state. Arnold Wolfers explained, for example, that collective defense arrangements are directed against an opponent known to the parties in the arrangement, although that opponent may not be named for diplomatic reasons. The parties can define geographically the danger they seek to thwart, and are thus able to work out their strategy in advance of any confrontation.[53]

While collective defense contemplates measures *against threats external to the subject states*, the MOU and the RSS countries clearly mean to address *both internal and external threats*.[54] There is, thus, a slight discrepancy between the collective defense posture in which the RSS is cast conceptually, and the exigencies of both internal and external security in which member-states are interested. A collective defense focus on threats external to the area is unrealistic since the capabilities of member-states do not permit them to provide credible military security against such, even if those external threats were defined.

No one in the Eastern Caribbean or elsewhere can realistically expect the RSS to be anything but a mechanism with limited utility. Political leaders in the region certainly do not.[55] And as we saw above, RSS officials themselves are under no misapprehension about the operational capabilities of the system. Thus, some of what one analyst said about small-state collective security efforts in Africa and the Persian Gulf is relevant to efforts in the Caribbean:

> Their strength lies in their ability to diffuse local conflagrations and thus to avoid superpower interference, in their ability to project a strong, collective voice, and in their talent for gaining support of major powers with compatible interests in the region. But the major threats to their areas—local powers or outside actors—will probably best such arrangements. They have not been able and will not be able to cope with them alone. In the near term, they will remain halfway houses on the road to security cooperation, dependent on the interest and support of outside powers, and absorbed, first and foremost, by their own political and economic instabilities.[56]

The RSS fits much of this characterization. Yet, the events of October 1983 in Grenada and the geopolitical realities of the region cast doubt on its ability to diffuse military tensions of any significance without the involvement of the proximate superpower or a middle power such as Venezuela. One cannot say categorically that it is the "strong collective voice" and "talent for gaining the support of major powers with compatible interests" of RSS states that would attract the United States or other military powers to "help" with conflict resolution in the region. Countries such as the United States, Britain, or Venezuela would be inclined to act because of their geopolitical interests, and because they can subordinate the Caribbean to those interests. Nevertheless, there is little doubt that the RSS is a security halfway house, dependent on the interests and support of outside powers, and preoccupied with the political and other challenges facing its members.

Conclusion

In sum, Caribbean states have gone beyond security self-reliance to security collaboration not merely by choice but by necessity. The RSS exemplifies the prescience of a statement made by Robert Rothstein more than two decades ago: "An alliance of small powers is an instrument of limited utility. It can [not], nor is it designed to handle major military threats."[57] Present measures in the Caribbean are, therefore, far from credible. The heavy reliance on external support that we saw here and in the two previous chapters detracts from the desired security self-sufficiency, creating a virtual security dependency on states and international agencies outside the Caribbean. Nevertheless, capability limitations have not stymied the quest for security in the Caribbean. Apart from the factors examined so far, this quest has been influenced by the geopolitics of the region, the subject of the next chapter.

Notes

1. "Communiqué and Addresses—Eleventh Meeting of the Heads of Government of the Caribbean Community," CARICOM Perspective (Special Supplement) 49 (July-December 1990), p. 6. Emphasis added.

2. See Government of Barbados, Address by the Prime Minister, the Right Honorable L. Erskine Sandiford, M.P., on the Occasion of the Closing Parade of the Sixth OECS/Caribbean Cadet Training Camp, St. Ann's Fort, Barbados, August 15, 1991.

3. AG/RES.456 (IX–0–79), in *OAS General Assembly Proceedings Vol. 1— Certified Texts of Resolutions* (1980), p. 120.

4. On the question of destabilization see Perry Mars, "Destabilization, Foreign Intervention, and Socialist Transformation in the Caribbean," *Transition* 7 (1983): 33–54; and Anthony J. Payne, *Politics in Jamaica*, New York: St. Martin's Press, 1988, pp. 50–59.

5. Lloyd Searwar, "Foreign Policy Decision-Making in the Commonwealth Caribbean," *Caribbean Affairs* 1 (January-March 1988): 78–79; and Andrés Serbin, *Caribbean Geopolitics: Toward Security Through Peace?* Boulder, CO: Lynne Rienner, 1990, pp. 99–100.

6. Caribbean Conference of Churches, *Peace: A Challenge to the Caribbean* Bridgetown, Barbados: Caribbean Conference of Churches, 1982, p. 20.

7. See Caribbean Conference of Churches, *Peace*, p. 20; Serbín, *Caribbean Geopolitics*, pp. 101–105; and Nina Maria Serafino, "The Contadora Initiative, the United States and the Concept of a Zone of Peace," in Augusto Varas, ed., *Hemispheric Security and the U.S. Policy in Latin America*, Boulder, CO: Westview Press, 1989.

8. See Rasul Rias, *The Indian Ocean and the Superpowers*, Totowa, NJ: Barnes and Noble Books, 1987, pp. 172–83.

9. "South Pacific Nuclear Free Zone," *U.S. Department of State Bulletin*, April 1987; and William T. Tow, *Subregional Security Cooperation in the Third World*, Boulder, CO: Lynne Rienner, 1990, pp. 97–99.

10. Searwar, "Foreign Policy Decision-Making," p. 78.

11. See "Treaty Establishing the Organization of Eastern Caribbean States," 20 *International Legal Materials* 1166 (September 1981). The treaty is also reproduced in Jack Hopkins, ed., *Latin American and Caribbean Contemporary Records 1981–1982*, New York: Holmes and Meier, 1983.

12. See U.S. Congress, House, Committee on Foreign Affairs, *U.S. Military Actions in Grenada: Implications for U.S. Policy in the Eastern Caribbean*, Hearings, Subcommittees on International Security and Scientific Affairs and on Western Hemisphere Affairs, November 2, 3 and 16, 1983, esp. pp. 2–4, 11–12, 23, 72, 79; Christopher C. Joyner, "Reflections on the Lawfulness of Invasion," *American Journal of International Law* 78 (January 1984): 131–44; and John Norton More, "Grenada and the International Double Standard," *American Journal of International Law* 78 (January 1984): 145–68, esp. 153–59.

13. For more on the OECS, see William Gilmore, "Legal and Institutional Aspects of the Organization of Eastern Caribbean States," *Review of International Studies* 11 (October 1985): 311–28; Patrick Emmanuel, "Community within a Community: The OECS Countries," in Inter-American Development Bank, *Ten Years of CARICOM*. Washington, D.C.: Inter-American Development Bank, 1984; Tow, *Subregional Security Cooperation in the Third World*, Boulder, CO: Lynne Rienner, 1990, pp. 15–16, 28–30, 57–63; and Vaughan Lewis, *A Decade of Accomplishment*, Castries, St Lucia: OECS Secretariat, 1991.

14. RSS Staff, "The Roles of the Regional Security System in the East Caribbean," *Bulletin of Eastern Caribbean Affairs* 11 (January-February 1986): 6.

15. Ibid, p. 7.

16. I am grateful to Lt. Commander Peter Tomlin of the RSS for his comments on my first draft of this chart.

17. Interview with Commander Schopp, Bridgetown, Barbados, August 12, 1987, and with Dr. Norman Antoika, Political Officer at the United States Embassy in Barbados, August 12, 1987.

18. See "Expansion of Security System Being Considered," *Sunday Advocate* (Barbados), February 24, 1991, p. 5.

19. Interview with Lt. Commander Peter Tomlin, Hastings, Barbados, July 21, 1988.

20. David Simmonds, "Militarization of the Caribbean: Concerns for National and Regional Security," *International Journal* 40 (Spring 1985): 368.

21. Rex A. Hudson, "Strategic and Regional Security Perspectives," in Sandra W. Meditz and Dennis M. Hanratty, eds., *Islands of the Commonwealth Caribbean*, Washington, D.C.: Library of Congress, 1989, p. 628.

22. Interview with Lt. Commander Tomlin, July 1988.

23. James Mitchell, "Address," Opening Ceremony of the 11th Meeting of the Authority of the OECS, British Virgin Islands, May 27, 1987, p. 2.

24. "Barbados Sends Letter for PMs," *Barbados Advocate*, September 15, 1986, p. 1.

25. Barrow himself did not attend the meeting. He sent Attorney General Maurice King. See "No Agreement on Caribbean Defense Treaty," *New York Carib News*, October 28, 1986, p. 4; Hudson, ibid; and "Barrow and Mitchell Put the Brakes on a Security Treaty," *Caribbean Insight* 9 (October 1986): 1–2.

26. "Communiqué and Addresses," p. 6.

27. "Communiqué and Addresses," p. 16.

28. Rickey Singh, "CARICOM Security," *New York Carib News*, July 16, 1991, p. 5.

29. Government of Barbados, *Remarks by the Right Honorable L. Erskine Sandiford, M.P., Prime Minister, to a Meeting of Chiefs of Staff of Member States of the Caribbean Community*, St. Ann's Fort, Barbados, June 4, 1991, p. 3.

30. West Indian Commission, *Time For Action: Report of the West Indian Commission*, Black Rock, Barbados, 1992, p. 472.

31. Government of Trinidad and Tobago, *Address by the Honorable A.N.R. Robinson, Regional Conference on Democracy, Subversion, and National Security*, Port of Spain, Trinidad, May 31, 1991, p. 15.

32. Mark Adkin, *Urgent Fury: The Battle for Grenada*, Lexington, MA: Lexington Books, 1989, pp. 92–93.

33. For full details see Adkin, pp. 93–95.

34. Ibid., p. 220.

35. Ibid., p. 131.

36. Ibid., p. 220.

37. Humberto García Muñiz, *Boots, Boots, Boots: Intervention, Regional Security, and Militarization in the Caribbean 1979–1986*, Río Piedras, Puerto Rico: Caribbean Project for Justice and Peace, 1986, pp. 8–9.

38. Dennis F. Caffrey, "The Inter-American Military System: Rhetoric or Reality," in Georges Fauriol, ed., *Security in the Americas*, Washington, D.C.: National Defense University Press, 1989, p. 46.

39. U.S. Congress, *U.S. Military Actions in Grenada*, p. 42.

40. Hudson, "Strategic and Regional Security Perspectives," p. 626.

41. "GDF Troops Leave for Trinidad," *Guyana Chronicle*, August 4, 1990, p. 1.

Also see "Caricom Troops Join in the Search," *Trinidad Express*, August 7, 1990, p. 3.

42. Hudson, pp. 627–28; and Earl Bousquet, "St. Lucia and its 'Loverly War,' " *Caribbean Contact*, October 1985, p. 2.

43. Earl Bousquet, "Chilling War Game Played in Hills of St. Lucia," *Guyana Chronicle*, September 16, 1985.

44. Ibid.

45. Joseph B. Treaster, "Caribbean War Games: Not Everyone Is Delighted," *New York Times*, September 16, 1985, p. 2. Treaster refers to the officer as Colonel Wayne Topp.

46. Hudson, "Strategic and Regional Perspectives," p. 628; and "Military Exercises in the Caribbean," *New York Carib News*, April 8, 1986, p. 4.

47. Hudson, ibid., p. 629; and "Jamaica Hosting Security Maneuvers," *New York Carib News*, September 15, 1987.

48. "Operation Tradewinds 89," *Grenada Tribune*, June 16–30, 1989, p. 12.

49. "Caribbean, U.S. Set Joint Military Exercise," *San Juan Star*, May 19, 1991, p. 11; "UK Will also Participate in Caribbean Military Exercise," *Guyana Chronicle*, May 21, 1991, pp. 2,7; and "War Games," *Sunday Advocate* (Barbados), June 23, 1991, p. 3.

50. "Barbados to get First Taste of Tradewinds," *Daily Nation* (Barbados), February 26, 1992, p. 23A; and Catherine Clarke, "Tradewinds Sink Gangs," *Weekend Nation* (Barbados), July 3, 1992, pp. 24A, 25A.

51. Adkin, *Urgent Fury*, p. 181.

52. Vaughan Lewis, "Small States, Eastern Caribbean Security, and the Grenada Intervention," in Jorge Heine, ed., *A Revolution Aborted: The Lessons of Grenada*, Pittsburgh: University of Pittsburgh Press, 1991, p. 260.

53. Arnold Wolfers, *Discord and Collaboration*, Baltimore, MD: Johns Hopkins, 1962, p. 183.

54. See MOU, Art. 2; OECS Treaty, Art. 8 (3), (4).

55. See "Communiqué and Addresses"; Lewis, "Small States," and Mary Eugenia Charles, "Isolation vs. One-ness: The Continuing Validity of the Monroe Doctrine," *Caribbean Affairs* 1 (April–June 1988): 150–54.

56. Mahnaz Zehra Ispahani, "Alone Together: Regional Security Arrangements in Southern Africa and the Persian Gulf," *International Security* 8 (Spring 1984): 175.

57. Robert Rothstein, *Alliances and Small Powers*, New York: Columbia University Press, 1968, p. 169.

7 GEOPOLITICS OF THE REGION

The geopolitical significance of the Caribbean lies, generally, in its possession of strategic materials, in the location of strategic access routes there, and in the security networks that powerful states have in the area. The geopolitical value of the Caribbean area varies for different countries depending on the military, economic, political, or other interests and stakes involved.

States with interests or stakes in the region are found at various parts of the international power hierarchy. There is the United States, a superpower. The USSR, recognized as a superpower from the end of World War II until close to its demise in 1991, also had strategic interests in the Caribbean. The strategic connection also involves big powers and middle powers. Britain and France are in the former category; Brazil, Mexico, and Venezuela in the latter. However, before looking at the geopolitical interests of these states and how they affect the Commonwealth Caribbean, some attention should be paid to the strategic character of the Caribbean Basin, defined here to include the littoral states plus the Guyanas.

Strategic Materials and Access

Caribbean states own and produce resources important for both military and civilian purposes. As Tables 7.1 and 7.2, and Figure 7.1 show (see pages 179, 180–81, and 183 respectively), there are oil, bauxite, gold, nickel, copper, cobalt, and other natural resources in the region. Neighboring Brazil has a variety of strategic and nonstrategic materials, including bauxite, manganese, dolomite, oil, uranium, tungsten, and chromium.[1] It is helpful to note the uses of some of these materials.

In the non-military area, petroleum is used for gasoline, heating, chemicals, and plastics. Cobalt is used in carbides, magnets, and alloys; manganese in batteries and in the steel industry. Bauxite is used for building materials, in aircraft, and to make household utensils; copper for coins, and to make electrical conductors. In the military area, bauxite is important in a variety of military vehicles, and for ammunition. For example, a single engine for the United States F–15 and F–16 fighters uses 720 pounds of aluminum, which is refined from bauxite. Cobalt is crucial for making jet turbine blades, landing gear, engine mounts, and other components. It is also vital for the production of missile controls, precision rollers, and recoil springs for war tanks. Uranium is crucial for the production of nuclear energy and nuclear weapons. In the case of chromium, every F–15 jet contains about 1,656 pounds of this material.[2]

Bauxite and oil are the two strategic resources found in the Commonwealth Caribbean, although, as noted in chapter three, they are found in few states there. Bauxite is produced as well as refined in the Caribbean, and both crude bauxite and alumina products are exported. These are exported primarily to the United States and Canada, but there have also been exports to Western Europe and the former USSR. As is evident from Table 7.2, there are several aspects of the petroleum industry in the Caribbean: production, refining, and transshipment. Barbados and Trinidad and Tobago are the region's two oil producers. Refining takes places there and in St. Lucia, Antigua-Barbuda, the Bahamas, the Dominican Republic, Jamaica, and elsewhere. Indeed, the largest refining operations in the world are in the U.S. Virgin Islands. Tom Barry and his colleagues explain: "The Caribbean has been highly regarded as a refining center because of its political stability, its deep harbors, its lack of environmental regulations and its proximity to major shipping lanes, and the Panama Canal."[3] Transshipment centers are found in the Bahamas, St. Lucia, and in the Netherlands Antilles.

The Caribbean Basin has two of the world's major "choke points"— the Panama Canal, and the Caribbean Sea.[4] The Panama Canal, completed in 1914, links the Atlantic and the Pacific oceans, thereby saving 8,000 miles and 20 to 30 days of steaming from ocean to ocean.[5] It was not a heavily used international trade artery prior to World War II. The trade volume was a mere 30 million cargo tons in 1929, the peak pre-war year. However, the post-war economic growth in the United States and other countries led to massive increases in world trade, and consequently in the use of the Canal. For example, while 30 million tons of cargo transited the Canal in 1950, some 152 million tons passed through in 1988.[6]

Ever since August 15, 1914, when the SS *Ancon* first transited the Canal, more than sixty nations have used this sea lane. In his November 2, 1989, congressional testimony, Dennis Philip McAuliffe, former Commander of the United States Southern Command in Panama and later Administrator of the Panama Canal Commission (until December 31, 1989), made this observation about the international use of the Canal:

> As important as the Panama Canal is to the United States, other countries are even more dependent on it. For example, over half of all of Ecuador's international trade passes through the Canal, as does some 40 percent of both Chile's and Peru's international commerce. Unlike the United States, most of the cargo moving to and from these countries does not have readily available alternatives in the event of a disruption to Canal service. . . . Japan is also a heavy user of the Canal, accounting for 34 million tons of Canal cargo. Although only 5 percent of Japanese trade passes through the Canal, for certain trades Japan depends extensively on the waterway. The vast majority of Japanese grain imports pass through the Canal as do more than half of all Japanese cars exported to the United States. . . .
>
> In sum, the Panama Canal clearly remains important to the United States and the maritime world. Over 93 percent of the world's ocean going vessels are able to pass through the waterway and each year, there are some 12,000 transits carrying more than 150 million tons of cargo to all parts of the globe.[7]

The Panama Canal has also been a vital military Sea Lane of Communication (SLOC). Indeed the motivation for American involvement in its construction had military roots. That motivation is traced to the experience of the United States Navy in 1898 during the Spanish-American War, when the Battleship *Oregon* took sixty-eight days to travel from San Francisco to Cuba, having to go around Cape Horn at the southern tip of South America.[8] The Canal was crucial to the movement of ships, men, and materiel to the European and North African theaters during World War II. Major General David Parker (Retired) of the United States Army even once remarked that "the Canal paid for itself several times over in World War II." It was also used heavily during the Vietnam War. At the peak of the conflict, over 1,500 United States ships passed through each year. The Canal was also vital to supply lines in the 1950–1953 Korean War.[9]

Once ships leave the Panama Canal from the Pacific Ocean they must use one or more of the Caribbean Sea passages shown in Table 7.3 and Figure 7.1, en route to destinations in the United States, Europe, Africa, and elsewhere. The Florida Strait, Mona Passage, Windward Passage, and the Yucatan Channel are the principal gateways for ships entering or leaving the Caribbean. Moreover, the Florida Strait offers the only open-sea link with the Gulf of Mexico. The strategic significance of the Caribbean Sea predates the creation of the Panama Canal. European leaders recognized its importance soon after the 1492 encounter between Europe and the Americas. The Caribbean lies at what José Martí called "the Vortex of the Americas," making it a bridge or a front between North and South America. It is, thus, quite natural that powers great and small, and near and far, would consider it strategically important.

Superpower Strategic Interests

The United States

The strategic interests of the United States in the Caribbean relate essentially to preventing extra-hemispheric powers from threatening its mainland, and to enhancing its global capabilities. Pursuit of these ends has involved the application of several basic principles. The first is to secure the Caribbean for American presence, power, and passage. The United States has also consistently sought to prevent potentially hostile foreign states from acquiring military bases and facilities in the area. Related to this have been efforts to exclude foreign balance-of-power struggles from the region. Yet, despite the importance of the Caribbean, the United States has dedicated few military resources to protecting interests and assets there.[10]

These interests and principles dictate emphasis on strategic resources, SLOCs, and potential threats by the former Soviet Union and by Cuba. Two scholars summarize the United States-Caribbean strategic connection this way:

> For the U.S. there are four distinct strategic perspectives on the Caribbean: militarily, in time of war, it could become a source of danger to Atlantic routes and indeed to the mainland itself . . .; commercially, it is a key transit zone for strategic and other raw materials; territorially, it is the location of the U.S. possessions and the Panama Canal, a major strategic artery; and politically, it serves as a base for subversive operations against U.S. interests in Central and South America.[11]

Table 7.1

Minerals in the Caribbean

LOCATION	OWNERSHIP	OPERATIONS
Bahamas	Marcona Industries	aragonite mining
Cuba	Cuban government	nickel mining, nickel refining
Dominican Republic	Alcoa	bauxite mining
	Falconbridge, Dominican government, others	nickel mining, nickel refining
	Dominican government	gold and silver mining
Guyana	Guyanese government, others	bauxite mining, alumina refining, gold and diamond mining
Haiti	First City International	gold and silver mining
Jamaica	Jamaican government, Anaconda	bauxite holdings
	Alcan, Jamaican government	bauxite mining, alumina refining
	Reynolds Metals, Kaiser, Jamaican government	bauxite mining, alumina refining
Surinam	Royal Dutch Shell	bauxite mining, alumina refining
	Alcoa	bauxite mining
	Alcoa, Billiton	bauxite mining, alumina smelting
Trinidad & Tobago	Alcan	alumina transshipment
U. S. Virgin Islands	Vialco	alumina refining

Source: Tom Barry et al., *The Other Side of Paradise,* New York: Grove Press, 1984.

The resource capacity of the Caribbean shown above, coupled with the resource needs of the United States, make it relatively easy to appreciate the region's strategic resource value to the United States. In the late 1980s, for example, 79 percent of the United States bauxite

Table 7.2 Oil in the Caribbean

LOCATION	COMPANY	OWNERSHIP	OPERATIONS
Antigua-Barbuda	West Indies Co.	National Petroleum, Antiguan government	refinery
Bahamas	Bahamas Oil Refining Co. (BORCO)	Charter Oil, Chevron	refinery, desulfurizer, distribution
	Burmah Oil	Apex Oil, Bahamas	transshipment
Barbados	Mobil Oil Barbados	Mobil Oil	refinery
	Barbados National Oil	Barbadian government	production
Cuba	Instituto Cubano del Petróleo	Cuban government	refinery
Dominican Republic	Falconbridge Dominica	Falconbridge	refinery
	Refinería Dominicana del Petróleo	Royal Dutch Shell, Dominican government	refinery
Guyana	Total (Guyana), LASMO-BHP, Mobil Oil, Hunt Oil	Total (France), London & Scottish Marine Oil (Britain), Mobil Oil, Hunt Oil	exploration
Jamaica	Petroleum Corporation of Jamaica	Jamaican government	refinery
Martinique	Société Anonyme de la Raffinerie des Antilles	Royal Dutch Shell, Exxon, Texaco, CFP, Erap	refinery
Netherland Antilles Aruba	Lago Oil and Transport	Exxon	refinery, transshipment
Bonaire	Bonaire Petroleum	Northville, Paktank	transshipment
Curaçao	Curaçao Oil Terminal	Northville, Paktank	transshipment
	Shell Curaçao	Shell	refinery

Puerto Rico	Caribbean Gulf Refining Corporation	Gulf Oil, others	refinery
	Petrolane of Puerto Rico	Gulf Oil, others	gas production
	Yubacoa Sun Oil	Sun Oil	refinery
	Clark Oil	Apex Oil	refinery
	Peerless Petro-Chemicals	Apex Oil	refinery
St. Kitts-Nevis	--------	planned by Canadian investors	refinery
St. Lucia	Hess Oil	Amerada Hess	transshipment
Trinidad & Tobago	Texaco Trinidad	Texaco, others	refinery
	Amoco Trinidad	Standard Oil of Indiana (AMOCO)	oil and gas
	Trinidad-Tesoro Petroleum	Trinidad & Tobago government, Tesoro	oil and gas production
	Trinidad & Tobago Oil (TRINTOC)	Trinidad & Tobago government	refinery
	Trinmar	AMOCO, Trinidad-Tesoro, TRINTOC	oil and gas production
	Occidental of Trinidad	Occidental Petroleum	production
U.S. Virgin Islands	Hess Oil - Virgin Islands	Amerada Hess	refinery

Source: Tom Barry et al., *The Other Side of Paradise*, New York: Grove Press, 1984, pp. 96–99; *Guyana Chronicle* (1991).

Table 7.3

Principal Straits and Passages in the Caribbean

PASSAGE	LOCATION	SOVEREIGNTY ON EACH SIDE	MINIMUM WIDTH (Nautical Miles)
Anegada Passage	Between Anegada and Sombrero	U.K.	48
Aruba-Paraguana Passage	Between Aruba and Venezuela	The Netherlands/Venezuela	15
Dominica Channel	Between Guadeloupe and Dominica	France/Dominica	16
Dragon's Mouth	Between Trinidad and Venezuela	Trinidad/Venezuela	6
Florida Strait	Between Key West and Cuba	U.S./Cuba	82
Guadeloupe Passage	Between Guadeloupe and Montserrat	France/U.K.	28
Martinique Passage	Between Dominica and Martinique	France/Dominica	22
Mona Passage	Between the Dominican Republic and Mona Island (Puerto Rico)	U.S./The Dominican Republic	33
			8
Serpent's Mouth	Between Trinidad and Venezuela	Trinidad/Venezuela	
St. Lucia Channel	Between Martinique and St. Lucia	France/ St. Lucia	17
St. Vincent Passage	Between St. Lucia and St. Vincent	St. Lucia/St. Vincent	23
Virgin Passage	Between Culebra (Puerto Rico) and the Virgin Islands	The United States	8
Windward Passage	Between Cuba and Haiti	Cuba /Haiti	45
Yucatan Channel	Between Cuba and the Mexican Yucatan	Cuba/Mexico	105

Source: Jorge Heine and Leslie Maniat, eds., *The Caribbean and World Politics*, New York: Holmes and Meier, 1988, p.31.

Figure 7.1 Oil Fields, Refineries, and SLOCs in the Caribbean

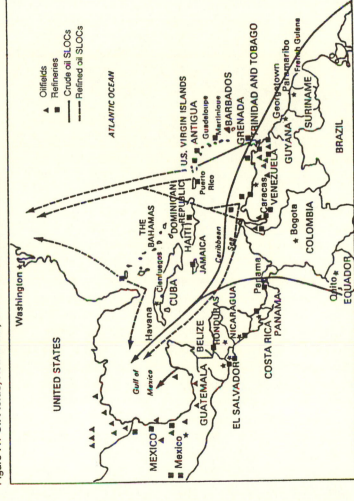

Source: Joseph H. Strodder and Kevin F. McCarthy, *Profiles of the Caribbean Basin in 1960/1980: Changing Geopolitical and Geostrategic Dimensions,* Rand Corporation, N–2058-AF, December 1983, p.4.

imports came from the Caribbean, including 52 percent from Jamaica, 9 percent from Surinam, and 4 percent each from Guyana and the Dominican Republic. Brazil, which has large undeveloped bauxite deposits, provided 4 percent.[12] Moreover, the Caribbean not only supplies a significant proportion of American oil, it also fulfills the need for petroleum products through refining operations, refining about 56 percent of all U.S. oil imports.

Countries close to the Caribbean also supply key minerals to the United States. Brazil and Mexico, for instance, provide some 16 percent of the United States' manganese imports. Manganese is one of the few minerals for which the United States is totally dependent on foreign sources since it has no deposits. Brazil supplies about one-third of the Unites States' columbium. There is 100 percent foreign importation of this mineral, which is essential for the aerospace industry. Brazil is also one of the eighteen sources of tantalum for the United States, second in importance only to Canada. In the 1980s, it fulfilled 17 percent of the Unites States' tantalum needs. Tantalum is used especially in the electronics, chemical, and aircraft industries. There is no substitute for its use in the control systems of jet engines.[13]

Caribbean SLOCs are also critical to American needs. The renowned American naval strategist Alfred Mahan is reputed to have declared: "One thing is sure. In the Caribbean Sea is the strategic key of two great oceans, the Atlantic and the Pacific." This is true in non-military as well as in military terms. In the non-military area, the Panama Canal is a boon to U.S. trade by shortening sea travel between San Francisco and New York by 7,800 miles. Thirty-three of the sixty-four standard U.S. ocean trade routes pass through the Caribbean. This is attributable largely to the importance of the Gulf ports, especially Gramercy, Louisiana, Houston, New Orleans, Baton Rouge, Corpus Christi, Tampa, Texas City, Beaumont, Mobile, and Galveston. These ports account for more than half of all U.S. maritime trade in the early 1980s.[14] Moreover, the United States provides a market for 60 percent of the Caribbean's exports.

Earlier I noted the role the Panama Canal played in World War II and the conflicts in Korea and Vietnam. In addition, during the 1962 Cuban missile crisis, eighteen warships made a dramatic overnight transit, jumping ahead of commercial shipping, to fortify the naval blockade of Cuba. Some military analysts argue that the military value of Caribbean SLOCs now rests primarily on the U.S. defense commitment to Europe.[15] The strategic value of the Canal to the United States has diminished over the years, though. One reason for this is the physical features of the Canal, given the increasing size of military vessels. The Canal has three sets of locks: the Gatun Locks on the Caribbean side, and the Pedro Miguel and Miraflores locks on the Pacific side. Lock chambers are 1,000 feet long and 110 feet wide, with a full-water depth of 42 feet. These dimensions limit the size of ships that can be accommodated: generally, 975 feet long, 106 feet wide, 40 feet draft, with a maximum tonnage of 65,000 deadweight tons.[16]

Some large military ships have been squeezed through the Canal, like the *Missouri*-class battleships with beams of 108 feet. In 1983, for instance, one battleship in this class, the USS *New Jersey*, transited to join the Sixth Fleet off Lebanon after completing a cruise in the Pacific. But in an age when the United States is emphasizing naval strategy centered around the projection of power through deployment of carrier task forces, the size of the Canal poses a limitation. Aircraft carriers are generally too big to pass through the Canal. A *Nimitz*-class carrier, for example, is 1,092 feet long, 252 feet wide, sits 37 feet in the water, and displaces 94,000 tons. Carriers in the *Enterprise* class are even longer—1,125 feet—although they displace only 75,000 tons.[17]

Thomas Anderson concedes that missile-carrying submarines, with the possible exception of the *Trident* class, can transit the Canal. Yet he notes that both the nature of their cargo and their high visibility make them rare users of this SLOC. According to Lars Schoultz, in a typical non-crisis year, about twenty-five navy vessels use the Canal, and most of them are "small" ships—destroyers, frigates, and submarines. Mary Kent was more specific: "In 1987 only 32 U.S. navy ships transited the Canal."[18] Nevertheless, for United States military and diplomatic officials, the Panama Canal remains a strategic SLOC. Two specialists have noted quite emphatically that "Caribbean SLOCs are absolutely vital to the United States. They constitute a primary security consideration."[19] On July 11, 1991 the Panama Canal Commission approved a plan to widen a narrow and hazardous stretch of the Canal, the Gaillard Cut. The project, to cost U.S. $200 million, will widen an eight-mile section to allow two-way traffic by larger vessels. The extension would permit between four and six additional ships to transit the Canal daily.[20]

Because of its strategic value, the Caribbean represents the United

States' "southern flank"; its "strategic rear." Traditionally, the region was defined as the area of highest U.S. security concern in the hemisphere, although it has suffered considerable political neglect. The United States maintains forces there, mainly in Puerto Rico, at the Atlantic threshold of the Caribbean; in Panama, at the southern rim of the Caribbean Basin; and in Cuba—at Guantánamo—on the northern perimeter. As Table 7.4 shows, the United States maintains 4,743 military and civilian personnel in Puerto Rico, occupying close to 35,000 acres of land. A Unites States Air Force Tactical Fighter Group is part of the establishment. In Panama, army, navy, and air force operations have a combined personnel strength of 20,709, occupying over 42,000 acres. At Quary Heights alone, headquarters of the United States Southern Command, there are some 16,000 military and civilian officials. The naval operations in Cuba have a personnel establishment of 3,401 occupying almost 29,000 acres of land.

These three force concentrations represent the northern, southern, and eastern points of a strategic triangle that stretches across the entire Caribbean Basin, and as Table 7.4 shows (see pages 188–89), there are also installations and personnel in many other parts of the region. The vertex of the triangle that most affects the English-speaking Caribbean is Puerto Rico. One Caribbean specialist notes: "The geographical mindset that became dominant with the Reagan administration served to emphasize the strategic military importance assigned to Puerto Rico as an Eastern Caribbean enclave, and so to accelerate and increase its integration into military policy towards the region."[21]

The importance of Puerto Rico has made the American military ascribe multidimensional roles to the installations there. Several of the communications facilities on the island have nuclear weapons-related functions: the low-frequency transmitter at Aguada; the high-frequency transmitter at Isabela; and the high frequency receiver at Sabana Seca. There is also the "Mystic Star" transmitter at Fort Allen, and a receiver at Salinas. These are part of the U.S. President's special communications network, used for communications with airborne command posts, including the National Emergency Command Post, which is designed to issue orders for nuclear weapons.[22]

In addition to the Camp Santiago training and surveillance facility, there is Fort Buchanan. Several functions are performed out of this facility: logistics, training, and other support for the United States National Guard, the Reserve, and the Reserve Officer Training Corps in

Puerto Rico; army intelligence; commissary and exchange benefits for retirees, their dependents and to veterans; and recruitment for the United States Armed Forces. In addition, there is Roosevelt Roads, long the coordinating center for military exercises in the Caribbean, including those discussed in the previous chapter.

García Muñiz provides a clear statement of the importance of Roosevelt Roads for United States military operations:

> Roosevelt Roads is seen as crucial in providing necessary port, airfield, and logistics facilities for supporting fleet and naval operations in Atlantic area contingencies, in the protection of the SLOCs from the United States to Latin America, and in facilitating force projection to South America and Africa. It has played an important role in U.S. intervention in Central America and the Caribbean, such as in Guatemala in 1954, in the Dominican Republic in 1965, and in the final rehearsal of the invasion of Grenada, which took place in Vieques (code-named Universal Trek I–83) just four months before that poorly executed military operation. During the Grenada invasion Tactical Air Command F–15s were positioned in Roosevelt Roads, "to provide surveillance and defense against possible interference by Cuban Forces."[23]

Operationally, United States bases in the Caribbean are part of the United States Atlantic Command (LANTCOM) whose Commander-in-Chief is also responsible for the United States Atlantic Fleet, and for a NATO command, as Supreme Allied Commander, Atlantic (SACLANT). LANTCOM is responsible for all joint United States military actions in the Atlantic area, from the North Pole to the South Pole, an area of 45 million square miles. All three of the major services (army, navy, and air force) have forces assigned to LANTCOM. As might be expected, the naval component is the largest. Until recently, LANTCOM had four subordinate integrated commands: the Iceland Defense Force; the United States Forces, Azores; the Special Operations Command, Atlantic; and United States Forces, Caribbean. The last command, which dealt with the Caribbean islands, was headquartered in Key West, Florida. However, in December 1989 it was disbanded, falling victim to the reorganization of the defense establishment in light of cuts in defense funds and new regional and international alignments. Its duties were assumed by the LANTCOM headquarters in Norfolk, Virginia.[24]

Table 7.4

U.S. Military Presence in the Caribbean

COUNTRY	CITY	MILITARY PERSONNEL	CIVILIAN PERSONNEL
Barbados	Bridgetown	5	----
Belize	Belize City	2	0
Bermuda	Bermuda	1,085	448
Costa Rica	San José	5	1
Cuba	Guantánamo Bay	2,468	933
Dominican Republic	Santo Domingo	5	0
El Salvador	San Salvador	13	2
Guatemala	Guatemala City	3	0
Haiti	Port-au-Prince	2	1
Honduras	Tegucigalpa	10	3
Jamaica	Kingston	3	1
Panama	Galeta Island	333	1
	Rod Man	698	484
	Balboa	2,559	597
	Quary Heights	10,000	5,997
Puerto Rico	Roosevelt Roads	3,163	857
	Sabana Seca	371	72
	San Juan	2	278

Sources: U.S. Department of Defense, *Department of Defense Worldwide List of Military Installations (Major, Minor, and Support 1990),* Washington, D.C., 1990; U.S. Department of State and Defense Security Assistance Agency, *Congressional Presentation for Security Assistance Programs Fiscal Year 1992,* Washington D.C. 1991.

LOCAL PERSONNEL	TOTAL PERSONNEL	SIZE OF INSTALLATION	MAJOR ACTIVITY
----	5	N.A.	Military Liaison Office
1	3	N.A.	Military Liaison Office
*	1,533	1,453 acres	Naval Patrol Aircraft
3	9	N.A.	Office of Defense Cooperation
*	3,401	28,817 acres	Naval Operating Base
3	8	N.A.	Military Assistance Advisory Group
13	28	N.A.	Military Group
3	6	N.A.	Military Group
1	4	N.A.	Military Liaison Office
10	23	N.A.	Military Group
0	4	N.A.	Military Liaison Office
*	374	707 acres	Naval Communications
*	1,182	3,166 acres	Naval Logistic Support
*	3,156	14,121 acres	U.S.A.F. Southern Air Division
*	15,997	24,143 acres	U.S. Army Southern Command HQ
*	4,020	32,161 acres	Naval Operating Base
*	443	2,618 acres	Naval Communications
*	280	44 acres	U.S.A.F. Tactical Fighter Group

* Figure not available
N.A. Not applicable

The USSR

December 21, 1991, marked the official demise of the USSR as a sovereign state, although the death of the Union was effectively signaled on December 12, 1991, when Russia, Ukraine, and Byelorussia ratified a treaty creating the Commonwealth of Independent States (CIS).[25] But for a great part of the forty-five years it existed as a superpower, the USSR had an interest in the Caribbean as part of a design for global power projection.[26]

One writer argued that under Soviet geopolitical thinking any geographical area could be designated a theater of war. These were not necessarily areas of actual conflict, but could represent regions politically, economically, or militarily crucial to competitive states. They were chosen based on SLOCs, sources of strategic materials, and geographic vulnerability. The area of Latin America and the Caribbean was identified as one of those theaters.[27] In this context, Soviet strategic interests in the Caribbean related directly to the region's proximity and geopolitical importance to the United States. Some analysts contended that the optimal Soviet strategy sought the creation, through naval and air presence complemented by the Cubans, of "an offensive interdiction capability effective enough to block the region's sea lanes," thereby upsetting the NATO "swing strategy" designed as a contingency for war in Europe. The "swing strategy" itself posited the movement of American reinforcements from Hawaii, Washington, and California through the Panama Canal.[28]

Edward Gonzalez claims the Soviets had three aims in the Caribbean:

- creation of greater dissension between the United States and the hemisphere and Western allies over the region;
- promotion of conflict situations that may entrap or encumber United States forces were they to intervene in the Central American conflict;
- fostering of political-military changes in the region to eventually facilitate Soviet-Cuban expansion there.

Nevertheless, most analysts conceded that the USSR lacked the required strength in the region to disrupt SLOCs important to the United States. Carl Jacobsen, for example, testified before Congress that while Moscow's presence was pervasive, its ability to control events was less than some observers feared. Moscow's authority among revolutionary groups and individuals was similarly less than often reputed, and less than the Soviets themselves desired.[29]

Soviet-American conflict scenarios featured the Caribbean in general and Cuba in particular playing important roles in the Soviet gameplan. One such scenario suggested four reasons for Soviet involvement in a large-scale interdiction campaign against Caribbean SLOCs. First, Cuban ports could have supported Soviet attack submarines and also obviate the need to transit the GIN (Greenland-Iceland-Norway) gap to fit and rearm the battle in the Atlantic and the Caribbean. In addition, airfields in the region could have been used to launch and recover TU–95 *Bear* and *Backfire* bombers and other aircraft. Also, the USSR could have initiated a Caribbean SLOC campaign to bolster the resolve of allies in the region. Finally, it was argued that by shifting the battle to the Western hemisphere, the USSR could have encumbered United States military assets and minimized the scope and intensity of hostilities in Europe, closer to the Soviet homeland.

The centerpiece of Soviet strategic interests in the Caribbean lay in the Soviet-Cuban nexus. Cuba's strategic location is undeniable. It "sits astride the Caribbean Sea," where it commands the entrance to the Gulf of Mexico, the Florida Strait, the eastern approaches to Central America, the northern region of South America, and the Eastern Caribbean. It was, thus, of considerable strategic value to the Soviet Union. The only significant Soviet military presence in the Caribbean was in Cuba. It included modern docks and repair facilities, airport facilities for reconnaissance aircraft, and satellite and other surveillance operations. The twenty-eight square-mile facility at Lourdes, for example, had three functions: monitoring United States missile tests; intercepting satellite communications; and relaying microwave communications between the USSR and its diplomatic posts in the Western hemisphere. This facility was reputedly the largest such operation the Soviets maintained outside the USSR. Nevertheless, according to Lars Schoultz, Soviet intelligence facilities in Cuba were more an annoyance that a serious threat to American security. They were convenient to the Soviets, but their functions could have been performed easily by satellite or naval reconnaissance units.[30]

The Soviets rendered military assistance to Cuba, including the delivery of MiG–29 advanced fighters, for close to three decades. Military deliveries for 1989 were valued at U.S. $1.2 billion; those for

1990, at U.S. $1.3 billion. Reconnaissance aircraft flew to Cuba in 1990, although the Soviet navy made no port call after 1989. Nevertheless, the USSR still maintained intelligence collection vessels in Cuban waters.[31] And according to the 1990–1991 edition of *The Military Balance*, in 1990 the USSR had 7,700 military personnel in Cuba, 2,800 of whom were part of a motorized rifle brigade, and another 2,800 of whom were military advisers.

The dramatic changes in the USSR following the advent of Mikhail Gorbachev in 1985 led to a transformation of relations with Cuba. The clearest statement of this came from Gorbachev, then Soviet President, and Boris Yeltsin, then President of the Russian Federation, in a televised "international town meeting" with the United States, broadcast in the United States on ABC News on September 5–6, 1991. The very next week President Gorbachev announced in Moscow that the USSR would shortly "discuss" with Cuba the withdrawal of 11,000 troops from the island. Speaking on September 11, 1991, after a meeting with United States Secretary of State James Baker, President Gorbachev also indicated that future Soviet-Cuban economic ties were to be based on free trade, eliminating the effective U.S. $2 billion annual subsidy to Cuba, granted through a barter of Soviet oil for Cuban sugar where the latter is greatly overvalued. The troop withdrawal began two months later, on November 24, 1991.

That new and dramatic chapter in Soviet-Cuban relations was the result of Soviet desperation for U.S. and other Western investment and economic and technical assistance. One condition for U.S. aid had been that the USSR cease underwriting Cuba. President Gorbachev explained that the Soviet move was intended to "transfer our relations with Cuba to a plane of mutually beneficial trade and economic ties and [we will] remove the other elements of that relationship—elements that were born of a different time in a different era."[32]

The Cuban-Soviet nexus did not prevent differences between the two over geopolitical issues, not even during the 1960s and the 1970s when ties were strongest. Over the years they had policy disputes regarding the defense of Cuba, American intervention in the region, military assistance to radical groups in the region, and Cuban-American relations.[33] Moreover, the Cuban-Soviet connection did not preclude Soviet maintenance of contacts with other Caribbean countries. Grenada, Jamaica, and Guyana had close contacts with the USSR in the 1970s and the 1980s.

The links with Grenada were the most dramatic, yet the most short-lived. In chapter three I discussed the extensive military agreements and military assistance program between the two. These, and Soviet-Grenadian relations in the Bishop era generally, gained momentum following the establishment of diplomatic relations between the two in December 1979, although the Soviet embassy was not opened in Grenada until September 1982. Grenada courted the Soviets intensively, consistently seeking Moscow's acceptance of its socialist-oriented credentials.[34]

Caribbean Middle Powers

Regional middle power analysis relating to the Caribbean often focuses on the "BVM" countries (Brazil, Venezuela, Mexico). However, for several reasons, attention is paid here to Brazil, Colombia, Cuba, Mexico, and Venezuela. First, these are the regional middle powers with the greatest geographic proximity to the Commonwealth Caribbean. Moreover, of all the states in the Caribbean Basin, their potential (and in some cases actual) impact on the economic capability and ideological posture of English Caribbean states is greatest. Because of these factors, these countries are able to affect directly the security of English Caribbean states, both negatively and positively.

Brazil

With an area of over eight-and-a-half million square kilometers, a population of 150 million, and a military establishment of 1.4 million men and women, as shown in Table 7.5 (see page 195), Brazil is the Leviathan of the area. It is credited with having the most sophisticated approach to geopolitical analysis in the region. That approach is rooted in notions of inevitable greatness—*grandeza*—which posit Brazil's eventual emergence as the first superpower in the southern hemisphere. National development policy is predicated on symbiosis between economic development and national security, a basic thrust being that a certain level of guaranteed security must precede development.

The small English Caribbean states harbor no fear of Brazil, partly because of its reluctance to capitalize on its size, capability, and proximity, and to exercise any influence over them. Historically, Brazil has been a low-profile operator in the Commonwealth Caribbean, except in relation to neighboring Guyana. Mirlande Manigat is, therefore, correct in saying "Brazil is . . . enjoying an odd but rewarding situation: it is sufficiently close to the region to play a role that can be justified by geographical proximity, but sufficiently remote for its intervention not to frighten."[35] Brazilian leaders have taken pains to correct any notions of ulterior motives in the area. They are also sensitive to claims of subordination to American interests. One Brazilian diplomat in the Caribbean repeatedly assured me that Brazil has no hegemonic designs toward the region. He also belabored the point that, contrary to suggestions by some writers, his country is not an American surrogate in the hemisphere.[36]

The relative passivity toward the Commonwealth Caribbean does not connote total lack of interest in the region. As Table 7.5 shows, there is a resident diplomatic presence in several Caribbean states. This suggests a certain degree of interest. Technical and financial assistance has been given to Guyana, Jamaica, Barbados, and other countries; state visits have been made by leaders from both sides; some trade goes on between Brazil and Caribbean nations, and there has been military cooperation with at least one country, Guyana. Moreover, as Anthony Bryan rightly observes, Brazil is also interested in Guyana's resource-rich Essequibo area; in the peaceful settlement of disputes between Guyana and Venezuela, and between Guyana and Surinam; and in constructing a highway between Boa Vista and Georgetown, the Guyana capital, for easy access to the Caribbean.[37]

Beyond these, a major Brazilian concern has been with the actual and potential role of Cuba in the area, especially in continental South America. In 1983 this concern about the Cuban role in Surinam led to the creation of a 20,000-member task force to deal with any contingency along the borders with Guyana and Surinam. Brazil also dispatched a high-level mission to Surinam, led by General Danilo Venturini, head of the National Security Council. He is reported to have offered the Surinamese leadership military credit; military supplies of boots, planes, and Cascavel armored cars; training; guaranteed rice imports; and a ban on Surinamese exile activity in Brazil, among other things. All this was part of a deal to reduce and eventually remove the Cuban presence.[38] Most of the Cubans—the Ambassador and 100 technicians—were later expelled. However, this resulted from the United States intervention in Grenada.

The Brazilians have also been concerned about Cuban-Guyanese

Table 7.5

Profile of Caribbean Middle Powers

COUNTRY	AREA (km²)	POPULATION (1989)	PER CAPITA GDP ($U.S. 1988)	ARMED FORCES (1991)		NATURAL RESOURCES
Brazil	8,511,965	150,051,784	2,449	A	296,700	bauxite, iron, manganese, lead, gold, dolomite, tungsten, silver, oil, copper, nickel, chromium, uranium
				R	1,115,000	
Colombia	1,138,914	30,241,000	1,739	A	134,000	gold, silver, oil
				R	116,900	
Cuba	110,861	10,576,921	2,000[a]	A	180,500	nickel, chromium, cobalt, oil (under exploration)
				R	135,000	
Mexico	1,972,547	84,274,992	2,588	A	175,000	oil, copper, manganese, barite, sulphur
				R	300,000	
Venezuela	912,050	19,245,522	2,544	A	75,000[b]	gold, diamonds, oil, bauxite

Sources: James W. Wilkie et al, *Statistical Abstract of Latin America*, vol. 28, Los Angeles, CA: UCLA Latin American Center Publications, 1990; *The Military Balance 1991–1992*, London: International Institute for Strategic Studies, 1991; *South America, Central America, and the Caribbean*, London: Europa Publications, 1991.

[a] 1989 per capita GNP figure
[b] Including National Guard of 48,000
A = Active Forces
R = Reserve Forces

contacts. The concern was acute following tensions between Guyana and Venezuela in 1981–1982 over Venezuela's non-renewal of the Protocol of Port of Spain, which had frozen, for twelve years, Venezuela's territorial claim against Guyana. Venezuela's intimidation led to speculation about Guyana's willingness to seek Cuban military assistance in the event of Venezuelan attack. The Brazilians were disturbed about this likelihood. Consequently, while striving to appear non-partisan in the dispute, they took diplomatic and military measures, such as limited arms sales to Guyana, and military maneuvers along the Brazil-Guyana-Venezuela border, to help deter Venezuela. Brazil's military contacts with Guyana have continued over the years. Indeed in January 1992, two Brazilian Navy Corvettes paid a three-day visit to Guyana as part of their training and operational links with Guyana's army.[39]

Colombia

Of the five middle powers examined here, Colombia has had the least contact with the Caribbean. Colombia has had diplomatic relations with Trinidad and Tobago, Guyana, and Jamaica since the mid-1960s. However, 1981 marked the adoption of the first conscious policy toward the English Caribbean. One writer attributed this shift to several factors: competition with Venezuela; the search for support in its dispute with Nicaragua; and pursuit of "democratic alternatives of government." Others have given different explanations: Colombia's Third World orientation; maritime boundary interests with Costa Rica, Haiti, Panama and other states; validation of the territorial claims once made by the United States and Nicagargua; growing Mexican and Venezuelan influence in the region.[40]

Colombia places more emphasis on its Pacific interests than its Caribbean ones. Part of the Pacific initiative is to become a trade bridge between the Atlantic and Pacific basins. In fulfillment of this aim, it has been trying to create a land bridge between the Pacific coast and the Caribbean Sea through a network of interconnecting roads and railways, as an alternative to the Panama Canal. Requests for Japanese financing of this plan have already been made.

Like Venezuela and Mexico, Colombia contributes to the Caribbean Development Bank. And apart from interest in stemming the tide of "communist model-building" in the region, Colombia's interest seems to lie in exploring economic opportunities. The more than U.S. $25 billion annual purchasing power of the Caribbean and the meager U.S.$80 million of it captured by Colombia seem to have made the pursuit of relations with the Caribbean economically desirable. It was also mainly for economic reasons that Colombia sought and received observer status with CARICOM at the 1991 CARICOM Summit in St. Kitts-Nevis.[41] It remains to be seen how sustained this economic interest becomes, and whether it will translate into more extensive and diversified bilateral and multilateral contacts.

Cuba

Over the years, Cuba's importance to the Commonwealth Caribbean became linked with its strategic location, noted above, its inordinate military strength given its size and resources, its activist foreign policy, and the model it offered many Caribbean leaders. Cuba's foreign policy pursuits in the region have been well-articulated, bold, and often pragmatic.[42] It was partly out of pragmatism that Cuba began focusing on the English Caribbean in the early 1970s. The failure of its guerrilla efforts in Latin America in the 1960s and the 1970s led to a reexamination of foreign policy in the hemisphere. Pursuit of links with the Commonwealth Caribbean resulted from that reevaluation.

Diplomatic relations were established simultaneously on August 12, 1972, with the Commonwealth Caribbean "Big Four": Barbados, Guyana, Jamaica, and Trinidad and Tobago. Over the years, ideological affinity and a convergence of national interests led to strong ties with some countries, especially Jamaica, Guyana, and later, strongest of all, Grenada during the Maurice Bishop era. Castro visited the Commonweath Caribbean several times, and Michael Manley of Jamaica, Forbes Burnham of Guyana, Eric Williams of Trinidad and Tobago, and Bishop of Grenada were among Caribbean leaders who visited Cuba, some of them several times. Cuba also participated in the first Caribbean Festival of Arts, CARIFESTA, held in Guyana in 1972.

Cuban-Caribbean relations began souring with the victory of Edward Seaga in Jamaica in 1980, and with the rise to power of several conservative parties in the Eastern Caribbean between 1979 and 1982. However, relations took a dramatic plunge following the 1983 Grenada intervention. Nevertheless, relations began to improve in the late 1980s. At the 1990 CARICOM Summit in Jamaica, many Caribbean leaders were sympathetic to Cuba's request for observer status with the organization. Some leaders were skeptical though, partly because of Cuba's non-recognition of any government in Grenada since the 1983 intervention, a position that Cuba subsequently changed. Guyana, the CARICOM country closest to Cuba, was mandated to follow up the matter, as was the West Indian Commission. The Commission was able to convince Cuba to recognize Grenada's government. As noted in chapter two, diplomatic ties were restored with Jamaica in July 1990. Cuba has reopened its embassy in Kingston, although Jamaica's ambassador to Cuba is resident in Kingston. In addition, Cuba and St. Vincent and the Grenadines established non-resident diplomatic relations in June 1992. Moreover, in July 1992, Cuba was granted full membership in the Caribbean Tourism Organization. (Mexico was also admitted.)

Part of the new Cuban-Caribbean contacts involved the visit of a Caribbean technical mission to Cuba during April and May 1991. The team included officials from the UWI, the Caribbean Agricultural Research Development Institute, the CARICOM Secretariat, and the Sugarcane Feeds Center in Trinidad and Tobago. The team explored prospects for closer and mutually beneficial relations in several areas, especially biotechnology, sugarcane utilization, dairy farming, and fisheries management.

The Cubans themselves have stressed the importance of bolstering Caribbean ties. Guyana is particularly important in this regard because of its natural resources and the long-standing closeness between the two countries. Speaking in Georgetown, Guyana, on September 11, 1991, the President of Cuba's State Economic Cooperation Council, Ernesto Meléndez Bach, acknowledged that developments in the USSR and elsewhere heightened the importance of ties with Guyana and the rest of the region. Meléndez spent three days in Guyana for the annual talks of the Cuba-Guyana Mixed Commission. In addition to government-to-government ties, Cuba is courting Guyanese businessmen for joint ventures in Cuba. According to one member of the Mixed Commission, "you do not have to be a foreign relations expert to realize that they are throwing out the lifeline to the Caribbean."[43]

Cuba's outreach has begun to pay political dividends, if not economic ones. At Cuba's request, during fall 1991 several Caribbean countries advocated the removal of United States trade sanctions against Cuba. Several Caribbean diplomats pressed Cuba's case at the

1991 session of the United Nations General Assembly. Among those who advocated removal of the embargo were Jamaica's Foreign Minister, David Coore, and the Permanent Representative of Trinidad and Tobago to the United Nations, Marjorie Thorpe. Trinidad and Tobago Foreign Minister Sahadeo Basdeo also expressed support, indicating that the initiative also had the full support of Barbados and Guyana. Guyana itself had long voiced support for the move. Grenada had reservations, while Dominica rejected it. In addition to CARICOM support, Cuba's new push has received the endorsement of Venezuelan President Carlos Andrés Pérez.[44] The U.N. resolution calling for an end to the embargo was adapted later, on November 24, 1992.

CARICOM countries have benefitted from Cuban technical assistance, and from its health, education, and cultural programs. Of course, there have been limits to Cuba's ability to extend the kind and amount of economic assistance needed by these countries, given Cuba's own limitations and problems. Cuba's "insertion" into the Commonwealth Caribbean has also been constrained by the region's political tradition of multiparty democracy.[45] Fear of "communist subversion" and "export of revolution" has led to concern about Cuban pursuits by both the United States and some Caribbean countries, especially those in the Eastern Caribbean. But as Leslie Manigat, no lover of Castro or admirer of communism, quite accurately remarked: "To speak of 'exporting' Cuban revolution as if it were a product imposed from abroad is misleading. Rather, what took place was a much more complex process, one from which the sheer human appeal to what happened in Cuba and the sympathetic response it evoked in the Caribbean were not alien."[46]

Several factors facilitated Cuban pursuits in the region over the years: the popularity of the Cuban revolution; the existence of a radical network in the Caribbean; and an active Cuban diplomatic and intelligence network. Contrary to what many observers believed, Cuba was not responsible for every act or policy antithetical to Western interests in the Caribbean. The Caribbean has had its own radical and Marxist bodies, and its own attempts to implement non-Western political precepts. Some of these predate the Cuban Revolution. For example, Dr. Cheddie Jagan of Guyana, until recently one of the region's most orthodox communists, began his work in the late 1940s. However, the Cubans do not overlook opportunities to extend influence, directly or indirectly. One Caribbean Foreign Minister told me that Cuba once engaged in the practice of handpicking citizens from his country for scholarships. This offered them a measure of control over both "the who" and "the what" of higher education in a country where who gets what higher education could have considerable long-term political and managerial consequences. Also, the OECS Director-General reported a similar approach to scholarships in relation to Eastern Caribbean countries.[47]

The Cubans have often been arrogant in dealing with CARICOM countries. One dramatic episode occurred on May 10, 1980, when the Royal Bahamas Defense Force (RBDF) patrol boat, *Flamingo*, seized two Cuban fishing vessels for violating the Bahamian economic zone by fishing in territorial waters south of Ragged Island. Before the *Flamingo* could reach its home port, Cuban air force MiGs strafed and sank it, killing four of the crew members and wounding three others. In addition, Cuban troops were transported by helicopter to Ragged Island in pursuit of the survivors. The following day MiGs buzzed the island for long periods. A Cuban statement later claimed that Cuba had responded to reports of piracy. Moreover, Cuba claimed the right to undertake similar measures against the pursuit of American interests by the Bahamas. An apology and U.S. $5.4 million in compensation to the Bahamas government and the families concerned were made only after the Bahamas threatened to present the issue to the United Nations Security Council as an act of aggression.[48]

Mexico

Mexico's approach to the region was once marked by passivity and relative indifference. This was due to several features of Mexico's foreign policy: a relatively isolationist policy; a preoccupation with self-determination and non-intervention in the affairs of others; and emphasis on relations with the United States. Its attitude was once such that one writer remarked: "Of all the regional powers with a[n active] role in the Caribbean, Mexico would seem to be the one most likely to acquiesce to the 'Finlandization' of some countries of the area, in the name of ideological pluralism and international neutralism."[49]

Mexico became increasingly conscious of the geopolitical importance of the Caribbean after 1970, as it began diversifying its foreign policy, playing a prime role in the search for a New International Economic Order. As part of this "new" foreign policy, President José López Portillo launched a "Global Energy Plan" in his September 1989 statement before the United Nations General Assembly. Among other things, the Plan anticipated cooperation between oil producers and oil consumers, and establishment of a system to help alleviate the burden felt by small oil importers. According to Portillo, the system was to guarantee the supply and honoring of contracts, stop speculation, provide for compensation for price increases, and ensure considerate treatment by exporting countries.[50]

Developments were such that the following year Mexico was willing to create a joint oil facility with Venezuela to help Caribbean countries facing massive oil bills and related economic difficulties. This was partly in fulfillment of the "Portillo Plan." The facility was created under the August 3, 1980, Economic Cooperation Program for Central American Countries, commonly known as the San José Agreement. Under the Agreement, Mexico and Venezuela pledged to ship 80,000 BPD (barrels per day) of oil on concessionary terms to nine (later ten) countries, including Barbados and Jamaica. They also promised beneficiaries credits of up to 30 percent of the commercial price of their purchases for up to five years, at an annual rate of four percent. Moreover, there were conditions under which the loans could be extended to twenty years at a 2 percent rate, with a five-year grace period.[51]

Since 1980 there have been spurts of personal diplomacy, such as visits by former President Luís Echeverriia to Guyana, Jamaica, and Trinidad and Tobago. Other contacts have included agreements with Jamaica to barter oil for bauxite, support for Belize in the dispute with Guatemala, and expanded diplomatic relations as more countries in the region became independent. Mexico's interest in the Caribbean became more intense as the decade of the eighties gave way to that of the nineties. Part of that renewed interest was reflected in appointment of a roving Ambassador for Caribbean Affairs.

The year 1990 was a landmark in recent Caribbean-Mexican relations. President Carlos Salinas de Gortari became the first Latin-American head of state to participate in a CARICOM Summit. The Summit, held in Jamaica from July 31 to August 2, 1990, granted observer status to Mexico, along with Venezuela, in several CARICOM institutions: the Conference of Ministers of Health; the Ministerial Conference on the Environment; and the Standing Committees of Ministers of Agriculture, Education, Science and Technology, Labor, and Transportation. While in Jamaica, President Salinas also signed bilateral agreements with Jamaica on narcotics control, trade, sports, culture, and tourism. Salinas invested acting Jamaican Prime Minister Percival Patterson with the Aztec Eagle of the Order of Banda, and Patterson reciprocated by granting Salinas the Order of Jamaica.[52] Mexico's links with Jamaica have been strongest among its contacts with CARICOM countries.

Venezuela

Of the regional powers examined here, Venezuela has the sharpest sense of a Caribbean identity and perhaps the greatest awareness of the region's geopolitical importance. This is understandable since Venezuela has 2,256 kilometers of Caribbean coastline, its major ports are along that coastline, and some 80 percent of its exports use Caribbean SLOCs.[53] Together, this sense of Caribbean identity and geopolitical consciousness have led to considerable activism since the late 1950s, even during periods of lull. As Table 7.6 shows, Venezuela has a very extensive diplomatic presence in the region. There are also Institutes of Culture and Cooperation in all CARICOM countries except Belize and the Bahamas. This activism, described by Carlos Méndez and others as "a diplomacy of projection," has been interpreted by some as an indication of subimperialist intentions, something the Venezuelans strenuously deny.[54]

Reference was made in chapter two to the apprehension among some Caribbean elites about ulterior motives Venezuela may have. This muted apprehension is not new. At times feelings have gone beyond muted expressions to open and direct criticism. The most dramatic and vocal critic of all Commonwealth Caribbean leaders over the years was the late Eric Williams of Trinidad and Tobago. In 1975, after an unsuccessful attempt at convincing Caribbean leaders other than Forbes Burnham of Venezuela's neocolonialist intentions, Williams convened a special convention of his ruling People's National Movement (PNM) to highlight the territorial, economic, and political jeopardy which he felt the Commonwealth Caribbean faced from Venezuela.

Williams, a renowned historian, made a lengthy analysis of Venezuelan foreign policy conduct since the colonial era. He cited

> Venezuela's Caribbean vision and ambitions, starting off from barren uninhabited rocks to a network of economic arrangements out of which

Table 7.6

Middle Power Representation in the Caribbean

CARIBBEAN / MIDDLE STATES	ANTIGUA	BAHAMAS	BARBADOS	BELIZE	DOMINICA	GRENADA	GUYANA	JAMAICA	ST. KITTS	ST. LUCIA	ST. VINCENT	TRINIDAD & TOBAGO
BRAZIL	NRDR	NRDR	RDM	NDR	NRDR	NRDR	RDM	RDM	NRDR	NRDR	NRDR	RDM
COLOMBIA	NRDR	NRDR	RDM	NRDR	NRDR	NDR	RDM	RDM	NDR	NDR	NDR	RDM
CUBA	NDR	NRDR	NRDR	NDR	NDR	NDR	RDM	RDM	NDR	NRDR	NRDR	NRDR
MEXICO	NDR	NRDR	NRDR	RDM	NRDR	NRDR	NRDR	RDM	NRDR	RDM	NRDR	NRDR
VENEZUELA	RDM	NRDR	RDM	RDM	RDM	RDM	RDM	RDM	RDM	RDM	RDM	RDM

Source: Compiled by author based on data from the CARICOM Secretariat, Latin American missions in New York, and *New York Carib News* (1992).

NDR No Diplomatic Relations
RDM Resident Diplomatic Mission
NRDR Non-Resident Diplomatic Representation

is emerging a Venezuela oil and industrial metropolis and an indebted Caribbean hinterland, the Caribbean as we know it integrated into Venezuela, the naval power of the future, the oil power of the present, the tourist mecca in the making, its position in its Venezuelan Sea fortified by its 200-mile exclusive economic zone: all to the plaudits of the Caribbean peoples themselves, with Trinidad and Tobago the odd man out.[55]

Williams' main concern, and something that has marked as well as marred Caribbean-Venezuelan relations, was territorial claims against Caribbean countries. There is one against Guyana for the Essequibo area—five-eights of the country, and rich in oil, gold, diamonds, and other resources. A claim exists for Bird Island, a small uninhabited island over which Dominica has jurisdiction. There was a dispute with Trinidad and Tobago over the Gulf of Paria.[56] Venezuela also has claims against Colombia for the Gulf of Venezuela, and against the Netherlands for part of the Netherlands Antilles.

Venezuela's dealings with the countries with which it has disputes have varied among the countries, as well as over time. In relation to Guyana, the active pursuit of the claim grew to intimidation and aggression during the presidency of Raul Leoni (1964–1969). In 1966, for example, troops occupied Ankoko Island, in Guyana's northwest region. Venezuelan President Rafael Caldera (1969–1974) adopted a more conciliatory approach. This was the period of the Protocol of Port of Spain (1970), which froze the dispute for twelve years. Relations were stable during the tenure of Carlos Andrés Pérez (1974–1979), and there was tension during the latter part of the Herrera Campins administration (1979–1983). Relations between the two countries improved during the rule of Jaime Lusinchi (1983–1988).

The upswing in relations started by Lusinchi continued under his successor, Carlos Andrés Pérez, and under President Desmond Hoyte, Guyana's leader between 1985 and 1992. The status of the dispute as of fall 1992 was one where the Good Offices Representative of the United Nations Secretary General was progressing with efforts to help the parties find a peaceful settlement. The representative is Alister McIntyre, former Secretary General of CARICOM, former Assistant Secretary General of the United Nations, and currently Vice Chancellor of UWI. Both Guyana and Venezuela are satisfied with McIntyre's efforts and with their improved relations.

Relations with Trinidad and Tobago also improved to the point where a maritime treaty was signed in Caracas on April 18, 1990, by Trinidad and Tobago Prime Minister A.N.R. Robinson, and President Pérez. The treaty abrogated a 1942 agreement between Venezuela and Britain. According to the Trinidad and Tobago Foreign Minister, the 1990 treaty results in a small northward shift of the 1942 submarine boundary line "in the Serpent's Mount and along the Columbus Channel" in favor of Venezuela, amounting to forty square nautical miles. Venezuela compensates for this acquisition by conceding forty-four square miles of territory off the southeast coast of Tobago where the Trinidad and Tobago government had previously granted several oil concessions without clearly delimiting the territory.[57]

Venezuela's improved relations with Guyana and Trinidad and Tobago reflect general advances with the Caribbean in recent times. Venezuela claims the distinction of being the first Latin American member of the Caribbean Development Bank (CDB). In addition to several bilateral state visits and agreements, a significant joint meeting was held in Tobago in August 1989. It involved the leaders of Barbados, Guyana, Jamaica, St. Vincent and the Grenadines, Trinidad and Tobago, and Venezuela. They agreed on stronger Caribbean-Venezuelan cooperation in technology, trade, transport and communications, education, mineral exploration, and other areas. They also agreed to establish a special cooperation committee bringing together Brazil, Colombia, Venezuela, and CARICOM in pursuit of greater Latin-American-Caribbean cooperation.[58]

As noted above, observer status was granted to Venezuela in several CARICOM institutions in 1990. Pérez also participated in the 1991 CARICOM Summit in St. Kitts-Nevis from July 2 to 4, 1991. He signed several agreements, including one for one-way free trade by CARICOM into Venezuela. Pérez also indicated that "Venezuela aspires to change its role of Observer to full membership of CARICOM."[59] Three months later Venezuela formally requested full membership in CARICOM in a letter to Trinidad and Tobago Prime Minister A.N.R. Robinson. The speed of Pérez's action astounded many Caribbean leaders. As one diplomat told me, "We know they wanted membership, but nobody expected that they would go right back home and send the application." The application was to be discussed by CARICOM leaders at their 1992 intersessional meeting. That meeting was held on February 26, 1992, in Jamaica, but no action was taken on the matter.

Extra-Regional Powers

There are several countries outside the Caribbean area with interest in the Commonwealth Caribbean. This interest derives from the strategic significance of the area in hemispheric or global terms, and from other factors. Among these states are Canada, Britain, France, and the Netherlands. They have clearly defined Caribbean policies and their actions affect the region's security.

Canada

Thomas Anderson made the important point that "in terms of strategic location or military capability, Canada is not an important geopolitical factor in the Caribbean."[60] Yet, as Kari Levitt, perhaps Canada's best known Caribbean scholar, declared:

> For Canada, the Commonwealth Caribbean constitutes perhaps the only place in the world where Canada enjoys a "presence," in the international relations sense of the term. The priority accorded to the Commonwealth Caribbean, "in the overall external policy of Canada" ... bear[s] testimony to the fact that Canada places an importance on its relations with the countries of the English-speaking Caribbean that is altogether disproportionate to their small size, and their rapidly diminishing importance in terms of trade and investment.[61]

This paradox is explained by the history of close Canadian-Caribbean trading relations, a wealth of trust and confidence by Caribbean leaders in Canadian policy and conduct over the years, and close contacts between Caribbean and Canadian leaders. One Canadian diplomat explained the impact of contacts between leaders in recounting the story behind the financing of the Grantly Adams International Airport in Barbados. Errol Barrow and Pierre Trudeau, then Prime Ministers of Barbados and Canada, respectively, had built up close personal and official relations from association in Commonwealth circles. They met at a traffic light in Toronto in the early 1980s, and during a brief conversation that ensued, Barrow indicated that airport financing was one of his reasons for visiting. Canada's commitment to assist was made there and then.[62] Canada enjoys a favorable image in the Caribbean. It has no territorial designs, and aid is not given with political conditions. Canada-Caribbean trade has diminished over the last decade, but since commerce is not the dominant motive, contacts are still extensive in several areas.

Within Canada there are three schools of foreign and security policy thinking about the Caribbean: the defense and security school; the peace and development school; and the national interest school. The first stresses the linkages between Western strategic interests and the Caribbean. The second is suspicious of military security assistance and regards economic cooperation as the best security guarantee. The third argues for a contribution to Caribbean security, but it seeks this contribution in the context of Canada's emphasis on economic and diplomatic cooperation, and non-entanglement in disputes that could damage the country's high reputation and positive image.[63]

Canada's Caribbean posture still follows the enunciations of former Prime Minister Pierre Trudeau. He felt countries have the right to follow whatever ideological path their people decide. For him, the internal systems adopted by countries of Latin America and the Caribbean, whatever their nature, do not in themselves threaten the Western hemisphere. "It is only when countries adopt systems which deliberately inject East-West rivalry or seek to destabilize neighbors that a threat is posed."[64] This perception guides the pursuit of what is essentially the third of the schools noted above. Canada offers security assistance, although in the context of development assistance, in communications, health and hospitals, airport security and maintenance, education, fire fighting, and disaster preparedness. It also provides police and coast guard training, pilot training, and training in infantry and combat driving, among other things. There is also intelligence sharing through the International Criminal Police Organization. Since 1982 the emphasis has been on coast guard training through the Caribbean Maritime Training Assistance Program (CMTAP). The program first provided assistance to Dominica, Grenada, St. Lucia, St. Kitts-Nevis, St. Vincent and the Grenadines, Antigua-Barbuda, Montserrat, Barbados, Trinidad and Tobago, and Jamaica. It has since been expanded to cater to Anguilla, Belize, the British Virgin Islands, the Caymans, and the Turks and Caicos.[65]

Canada's economic security assistance was boosted dramatically in 1990 when it "forgave" Can. $182 million in debt by CARICOM countries. The debt forgiveness was announced following a meeting of Caribbean leaders with Canadian Prime Minister Brian Mulroney in

Barbados on March 19 and 20, 1990. Little more than half of the debt was owed by Jamaica—Can. $93.4 million. Guyana had the second largest liability—Can. $37.2 million. The other countries owed as follows: Barbados—Can. $23.4; Trinidad and Tobago—Can. $7.2 million; Antigua-Barbuda—Can. $5.1 million; Dominica—Can. $1.6 million; St. Vincent and the Grenadines—Can. $966,000; Grenada—Can. $774,000; Montserrat—Can. $632,000; and St. Lucia—Can. $453,000. The Can. $182 million was originally given over a period of years under highly concessional terms, repayable over fifty years without interest.[66]

Britain, France, and the Netherlands

The historical, political, military, and economic connections involving Britain, France, and the Netherlands in the Caribbean are too well known to require examination here. And although the passage of time has witnessed a contraction of their power and influence, these countries still have contacts and interests in the region.

Politically, all three have Caribbean dependencies. These differ both in their constitutional and administrative linkages with the "motherland," and in the degree of "maturation" toward independence. The British dependencies are Anguilla, Bermuda, the British Virgin Islands, Montserrat, the Turks and Caicos Islands, and the Cayman Islands. All of these territories have internal self-government. Yet, whereas in the past it was assumed that sooner or later the dependencies would progress to independence, the future of these dependencies seems to be one of indefinite British control, and by their own choice.

In the French Caribbean, the *vieilles colonies* of Guadeloupe, Martinique, and Guyane (French Guiana) were transformed into *Départements d'Outre-Mer* (DOMs) in 1946. The DOMs are spread over an area of 92,882 km², about 8.4 percent of the entire territory of France. While there are nationalist forces in some places, most people seem desirous of retaining French citizenship and departmental status. This is primarily because a more credible alternative is yet to be presented. Citizens in the DOMs do not obtain socioeconomic benefits from the French republic comparable with those in Europe. However, even with the recent recession and consequent budgetary cutbacks, France did not reduce financial outlays to the DOMs. According to one observer, "Between 1985 and 1987, when budgets were being tightly controlled in many ministries, public expenditure in the DOM increased by a third." This was attributed to "both the strategic importance of the DOM for France and the concomitant commitment to continue making efforts to improve living standards in these territories."[67]

Presently, Bonaire, Curaçao, Saba, St. Eustatius, and St. Maarten comprise the Netherlands Antilles. Aruba gained a separate status on January 1, 1986, and will become independent in 1996. There are three levels of government over the Dutch territories: the Kingdom (the Netherlands, the Netherlands Antilles, and Aruba), the Land (the Antilles-of-five), and the individual islands. Foreign affairs and defense are handled by the Kingdom. Theoretically, the Land controls judicial, postal, and financial affairs, while the islands deal with education, economic development, and so forth. However, there is often no precise definition of jurisdiction, resulting in considerable overlapping and inefficiency.[68]

In the military area, I dealt with Britain's military commitments in the region in chapter three and elsewhere. France maintains naval basing operations in Guadeloupe, but its Caribbean interests are far more extensive. In stressing the strategic importance of the area to France, Helen Hintjens noted:

> Both Martinique and Guadeloupe are essential stopping-off points in the transportation of nuclear weapons to the test sites in the French Pacific (Mururoa). Apart from the nuclear test sites in Polynesia, the CSG (*Centre Spatial Guyanais*—Guyana Space Center) in Guyane is the most important strategic asset of France overseas. The location of the Kourou base (near the Equator, outside the cyclonic belt, and on the eastern rim of the Atlantic Ocean) makes it ideal for rocket launching. By 1989 thirty Ariane rockets had been launched, and the Ariane space program controlled almost two-thirds of the world market in commercial satellite launches.[69]

Since the decommissioning of the Kammaguir base in Algeria in 1964 following Algeria's independence, the Kourou base has become key to French and European aerospace programs as well as telecommunications and military intelligence systems. These include *Syracuse 1* and *Helios*, the Columbus space station, and the *Hermes* space craft. The French military establishment in the Caribbean is partly intended to protect these installations and facilities, and partly to permit France a certain global reach. French military presence in the region involves about 9,000 troops drawn from their army, air force, navy, and gendarmerie. This permanent force is commanded by a full general, designated *Commandant Superieur des Forces Armées Antilles-Guyane* and called ComSup for short. He is stationed in Martinique.

This French Caribbean army has an estimated ground force of 4,700 men. The operational forces comprise one marine regiment, two marine battalions, one logistical unit, and one Foreign Legion regiment. The gendarmerie of 1,630 has a special operations unit designed for terrorist, riot, and hostage operations. They have their own helicopters, armored cars, and boats. The air force complement, about 320 in 1992, is equipped with conventional armed helicopters and transport aircraft. The 700-member navy component has two high-speed patrol boats, and transport and supply boats, in addition to light ships. Part of the mission of the French Caribbean navy is to protect France's 300,000 km^2 exclusive maritime economic zone in the area, and to undertake a host of other functions, including search and rescue, antipollution operations, and mail delivery.[70]

It is difficult to fault the assertion that "In pragmatic terms, the Netherlands Antilles and Aruba constitute a liability rather than an asset to the Netherlands."[71] Nevertheless, as a member of NATO, Holland has commitments that make access to the Caribbean a great advantage. Partly because of this, the Netherlands retains a naval basing presence in Curaçao. In 1982 they also reactivated the 336th Royal Netherlands Air Force squadron and deployed it there.[72]

Conlusion

The geopolitical milieu in which Caribbean countries exist is such that several states, both contiguous and distant, have capabilities, interests, and stakes in the area. These countries influence Commonwealth Caribbean developments generally and its security pursuits in particular. They have both capability and the will to act. They have done so—and will continue to do so—according to their national interests, and because they can subordinate Commonwealth Caribbean countries to those interests.

The United States, of course, is *the* dominant state in the area. We saw in chapter two what dominance means in terms of influence on elite perceptions. United States economic and military might is made all the more overwhelming by that country's proximity to the Caribbean. Guyana, the CARICOM country furthest south of the United States, is only 4,027 miles away from it. (Interestingly enough, it takes longer to fly from New York to California by commercial jet than it does to fly from New York to Guyana.) The Bahamas, the closest country, is merely 1,532 miles away.[73] Moreover, technological innovations in transport and communications are progressively making distance relatively unimportant. However, it is not merely the geographic proximity of a dominant state that influences the security perceptions and pursuits of subordinate ones. As the above discussion suggests, historical contacts, trade patterns, transportation and communications linkages, the strategic interests of the larger state, and ideology are all considerations that affect the nature and extent of the geography-security nexus and the policy options that small states adopt. (Incidentally, this is also true of geopolitical relationships among big powers.)

Small states cherish their sovereignty. Their leaders sometimes attempt to assert it in ways antithetical to the interests of proximate big powers or of the dominant state in the area. Ideological, strategic, or other factors may cause a dominant state to thwart or destabilize sovereign pursuits that actually or potentially threaten its interests. There is abundant evidence of this in the Caribbean, as we have seen in other chapters. United States intervention and destabilization are, perhaps, the most dramatic actions in this regard. Therefore, whether and how a small state deploys its forces, the kind of military relations it maintains, the quantity, nature, and source of its arms, and the character of its political alignments internationally would be of direct interest to the dominant state and to proximate big powers. Caribbean small states have to be mindful of such concerns by the United States and by proximate, and even distant, big and middle powers.

Yet, as we have seen above, not all the actions of countries with geopolitical and other interests in the Caribbean have negative-sum consequences. Canada is the outstanding example of positive-sum action. Relations with Cuba, Mexico, Venezuela, and other middle powers have paid off in economic areas, despite apprehensions about Cuba and Venezuela in parts of the region. In addition, disdain for United States arrogance, its intervention, and its destabilization should not cloud recognition of the positive aspects of Caribbean-United States relations over the years. We saw some of this also in previous chapters.

For all of its importance, geopolitics helps us to understand only some dimensions of the Caribbean security situation. To complete the picture we must add a fourth conceptual reference point to the three examined thus far (perception, capability, geopolitics). This fourth one is ideology, the subject of the next chapter.

Notes

1. See *South America, Central America, and the Caribbean 1988*, London: Europa Publications, 1987, pp. 197–98, 203.

2. See Lars Schoultz, *National Security and United States Policy toward Latin America*, Princeton, NJ: Princeton University Press, 1987, pp. 149–51; and the *McGraw-Hill Encyclopedia of Science and Technology*, 6th ed., New York: McGraw-Hill Books, 1987, p. 232.

3. Tom Barry, Beth Wood, and Deb Preusch, *The Other Side of Paradise*, New York: Grove Press, 1984, p. 89.

4. Some other major "choke points" are: the South China Sea; the North Sea; the Mediterranean Sea; the Suez Canal; the Straits of Malacca; the Horn of Africa; the Straits of Gibraltar; the Sri Lanka Straits; and the Cape of Good Hope. See Jack Child, *Geopolitics and Conflict in South America*, New York: Praeger, 1985, pp. 24–25.

5. U.S. Congress, House, Committee on Merchant Marine and Fisheries, *Strategic Importance of the Panama Canal*, Hearing, Subcommittee on Panama Canal/Outer Continental Shelf, 101st Congress, 1st. Sess., November 2, 1989, p. 4.

6. Thomas D. Anderson, *Geopolitics of the Caribbean*, New York: Praeger, 1984, p. 17; and *Strategic Importance of the Panama Canal*, p. 58.

7. *Strategic Importance of the Panama Canal*. pp. 61, 62. Also see Schoultz, *National Security*, pp. 218–22; and Anderson, *Geopolitics*, pp. 18–20.

8. Mary Day Kent, "Panama: Protecting the United States Backyard," in Joseph Gerson and Bruce Birchard, eds., *The Sun Never Sets*, Boston: South End Press, 1991, p. 333.

9. See *Strategic Importance of the Panama Canal*, pp. 61–62, 5–6; and Schoultz, *National Security*, pp. 216–18.

10. David Ronfeldt, *Geopolitics, Security, and U.S. Strategy in the Caribbean Basin*, Rand Corporation, R–2997-AF/FC, November 1983, pp. 7–8; and David Ronfeldt, "Rethinking the Monroe Doctrine," *ORBIS* 28 (Winter 1985): 687–88.

11. Richard Sim and James Anderson, "The Caribbean Strategic Vacuum," *Conflict Studies* 121 (August 1980): 1.

12. Schoultz, *National Security*, p. 155.

13. Ibid. pp. 150–54.

14. See Rex A. Hudson, "Strategic and Regional Security Perspectives," in Sandra W. Meditz and Dennis M. Hanratty, eds., *Islands in the Commonwealth Caribbean*, Washington, D.C.: Library of Congress, 1989, pp. 589–91; and Schoultz, *National Security*, pp. 199–200.

15. See, for example, Michael C. Desch, "Turning the Caribbean Flank: Sea-Lane Vulnerability during a European War," *Survival* 29 (No. 6, 1987): 530.

16. Anderson, *Geopolitics*, p. 18.

17. Schoultz, *National Security*, p. 217.

18. Kent, "Panama," p. 333.

19. Thomas H. Moorer and Georges A. Fauriol, *Caribbean Basin Security,. The Washington Papers/104, Vol. XI, 1984, p. 16.*

20. *Facts on File*, vol. 51, No. 2645, August 1, 1991, p. 569.

21. Jorge Rodríguez Beruff, "Puerto Rico and the Militarization of the Caribbean 1979–1984," *Contemporary Marxism* 10 (1985): 74.

22. Humberto García Muñiz, "Decolonization, Demilitarization, and Denuclearization in the Caribbean," in Ivelaw L. Griffith, ed., *Strategy and Security in the Caribbean*, New York: Praeger, 1991, p. 38.

23. Ibid.

24. García Muñiz, p. 33; and telephone interviews with Janice Simms, Department of Defense Public Affairs Officer, August 30, 1991, and with Van Steuben, Naval Archivist, LANTCOM, September 13, 1991. For more on the U.S. military network in the Caribbean, see Schoultz, pp. 160–90; Kent; Jorge Rodríguez Beruff, "U.S. Caribbean Policy and Regional Militarization," in Augusto Varas, ed., *Hemispheric Security and U.S. Policy in Latin America*, Boulder, CO: Westview, 1989, esp. pp. 105–15; and James R. Blaker, *United States Overseas Basing*, New York: Praeger, 1990, esp. pp. 9–132. For a concise description of the organization and functioning of the United States military establishment, both in policy and operational terms, see U.S. Department of Defense, *Office of the Secretary of Defense, Defense Agencies, and DOD Field Activities Organization and Functions Handbook*, Washington, D.C., April 1991.

25. See Francis X. Clines, "Five Asian Republics Join Slavs in Plan for Commonwealth Replacing the Soviet Union," *New York Times*, December 14, 1991, pp. 1, 6; and Francis X. Clines, "Soviet States Form Commonwealth without Clearly Defining its Powers," *New York Times*, December 22, 1991, pp. L1, L12.

26. See Gordon Sumner, "Strategic Military Issues for the Free World," in *The Caribbean Basin and Global Security: Strategic Implications of the Soviet Threat*, Report of a conference held by the International Security Council, Paris, France, 1985; Heinz Von Zur Gathen, "The Caribbean Basin and Global Strategy," in *The Caribbean Basin and Global Security*; and Timothy Ashby, *The Bear in the Backyard: Moscow's Caribbean Strategy*, Lexington, MA: Lexington Books, 1987.

27. The other theaters were the European subcontinent; the United States of America; the Middle East and the Horn of Africa; the South Atlantic; and South Asia. See Álvaro Valencia Tovar, "Soviet Strategy in the Caribbean," in *The Caribbean Basin and Global Strategy*, p. 11.

28. Howard Wiarda, Mark Falcoff, et al., *The Communist Challenge in the Caribbean and Central America*, Washington, D.C.: American Enterprise Institute, 1987, p. 16.

29. Edward González, *A Strategy for Dealing with Cuba*, Rand Corporation, R–2954-DOS/AF, September 1982, p. 288; and U.S. Congress, House, Committee on Foreign Affairs, *Soviet Posture in the Western Hemisphere*, Hearings, Subcommittee on Western Hemisphere Affairs, 99th Congress, 1st Sess., February 1985, p. 43.

30. See González, *A Strategy for Dealing with Cuba*, p. 3; Desch, "Turning the Caribbean Flank," p. 532; and Schoultz, *National Security*, p. 227.

31. U.S. Department of Defense, *Soviet Military Power 1990*, Washington,

D.C., 1990, p. 19; and personal communication from Donald R. Lenker, Chief Public Affairs Officer, Defense Intelligence Agency, July 10, 1991.

32. Thomas L. Friedman, "Gorbachev Says He's Ready to Pull Troops Out of Cuba and End Castro's Subsidy," *New York Times*, September 12, 1991, pp. A1, A12. Also see Craig R. Whitney, "Aid at Any Price," *New York Times*, September 12, 1991, p. A12; and David Binder, "The Cuban-Soviet Connection: 31 Year Irritant to the U.S.," *New York Times*, September 12, 1991, p. A12.

33. See Cole Blasier, *The Giants Rival: The USSR and Latin America*, Pittsburgh: University of Pittsburgh Press, 1983, pp. 103–28; and W. Raymond Duncan, *The Soviet Union and Cuba: Interests and Influences*, New York: Praeger, 1985, pp. 169–77.

34. See Ashby, pp. 93–98; and Anthony Payne, "The Foreign Policy of the People's Revolutionary Government," in Jorge Heine, ed., *A Revolution Aborted: The Lessons of Grenada*, Pittsburgh: University of Pittsburgh Press, 1991, pp. 93–98.

35. Mirlande Manigat, "Brazil and the Caribbean," in Jorge Heine and Leslie Manigat, eds., *The Caribbean and World Politics*, New York: Holmes and Meier, 1988, p. 262.

36. Interview with Amaury Bier, Brazil's Ambassador in the Eastern Caribbean, Bridgetown, Barbados, July 29, 1987. American diplomatic officials in the Caribbean also sought to dispel the notion of Brazil's subservience to American interests in the Caribbean. However, such notions are historically not unfounded. See Child, *Geopolitics and Conflict*, p. 35.

37. Anthony T. Bryan, "The Geopolitical Environment: Latin America," in Anthony T. Bryan, J. Edward Greene, and Timothy M. Shaw, eds., *Peace, Development, and Security in the Caribbean*, New York: St. Martin's Press, 1990, p. 98.

38. Leslie Manigat, "The Setting: Crisis, Ideology and Geopolitics," in *The Caribbean and World Politics*, pp. 67–68; and Mirlande Manigat, in Heine and Manigat, p. 269.

39. See "Brazilian Naval Vessels Arrive," *Guyana Chronicle*, January 18, 1992, p. 7.

40. See Leslie Manigat, "The Setting," p. 65; Fernando Cepeda, "Colombia: A Caribbean Vocation?" in *The Caribbean and World Politics*, pp. 248–52; and Andrés Serbín, *Caribbean Geopolitics: Toward Security Through Peace?* Boulder, CO: Lynne Rienner, 1990, p. 64.

41. Andrés Serbín, "The CARICOM States and the Group of Three: A New Partnership between Latin-American and the Non-Hispanic Caribbean?" *Journal of Interamerican Studies and World Affairs* 33 (Summer 1991): 65; and "CARICOM Plans its Common Market," *Latin American Weekly Report*, July 18, 1991 (WR–91–27): 9.

42. See Duncan, *The Soviet Union and Cuba*, pp. 119–90; Jorge Domínguez, "Cuba's Relation with Caribbean and Central American Countries," in Alan Adelman and Reid Reiding eds., *Confrontation in the Caribbean Basin*, Pittsburgh: University of Pittsburgh Press, 1984; and Anthony Maingot, "Cuba and the Commonwealth Caribbean: Playing the Cuba Card," in Barry Levine, ed., *The New Cuban Presence in the Caribbean*, Boulder, CO: Westview, 1983.

43. See "Visit to Cuba," *CARICOM Perspective* 50 & 51 (January-June 1991): 74; Sharief Khan, "Cuba Seeking Closer Regional Ties," *Stabroek News*,

September 12, 1991, pp. 1, 2; and "Guyana to Invest in Cuba," *New York Carib News*, September 24, 1991, p. 32.

44. "Jamaica: Change U.S.-Cuba Relations," *New York Carib News*, October 15, 1991, p. 30; "Trinidad Urges Support for Cuba," *New York Carib News*, October 15, 1991, p. 31; Canute James, "Neighbors Rally to Cuba's Call," *Financial Times* (London), October 17, 1991; and "Guyana Backs Lifting U.S. Trade Embargo," *Stabroek News*, October 1, 1991, p. 1.

45. See Duncan, *The Soviet Union and Cuba*, pp. 177–84.

46. Leslie Manigat, "The Setting," p. 42.

47. See U.S. Congress, House, Committee on Foreign Affairs, *The English-speaking Caribbean: Current Conditions and Implications for U.S. Policy*, Report by the Congressional Research Service for the Subcommittee on Western Hemisphere Affairs, 99th Congress, 1st Sess., Sept. 13, 1985, pp. 96–97.

48. Domínguez, "Cuba's Relations," p. 183; and Hudson, "Strategic and Regional Security Perspectives," pp. 620–21.

49. Leslie Manigat, "The Setting," p. 65. Also, see René Herrera and Mario Gómez, "The Policy of Mexico in the Caribbean Basin," in Adelman and Reading, *Confrontation in the Caribbean Basin*, pp. 29–30.

50. George W. Grayson, "The Joint Oil Facility: Mexican-Venezuelan Cooperation in the Caribbean," *Caribbean Review* 12 (No. 2, 1983): 20.

51. Ibid., p. 20.

52. "Jamaica, Mexico Sign Bilateral Agreements," *Jamaican Weekly Gleaner*, August 6, 1990, p. 9; and "Communiqué and Addresses—Eleventh Meeting of the Heads of Government of the Caribbean Community," *CARICOM Perspective* (Special Supplement) 49 (July-December 1990): 17.

53. Serbín, *Caribbean Geopolitics*, p. 65.

54. Orieste de Giacomo, Venezuela's Ambassador to Barbados, took pains to dispel such fears in an interview on August 13, 1987 in Bridgetown, Barbados.

55. "The Threat to the Caribbean Community: Speech of Dr. Eric Williams, Political Leader, at the Special Convention of the People's National Movement, Chaguaramas Convention Center, Trinidad, June 15, 1975," in Leslie F. Manigat, ed., *The Caribbean Yearbook of International Relations 1975*, St. Augustine, Trinidad: Institute of International Relations, 1976, pp. 600–601.

56. See Government of Guyana, Ministry of Foreign Affairs, *Memorandum on the Guyana/Venezuela Boundary*, Georgetown, 1981; Government of Venezuela, Ministry of Foreign Relations, *Summary of the Boundary Question with British Guiana, now Guyana*, Caracas, 1981; J. Braveboy-Wagner, *The Veneluela-Guyana Border Dispute*, Boulder, CO: Westview, 1984; Henry Gill, "Conflict in Trinidad and Tobago's Relations with Venezuela," in *Caribbean Yearbook of International Relations 1975*, esp. pp. 466–74, 481–85; Anselm Francis, "The Gulf of Paria: Area of Conflict," *Caribbean Affairs* 3 (January-March 1990): 26–37; and "The Threat to the Caribbean Community," in Manigat, *The Caribbean Yearbook of International Relations 1975*.

57. Government of Trinidad and Tobago, Parliament, *Speaking Notes for Dr. the Hon. Sahadeo Basdeo, Minister of External Affairs and International Trade on the 1990 Trinidad and Tobago-Venezuela Maritime Boundary Agreement*, Trinidad and Tobago House of Assembly, June 18, 1990, p. 2. I am grateful to Patricia Phillips of the Trinidad and Tobago Mission to the United Nations for

copies of the 1990 treaty and Dr. Basdeo's notes.

58. Lindsay Mackoon, "A Meeting of Neighbors," *Caribbean Contact*, September, 1989, p. 2.

59. "CARICOM, Venezuela Sign Trade Pact," *Trinidad Guardian*, July 2, 1991, p. 1; "Pérez Interested in Full Membership in CARICOM," *Trinidad Express*, July 2, 1991, p. 4; and "Pérez Ends Historic State Visit to St. Kitts," *Trinidad Guardian*, July 3, 1991, p. 6.

60. Anderson, *Geopolitics of the Caribbean*, p. 142.

61. Kari Levitt, "Canada and the Caribbean: An Assessment," in *The Caribbean and World Politics*, p. 229.

62. Interview with James Puddington, Counselor, Canadian High Commission to Barbados, St. Michael, Barbados, August 4, 1987.

63. Steven Baranyi and Edgar Dosman, "Canada and the Security of the Commonwealth Caribbean," Paper presented at Conference on Peace, Development, and Security in the Caribbean Basin: Perspectives to the Year 2000, Kingston, Jamaica, March 22–25, 1987, pp. 4–5. A revised version of this paper appears as chapter five of the conference volume, *Peace, Development, and Security in the Caribbean*.

64. Levitt, "Canada and the Caribbean," p. 244.

65. For more on Canadian-Caribbean security cooperation see Baranyi and Dosman, cited in note 63; and Levitt, ibid., esp. pp. 229–39.

66. Rickey Singh, "Canada Eases Caribbean Debts," *Caribbean Contact*, April 1990, p. 1.

67. Helen Hintjens, "France in the Caribbean," in Paul Sutton, ed., *Europe and the Caribbean*, London: Macmillan Caribbean, 1991, p. 65.

68. Rosemarijn Hoefte and Gert Oostindie, "The Netherlands and the Dutch Caribbean: Dilemmas of Decolonization," in *Europe and the Caribbean*, pp. 89–90.

69. Hintjens, "France in the Caribbean," p. 64.

70. Michel L. Martin, "French Presence and Strategic Interests in the Caribbean," Paper Delivered at the Fourth Meeting of the Caribbean International Relations Working Group of the Latin American Social Sciences Council, St. Thomas, United States Virgin Islands, June 9–13, 1992, pp. 4–7.

71. Heofte and Oostindie, "The Netherlands and the Dutch Caribbean," p. 90.

72. Paul Seidenman and David Spanovich, "Dutch Involvement in Latin America," in William Perry and Peter Wehner, eds., *The Latin-American Policies of U.S. Allies*, New York: Praeger, 1985, p. 85.

73. The distances between the United States and the other Caribbean countries are as follows: Antigua-Barbuda, 2,803 miles; Barbados, 3,334 miles; Belize, 2,660 miles; Dominica, 3,189 miles; Grenada, 3,336 miles; Jamaica, 2,315 miles; St. Kitts-Nevis, 2,767 miles; St. Lucia, 3,175 miles; St. Vincent and the Grenadines, 3,249 miles; Trinidad and Tobago, 3,487 miles. Distances are calculated on the basis of air distances between Washington and the respective Caribbean capitals from Gary Fitzpatrick and Marily Modelin, *Direct Line Distances*, Metuchen, NJ: Scarecrow Press, 1986.

8 IDEOLOGY IN THE CARIBBEAN

Many of the internal security problems experienced by Caribbean states have involved ideological disputes. Ideological differences also affected regional harmony in the late 1970s and early 1980s. This disrupted the CARICOM machinery, with the result that no summit was held between 1975 and 1982. Moreover, as I noted in chapter two and elsewhere, the socialist posture of Guyana and Jamaica incurred United States destabilization during the 1970s. In Guyana's case, it carried over into the early 1980s.

The rise to power of the leftist New Jewel Movement (NJM) in Grenada in 1979 led to considerable antipathy toward the leaders of the People's Revolutionary Government (PRG) by other Caribbean heads. Especially in the Eastern Caribbean, these leaders were mostly conservative and thus disdained the PRG's Marxist orientation. In addition, it was ideologically based factionalism within the PRG in 1983 that precipitated the crisis in Grenada, leading to United States intervention and the abortion of their revolution. Understanding the linkage between ideology and security in the region is, therefore, not merely useful, but necessary. This requires an initial examination of the region's ideological profile.

Ideological Doctrines In The Caribbean

In historical terms, ideological doctrines in the Caribbean may be placed in two "traditions." The first developed in the context of the Old Representative System, the system of colonial government that predominated in the seventeenth and eighteenth centuries. This tradition was confined to the white planter class. It elaborated a philosophy in defense of the economic and political privileges of that class, following efforts by the British imperial government to tighten control over the colonies for economic and political reasons. Edward Long (1734–1813) and Bryan Edwards (1743–1800), two of the earliest and most important writers on Caribbean politics and society, represented the core beliefs of that tradition. Denis Benn argues: "Both Long and Edwards attempted to systematize the world view of the planter class of the period, with whom they were closely identified and, as such, may be seen as ideologists of that class."[1]

The second tradition developed in the framework of the Crown Colony system of colonial government. Under this system the elected legislature was eliminated. Legislative as well as executive power was vested in a colonial governor assisted by an appointed Legislative Council. Of course, the actions of the governor and the council were subject to the veto of the imperial government, exercised by the Secretary of State for the Colonies.[2] Marcus Garvey (1887–1940) of Jamaica, and C.L.R. James (1901–1989) and Eric Williams (1911–1981) of Trinidad and Tobago are considered the three major intellectual influences on this tradition. Garvey influenced race consciousness as the basis for political action. James's role was in evoking radical intellectual discourse based on Marxist and neo-Marxist interpretations of reality. And Williams epitomized "the nationalist intellectual ethos which sees the local community as an indivisible entity and as the ultimate basis of political allegiance . . . "[3] Benn explains the development of social and political doctrines by showing how colonial history gave rise to a series of intellectual and political ferments out of which grew various doctrinal propositions.

Political ideas in the second tradition were shaped mainly by three ideological currents, especially after the Second World War: anticolonial nationalism; Black Power; and Marxism-Leninism.[4] The first was facilitated by the decline of the British empire, the advent of universal adult suffrage, and the rise of mass based parties. Nationalist pursuits led to political independence, beginning with Jamaica and Trinidad and Tobago in 1962. Some countries subsequently altered their constitutional and administrative systems to reflect what the leaders considered necessary or appropriate for the fulfillment of new national ideals.[5] Guyana stands out in this regard.[6]

Undoubtedly, nationalism led to significant transformation of both state and society. But as the late Gordon Lewis warned, "nationalism can be conflictive as well as creative." Quite accurately, he argued:

> It [nationalism] can encourage a narrow minded "my country right or wrong" attitude in both leaders and electorates. Especially in small ministates as in the Caribbean it can give rise to an inward-turned, psychologically crippling insularity of temper, mixed with feelings of suspicion and jealousy of neighboring countries. It can persuade governments, in their national economic policies, to embrace protectionist policies, thus jeopardizing regional economic integration. It also burdens them with a whole set of the paraphernalia of sovereignty which is cumbersome and costly.[7]

Black Power, the second of the post-war currents, was affected by several political and doctrinal developments, including Garveyism and the United States civil rights movement. It found expression in symbolic slogans such as "Black is Beautiful," in new and renewed pride in African heritage, and new interest in black history. It heightened political activism, leading to the formation of several black-based parties and interest groups. It also contributed to the 1970 crisis in Trinidad and Tobago, one aspect of which was examined in chapter four. Poetry, art, and theater, music, and literature were all means through which Black Power found expression. Among the more noted writers in this regard were Lloyd Best, C.L.R. James, Amié Césaire, Jean Price Mars, Walter Rodney, George Padmore, and Eric Williams.

The experience of countries in the Caribbean and elsewhere has shown that emphasis on race could cause neglect of social class issues. The result could be that class conflict becomes obscured by ethnic differentiation. Gordon Lewis correctly observed that Black Power has often been used as a slogan for political empowerment of the black bourgeoisie who are not necessarily better rulers than the white bourgeoisie they supplant. As a matter of fact, their better appreciation of black psychology has often facilitated more successful class suppression. Moreover, in plural societies such as Guyana and Trinidad and Tobago, Black Power often aggravated tensions between people of African descent and other non-white groups.[8]

The last of the post-war ideological currents led to a multiplicity of socialist "tendencies" and "interpretations," including Fabian socialism, Trotskyism, Leninism, Democratic socialism, Cooperative socialism, and Scientific socialism. Some of these tendencies and interpretations found practical expression in attempts to build socialism in places where adherents secured political power: Grenada, Guyana, and Jamaica. The tendencies and orientations have been supported by a variety of political parties and interest groups, some of which have been pro-Soviet and others Maoist. Some have been pro-Albanian; still others have been pro-Cuban. Some have defined themselves as "independent."

Among the more known parties and groups have been the National Joint Action Committee (NJAC) of Trinidad and Tobago, the Working People's Alliance (WPA) of Guyana, the People's National Party (PNP) of Jamaica, the People's National Congress (PNC) of Guyana, Movement for National Liberation (MONALI) of Barbados, the Workers' Party of Jamaica (WPJ), the Workers' Party of Barbados (WPB), the United Labor Front (ULF) of Trinidad and Tobago, the Youlou United Liberation Movement (YULIMO) of St. Vincent and the Grenadines, the Antigua-Caribbean Liberation Movement (ACLM), the NJM, the St. Lucia Labor Party (SLP), the People's Progressive Party (PPP) of Guyana, the Vanguard Party of the Bahamas, and the United People's Movement (UPM) of St. Vincent and the Grenadines.[9]

There have been several assessments of the ideological climate of the contemporary Caribbean. In focusing on the "Caribbean left spectrum," Perry Mars found three kinds of tendencies: the reformist; the radical; and the revolutionary. The reformists espoused piecemeal evolutionary change, while the latter two articulated fundamental structural transformation in the political, economic, and social aspects of state and society. The difference between the radicals and the revolutionaries lay in the different degrees of commitment to class struggle, with the revolutionary advocates offering more specificity and consistency about it.[10] The three Marxist-Leninist tendencies found institutional expression in various parts of the Caribbean, but especially in the larger countries. Mars found that the PNC and the PNP demonstrated reformist tendencies. The WPA, the ULF, and NJAC fell in the radical category, and the PPP and the WPJ were representative of the revolutionary one.[11]

Carl Stone offered four ideological trends in describing the ideological profile of the Caribbean Basin: the conservative (example, Haiti); the reformist (example, Barbados); the socialist (example, Guyana); and the Marxist (example Cuba). The first trend focused on economic growth and spurned strategies to alter the society or its institutions fundamentally, or to redistribute income or wealth in ways significant enough to alter the balance of class forces. The second operated on the assumptions and postulates of the first, but agitated for social change to relieve the poor. The third trend advocated the redistribution of wealth and power in favor of the poor through cooperatives, land reform, nationalization, and social welfare programs. The fourth went beyond the third, seeking to establish a planned economy.[12]

Lloyd Searwar, on the other hand, suggested that there were two ideological "stances" in the region: one radical; the other conservative. The first was "characterized by objectives which require levels of change with a focus on state action for development, usually projected in terms of 'socialist' ideology." The second involved acceptance and pursuit of market economies as the prime development instrument. Guyana (under Burnham) demonstrated the first, and Jamaica (under Seaga) the second.[13]

The typologies by Mars, Stone, and Searwar are all excellent analytic interpretations of the Caribbean scene, although in focusing only on the "left" Mars neglected a sizable part of the political spectrum. They go beyond probing doctrinal nuances to consider questions of "ideology in politics" in the sense used by Giovanni Sartori.[14] Moreover, they all pay attention to the links between internal political action and international factors that affect Caribbean societies. However, apart from Searwar's analysis, these assessments reflect the region's political and ideological matrix during the 1970s and the early 1980s. This suggests the need for an additional sketch of the region's ideological-political scene.

As Table 8.1 indicates (see page 222), the 1970s witnessed the empowerment of several leftist parties. Some of them experimented with different forms of socialism. In 1970 Forbes Burnham of Guyana began his "peaceful" revolution in the experiment with Cooperative Socialism.[15] Michael Manley's rise to power in 1972 saw the beginning of Democratic Socialism in Jamaica.[16] And the NJM coup in 1979 led to the launching of Grenada's non-capitalist revolution.[17] As Table 8.2 shows (see page 223), these experiments had differing economic and political features.

Socialist-oriented parties also ruled for short periods in Antigua-Barbuda, Dominica, St. Lucia, and St. Vincent and the Grenadines during the 1970s. Moreover, there were socialist or socialist-oriented groups that influenced the region's leftist posture through eloquent

Table 8.1 Caribbean Ruling Parties and Postures, 1972–1992

COUNTRY	1972 PARTY	POSTURE	1977 PARTY	POSTURE	1982 PARTY	POSTURE	1987 PARTY	POSTURE	1992 PARTY	POSTURE
Antigua-Barbuda	Progressive Labor Party	S-R	Antigua Labor Party	C-C	Antigua Labor Party	C-C	Antigua Labor Party	C-C	Antigua Labor Party	C-C
Bahamas	Progressive Liberal Party	C-L	Progressive Liberal Party	C-L	Progressive Liberal Party	C-L	Progressive Liberal Party	C-L	Free National Movement	C-C
Barbados	Democratic Labor Party	C-L	Barbados Labor Party	C-C	Barbados Labor Party	C-C	Democratic Labor Party	C-L	Democratic Labor Party	C-L
Belize	People's United Party	C-L	People's United Party	C-L	People's United Party	C-L	United Democratic Party	C-C	People's United Party	C-L
Dominica	Dominica Labor Party	S-R	Dominica Labor Party	S-R	Dominica Freedom Party	C-C	Dominica Freedom Party	C-C	Dominica Freedom Party	C-C
Grenada	Grenada United Labor Party	C-L	Grenada United Labor Party	C-L	New Jewel Movement	S-Ra	People's National Party	C-C	National Democratic Congress	C-C
Guyana	People's National Congress	S-R	People's National Congress	S-R	People's National Congress	S-R	People's National Congress	C-L	People's Progressive Party	C-L?
Jamaica	People's National Party	S-R	People's National Party	S-R	Jamaica Labor Party	C-C	Jamaica Labor Party	C-C	People's National Party	C-L
St. Kitts-Nevis	Labor Party	S-R	Labor Party	S-R	People's Action Movement	C-C	People's Action Movement	C-C	People's Action Movement	C-C
St. Lucia	United Workers' Party	C-C	United Workers' Party	C-C	Progressive Labor Party	S-R	United Workers' Party	C-C	United Workers' Party	C-C
St. Vincent & The Grenadines	People's Political Party	C-C	St. Vincent Labor Party	S-R	St. Vincent Labor Party	S-R	New Democratic Party	C-L	New Democratic Party	C-L
Trinidad & Tobago	People's National Movement	C-L	People's National Movement	C-L	People's National Movement	C-L	National Alliance for Reconstruction	C-L	People's National Movement	C-L

C-C Capitalist-Conservative
C-L Capitalist-Liberal
S-R Socialist-Reformist
S-Ra Socialist-Radical

Sources: Arthur S. Banks, ed., *Political Handbook of the World*, Binghamton, N.Y.: State University of New York at Binghamton, various years; Europa Publications, *The Europa Year Book*, London: Europa Publications, various years; Foreign and Commonwealth Office, *The Commonwealth Year Book 1991*, London: Her Majesty's Stationary Office, 1991; *New York Carib News*, 1992; *Guyana Chronicle*, 1992.

Table 8.2

Main Features of Caribbean Socialist Regimes

SOCIALIST FEATURES	GRENADA	GUYANA	JAMAICA
ECONOMIC			
State Ownership	Low	High	Medium
Economic System	Market	Market	Market
Policy Priority	Redistribution	State Ownership	Redistribution
External Economic Ties	Capitalist	Capitalist	Capitalist
POLITICAL			
International Alignment	East	Non-Aligned	Non-Aligned
Support Basis	Youth	Race	Class
Political Style	Limited Participatory	Authoritarian	Participatory
Individual Freedom	Low	Low	Medium
Power Structure	Party-State	Liberal-Democratic	Party-State

Source: Carl Stone, "Wither Caribbean Socialism? Grenada, Jamaica, and Guyana in Perspective," in Jorge Heine, ed., *A Revolution Aborted: The Lessons of Grenada*, Pittsburgh, PA: University of

articulation of socialist doctrine and through political activism, although they held no state power. Included here were the WPJ, the WPA, the PPP, and the ACLM. However, by the mid-1980s the ascendancy of the left had given way to shifts to the right; liberal and conservative capitalists had gained control of both state power and the ideological agenda in the region.

United States destabilization, which was discussed in chapter two and elsewhere, paid the United States dividends in both Guyana and Jamaica. It aided curtailment of foreign investment and assistance, aggravated domestic labor and political disputes, and it created a negative political press. Guyana's own economic mismanagement and the authoritarian practices of the Burnham regime also helped to increase the economic deprivation there. Consequently, political discontent increased. Problems were compounded by adverse international public opinion and the negative impact of the global economic recession.

Because of all this, following Burnham's death in August 1985 his successors were forced to abandon the socialist experiment, long deemed a fraud by some analysts.[18] Burnham's successor initially paid allegiance to Burnham's ideals and programs, but the scope of the failure and the compelling necessity for change were soon impressed on him, leading to drastic domestic and foreign policy changes. These included privatization, pursuit of foreign investment, rapprochement with the United States and the IMF, electoral reforms, and the easing of press and other restrictions. The reforms were such that when the first set of free and fair elections in more than two decades were held on October 5, 1992, the ruling P.N.C. lost power.[19] In the case of Jamaica, several factors other than United States destabilization contributed to the failure of the socialist experiment. Included here were the international recession, the high incidence of crime, and self-destructive political violence. The subculture of violence was reflected in holdups, arson, shoot-outs, and other criminal activity. The nature of the violence became political around the times of general elections and later resumed the character of general social crime.

This was the pattern around the elections of 1972, 1976, and 1980. As Neville Duncan observed, "Indeed the six-month period leading to the 1980 general elections constituted an unbridled orgy of partisan violence in which over 800 persons were killed, including a PNP candidate. This was virtually a civil war in all important urban centers in Jamaica . . ."[20] The net result of all this was the disastrous defeat of Michael Manley and the PNP at the October 30, 1980, elections. Democratic Socialism was, thus, dead, despite Manley's return to power in February 1989. As we saw in chapter five, on his return Manley not only abandoned his earlier postulates and programs, but began adopting economic and political positions that challenged the conservatism of his predecessor and erstwhile ideological opposite, Edward Seaga.

The Grenadian experiment aborted in October 1983 following United States intervention, precipitated by ideologically based conflict within the NJM. It was the most dramatic end of the socialist experiments. It was also the most costly in human terms, and not only to Grenada. Sixty-seven Grenadians died and some 358 were wounded or injured. Twenty-four Cubans were killed and fifty-nine were wounded in combat. On the United States side, nineteen were killed in battle or from injuries later. About 152 were wounded, a large proportion of them due to accidental injuries. Curiously enough, the United States military awarded 812 Bronze Stars, 5,079 Army Commendation Medals, 2,946 Army Achievement Medals, 1,649 Air Force Commendation Medals, and 311 Air Force Achievement Medals in the Grenada operation, code-named "Operation Urgent Fury." In all, between 30,000 and 35,000 medals were distributed.[21]

Because of its high human cost, foreign and security policy implications, and its threat to the hopes of Caribbean leftists, the death of the Grenada experiment evoked considerable debate on the future of socialism in the Caribbean. Many observers accept tacitly if not openly that the prospects for socialism are very grim. Clive Thomas, one of the region's most respected intellectuals, who is also leftist, underscored the importance of legitimizing radical experiments: "No regime, no matter how popular it may be, will be able to sustain the support of the popular forces of the region if its political rule is not grounded in constitutionality, legality, and due legal process."[22] As Gordon Lewis put it: "The lesson of all this for Caribbean progressive movements is clear. It must rediscover its conviction that socialism must go hand in hand with democracy."[23]

There was almost universal agreement among Caribbeanists that, to quote Benn, "advocacy of Marxism in the Caribbean would need to be tempered with a strong dose of pragmatism if it is to serve as a guide to political change in the region."[24] Many analysts also felt that socialist practitioners should be able to recognize those among them whose blind power ambition portend danger, both for the group in question and for the movement in the region generally. In addition, there was widespread belief that the PRG was extremely naive regarding questions of the geopolitics of the area.

The dim prospects for the future of Caribbean socialism, however, go beyond domestic political factors in Grenada or in any single country. As suggested repeatedly, because Caribbean states are subordinate to others, the future of socialism or any doctrine or development there would have hemispheric and international ramifications. The ramifications themselves would be multidimensional: economic, political, military, cultural, and other. Carl Stone's analysis reflects many of these dimensions:

> Development of a basic needs socialist economy requires a hegemonic one party state, a strong dominant Marxist ideology, and a mass party or movement with a highly developed capacity for mobilization and administration. Organizational weaknesses within Caribbean leftist parties, fratricidal contentions for power among ruthless, leftist, intelligentsia, low levels of organizational discipline, and weak leadership at the grass roots level, as in Grenada, all suggest that prospects for socialist development in this direction are not very promising.
>
> The failure to consolidate power in Grenada and the murder of the regime's popular leader has left an indelible scar on the image of Marxist-oriented socialism. This has served to exacerbate the strong anticommunist political tendencies in the region, based on conservative and fundamentalist church influences, [and] peasant values (which are skeptical of state ownership or control of productive assets). . . . The penetration of the region by North American media, extensive networks of family connections with the North American mainland through migration, and strong social traditions that encourage excessive consumerism and individualism, private accumulation and upward social mobility into middle-class life styles, all render the basic needs model incompatible with the value system of most Caribbean peoples.[25]

Thus, the 1990s began with most Caribbean leftists resigned to the death of Caribbean socialism. This sense of acceptance was clearly demonstrated by the March 8, 1992, resignation of Trevor Munroe as General Secretary of the fourteen-year-old WPJ. Munroe, a distinguished political scientist at the University of the West Indies (UWI), admitted that there was little hope for the party's future.[26] However, several factors besides the failure of the socialist experiments contributed to the strong resurgence of the right in the region. The disruption in the world economy in the early 1970s was one such factor. It led to a quadrupling of oil prices, a decline in the prices and values of Caribbean exports and hence drastic cuts in imports, price increases, wage freezes, and contraction in the labor force in most places. The resulting economic deprivation was reflected in actions by electorates. They sought change, ousting political leaders in many places. These new leaders, who had already been jockeying for leadership, began to use the international political climate to align politically with Western patrons capable of providing the needed economic assistance.

For example, in Antigua-Barbuda, the reform-socialist Progressive Labor Movement led by George Walter lost power in 1976 to the Antigua Labor Party (ALP) headed by Vere Bird, Sr. Bird's economic policies emphasized attracting United States and other foreign investment, especially in the tourist industry. On April 27, 1980, the ALP again swept the polls, winning 13 of the 17 parliamentary seats. Bird and the ALP have been in control ever since. In Barbados, Tom Adams's strong advocacy of capitalist policies and his staunch pro-American foreign policy advocacy while he led the opposition helped his dramatic electoral victory over the Democratic Labor Party (DLP) in 1976.

In Dominica's case, political instability due to economic deprivation, squabbling among the leftists, and repression by Patrick John led to the emergence of Mary Eugenia Charles of the Dominica Freedom Party (DFP) in the July 1980 elections. Charles, known as the "Caribbean Iron Lady," has a strong antipathy for socialism. She is a firm believer in free enterprise and in "the American way." As noted in chapter two, she is not only proud of her United States contacts, but has endorsed the application of the Monroe Doctrine to all Caribbean countries.

In addition, there were geopolitical developments during the latter part of the Jimmy Carter administration and during Ronald Reagan's tenure as president where an offensive was launched against "the communist menace" internationally, and its manifestations in the Caribbean Basin particularly. The shift to the right was thus the result of economic, political, and other factors, both within the region and in the international system. It was very dramatic between December 1979 to November 1980, when new elites were elected in five countries:

- Milton Cato in St. Vincent and the Grenadines won 11 of the 13 seats in the December 5, 1979 elections.
- Dr. Kennedy Simmonds and the People's Action Movement (PAM) won 5 of the 9 seats in the St. Kitts-Nevis elections of February 18, 1980.
- Vere Bird, Sr., and the ALP won as noted above.
- Mary Eugenia Charles and the DFP won 17 of 27 seats in Dominica on July 21, 1980.
- Edward Seaga and the JLP won 51 of the 60 seats in Jamaica's October 1980 elections.[27]

Thus, as the 1990s continue there are two basic sets of doctrinal beliefs in the Caribbean: capitalism and socialism. They both have central economic and political tenets. Capitalism advocates a political economy based on free enterprise and a climate conducive to foreign investment. It admires individualism and spurns massive social welfare practices. Politically, it espouses social democratic principles and places a premium on civil and political rights such as freedom of the press, speech, and movement, and free and fair elections. Transformation of the economic and political substructure and superstructure of society is a cardinal feature of the socialist doctrine. It considers state involvement in the economy to be critical to this aim, and takes the position that the changes should be led by a political party that is competent and legitimately entitled to do so, based on class interests. It stresses collective, as opposed to individual interests, and tends to subordinate political and civil rights to economic and social rights.

As might be expected, there are doctrinal variations on both sides. Moreover, adherents to these beliefs vary both in the degree of commitment to them and in their "ideology in politics," making some in the capitalist category conservative while others are liberal. Similarly, some socialists are radical; others are reformist. As Table 8.1 shows, in marked contrast to 1972 and 1982, no socialists control state power in 1992, although many people question whether Cheddie Jagan in Guyana, an avowed Marxist from the 1940s until 1990, has really undergone the ideological change he pretends to have undergone. While there was some continuity in Guyana, where the PNC held power until October 1992, the political and economic changes introduced there between August 1985 and October 1992 placed the PNC outside the socialist camp. And as noted above, while the PNP is again in control of Jamaica's affairs, the metamorphosis in the thinking and policies of that party clearly puts it outside the socialist group. The ascendancy of the liberal and conservative capitalists is, therefore, now firmly established.

Ideology-Security Nexus

The noted international politics scholar Alexander George explains an important connection between ideology and security:

> Philosophical and instrumental beliefs serve as a cognitive and affective prism that influences an actor's perceptions and diagnoses of the flow of political events, his estimate of threat and opportunity, his definitions of situations. These beliefs also provide general norms, standards and guidelines that influence the actor's judgments of preferred strategies and tactics. Such beliefs influence policy preferences, but do not by themselves determine decision.[28]

George makes several related propositions. The first is that links exist between beliefs and policy choice. He also suggests that the links are more than inconsequential. Yet, he warns against overstatement of causal relationships between doctrine and strategy. Although Caribbean political elites may not deny such links, except for the avowed socialists, they have been reluctant to address the interests and pursuits of their countries in ideological terms.

One exception was Rashleigh Jackson, Guyana's Foreign Minister from 1978 until November 26, 1990, when he resigned following the indictment of his son, Martin, on narcotics possession charges. After noting the mutual dependence of domestic policy and foreign policy, Jackson argued that states must take account of their "class ideological as well as strategic-national interests." Jackson defined the role of the foreign policy establishment as being to promote the creation of external conditions to facilitate the achievement of political and socioeconomic objectives set by the ruling party. He explained: "There is a link between our ideology, our national interests, and our national policy, of which foreign policy is an important dimension."[29]

Whether the importance of ideology is stated with the conceptual clarity of George or with the diplomatic flair of Jackson, there is an undeniable nexus between ideology and security. In the Caribbean, as in many other places, the relationship between the two has had domestic and international ramifications, often triggering concerns about both internal and external security. Based on how they define their internal security problems, Caribbean regimes may take measures against actual or potential threats, with economic as well as political consequences. For example, the increases in Guyana's military expenditure between 1970 and 1985 were intended partly to create a security establishment capable of dealing with national security threats. Unquestionably, one threat was external, coming from Venezuela, as noted in chapters two and four. But the political elites also perceived threats to be emanating from within the society: threats to the political survival of the regime.

Consequently, among other things, the PNC government increasingly curtailed political and civil rights—to speech, movement, and assembly—and entrenched itself in power, partly with the help of the military. In doing so, the regime progressively created the basis for a groundswell of opposition and hence real threats to its political survival. There was, thus, a kind of circular situation where threat definition colored by doctrine led to an enlarged security establishment that facilitated the suppression of political rights, especially as economic woes increased. This evoked greater opposition to the regime, thereby threatening the nation's internal stability.

Guyana is not the only country where ideology was part of the internal security scenario. This was true also of the 1970 crisis in Trinidad and Tobago, part of which was the army mutiny discussed in chapter four. The crisis started with a February 26, 1970, protest by students of the UWI campus at St. Augustine, Trinidad. It had few ideological overtones initially. However, it quickly became the centerpiece of the political agenda of the Black Power movement led by NJAC, and involving the Black Panthers and the Young Power Movement. NJAC sought fundamental socioeconomic change in the country, arguing that white racism was the main cause for the economic deprivation suffered by people of African and Indian descent. The crisis involved several marches, some attracting more than 10,000 people, arson, vandalism, strikes, and the army mutiny. There was also an impasse in the government following the April 13, 1970, resignation of A.N.R. Robinson, then Deputy Prime Minister and Minister of External Affairs.

As the crisis developed and threatened to plunge the twin-island nation into chaos, the government declared a state of emergency on April 21. According to one participant-observer: "On the morning of April 22, 1970 an eerie calm hung over the streets of Port of Spain which, for the first time in 55 days, did not resound to the shuffle of marching feet or shouts of 'Power to the People.' "[30] The state of emergency was maintained until November 1970. And, as was explained in chapter four, the crisis gave rise to several laws to control "dissident groups," and to a major restructuring of the security establishment.[31]

Part of Dominica's internal instability during the 1970s also had ideological dimensions. Apart from the squabbling among leftist groups, the ideological leanings of the ruling Dominica Labor Party (DLP) caused friction within the party and puzzlement within the society as well as in the region. Prime Minister Patrick John made frequent ideological shifts when he felt it politically expedient. This led to both concern and uncertainty over his policies toward left-wing politics in the region. There was particular concern over John's close ties with Guyana, leading to considerable apprehension over the possibility of the introduction of Guyanese-style socialism. John later compounded the confusion by dismissing two leftist government ministers, Michael Douglas and Ferdinand Parillon, on grounds that they manifested "communist tendencies" and had engaged in a communist plot to usurp power.[32]

The voluminous literature on the self-destruction of the Grenada revolution obviates the need to elaborate on that crisis. Suffice it to observe that among the accepted causal explanations is ideologically based factionalism within the NJM. The charismatic Maurice Bishop embodied a more populist, mass-based conception of the NJM. On the other hand, Bernard Coard, his deputy and challenger, sought a vanguardist, Leninist party structure. While both men were committed to Marxism-Leninism, there were differences over interpretation and strategy. Of course, the ideologically based conflict was not the sole contributor to the death of the Grenada revolution. Some other factors were the power pursuits of Coard, the organizational weaknesses of the NJM, and errors of foreign policy judgment.

The NJM's rise to power itself, through the March 13, 1979, coup, generated security concerns at the regional level. As was shown above, by the late 1970s the region's ideological profile had begun to assume a significantly conservative character. Indeed, in 1979 most Caribbean ruling parties were capitalist oriented, many of the conservative ilk, as

Table 8.1 shows. The NJM's radical socialist posture was anathema to most leaders in the region, although they demonstrated tolerance, within the framework of Ideological Pluralism.

In addition, there was the question of the manner in which the NJM had come to power. The Commonwealth Caribbean has long prided itself on having the kind of political culture where legitimacy is conferred by democratic elections and where political violence is deemed deviant.[33] Most Caribbean leaders deplored Eric Gairy's rule in Grenada, in part because of the political violence visited on the society. Yet they were not prepared to countenance his removal through a coup. Moreover, the NJM aggravated the state of relations by dishonoring the pledge to hold "early" elections. The NJM took the position that elections were part of "the dysfunctional elitist and alienated structures that were inherited from British colonialism," one of several "crippling undemocratic institutions of the decrepit and exploitative past."[34]

The net result of all this was a heightened sense of political vulnerability, leading partly to the formation of the RSS, examined in chapter six. Except for Burnham in Guyana and Manley in Jamaica, Caribbean leaders did not embrace Maurice Bishop, although they admired his charisma. For instance, Manley was the only Caribbean head of government who attended the first anniversary celebrations of the PRG in March 1980. The Jamaican embrace was short-lived, though, as Manley lost power in October 1980. In the case of Guyana, there was considerable change in the relations after Bishop openly accused the Burnham government of complicity in the June 1980 death of Walter Rodney, renowned historian and leftist political activist.

After 1980, Tom Adams of Barbados and Edward Seaga of Jamaica, then the region's leading capitalists-conservatives, were Bishop's main antagonists. The antagonism even assumed the form of very uncomplimentary public exchanges. Bishop often referred to Adams as "Uncle Tom Adams," and once equated him with "an expectant dog barking for his supper." There were also uncomplimentary exchanges involving Burnham and Adams. Eric Williams of Trinidad and Tobago and his ministers gave the PRG the cold shoulder by not responding to letters, not even those from Bishop himself. In addition, Adams and Seaga clearly were aiming at Grenada, but also Guyana, when they proposed the amendment of the CARICOM treaty to make CARICOM membership conditional on the maintenance of parliamentary democracy. The proposal was later abandoned.[35]

We saw in chapter six that the Mutual Assistance Scheme (MAS) and the Zone of Peace proposal are practically dead as regional security initiatives. This has resulted primarily from the inability of states to agree on a common basis for operation due to perceptual differences and national interest dictates. But the ideological factor was clearly also present. It was particularly present in influencing "the definition of the situation" and in the assessment of security measures. Several states were uncomfortable with Bishop's government as prime sponsor and activist for the Zone of Peace resolution. Others, while paying lip service or honestly supportive of the resolution, were suspicious that Grenada might have been serving Cuban or Soviet interests in the Caribbean. They were, thus, reluctant to exercise the kind of political will in both initiatives that may have led to some positive actions, at least with the MAS.

United States intervention in Grenada in 1983, and more so the coat-tail involvement of the RSS states and Jamaica, caused a polarization within CARICOM, which saw opposition to the intervention by the Bahamas, Belize, Guyana, and Trinidad and Tobago. The other states publicly supported the intervention, some participating in it, as we saw in chapter six. One cannot directly attribute the polarization to ideological differences since opposing states did not share a common doctrine. Guyana then stood to the left of the Bahamas, Belize, and Trinidad and Tobago. However, the ideological factor is not to be discounted.

Guyana, the most strident critic among the four, had then been known for its anti-imperialism and anti-Americanism. These certainly entered into the calculus of the Guyana decision. In a national radio broadcast on October 25, 1983, Burnham said:

> However unfortunate may be the events over the past twelve days in Grenada ... they cannot justify military intervention and aggression. The Government of Guyana condemns the invasion and seeks to have an immediate withdrawal of all U.S. forces. Today Grenada, tomorrow Guyana and the day after tomorrow someone else....
>
> We in the Caribbean are witnessing such outside interference instigated and/or supported by a group of Caribbean countries, a group that has not thought its position through, has not recognized that there we have a case of the reintroduction of colonialism and imperialism by invitation here today in the Caribbean. ...[36]

Ideological differentiation can lead to the frustration of attempts at regional cooperation. In the Caribbean it contributed to disruption of the CARICOM machinery, leading to the inability of leaders to hold any summit between 1975 and 1982. One Caribbean scholar-turned-diplomat observed: "Differing ideological orientations, masked for a while by the concept of ideological pluralism, inhibited any harmony in foreign relations. By the late seventies, differences in ideological orientation had separated Guyana and Jamaica from most Caribbean countries."[37] Moreover, ideological rancor can facilitate fragmentation and create the basis for countries such as Cuba and the United States to exploit the fragmentation, in the process harming individual nations and the region as a whole. This is partly the situation stemming from Bishop's pursuits. The NJM posture and rhetoric were somewhat extreme in the degree of alignment with Cuba and the USSR, and the extent of hostility to the United States. Some countries, therefore, distanced themselves from Grenada, thereby weakening the region's collaborative and supportive network. This allowed both Cuba and the United States to exploit the situation in different ways.

The concept of Ideological Pluralism referred to above was once recognized as more than the mere existence of several doctrines at any one time. For many, it was an article of faith. It dates to the 1979 OAS Zone of Peace resolution. As we saw in chapter six, among other things, the Grenada-sponsored resolution stressed "support for the principles of ideological pluralism and peaceful coexistence, which are essential to the peace, stability and development of the region." The February 1980 meeting of the CARICOM Foreign Ministers in St. Lucia declared Ideological Pluralism an "irreversible fact of international relations" and sought to make its preservation and consolidation a goal of CARICOM member-states.

Guyana was among the states that staunchly supported the principle. Guyana's Foreign Minister once declared: "The foreign policy of Guyana has, as principal elements, peaceful coexistence and ideological pluralism. We shall continue to struggle for their universal acceptance."[38] The ascendancy of the right in the region, however, seems to have jeopardized the prospects for this ideological coexistence. The tolerance for ideological diversity certainly has been lowered. The views of one Caribbean diplomat expressed in 1984 seem even more appropriate now. He felt Ideological Pluralism may have been "a thin veil which when buffeted by the winds of change quickly fell away."

Consequently, "what this new scenario has exposed is an inherent unwillingness to tolerate different political persuasions in the hemisphere."[39]

Shridath Ramphal, former Guyana Foreign Minister and Commonwealth Secretary-General, now Chancellor of UWI, offered this analysis of the subject:

> In a curious way, that early manifestation of regional unity in areas where it mattered most was achieved in an environment within the region that was tolerant of pluralism; tolerant of shades of difference—ideological and otherwise—among countries of the region. Ironically, that unity fell away when the environment of the region became unpropitious to pluralism. It might be seen as paradoxical but it is really intelligible, that when a group becomes intolerant of the differences within itself, it moves not to homogeneity, but fragmentation—the very environment of intolerance encouraging fissiparous trends. The differences tolerated before, and here and there overcome in the interest of joint positions, become now ever deeper divisions. And that in large measure has been the fate of the Caribbean over something like the last decade.[40]

The absence of significant ideological differentiation in the region now has led to a certain sense of security; perhaps a false security. There is the feeling in some nations, especially in the Eastern Caribbean, that the ideological dominance of the right displaces any significant threats to their internal political security. The danger of this is that governments there may become both overconfident and complacent, and take their internal political security for granted. The 1990 coup attempt in Trinidad and Tobago, which, according to its architect, Abu Bakr, was precipitated by the country's increasing economic deprivation, clearly demonstrates that internal security threats need not be ideological in origin.

Ever since 1986, this sense of security has been bolstered by the coalition called the Caribbean Democratic Union (CDU). The CDU was formed as a branch of the International Democratic Union on January 17, 1986, in Jamaica by eight political parties, all of which held power. According to Article 1(b) of the CDU Rules, the organization "shall advocate the promotion of freedom and an economic system based on a social market economy."[41] The CDU's Charter, also called "The Kingston Declaration," outlines the guiding principles of the organization under five headings: Democracy; Freedom and the Individual; the Individual and the Community; Private Property and Private Enterprise; and International Relations.

Edward Seaga explained the organization's background while speaking at a Dominica Freedom Party (DFP) conference in Dominica in July 1988:

> During the days in which I was in opposition in Jamaica, and during my travels in other regions of the world, I continued to ask myself why is it that all the socialist parties in the world have banded themselves into one family, under one organization which they call Socialist International. And we who are non-socialist parties have no roof, have no organization in which we can embrace each other and help each other.
>
> I visited [West] Germany at the time and found that there was an organization that embraced many like-minded parties of Europe. And they call it the European Democratic Union.
>
> On this side of the world, other democratic nations were never part of that union. I took the message to the United States and to other areas, and I asked why? and eventually in the early 1980s, a world democratic organization was formed which embraces all freedom-loving democratic nations, called the International Democratic Union.
>
> That union has many regional unions, one in Europe, one for the Pacific, and it came a time when we said to ourselves, we in the Caribbean who are so richly blessed with so many parties that are democratic and freedom-loving must have our own union too, and so we established the Caribbean Democratic Union.[42]

The CDU is headed by a Chairman, with the Party Leaders Conference as the governing body. There is also an Executive Committee comprised of the Chairman, the Vice-Chairmen, the Treasurer, and the Executive Secretary. The Conference meets biennially, while the members of the Executive Committee confer annually. Seaga was elected the first Chairman, with Kennedy Simmonds of St. Kitts-Nevis, the late Herbert Blaize of Grenada, and Manuel Esquivel of Belize as Vice-Chairmen. Mary Eugenia Charles of Dominica was elected Treasurer. The second conference of leaders was held in July 1988 in Antigua. All the officers were reelected and two new parties joined the grouping: the Anguilla National Alliance; and the Nevis Reform Party.

That conference was held during the period of the Ninth CARICOM Summit, July 4–8, also held in Antigua. This prompted charges that Seaga and others were attempting to subordinate the interests of CAR-

ICOM to those of the CDU by taking time and attention away from CARICOM matters. CDU leadership underwent significant change in September 1991: James Mitchell, Prime Minister of St. Vincent and the Grenadines and leader of the New Democratic Party succeeded Seaga; Keith Mitchell of Grenada's New National Party was elected as one of three Vice-Chairmen; St. Lucia's Prime Minister, John Compton, replaced Charles as Treasurer; and former Jamaican diplomat Hector Wynter was confirmed as Executive Secretary.

The CDU now comprises:

- Anguilla National Alliance (Anguilla)
- United Democratic Party (Belize)
- Dominica Freedom Party (Dominica)
- New National Party (Grenada)
- Jamaica Labor Party (Jamaica)
- People's Liberation Movement (Montserrat)
- Nevis Reformation Party (St. Kitts-Nevis)
- People's Action Movement (St. Kitts-Nevis)
- United Workers Party (St. Lucia)
- New Democratic Party (St. Vincent and the Grenadines).[43]

CDU member-parties have received financial and political support from within the Caribbean, notably from the JLP, and from Venezuela and the United States. The CDU gives member-parties financial and organizational support, especially for electoral contests, but also for organizational sustenance between elections. Member-parties also contribute financially to the CDU, but the CDU depends on the National Republican Institute for International Affairs in the United States for most of its finances. The institute itself is funded by the National Endowment for Democracy (NED), a private foundation chartered and funded by the United States Congress and mandated to promote democracy internationally. According to the CDU Executive Secretary, NED money "does not allow for any outside interference in the conduct of the CDU."[44] Regarding CDU funding sources, one observer noted: "Since 1986 this collection of right-wing parties has received more than [U.S.]$800,000 in NED [National Endowment for Democracy] funds."[45] Part of the 1989 funding was used to organize seminars including one on "communist infiltration," held in June 1989 in St. Vincent and the Grenadines.

Thus the CDU offers member-parties, five of which in 1992 are ruling parties, a sense of solidarity and security. More than this, though, some Caribbean states are also likely to take the security of the region for granted because of the ideological affinity of most states with the United States, the dominant state in the area, and with Venezuela, an important middle power. Some Caribbean leaders consider American power and their ideological coincidence with the United States as sufficient for American protection from possible Cuban, and perhaps even Venezuelan, threats.[46]

This is a somewhat dangerous position to adopt. It can lead eventually to total security dependency, which itself can undermine sovereignty. The history of inter-state conduct, both in the hemisphere and internationally, shows that states act according to national interests when it comes to their security, and not necessarily based on ideology. As Ivo Duchacek once noted, "National interest, not ideology becomes the last word . . . when the leader concludes that it would be suicidal to sacrifice the national interest on the altar of ideological purity."[47] Of course, the national interest may be defined to include ideological elements, as happens with the United States.

Conclusion

Ideology has been a factor of considerable import for Caribbean security over the past two-and-a-half decades. It has featured in internal instability, affected militarization, and helped to precipitate the first United States intervention in the Commonwealth Caribbean. In addition, ideology once helped to undermine the regional integration movement by leading to personal animosity among leaders and derailing efforts at foreign policy harmonization. Further, the significance of ideological questions pertains to the important relationship between ideological and economic security. Ideological posture has affected economic security because the United States has rewarded governments sharing its orientation and has leveled sanctions against those to the left.

Destabilization, for example, involved varying economic pressures. These undermined economic security, and consequently, political security. Moreover, as seen in chapter five, the passage of power from the socialist PNP to the capitalist-conservative JLP in 1980 saw a dramatic increase in economic and technical assistance to Jamaica.

This is also true for Eastern Caribbean countries where, especially after 1983, most governments underwent a kind of rightist ideological rebirth and secured economic rewards from the United States. Yet in the contemporary Caribbean, certain security challenges have no ideological parameters, are not necessarily disposed to any ideological orientation, and are not better met by governments of any particular ideological persuasion. One such challenge relates to drugs, to which I turn my attention in the next chapter.

Notes

1. Denis Benn, *Ideology and Political Development: The Growth and Development of Political Ideas in the Caribbean 1774–1983*, Kingston, Jamaica: Institute of Social and Economic Research, 1987, p. 7.

2. For more on the Old Representative System and Crown Colony government see Morley Ayearst, *The British West Indies: The Search for Self-Government*, New York: New York University Press, 1960; and H.A. Will, *Constitutional Change in the British West Indies 1880–1903*, Oxford: Clarendon Press, 1970.

3. Benn, *Ideology and Political Development*, p. 163.

4. Gordon K. Lewis, "Some Reflections on the Leading Intellectual Currents That Have Shaped the Caribbean Experience: 1950–1984," *Cimarrón* 1 (Spring 1985): 23–40.

5. See Wendell Bell, ed., *The Democratic Revolution in the West Indies*, Cambridge, MA: Schenkman, 1967; Paul G. Singh, *Local Democracy in the Commonwealth Caribbean*, London: Longman Caribbean, 1972; Trevor Farrell, "Decolonization in the English-speaking Caribbean: Myth or Reality?" in Paget Henry and Carl Stone, eds., *The Newer Caribbean: Decolonization, Democracy, and Development*, Philadelphia, PA: Institute for the Study of Human Issues, 1983; Francis Alexis, *Changing Caribbean Constitutions*, Bridgetown, Barbados: Antilles, 1983; and Fred Phillips, *West Indian Constitutions: Post-Independence Reforms*, New York: Oceana, 1985.

6. See Harold Lutchman, *From Colonialism to Cooperative Republic*, Río Piedras, Puerto Rico: Institute of Caribbean Studies, 1974; Ivelaw L. Griffith, "New Approaches to Political Change and Development in the Third World: An Assessment of Guyana's System of Local Democracy," Unpublished Paper, 1982; and Rudolph James and Harold Lutchman, *Law and the Political Environment in Guyana*, Georgetown, Guyana: Institute of Development Studies, University of Guyana, 1984.

7. Lewis, "Some Reflections," p. 26.

8. Lewis, p. 30.

9. George Black, "MARE NOSTRUM: U.S. Security Policy in the English-speaking Caribbean," *NACLA Report on the Americas* 19 (July-August 1985): 23; Leslie Manigat, "The Setting: Crisis, Ideology, and Geopolitics," in Jorge Heine and Leslie Manigat, eds., *The Caribbean and World Politics*, New York: Holmes and Meier, 1988, p. 43; and Roger East, ed., *Communist and Marxist Parties of*

the World, 2d ed., Harlow, England: Longman, 1990, pp. 371–413, 442–44.

10. Perry Mars, "Political Mobilization and Class Struggle in the English-speaking Caribbean," *Contemporary Marxism* 10 (1985): 131–32.

11. Ibid. p. 132.

12. Carl Stone, *Power in the Caribbean Basin*, Philadelphia, PA: Institute for the Study of Human Issues, 1986, p. 65.

13. Lloyd Searwar, "Dominant Issues in the Role and Responses of Caribbean Small States," in Anthony T. Bryan, J. Edward Greene, and Timothy M. Shaw, eds., *Peace, Development, and Security in the Caribbean*, New York: St. Martin's Press, 1990, p. 6.

14. For Sartori, "ideology in politics" focuses on actions and has efficacy as the central issue. On the other hand, "ideology in knowledge" or doctrine is concerned with thinking, a central issue being validity. See his *Theory of Democracy Revisited, Part Two: The Classical Issues*, Chatham, NJ: Chatham House, 1987, p. 500.

15. For assessments of this experiment see Paul G. Singh, *Guyana: Socialism in a Plural Society*, London: Fabian Society, 1972; Perry Mars, "Cooperative Socialism and Marxist Scientific Theory," *Caribbean Issues* 4 (August 1978): 71–106; and Clive Y. Thomas, "Guyana: The Rise and Fall of Cooperative Socialism," in Anthony Payne and Paul Sutton, eds., *Dependency Under Challenge*, Manchester: Manchester University Press, 1984.

16. See Michael Manley, *The Politics of Change: A Jamaica Testament*. London: Andre Deutsch, 1974; Michael Kaufman, *Jamaica under Manley*, London: Zed Books, 1985; and Anthony Payne, "From Michael with Love: The Nature of Socialism in Jamaica," *Journal of Commonwealth and Comparative Politics* 14 (March 1976): 82–100.

17. See Tony Thorndike, *Grenada: Politics, Economics, and Society*. Boulder, CO: Lynne Rienner, 1985; Jay Mandle, *Big Revolution, Small Country: The Rise and Fall of the Grenada Revolution*, Lanham, MD: North-South, 1985; and Jorge Heine, ed., *A Revolution Aborted: The Lessons of Grenada*, Pittsburgh: University of Pittsburgh Press, 1991.

18. See Clive Y. Thomas, "State Capitalism in Guyana: An Assessment of Burnham's Cooperative Socialist Republic," in Fitzroy Ambursley and Robin Cohen, eds., *Crisis in the Caribbean*, New York: Monthly Review Press, 1983; and Latin America Bureau, *Guyana: Fraudulent Revolution*, London: Latin America Bureau, 1984.

19. See David de Caires, "A New Era? Or Is President Hoyte Trapped in the Skin of the Old PNC?" *Caribbean Affairs* 1 (January-March 1988): 183–98; Ivelaw L. Griffith, "The Military and the Politics of Change in Guyana," *Journal of Interamerican Studies and World Affairs* 33 (Summer 1991): 141–73; "PPP/Civic Enters House with 3-Seat Majority," *Guyana Chronicle*, October 10, 1992, pp. 1, 6; and "Brand New Faces in President Jagan's Brand New Government," *Guyana Chronicle*, October 14, 1992, p. 1.

20. Neville C. Duncan, "Political Violence in the Caribbean," in Ivelaw L. Griffith, ed., *Strategy and Security in the Caribbean*, New York: Praeger, 1991, p. 58.

21. Mark Adkin, *Urgent Fury: The Battle for Grenada*. Lexington, MA: Lexington Books, 1989, pp. 308–09, 321–23.

22. Clive Thomas, "Hard Lessons for Intellectuals," *Caribbean Contact*, September 1984, p. 7.

23. Lewis, "Some Reflections," p. 38.

24. Bonn, *Ideology and Political Development*, p. 196.

25. Carl Stone, "Whither Caribbean Socialism? Grenada, Jamaica, and Guyana in Perspective," in *A Revolution Aborted*, pp. 305–306.

26. Balford Henry, "WPJ On the Way Out," *Jamaican Weekly Gleaner*, March 9, 1992, p. 1.

27. Leslie Manigat, "The Setting," p. 55. Also, see Percy C. Hintzen, "From Ideology to Pragmatism: The Evolution of Political Leaders in the Anglophone Caribbean," Paper Delivered at the 12th Annual Conference of the Caribbean Studies Association, Belize, May 1987, esp. pp. 48–58; Black, "MARE NOSTRUM," pp. 20–26; and Fitzroy Ambursley and Robin Cohen, "Crisis in the Caribbean: Internal Transformations and External Constraints," in *Crisis in the Caribbean*.

28. Alexander George, "Ideology and International Relations: A Conceptual Analysis," *Jerusalem Journal of International Relations* 9 (No. 1 1987): 18.

29. Rashleigh Jackson, *The International Question*, Georgetown, Guyana: People's National Congress, 1981, pp. 5–6.

30. Raoul Pantin, "Black Power on the Road: Portrait of a Revolution," *Caribbean Affairs* 3 (January-March 1990): 185.

31. For more on the 1970 crisis see Pantin, "Black Power on the Road"; Lt. Rafique Shah, "The Military Crisis in Trinidad and Tobago During 1970," in Trevor Munroe and Rupert Lewis, eds., *Readings in Government and Politics in the West Indies*, Kingston, Jamaica: University of the West Indies, 1971; and Lloyd Best, "The February Revolution," in David Lowenthal and Lambros Comitas, eds., *The Aftermath of Sovereignty*, Garden City, NY: Anchor Books, 1973.

32. Lennox Honychurch, *The Dominica Story*, 2d ed., Roseau, Dominica: The Dominica Institute, 1984, pp. 202–03.

33. For a discussion on Caribbean political culture see George Danns, *Leadership, Legitimacy, and the West Indian Experience*, Working Papers Series No. 1, Institute of Development Studies, University of Guyana, 1978; Duncan, "Political Violence in the Caribbean"; Clifford E. Griffin, "Postinvasion Political Security in the Eastern Caribbean," in *Strategy and Security in the Caribbean*, pp. 78–81; Arend Lijphart, "Size, Pluralism, and the Westminster Model of Democracy: Implications for the Eastern Caribbean," in *A Revolution Aborted*; and Donald C. Peters, *The Democratic System in the Eastern Caribbean*, Westport, CT: Greenwood Press, 1992.

34. Tony Thorndike, "People's Power in Theory and Practice," in *A Revolution Aborted*, p. 45.

35. Anthony Payne, "The Foreign Policy of the People's Revolutionary Government," in *A Revolution Aborted*, pp. 142–44.

36. Forbes Burnham, "Address to the Nation," in Mohamed Shahabuddeen, *The Conquest of Grenada: Sovereignty in the Periphery*, Georgetown, Guyana: University of Guyana, 1986, pp. 194–95.

37. Vaughan Lewis, "Small States, Eastern Caribbean Security, and the Grenada Intervention," in *A Revolution Aborted*, p. 259.

38. Rashleigh Jackson, *The Right to a Peaceful World*, Georgetown, Guyana: Ministry of Foreign Affairs, 1985, p. 54.

39. Cedric Grant, "Ideological Pluralism in the Caribbean: Challenges and Prospects," *Transafrica Forum* 2 (No. 3, 1984): 6–7.

40. Cited in Shahabuddeen, *The Conquest of Grenada*, p. 160.

41. Caribbean Democratic Union, *Composition and Rules*, Kingston, Jamaica, January 17, 1986, p. 1. I am grateful to Executive Secretary Hector Wynter for providing copies of the Rules, the Charter, and other data.

42. R.B. Manderson-Jones, *Jamaican Foreign Policy in the Caribbean 1962–1988*, Kingston, Jamaica: Caricom Publishers, 1990, p. 167.

43. "Seaga Heads New Grouping of Region's Conservative Parties," *Caribbean Insight* 9 (February 1986): 5; "Seaga Reelected Head of CDU," *Daily Nation* (Barbados), July 6, 1988, p. 10; "Mitchell Replaces Seaga as CDU Head," *Stabroek News* (Guyana), September 10, 1991, p. 9; and personal communication from Executive Secretary Hector Wynter, October 1, 1991.

44. Personal communication from the Executive Secretary, October 1, 1991.

45. David Corn, "Foreign Aid for the Right," *The Nation* (United States), December 18, 1989, p. 746.

46. See, for example, Mary Eugenia Charles, "Isolationism vs. One-ness: The Continuing Validity of the Monroe Doctrine," *Caribbean Affairs* 1 (April-June 1988): 150–54.

47. See his *Nations and Men*, 3d ed., Hinsdale, IL: The Dryden Press, 1975, p. 223.

9

DRUGS AND SECURITY

> Nothing poses greater threats to civil society in CARICOM countries than the drug problem; and nothing exemplifies the powerlessness of regional governments more. That is the magnitude of the danger that drug abuse and drug trafficking hold for our Community. It is a many-layered danger. At base is the human destruction implicit in drug addiction; but, implicit also, is the corruption of individuals and systems by the sheer enormity of the inducements of the illegal drug trade in relatively poor societies. On top of all this lie the implications for governance itself—at the hands of both external agencies engaged in international interdiction, and the drug barons themselves—the 'dons' of the modern Caribbean—who threaten governance from within.
>
> —West Indian Commission

In our chapter two examination of how Caribbean political elites define the region's security problems, we observed that drugs present the single most critical security challenge to the region. Contrary to a popular misconception, there is no single "drug problem." The main problems relate to drug production, abuse, and transshipment, and to money laundering. This chapter examines the security implications of these for the Commonwealth Caribbean.

Prime Minister Lloyd Erskine Sandiford of Barbados deemed the drugs issue "perhaps the single most serious problem for the region in the next decade." Michael Manley, former Prime Minister of Jamaica called illicit drugs a "scourge" and described the drug network as "probably the most highly organized and successfully interfaced collection of interlocking cartels of criminal purpose in human history."[1]

The perception of the grave actual and potential dangers of drugs is not confined to Caribbean decisionmakers, though. Indeed, the 1990 Special Session of the United Nations General Assembly declared the concern by the international community to be justifiable:

> [T]he magnitude of the rising trend in the illicit demand, production, supply, trafficking, and distribution of narcotic drugs and psychotropic substances [is] a grave and persistent threat to the health and well-being of mankind, the stability of nations, the political, economic, social, and cultural structures of all societies, and the lives and dignity of millions of human beings, most especially our young people. . . .[2]

Problem Areas

Production and Abuse

The use and misuse of drugs like alcohol and tobacco have long been problematic for countries in the Caribbean. Yet the drugs with security implications are primarily cocaine, marijuana, heroin, and their derivatives, such as crack. There is considerable variation in the production and use of these drugs. Only marijuana is produced in the Commonwealth Caribbean, and then not everywhere in the region. Moreover, production varies among those places where there is cultivation.

Belize, Guyana, Jamaica, and Trinidad and Tobago are among the places with the highest levels of marijuana production. In March 1992, joint army-police operations in Guyana uncovered 60,000 pounds of marijuana in the Mahaica River area, and ten fields, with an estimated 160,000 marijuana plants, along the Maduni Creek. Two months later there was an even larger discovery, this time along the Berbice River in eastern Guyana: 799,700 pounds of marijuana, valued at over G$1 billion.[3] However, among the four states named above, Belize and Jamaica stand out for the levels of production and for their export of the drug. Marijuana has been the largest cash crop in both countries, producing some U.S. $350 million annually in Belize, and about U.S. $2 billion in Jamaica.[4] The Bahamas, which features prominently in the drug transshipment, has traditionally been neither a drug-producing nor a drug-refining country. However, the production alarm was sounded in 1991 following the discovery of 40,000 cannabis seedlings and 1,000 medium-size plants, and the seizure of twenty-two kilos of prepared marijuana, all on Andros Island.

Marijuana is cultivated mostly in the north and west of Belize, in small plots of about one acre or less. Significant cultivation began in the 1960s, mainly for the United States market. By the early 1980s Belize was the fourth largest United States supplier, behind Colombia, Mexico, and Jamaica. But production has plummeted since 1985, largely due to eradication measures by the Belize government, often under pressure from the United States. The Belize government began aerial spraying in 1982, with the help of Mexico and the United States. Prime Minister George Price found it politically expedient to discontinue the spraying in 1984, given the impending general elections. The spraying operations generated a storm of protest from environmentalists and farmers. Belize specialists believe that the loss of the 1985 elections by the People's United Party (PUP) was due partly to the anger generated by farmers. However, spraying resumed in 1986 by the new government. The new Prime Minister, Manuel Esquivel, defined the drug problem as a serious national security threat, justifying an "all-out war." He perceived the drug trade as a greater threat to the country's sovereignty and democracy than the territorial claims by Guatemala.[5]

Eradication measures have drastically reduced marijuana production. Most marijuana that is discovered is destroyed immediately by aerial eradication, or by hand where there is close proximity to residences or to legitimate crops. The United States Department of State proudly reported in 1991 that "After three years of intensive eradication efforts and the maintenance of an effective suppression program supported by the USG [United States Government], Belize is now only a marginal producer of marijuana."[6] Personnel from the Belize Defense Force (BDF) now fly in aircraft of the American State Department's Bureau of International Narcotics Matters (INM) as part of the eradication program.

INM officials believe that Belize may be near the maximum achievable level of suppressible marijuana production. Indeed, it is estimated that only 54 hectares were harvested in 1991, compared with 67 hectares in 1990, and 132 hectares in 1988. The decline in marijuana production is due not only to herbicide application. There have been other measures, including improvement in the sugar, banana, and citrus industries. In addition, marijuana is continually available from the

Peten Region of neighboring Guatemala. Belize suppliers can, therefore, easily acquire the product for their own buyers. However, in spite of overall reduction, there is some concern about the cultivation of the new *indica* variety of cannabis, which is shorter than the six-foot-tall indigenous plants, and grows much faster.

Jamaica's subtropical climate makes the entire island ideal for cannabis cultivation. "Ganja," as marijuana is popularly called there, grows year-round and traditionally is harvested in two main annual seasons, of five- to six-month cycles. However, the *indica* variety mentioned above matures in three to four months, making four harvests possible. Large-scale cultivation, of five- to fifty-acre plots, were once common, but because of eradication measures, most cultivation is now done in plots one acre or less, with yields of about 1,485 pounds per hectare. Cultivation was once highly concentrated in the wetlands of western and central Jamaica, but production countermeasures have resulted in shifts to remote highland areas, including the Blue Mountains in the eastern part of the country. Most of the cultivation is now on inaccessible mountain sides, ridges, or valleys.[7]

Cannabis production in Jamaica was on a continuous rise until, in response to United States pressure and with its assistance, eradication measures began to reduce cultivation. The campaign, called Operation Buccaneer, is still undertaken annually. One dramatic success of the campaign saw a drop in production from an estimated 405 metric tons in 1988 to 190 metric tons in 1989. Yet shifts in cultivation patterns, a change in crop variety, and reduced resources for aerial spraying led to a dramatic rebound in the 1990s. Although Operation Buccaneer eradicated about 1,000 hectares of marijuana in 1990, cultivation actually expanded from 280 hectares in 1989 to 1,220 hectares in 1990.[8] Aerial spraying of cannabis in Jamaica is more controversial than in Belize because marijuana is an even larger source of income in Jamaica. One estimate for the 1980s placed the number of farmers cultivating the crop at 6,000. In the late 1980s it is said to have contributed between U.S. $1 and U.S. $2 billion to the island's foreign exchange earnings, in excess of all other exports combined, including bauxite, sugar, and tourism.[9]

The narcotics used illegally in the Commonwealth Caribbean are mainly marijuana and cocaine. Like production, drug use differs from place to place. The greatest concern seems to be in Jamaica, the Bahamas, Barbados, Guyana, Trinidad and Tobago, and in parts of the

Eastern Caribbean. While marijuana is abused in many places, it has had a long history of accepted socioreligious use, dating to the introduction of indentured workers from India following the abolition of slavery by the British in 1834. The socioreligious use has changed over the years. It is now predominantly associated with the Africa-oriented social-religious group called the Rastas, and thus is found in places with large numbers of Rastas, including Jamaica, Guyana, Trinidad and Tobago, Barbados, and Grenada. One writer explained: "Part of the Rastafari faith condones the use of *ganja* . . . [T]hey smoke, eat, or drink *ganja* . . . Rastas argue that there is a Biblical justification for *ganja* use and cite the following passages: Genesis 1:12, 3:18; Exodus 10:12; and Psalms 104:14. To the Rastas, *ganja* is not a drug, but an herb."[10]

Cocaine abuse in the region is primarily a spillover from the illicit cocaine trade. This problem is found mainly in the principal transit states: Bahamas, Jamaica, Belize, Trinidad and Tobago, and to a lesser extent, Guyana. In the case of the Bahamas, the INM has declared: "The Bahamas suffers from a serious drug abuse and addiction problem brought about by the ready availability of drugs as they transit the country. Cocaine is the drug of choice for addicts."[11] Belize continues to suffer from an increase in the availability of crack. Indeed, one official source reported that cocaine and crack use has increased since 1990, contributing to increased crime and violence. The increase was clearly demonstrated during the September 1991 Belize Games when forty-four of the 180 winning athletes tested positive for illegal drug use.[12] Data from elsewhere also suggest the extent of the cocaine problem: cocaine seizures in Guyana rose from 400 grams in 1987 to 3,575 grams in 1988; the registration of addicts seeking rehabilitation in Barbados rose from seven in 1986 to 115 in 1988; hospital admission of cocaine and marijuana addicts in Trinidad and Tobago rose from 376 in 1983 to 1,041 in 1989; and the number of "crack bases" in Jamaica has been increasing dramatically.[13]

In a 1990 study, Carl Stone concluded that the cocaine discovery trends in Jamaica suggest that Jamaica has become a cocaine and crack market for both residents and tourists. He considered the use of those drugs, combined with the long tradition of marijuana use, as creating an increasingly serious drug abuse problem in Jamaica. The Stone survey, conducted from August to October 1990, revealed that Jamaican public opinion has a very favorable view of ganja, alcohol, and cigarettes, and reserves most of its concern over cocaine use. Drugs are used increasingly by the youth, in urban areas such as Kingston, St. Andrew, Spanish Town, Portmore, and in tourist centers such as Ocho Rios, Negril, and Montego Bay.

Stone found that crack and cocaine are used more by people in the country's upper and lower income groups. He also detected that ganja, once used mainly by the lower class and by the Rastas, has become part of the life-style of the "fast-moving uptown yuppies." The study also indicated a sharp contrast between the frequency of cocaine and crack use, and that of marijuana. Among users of the former drugs there is a greater concentration of daily and weekly users, reflecting the compulsive nature of cocaine use. For cocaine, there was 2 percent occasional use; 21 percent monthly use; 37 percent weekly use; and 40 percent daily use. For marijuana, the results were: occasional use, 38 percent; monthly, 14 percent; weekly, 27 percent; and daily, 21 percent.[14]

Quite important for Stone, the survey showed a close relationship between the use of various drugs to a degree that "one can define a syndrome of multiple drug use as a central feature of Jamaica's drug culture." He considered this finding a contradiction of analysts who argued previously that ganja use in Jamaica was resistant to the use of "hard drugs." According to Stone, the previous approach was flawed in looking at the use of the varying drugs as separate and distinct phenomena. Stone argued: "Jamaican society at all class and societal levels is highly disposed to consume drugs which relax tensions, suppress worries and problems, manage stress in their lives, and give them a feeling of overcoming their problems and being on top of the world."[15] This may well be true for many other places in the Caribbean.

Transshipment

Apart from trading their own marijuana in the United States, some Caribbean countries have become important transshipment centers for South American cocaine, heroin, and marijuana bound for Europe and North America. For more that two decades the Bahamas, Belize, and Jamaica dominated this business, but recently Barbados, Guyana, Trinidad and Tobago, OECS countries, and the Caymans and other British dependencies have featured more prominently in the illicit trafficking.[16] On July 4, 1992, for instance, a joint police-Coast Guard interdiction in Barbados confiscated over 2,000 pounds of marijuana, worth about B. $6 million, and arrested three Barbadians and one Canadian with arms and ammunition. Later that same month, 26.5 kilos of cocaine, worth about TT. $35 million, were seized at Cali Bay, Tobago following transshipment from Venezuela. Two months after that, on September 11, 1992, a Barbadian national was caught trying to smuggle 20 pounds of cocaine out of Guyana.[17]

The geography of the Bahamian archipelago makes it an excellent candidate for drug transshipment, given its 700 islands and cays, and its strategic location in the airline flight path between Colombia and South Florida. While most of the Bahamian islands could be used for smuggling, over the years the trade was concentrated in a few strategic places: Bimini; the Exumas; Andros; Grand Bahama; Abaco; Berry Islands; Cat Islands; Crooked Island and Acklins; Ragged Island; Mayaguana; Eleuthera; Long Island; San Salvador; and Inagua. Bimini, for example, is a mere fifty miles from the United States mainland.[18] One writer makes an uncomplimentary, but valid point about the country: "In a way, geography had always been the Bahamas' main commodity, and they had always marketed it with great skill."[19] This, of course, is true of other countries in the region.

Typically, aircraft depart the north coast of Colombia, arriving in the Bahamas five hours later. The cocaine or heroin is dropped for awaiting vessels for the final leg, a United States port of entry. The Bahamas has also become (in)famous for marijuana and hashish traffic from South American as well as Jamaica. As a matter of fact, when the Bahamas first became a transshipment center, the drug involved was mainly marijuana, with a few consignments of hashish. The 1983–1984 drug inquiry found evidence of drug trafficking as far back as 1968, when Jack Devoe and Robert Bireck undertook a fly-drop mission with 250 to 300 pounds of marijuana from Jamaica to Bimini. One of the earliest cocaine seizures was made in 1974: 247 pounds of pure cocaine, with a 1974 street value of U.S. $2 billion, at an airport in George Town, Exuma. That same year, the Bahamas police discovered a store of marijuana off Grand Bahama Island. It was over six feet high and more than two miles long.[20]

One measure of the amount of trafficking in the Bahamas is the extent of drug seizures and related arrests. Table 9.1 suggests that the Bahamas is a major part of the illicit network. American citizens are always the largest group of foreigners arrested, followed by a combination of Jamaicans, Colombians, and Haitians. For example, more

Table 9.1

Bahamas Drug Seizures (pounds), Arrests, and Convictions

ACTIVITY	1983	1984	1985	1986	1987	1988	1989	1990	1991	TOTALS
Cocaine Seizures	3,354	3,701	14,469	6,687	23,126	20,620	12,088	5,569	7,981	97,595
Marijuana Seizures	705,554	180,468	83,413	12,583	171,408	19,587	1,015	5,249	2,623	1,181,900
Number of Arrests	NA	1,501 [1,130]	1,580 [1,218]	1,530 [1,212]	1,596 [1,172]	1,277 [1,040]	1,255 [1,043]	1,443 [1,241]	1,085 [NA]	11,267 [NA]
Percentage Convicted	NA	NA	NA	66	69	71	67	36	NA	NA

Sources: Government of the Bahamas, Ministry of National Security, *Summary Report on the Traffic in Narcotic Drugs Affecting the Bahamas in 1990*, 28 March 1991; Government of the Bahamas, Ministry of Foreign Affairs, *Bahamas Narcotics Control Report 1991*, March 1992.

NA Not available.
[ ] Number of Bahamians arrested.

than 50 percent of the 202 foreigners arrested in 1990 were American—120. The next largest groups were Haitians and Jamaicans. However, there is also trafficking by nationals of places far from the Bahamas. In one case, a Nigerian woman was given a seven-year sentence by the Bahamas Supreme Court, on August 29, 1990, following a 1989 arrest for attempting to smuggle 4.1 pounds of heroin and 1.25 pounds of cocaine out of the country.[21]

Bahamian National Security authorities noted a steep decline in cocaine seizures from June 26, 1989 to November 14, 1990: a mere 3,479 pounds. But there was a dramatic upsurge in seizures in the one month from November 14 to December 14, 1990: 3,617 pounds of cocaine seized in three air delivery interceptions. In 1991, Bahamas officials were convinced that use of the country as a transit center for marijuana from Colombia and Jamaica to Florida by air and sea had virtually ended. However, in 1992 they concluded that the major seizures of cocaine in Bahamian and adjacent international waters during late 1990 and early 1991 indicated that the traffic from Colombia has returned to pre-1989 levels.[22]

The geography and topography of Belize also make that country ideal for drug smuggling. There are large jungle-like areas, sparse settlements, and about 140 isolated airstrips that facilitate pitstops on flights from South America to North America. Moreover, there is virtually no radar coverage beyond a thirty-mile radius of the international airport in Belize City. The 1992 *International Narcotics Control Strategy Report* noted: "Belize is now a marginal producer of marijuana. [However,] its growing importance as a transshipment point for South American cocaine is now the most important narcotics-related challenge confronting Belize."[23] Evidence of the increasing traffic is reflected in the growing number of drug seizures, numerous crashed and or seized aircraft, and increased availability of cocaine and crack in Belize. Trafficking arrests for 1987, 1988, and 1989, for example, numbered 1,540. In 1989 alone, 539 people were arrested.

Table 9.2 gives an idea of the scope of the Jamaican smuggling problem. The island has long been a linchpin in the drug trade, given its long coastline, proximity to the United States, its many ports, harbors, and beaches, and its closeness to the Yucatan and Windward Passages. There is both air and maritime trafficking. For maritime traffic, use is made of pleasure boats with storage compartments to ferry small quantities of drugs. Bigger loads are put aboard commer-

Table 9.2

Jamaica Drug Seizures (pounds) and Arrests

ACTIVITY	1986	1987	1988	1989	1990	1991	TOTALS
Cocaine Seizures	1,213	18,960	22	287	1,676	132	22,290
Marijuana Seizures	–	473,989	1,168	83,775	63,933	94,799	717,664
Foreigners Arrested	782	567	625	638	524	674	3,810
Jamaicans Arrested	3,341	3,400	3,100	2,956	4,908	4,353	22,058
Total Number of Arrests	4,123	3,967	3,725	3,594	5,432	5,027	25,868

Sources: U.S. Department of State, *International Narcotics Control Strategy Report*, Washington, D.C., March 1992; March 1991; March 1990.

cial cargo and fishing vessels. Both large and small amounts of drugs are smuggled by air, with arrests of couriers at the two international airports almost daily occurrences.

Between 1984 and 1989 there were five major drug seizures by United States Customs on board Air Jamaica flights, involving 15,000 pounds of marijuana alone. After a significant drop in both marijuana and cocaine seizures, there were dramatic increases for both substances in 1989. Two astronomical finds in 1989 contributed to the increase:

- On April 1, 1989, United States Customs found 4,173 pounds of marijuana on an Air Jamaica A–300 AirBus in Miami. The drugs were packed in 88 boxes labeled "wearing apparel," and consigned to Joseph and Schiller, Inc. of Miami. The "garment" consignment was from Threadways Garments of Jamaica.
- On April 8, 1989, a seizure of 5,000 pounds of marijuana was made in Gramercy, Louisiana, on board *MV Kotor*, which was there to deliver a shipment of Jamaican bauxite. The smuggling was discovered after violent clashes by two rival drug gangs over ownership of the marijuana.[24]

Money Laundering

Money laundering is the conversion of profits from illegal activities, in this case drug activities, into financial assets that appear to have legitimate origins. There are several different techniques and methods of doing this. One way was outlined by William Rosenblatt, Assistant Commissioner of the United States Customs Service. According to Rosenblatt, money laundering has three stages: placement, layering, and integration.

Placement refers to the physical disposal of bulk cash, either by commingling it with revenues from legitimate businesses, or by converting currency into deposits in banks, securities companies, or other financial intermediaries. Layering involves transferring the money among various accounts through several complex transactions designed to disguise the trail of illicit takings. Integration, the last stage, requires shifting the laundered funds to legitimate organizations with no apparent links to the drug trade.[25] It is estimated that about U.S. $300 billion in drug revenues are laundered annually.

The Caribbean countries involved in this aspect of the drug business are Anguilla, the Bahamas, Cayman Islands, Montserrat, and the Turks and Caicos Islands. Antigua-Barbuda, Dominica, Grenada, St. Lucia, St. Vincent and the Grenadines, and Trinidad and Tobago are designated as "sleepers," countries with "the potential to become more important financial centers and havens for exploitation by money launderers, as the game of global musical chairs by narcotics money launderers continues."[26] For the INM, these countries have the appropriate qualifications for money laundering: bank secrecy; willingness to cooperate; and limited, usually poorly trained, enforcement resources. During fall 1991 there were several allegations of money laundering in Grenada where the number of offshore banks had grown from three in early 1990 to 118 by late 1991.[27]

The money laundering allegations have centered mainly around the British dependencies. A 1989 study by Rodney Gallagher of the international accounting firm Coopers and Lybrand revealed some telling reasons for this. According to the Gallagher Report, over 525 international banks and trust companies have offices in the Cayman Islands. With 26,000 people, 10,000 of whom are foreigners, the Caymans accommodated 46 of the world's 50 largest banks, including Dai Ichi Kangyo and Fuji, Japan's two largest banks; Bank America; Barclays of the United Kingdom; Swiss Bank Corporation; and Royal Bank of Canada. Registration data for 1987 showed 18,264 companies registered in the areas of international investment, sales trading, shipping, insurance, real estate, and related areas. This amounted to a ratio of one international bank for every forty-nine residents. The 1987 banking sector assets stood at U.S. $250 billion.

There are many incentives and benefits of doing business in the Caymans and other dependencies. The Caymans have no income, corporate, or withholding tax. Companies that operate mainly outside the Caymans can register there as non-resident companies or incorporate as exempt ones, with the ability to issue bearer shares to non-resident ones and thus avoid disclosure of beneficial owners. In addition, bank secrecy is guaranteed under the 1976 Preservation of Confidential Relations Act. The offshore financial industry itself is critical to the economic security of the Caymans, having grown to U.S. $360 billion in one decade. It provides one-third of the jobs in the Caymans and about the same proportion of their GDP.[28]

Anguilla was home to 2,400 registered companies in 1988, including 38 banks and 80 insurance companies. The inducements are freedom to move capital without exchange controls, no domestic taxes, minimum disclosure requirements, and the availability of professional services. The British Virgin Islands (BVI) have a tax regime, but a light one. They had 13,000 companies registered in 1988. Although they now have only six major banks, reports are that money launderers use their services extensively. However, BVI and United States authorities have been able to obtain vital bank records and have frozen drug-related money. In 1991, for example, over U.S. $3 million were transferred to the United States for forfeiture and sharing between the United States and the BVI. Of all the British dependencies, the Turks and Caicos Islands have the least developed financial services sector.[29]

Security Implications

Political Security

The various narcotics-related problems discussed above present Caribbean countries with security challenges that are political and military as well as economic in nature. One of the most critical political security aspects is the corruption of government officials. Drug corruption not only undermines the credibility of governments, it also impairs the ability of government agencies to protect the public interest. It can even warp the ability of politicians and bureaucrats to define the national interest adequately. Moreover, it can lead to the development of cynicism within the general society, and to an increase in the level of public tolerance for corruption, both of which are dangerous. As such, corruption subverts political security.

Corruption has been unearthed in the Bahamas, Jamaica, Trinidad and Tobago, St. Lucia, the Turks and Caicos, and elsewhere. Even more dangerous than general government corruption is the corruption of law enforcement officials in police and defense forces, immigration and customs services, and internal revenue agencies. For example, on August 16, 1988 I had an extensive interview with Cuthbert Phillips, then Police Commissioner of St. Lucia, on Eastern Caribbean security concerns. The drug problem consumed much of our attention, and Phillips waxed eloquent in declaiming against the drug barons and those who aid them. Less than a month later Phillips was dismissed for being implicated in drug-related corruption and inefficiency in the Royal St. Lucia Police Force. And as we saw in chapter five, he was imprisoned also later, following a manslaughter conviction.

In some cases, law enforcement officials go beyond facilitating smuggling; they themselves become couriers. One of many such cases recently involved the arrest of a Barbadian immigration officer at London's Heathrow International Airport, on May 14, 1990, with a large quantity of cocaine he had brought from Barbados. And in March 1992 Sargeant Roger Newman of the Royal Bahamas Police Force (RBPF) was charged with possession and intent to supply six kilos of cocaine. Interestingly enough, Sergeant Newman worked with the Bahamas special drug court where he often acted as a prosecutor.[30]

Some of the region's most notorious corruption cases were in the Bahamas. Continuous allegations about high-level drug-related corruption involving the Prime Minister and other government officials prompted an official inquiry in 1983. In its 1984 report, the Commission of Inquiry noted that widespread transshipment of drugs through the Bahamas had adversely affected almost all strata of the society. Several top officials were indicted. Five government ministers either resigned or were dismissed. The Commission noted several questionable practices by the Prime Minister, and the fact that between 1977 and 1984 his expenditures and assets far exceeded his official income. For example, his bank deposits reflected U.S. $3.5 million in excess of his salary for that period. Yet there was no firm evidence of his being on a drug payroll as alleged.

The Commission reported:

> We were also alarmed by the extent to which persons in the public service have been corrupted by the illegal trade. We have given our reasons later in this report for concluding that corruption existed at the upper and lower levels of the Royal Bahamas Police Force and we have concluded that certain Immigration and Customs officers accepted bribes. We were particularly concerned to discover that those corrupting influences made their presence felt at the levels of Permanent Secretary and Minister.... In our opinion, the whole nation must accept some responsibility. Apathy and a weak public opinion have led to the present unhappy and undesirable state of affairs in the nation.[31]

The Commission's report and the implementation of some of its recommendations have improved the picture in the Bahamas considerably, but drug corruption still exists there. In President George Bush's March 1989 Statement of Explanation for the Bahamas to the United

States Congress—part of the foreign assistance certification procedure—he noted: "While the Government of the Commonwealth of the Bahamas is more active in investigating allegations of corruption, we are concerned by reports that corruption still exists. Prime Minister Pindling and his ministers must forcefully address this issue." The Statement also called for "stronger unilateral efforts to curb drug trafficking and consumption within the Bahamas."[32]

Three months after the publication of the Bahamas inquiry report, Chief Minister Norman Saunders and Commerce and Development Minister Stafford Missick of the Turks and Caicos were among several people arrested in Miami on drug-related charges. The March 1985 arrests followed three months of investigations by the United States Drug Enforcement Administration (DEA), in cooperation with the British government, and Turks and Caicos law enforcement agencies. The charges included conspiracy to import narcotics into the United States, conspiracy to violate the United States Travel Act, and the conduct of interstate and foreign travel to aid racketeering enterprises.

During the trial, the DEA alleged that Saunders had accepted U.S. $30,000 from undercover DEA agents to guarantee safe stopover refueling on flights from Colombia to the United States. Moreover, the prosecution showed a video tape, filmed before the arrests, where Saunders was shown receiving U.S. $20,000 from a DEA undercover agent. The money was allegedly to protect drug shipments passing through South Caicos Island, en route to the United States. All the defendants were convicted in July 1985 on the conspiracy charges, although Saunders was acquitted of the more serious charges of conspiring to import cocaine into the United States. Missick was convicted of the additional charge of cocaine importation. Saunders and Missick were sentenced to eight and ten years, respectively, and each was fined U.S. $50,000.

As might be expected, all of this had tremendous political repercussions in the Turks and Caicos. An official inquiry into arson, corruption, and other malpractice in the dependency provided a scathing commentary on the state of affairs there. The net result was the suspension of the constitution by Britain, and the imposition of direct rule by the Governor, assisted by a four-member advisory council. Britain also established a constitutional reform commission, headed by University of the West Indies Vice-Chancellor, Sir Roy Marshall, to consider possible changes in the dependency's governmental structure and operations.[33]

In April 1992, Assistant COP Rodwell Murray of the TTPS went public with an allegation he had made in 1991 to top National Security Ministry officials: that there is a drug-trafficking cartel operating within the police force. Drug corruption has been uncovered before in Trinidad and Tobago. In 1987, the Scott Commission report led to the suspension of 51 police officers and the eventual resignation of COP Randolph Burroughs who had earlier been indicted on bribery and other charges, but later acquitted. In March 1991, the La Tinta Commission investigation into an aborted sting operation where one policeman was killed led to the suspension of sixteen officers. Because of the increasing scale of trug trafficking in Trinidad and Tobago, and the seniority of the police official making the allegation this time, Prime Minister Patrick Manning has invited Britain's Scotland Yard to investigate the allegation.[34]

There is another important political security dimension of the narcotics operations. While there is no imminent threat of the "Colombianization" of the Caribbean in terms of violence waged by the drug barons against government officials and institutions, the openness and vulnerability of Caribbean societies are such that drug barons can easily subvert their sovereignty and governability. Indeed, some analysts contend that the April 1, 1989, Air Jamaica drug discovery, coming just one week after Prime Minister Manley had declared a "war on drugs," resulted from a deliberate act, and was meant to challenge the Jamaican government.[35]

Ron Sanders made a very pertinent observation: "A handful of well-trained narcotic soldiers or mercenaries could make a lightening trip to a country, wreak destruction, and fly out before a defense could be mounted by states friendly to the small island."[36] Shridath Ramphal, former Commonwealth Secretary-General, once put it more poignantly: "It only takes twelve men in a boat to put some of these governments out of business." This is precisely one of the points made to me by the former St. Lucia COP in our August 1988 interview. Officials within and outside the British Virgin Islands harbored this very concern in January 1989 after a group of Colombian traffickers had been arrested. The apprehension would be even greater where there is suspicion of significant collusion of government officials, especially in law enforcement agencies, with traffickers.

Military Security

The corrupting of law enforcement officials noted above has a distinct military security dimension: it compromises the agents of national security, with the implication that (a) their capacity for effective action is undermined, and (b) individuals and groups become inclined to resort to vigilante tactics because of that diminished capacity. Moreover, drugs have precipitated a sharp increase in crime generally and gang warfare in particular. Jamaica has suffered the brunt of this increase. One writer explains: "Indeed, Jamaica over the past few years has experienced, through an upsurge in violent crime, the effects of a combination of drugs and money in the form of the naked display of power through the use of arms."[37]

Perhaps even worse, in some places the drug business facilitates a dangerous ancillary operation: gun running. In one case, a ten-ton shipment of arms, with an estimated value of J. $8 million, arrived in Jamaica on December 22, 1988. It was to be airlifted later to Colombia. The shipment, from Heckler and Koch of West Germany, included 1,000 G3A3 automatic assault rifles, 250 HK21 machine guns, ten 60-millimeter commando mortars, and 600 rounds of high explosive 60-millimeter mortar shells. The planned operation involved West Germans, Englishmen, Panamanians, Colombians, and Jamaicans. Interrogation of the conspirators on January 4 and 5, 1989, revealed that the arms were destined for a leftist insurgent group called the Revolutionary Armed Forces of Colombia (FARC). The operation was underwritten by Colombian cocaine dealers who finance FARC. The arms had been paid for out of a special drug shipment made earlier to Europe.

The affair ended on January 6, 1989, when the arms were placed on a Colombian military aircraft and sent to Bogota. The foreigners were extradited and the Jamaicans were held on a variety of charges. That, of course, was not the first or only reported incident of gun running in the region. Scott MacDonald documents the involvement of "Mickey" Tolliver, an American pilot, in a July 1986 operation. It began in Haiti where he picked up a DC–3 aircraft with weapons and ammunition. He then flew to Costa Rica, then to Colombia where he took a consignment of 4,000 pounds of marijuana and 400–500 kilos of cocaine. Then, said Tolliver, he flew to the Bahamas where he watched Bahamian police unload the guns and weapons.

This narcoterrorism aspect of drug operations was even more dramatic in the Antigua-Barbuda case, and warrants some extended discussion. On December 15, 1989, the Colombian police killed Rodríguez Gacha and his son Freddy, both of the Medellin drug cartel. One of the raids made on several of Gacha's properties uncovered hundreds of Israeli-made Galil rifles and supporting ammunition. The disclosure by Israel that the weapons were part of a larger sale to the Antigua-Barbuda government for the Antigua-Barbuda Defense Force (ABDF) led to a Colombian diplomatic protest to Antigua-Barbuda on April 3, 1990. The protest prompted Antigua-Barbuda on April 10, 1990, to retain United States attorney Lawrence Barcella to investigate the matter. Shortly afterwards, there was an extensive public inquiry by a one-man Commission of Inquiry.

The inquiry, by British jurist Louis Blom-Cooper, uncovered an incredible scheme involving Israelis, Antiguans, Panamanians, and Colombians. Yair Klein, a retired Israeli army Colonel, and Pinchas Schachar, a retired Brigadier-General, then a representative of Israel Military Industries (IMI), were told by Maurice Sarfati, another Israeli, that the Antigua-Barbuda government was interested in acquiring weapons and ammunition. Sarfati presented forged documents showing (a) he was an authorized Antiguan government representative, and (b) an arms purchase had been authorized by Vere Bird, Jr., Antigua's "National Security Minister," the son of Prime Minister Vere Bird, Sr., and Colonel Clyde Walker, the head of the ABDF. Consequently, the relevant End-User Certificate, the official weapons requisition by an arms purchaser, was forwarded to Israel.[38] It should be noted that Sarfati had indeed been a government representative at one time, but in this case the documents were forged. Moreover, there was no person in the Antiguan government designated "National Security Minister."

United States Senate investigations into the affair revealed that the initial order was for 500 weapons and 200,000 rounds of ammunition, valued at U.S. $353,700. The final order total was U.S. $324,205. A down payment of U.S. $95,000 was made, and between November 14, 1988, and February 13, 1989, thirteen financial transactions, ranging between U.S. $44,000 and U.S. $100,000, were made on the deal. The banks used were Banco Aleman-Panameño; Philadelphia International Bank; Manufacturers Hanover Trust; Bank Hapoalim of Israel; and American Security Bank of Washington, D.C.[39] The weapons were placed aboard a Danish ship, MV *Else TH*, which sailed from Haifa,

Israel, on March 29, 1989, bound for Central and South America via Antigua. The Antigua consignment was transshipped at Port Antigua to the MV *Seapoint*, a Panamanian ship. The *Seapoint* then took the arms to Colombia to the real consignee, the Medellin drug cartel. The Antiguans implicated were: Vere Bird, Jr., Minister of Public Works and Communications; Lt. Colonel Clyde Walker, ABDF Commander; Vernon Edwards, Managing Director of a shipping and brokerage agency; and Glenton Armstrong and Sean Leitch, Customs officers.

Sarfati, the leading Israeli figure, first went to Antigua in April 1983. He cultivated a friendship with Vere Bird, Jr., then an attorney in private practice, who was instrumental in the granting of official approval for a melon cultivation project, one of Sarfati's pet schemes. The Bird-Sarfati friendship produced many advantages for Sarfati between 1983 and 1990: appointment in October 1984 by Vere Bird, Jr., as Special Adviser on Civil Aviation; appointment in May 1985 as Special Envoy in the Ministry of External Affairs, Economic Development, and Tourism; a 1985 OPIC ([U.S.] Overseas Private Investment Corporation) loan of U.S. $700,000; a supplemental loan from OPIC for U.S. $600,000 in 1986; appointment in February 1986 as Managing Director of Antigua-Barbuda Airways, with a token annual salary of U.S. $100, but a U.S. $70,000 expense account; and a series of 1987 promissory notes by the Antiguan government, amounting to U.S. $4 million.[40]

Thus, Sarfati had developed a relationship with the Antiguan government, and with Vere Bird, Jr., in particular, enabling him to exploit the relationship and not account meaningfully for any of his actions. Vere Bird, Jr., also benefitted from the links. For example, his law firm, Bird and Bird, handled the legal interests of Sarfati's corporate holdings—Roydan Ltd. and Antigua Promoters Ltd. In addition, Sarfati guaranteed Bird's loans, amounting to U.S. $92,000 in November 1988. Blom-Cooper observed: "It seems to me a matter of some significance that at the time the conspiracy was negotiated, Mr. Vere Bird, Jr. was in financial difficulties and was beholden to the bankrupt Mr. Sarfati. Not only did he need money, but he also needed to help Mr. Sarfati earn money." The Commissioner made an even more damaging observation: "I entertain no doubt Mr. Vere Bird, Jr. was paid by or at least with, money emanating from Señor Rodríguez Gacha, for the services rendered to the arms transshipment."[41]

The arms transshipment was, however, only part of a larger scheme, which was initiated in September 1988 to create a mercenary training establishment using the ABDF as an organizational cover. According to the brochure produced by Spearhead Ltd., the project's corporate entity, the aim was to establish a central civilian security school to train "corporate security experts, ranging from the executive level to the operational level, and bring them to the highest professional capacity in order to confront and defuse any possible threat." A central part of the enterprise was to be a "speciality shop" to sell small arms, among other things. The planners were catering to a special clientele, including "local private and official entities"; international banks; international oil and industrial companies; and "international private business people." Blom-Cooper asserted: "To any one with the slightest knowledge of armed forces it was obvious that the training school proffered by Spearhead Ltd., was intended, among other things, to train mercenaries in assault techniques and assassination."[42]

Both Vere Bird, Jr., and the ABDF Commander were involved in the scheme, having made several trips to Miami do discuss details, allowed their offices and phones to be used for the project, and having provided, in the case of the ABDF Commander, inspections of ABDF facilities to visiting Spearhead officials. Antigua and Antiguan public officials were thus deeply implicated in schemes with direct and indirect connections to the devious and nefarious pursuits of the drug underworld. Blom-Cooper summed up the motives quite well:

> The scandal which surfaced in Antigua in April 1990 around the plot to provide a school to train mercenaries for the illegal armed forces of the Medellin drug cartel, and which led to the criminality, not only of a prominent Minister . . . in unholy alliance with the Commander of the Defense Force, but also with the assistance of a prominent shipping agent and a customs officer, reflect the age-old pressures of human nature, greed, the thirst for power, and finally, unbridled corruption.[43]

Economic Security

As it happens elsewhere, much of the Caribbean's drug corruption springs from greed. However, some of it relates to the relative economic deprivation in parts of the region where unemployment in 1989 was 19 percent in Jamaica, 23 percent in Trinidad and Tobago, and 26 percent in Guyana. GDP growth has generally been low. Indeed in

Barbados, Guyana, and Trinidad and Tobago, the economy actually declined in 1990. Moreover, as was observed in chapters two and three, the Caribbean has a huge public debt—U.S. $10.2 billion in 1990. This debt and the related high debt service ratios are a virtual economic albatross. In addition, high inflation drives up prices, even of basic commodities.

Under these circumstances, one can appreciate that some people who engage in drug production and trafficking are driven by basic economic needs. Even for those without such motives, like public officials, it is often difficult to resist the temptation to earn "easy money" to supplement low incomes. For example, in Antigua, one of the more economically comfortable islands in the Eastern Caribbean, the average 1990 monthly salary of a police officer was around U.S. $456, while the Police Commissioner earned about U.S. $2,000 a month. Junior customs officials got about US$365 per month, and senior officers, U.S. $483. It should be borne in mind, also, that prices are high. Moreover, compared with other government workers, the police "have it made." Thus, while not condoning bribery, one could understand the susceptibility to it, considering that these officials could make four or five times their monthly income for facilitating just one transaction. The average pilot, for example, reportedly earns about U.S. $5,000 per kilo for his services.[44]

The drug trade takes a heavy toll on the already weak Caribbean economies. One respect relates to the charges and fines levied against the owners of carriers on which drugs are found. In January 1992, for instance, a U.S. $1.2 million fine was imposed by the United States Customs against the Guyana Airways Corporation (GAC) after a GAC flight had arrived in New York with close to 100 pounds of marijuana.[45] The toll has been heaviest for Jamaica, with several noteworthy instances:

- In 1986 two Air Jamaica planes were impounded in Miami and New York and a U.S. $657,000 fine was levied.
- In 1986, the now defunct Eastern Airlines was fined U.S. $900,000 after marijuana was found on a cargo flight. Three weeks later it was fined U.S. $1.6 million for the same infraction. Cargo flights from Jamaica were then suspended.
- In 1987, Evergreen, a Korean-owned shipping line, paid U.S. $135 million in fines to the United States Customs.

- In 1988, Sea-Land Services paid the United States Customs U.S. $85 million in fines.
- In 1989 the United States Customs imposed a U.S. $96 million charge against Sea-Land Services following the discovery of 12,000 pounds of marijuana shipped from Jamaica. Sea-Land subsequently withdrew its services from Jamaica.
- In April 1989 an Air Jamaica plane was impounded in Miami and a U.S. $28.8 million fine imposed.
- Two boats belonging to the Jamaica Banana Cooperative Association were impounded for most of spring 1989, unable to pay the heavy fines imposed following the discovery of marijuana aboard them.[46]

Both state and commercial enterprises have, therefore, felt the crunch. The fines have been devastating for Air Jamaica, contributing to its 1988–1989 losses of U.S. $14 million, 20 percent more than the losses for the previous year. Between 1989 and 1991, Air Jamaica was fined about U.S. $37 million for illegal drugs found on its planes entering the United States. The fines were, however, reduced to U.S. $3 million with agreement that the remaining money be used to upgrade security at the country's airports. The security measures introduced to curb the trafficking also have a high financial burden. For example, in Jamaica, all container cargo is now subject to a 100 percent search (or close to it), resulting in about 85 percent shipping delays. Moreover, it costs about J$3,000 to strip and search each container. The overall costs of this operation to businesses in any single year are astronomical, considering that Jamaica operates between 850,000 and one million containers annually.[47] Obviously, these costs are passed on to the consumer. The campaigns to eliminate production and curb the trafficking of drugs also require Caribbean states to devote considerable portions of their already scarce financial resources to the drug problem. For instance, since 1989 the Bahamas has spent about 15 percent of its annual national budget on drug countermeasures. Eighty-five percent of the RBDF 1990 expenditure of B$18.5 million was devoted to combating drug trafficking.[48]

We saw in chapter three that because of internal capability limitations, Caribbean countries are forced to rely significantly on foreign economic and technical assistance, at both the bilateral and the multilateral levels. At the bilateral level, United States assistance is important to many countries. However, drug operations have often jeopardized the assistance to some.

Under the 1986 United States Anti-Drug Abuse Act (PL 99–570), the President is allowed to impose trade sanctions, including duties, loss of tariff benefits, 50 percent withholding of bilateral aid, and suspension of air services on "offending countries." In the Western Hemisphere the list of "offending countries" includes the Bahamas, Belize, Bolivia, Brazil, Colombia, Ecuador, Jamaica, Mexico, Panama, Paraguay, and Peru. Congress can reverse presidential action to grant aid or impose sanctions by passing a joint resolution within forty-five days of the president's determination on the matter, due on March 1 of each year.[49] Ever since the passage of PL 99–570, the Commonwealth Caribbean countries concerned have managed to receive certification. Congress, however, did not always agree with the President's assessment and certification efforts. In 1988, for instance, Congress attempted to overturn the certification for the Bahamas. And in 1989 Senator John Kerry (D-Mass) led another effort to decertify the Bahamas. Fortunately, his effort was defeated, by a 57 to 40 vote.[50] What is troubling about the drugs-aid link is that the United States pressures countries into specific kinds of cooperation, using the aid suspension as a threat.

The economic security implications of drug operations discussed above, however, reflect only part of the economic security matrix. Tourism, a key sector in many Caribbean countries, has been adversely affected in many places. The linkage between drugs and tourism needs substantive assessment, but evidence suggests that the adverse effect is a consequence of the negative press that scares away potential tourists, and the high incidence of drug-related crime in some places. In addition, drug use contributes to the loss of employment man-hours due to addiction, rehabilitation, and incarceration. It also affects the shaping of attitudes and values in societies that are highly vulnerable to American materialism.

Countermeasures

While the main purpose here is to discuss the nature of the drug problems and their security implications, it is useful to conclude by noting some of the responses to the various problems, in addition to those mentioned above.

Countermeasures have been taken at the domestic, regional, and international levels. The importance attached to the regional and international efforts reflects the recognition that Caribbean countries do not possess the capabilities to deal adequately with the problems individually. But perhaps, more importantly, it also reflects acceptance by states in the Caribbean and, indeed, throughout the world, that the international scope of the problems demands international responses. It is also important to note that responses come not only from governments and international governmental agencies, but also from nongovernmental organizations. This is a demonstration by these organizations that the implications of the problems are such that the collective will and the resources of all are required.

Countermeasures include campaigns to reduce drug production, rehabilitate addicts, and to educate the public on the dangers of drug use. Interdiction and law enforcement have been boosted, and several countries have found it necessary to introduce draconian laws to deal with aspects of the problem. For instance, the Jamaica Parliament passed the Dangerous Drugs Act in 1987; the Narcotic Drugs and Psychotropic Substances Act was approved in Guyana in 1988; Barbados had the Drug Abuse (Prevention and Control) Act okayed in 1990; and in 1991 Trinidad and Tobago's Dangerous Drug Act became law.

Calls have been made for capital punishment for some drug offenses.[51] But generally, these new laws impose stiff fines and terms of imprisonment for drug use and trafficking. They also provide for the confiscation of property acquired through drug trading, and they create or expand institutions to deal with different aspects of the problem. In Guyana, for example, the 1988 legislation imposes heavy fines and prison terms for the possession, sale, dispensing, and trafficking of illicit drugs. In some cases the penalty is life imprisonment. The law also sanctions seizure of drug acquired property, and allows bail for drug offenders only under special circumstances. These laws are often applied fully, as when, in March 1992, Guyana's Chief Magistrate, Claudette La Bennett, refused bail to a nine-month pregnant woman accused of possessing six pounds of cocaine and weapons and ammunition. The woman, Sharon Morgan, who had been charged along with Colombian and Venezuelan accomplices, appealed La Bennett's decision and was released on G$100,000 bail. During her release she delivered her baby, but then failed to show for trial on three occasions. She was later convicted and sentenced to four years in prison, *in absentia*.[52]

Some of the provisions of the new laws border on the violation of the civil rights of citizens. Two examples will suffice. Section 24(1) of the Jamaica legislation permits *any constable* to search, seize, and detain, *without a warrant*, any conveyance he reasonably suspects is "being or has been used for the commission of any offense under this Act." The Guyana law has a similar provision—Section 93(1). These provisions permit considerable police power, which, regrettably, has often been misused. The second example is that under Section 26 of the 1987 Jamaica legislation, Section 78 of the Guyana legislation, and under Section 20 of the Trinidad and Tobago law, the burden of proof rests on the accused. This is an exception to the normal provision for the state to have the burden of proof.

There are obvious and not so obvious dangers in all this. The Jamaica Justice Minister alluded to some of them, even before the Trinidad and Tobago legislation was passed. Precedents had already been set in Jamaica and Guyana. The Minister observed:

> In our effort to rid our societies of the scourge of drugs and with some international pressures we are being invited to reverse burdens of proof and adopt a retroactive confiscatory regime. All this is understandable. The perceived danger is real, the consequences of the mischief which we would excise disastrous. As we contemplate effective measures, the nagging question though for all of us remains: Are they just?
>
> I remember too that in Jamaica, the mongoose was imported from India to kill out the snakes. It did a very good job. The snakes were eliminated. The mongoose then turned its attention to the chickens. There is a lesson in this. Effective measures against vermin may be turned to effective use by the ill-intentioned against decent and law-abiding citizens.[53]

Jamaica's National Security Minister, K.D. Knight, reported to the Jamaican Parliament in July 1991 on a special anti-cocaine trafficking strategy introduced in 1990. The strategy consists of identifying organizations in Jamaica and the United States involved in the trade; targeting high-risk flights; profiling legitimate Jamaican entrepreneurs suspected of trading; and using the intelligence capability of the newly created National Firearms and Drug Intelligence Center. The strategy began to pay off, with cocaine seizures totaling sixteen pounds at the Norman Manley International Airport alone between June and December 1990. Minister Knight also reported two other major cocaine seizures in 1990: one of 400 kilos, and the other of 300 kilos. Between January and November 1991, more than 2,534 kilos of marijuana, 3 kilos of cocaine, and 36 kilos of hashish oil were seized at the country's two international airports. Jamaica also increased the manpower of the Port Security Corps (PSC) in 1991 to 900, and allowed the United States National Guard to install a radar on the island. The success of the initial radar operations, which ran from August to October 1991, convinced Jamaican and United States authorities to make the operations permanent.[54]

As a result of the Gallagher Report mentioned above and investigation by Britain's Scotland Yard following inquiries by the United States Office of the Comptroller of the Currency, measures were taken to curb money laundering in Montserrat. Montserrat had been using the offshore banking industry as part of a strategy to reduce dependency on Britain. Banking licenses were sold for U.S. $10,000 and the island soon became a haven for money laundering and other financial irregularities. The most dramatic measure to curb irregularities was the March 1991 revocation of 311 banking licenses. Many of the institutions whose licenses were revoked were described as "little more than a smart title and a letterhead," and "nothing more than a few documents in a lawyer's filing cabinet." Yet they provide the legal basis for moving money around the world. In addition to the bank closures, Britain amended the island's constitution, assigning responsibility for the financial sector, previously held by local politicians, to the Governor of the dependency. Further, a British adviser was appointed to oversee a new financial supervisory agency.[55]

At the regional level there are several joint initiatives in education, intelligence, rehabilitation, law enforcement, and other subjects under the CARICOM High Level Ad Hoc Group on the Regional Drug Program.[56] One significant initiative was the endorsement by CARICOM leaders at their 1991 Summit in St. Kitts-Nevis of Jamaica's proposal for a Regional Training Center for Drug Law Enforcement. The Jamaica plan is for a regional agency to serve as a resource base for technical advice to Caribbean governments, and to systematize the region's anti-narcotic law enforcement training. Jamaica argued: "A Regional Drug Training Center, by helping to establish a common approach to drug control strategies, [will] minimize the possibilities of narco-criminals transferring their activities from one country to another within the region."[57]

The Center will be financed by the Jamaican government, the United Nations Drug Control Program (UNDCP), the Inter-American Drug Abuse Control Commission (CICAD), and other sources. The plan is to locate it in St. Catherine, 134 miles outside the Jamaican capital, Kingston, as part of an existing criminal justice complex that includes the Police Staff College and the Jamaica Police Academy. Training at the Center will focus on drug identification, interdiction procedures, surveillance techniques, money laundering investigation, intelligence data collection and analysis, risk assessment, procedures for tracking and seizing drug assets, and other subjects.

The UNDCP secured the services of Robert Simmonds, a former Commissioner of the Royal Canadian Mounted Police (RCMP), to advise on the establishment of the institution. Simmonds made his first visit to Jamaica in June 1991. Jamaica plans to put at the disposal of the Center some of its own counter-narcotics resources and facilities. These include the computerized National Firearms and Drug Intelligence Center; a Joint Information and Coordination Center with computer links to similar centers in the United States and elsewhere; a Contraband Enforcement Team; and a specially trained anti-narcotics Port Security Corps.[58]

Some Caribbean countries have signed Mutual Legal Assistance Treaties with the United States in the counter-narcotics effort. Treaties have been signed by Jamaica, the Bahamas, Belize, and by Grenada, on September 18, 1991. These treaties provide for training, joint interdiction, asset sharing, intelligence, and material and technical assistance. Air Jamaica and the United States Customs signed an agreement on December 13, 1991 to bolster drug countermeasures. And on August 14, 1992 the United States gave Guyana an additional U.S. $50,000 in assistance to combat trafficking. The sum augments the U.S. $300,000 given to Guyana in 1989 to aid the drug battle, and is to be used to repair GDF Coast Guard radar equipment and upgrade army and police computer facilities. There are also other bilateral narcotics treaties. One between the Bahamas and Canada, for example, came into force in July 1990. There is also one between the Bahamas and Britain. Belize has four agreements with Mexico for improved narcotics cooperation, including intelligence exchange, and Mexican assistance for prevention and rehabilitation programs.

There are also some multilateral treaties. The Bahamas, Britain, and the United States, for instance, signed one on July 12, 1990, providing for joint law enforcement involving the Bahamas, the Turks and Caicos, and the United States. This treaty extends the basing network of OPBAT—Operation Bahamas and the Turks and Caicos—from three bases to four. The new base is at Great Inagua, the southernmost island in the Bahamas. Also of interest is the fact that during July 1991, Trinidad and Tobago and Venezuela agreed to establish joint air and naval interdiction operations. Moreover, in September 1991, the Bahamas and Cuba initiated talks about joint trafficking countermeasures, and in April 1992 Guyana and Venezuela agreed on joint measures to combat trafficking and use.[59]

For all the successes in eradication and interdiction programs, there is a certain futility in efforts to halt drug trafficking completely. One writer explains it in very practical terms:

> Even if the United States can increase the risk of capture and conviction for traffickers, drug smuggling's tremendous profitability guarantees that there will be thousands of willing replacements for the traffickers that are successfully prosecuted. A payment of $50,000 per trip to the masters of these ships is common. The engineers make about $25,000 and each of the crewmen receives between $5,000 and $10,000.[60]

The way the United States pursues its drug eradication and interdiction policies in the Caribbean is itself a problem for many countries in the region. United States law enforcement officials have often pursued suspects into Caribbean territorial waters, at times arresting individuals in Caribbean jurisdictions without even courtesy notification of the arrests. There has often been virtual coercion by United States agencies in the selection of local personnel for local drug enforcement units and in the planning and directing of drug operations. Caribbean governments consider all these affronts to their sovereign authority and indicated this to President Ronald Reagan. In pursuit of a mandate by CARICOM leaders, Prime Minister Vere Bird, Sr., of Antigua-Barbuda wrote President Reagan in July 1988, in his capacity as Chairman of CARICOM. He rebuked "attempts to extend domestic United States authority into the neighboring countries of the region without regard to the sovereignty and independent legal systems of those countries."[61] Nevertheless, there is greater affront in relation to Latin American countries.[62]

At the international level, Caribbean countries are party to several agreements designed to facilitate information-sharing, education, and joint countermeasures, to name a few. Among these are the 1961 Single Convention on Narcotic Drugs; the 1971 Convention on Psychotropic Substances; the 1972 Protocol amending the 1961 Convention; and the 1988 United Nations Convention Against Illicit Traffic in Narcotic Drugs and Psychotropic Substances. Indeed, the Bahamas has the distinction of being the first country to ratify the 1988 Convention. States in the region also participate in many hemispheric and international agencies and networks. These include the OAS Money Laundering Experts Group; UNDCP; CICAD; the United Nations Fund for Drug Abuse Control (UNFDAC); the International Narcotics Control Board (INCB); the Caribbean Drug Money Laundering Conference; the Meeting of Heads of National Law Enforcement Agencies (HONLEA); and the Maritime Security Council.

Caribbean countries are, thus, engaged in a wide range of domestic, regional, and international initiatives and measures to help counter the problems of illicit drug production, abuse, and trafficking, and of money laundering. There is now even greater acceptance of the validity of an assertion made in 1980 by Linden Pindling while he was Prime Minister of the Bahamas: "I have no doubt . . . that it's the greatest single threat to the social, economic fabric. . . . Unchecked it will destroy us . . . the money available is just too great."[63] Narcotics operations provide the Commonwealth Caribbean with its greatest security challenge. Caribbean governments and decent, law-abiding citizens have to win the battles against narcotics. The consequences of failure are too horrendous even to contemplate, and it is clear that when the final reckoning is made, Caribbean people and government will have sustained severe political, military, and economic casualties in the war on drugs.

Notes

1. "Sandiford Addresses Caribbean Coast Guards," *New York Carib News*, July 31, 1990, p. 36; and "Statement of Honorable Michael Manley, Prime Minister of Jamaica," p. 7, in U.S. Congress, Senate, Committee on the Judiciary and the Caucus on International Narcotics Control, *U.S. International Drug Policy—Multilateral Strike Forces—Drug Policy in the Andean Nations*, Joint Hearings, 101st Cong., 1st and 2nd Sess., November 6, 1989, and January 18 and March 27, 1990. Manley's testimony was given on November 6.

2. United Nations General Assembly, *Political Declaration*, XVIIth Special Session, A/RES/S-17/2. 15 March 1990, p. 2.

3. Gitanjali Persaud, "Police Uncover Biggest Ganja Plot Yet," *Stabroek News* (Guyana), March 15, 1992, p. 1; and Frederick Gilbert, "Police Discover G. $1 Billion of Ganja in Berbice," *Stabroek News* (Guyana), May 23, 1992, p. 1.

4. Scott B. MacDonald, *Dancing on a Volcano: The Latin American Drug Trade*, New York: Praeger, 1988, p. 89.

5. Alma H. Young, "Territorial Dimensions of Caribbean Security: The Case of Belize," in Ivelaw L. Griffith, ed., *Strategy and Security in the Caribbean*, New York: Praeger, 1991, pp. 142–43; and U.S. Department of State, *International Narcotics Control Strategy Report*, March 1991, p. 135. This document is referred to hereafter as *International Narcotics Report*.

6. *International Narcotics Report*, 1991, p. 133.

7. *International Narcotics Report*, 1991, pp. 198–99.

8. "Ganja Growers Finding New Ways to Harvest," *Sunday Sun* (Barbados), November 5, 1989, p. 24A; and *International Narcotics Report*, 1991, p. 195.

9. MacDonald, *Dancing on a Volcano*, p. 90.

10. Ibid., p. 91.

11. *International Narcotics Report*, 1991, p. 182.

12. *International Narcotics Report*, 1992, p. 142. Also see, Howard Frankson, "An Upsurge of Crime in Belize," *Caribbean Contact* (Barbados), July/August 1992, pp. 5, 8.

13. "Police Reports Alarming Increase in Cocaine Seizures," *Guyana Chronicle*, December 15, 1989; Ronald Sanders, "The Drug Problem: Social and Economic Effects—Policy Options for the Caribbean," *Caribbean Affairs* 3 (July-September 1990): 20; and "Crack Bases on the Rise," *Jamaican Weekly Gleaner*, May 18, 1992, p. 4.

14. Carl Stone, "National Survey on the Use of Drugs in Jamaca (1990)," Kingston, Jamaica: USAID, 1990, p. 35. I am grateful to Anne Langhaug of USAID headquarters, Washington, for going to great trouble to secure a copy of this study.

15. Stone, "National Survey," p. 40.

16. Rickey Singh, "Barbados Named in Trinidad Drug Report," *Daily Nation* (Barbados), February 3, 1987; Roy Morris, "Bajan Connection Arrested in London Cocaine Catch," *Daily Nation*, May 16, 1990, p. 1; Ron Sanders, "Narcotics, Corruption, and Development: The Problems in the Smaller Islands," *Caribbean Affairs* 3 (January-March 1990): 79–92; "Bellyful of Dope is Fatal," *Barbados Advocate*, April 11, 1990; "$30 Million in Cocaine is Seized in Trinidad," *New York Carib News*, February 29, 1990, p. 4; "10 Arrested in Drugs Shootout [in St. Lucia]," *New York Carib News*, October 16, 1990, p. 4; "$300M in Illegal Drugs Seized Last Year," *Sunday Chronicle* (Guyana), January 6, 1991, pp. 6,7; Gitanjali Persaud, "Witness Tells of Cocaine Found in Soap Box," *Stabroek News*, January 14, 1992, pp. 1, 12; and "Cops Tell of Finding Coke among Panties," *Stabroek News*, February 15, 1992, p. 3.

17. Janice Griffith, "$6M Ganja Haul," *Sunday Sun*, July 5, 1992, p. 1; "Trinidad and Tobago Police Make Big Cocaine Seizure," *Stabroek News*, July 29, 1992, p. 7; and "Cops in U.S.$12 Million Cocaine Timehri Haul," *Stabroek News*, September 12, 1992, p. 1. The police detective responsible for canine drug detection at the airport was charged as an accomplice of the Barbadian national. See "Sniffer Dog Handler Charged in Timehri Coke Case," *Stabroek News*, September 29, 1992, p. 20.

18. For a detailed examination of the use of Bimini and other areas for trafficking, see Government of the Bahamas. *Report of the Commission of Inquiry,* Nassau, Bahamas, 1984, pp. 9–51.

19. Anthony P. Maingot, "Laundering the Gains of the Drug Trade: Miami and Caribbean Tax Havens," *Journal of Interamerican Studies and World Affairs* 30 (Summer-Fall 1988): 168.

20. *Report of the Commission of Inquiry,* pp. 7–8.

21. Government of the Bahamas, Ministry of National Security, *Summary Report on the Traffic in Narcotic Drugs Affecting the Bahamas in 1990,* Nassau, the Bahamas, March 28, 1991, pp. 13–14, 66.

22. *Summary Report,* p. 31; and Government of the Bahamas, Ministry of Foreign Affairs, *Bahamas Narcotics Control Report 1991,* Nassau, the Bahamas, March 1992, p. 7.

23. *International Narcotics Report,* 1992, p. 141.

24. "Jamaica under Drug Siege," *New York Carib News,* May 2, 1989, p. 4; "Questions Surround Air Jamaica Drug Find," *New York Carib News,* May 16, 1989, p. 3; and "Politicians United against Drugs," *New York Carib News,* May 16, 1989, p. 3.

25. U.S. Congress, Senate, Committee on Foreign Relations, *Drug Money Laundering, Banks, and Foreign Policy,* Report by the Subcommittee on Narcotics, Terrorism, and International Operations, 101st Cong., 2nd Sess., September 27, October 4, and November 1, 1989, p. 5.

26. *International Narcotics Report,* 1991, pp. 364–65.

27. See Michael D. Roberts, "Grenada's Second Invasion," *New York Carib News,* November 12, 1991, p. 3.

28. *International Narcotics Report,* 1991, pp. 366–67. See also Steve Lohr, "Where the Money Washes Up," *New York Times Magazine,* March 29, 1992, pp. 27ff.

29. *International Narcotics Report,* 1991, pp. 367–68; and *International Narcotics Report,* 1992, pp. 421–22.

30. See Morris, "Bajan Connection." See also "Two [Bajan] Cops Detained Following Ganja Bust," *Guyana Chronicle,* January 21, 1992, p. 7; and "Bahamian Policeman Charged for Cocaine," *Stabroek News,* March 18, 1992, p. 7.

31. *Report of Commission of Inquiry,* p. 35.

32. "Statement of Explanation: The Bahamas," Appendix C of Raphael Perl, *International Narcotics Control: The President's March 1, 1989 Certification for Foreign Assistance Eligibility and Options for Congressional Action,* Congressional Research Service Report for Congress 89–141F, April 7, 1989.

33. MacDonald, *Dancing on a Volcano,* pp. 120–22; and Deborah Cichon, "British Dependencies: The Cayman Islands and the Turks and Caicos Islands," in Sandra W. Meditz and Dennis M. Hanratty, eds., *Islands in the Commonwealth Caribbean,* Washington, D.C.: Library of Congress, 1989, pp. 579–81.

34. Camini Marajh, "Police 'Drug Cartel' Charges Made in 1991—Murray told NAR Government," *Sunday Guardian* (Trinidad and Tobago), April 12, 1992, pp. 1,5; Anabel Thomas, "DPP to Act on Suspended Cops," *Daily Express* (Trinidad and Tobago), April 14, 1992, pp. 1,10; "Scotland Yard to Investigate Trinidad Drug Cartel," *Stabroek News,* May 10, 1992, p. 24.

35. See, for example, testimony by Anthony Maingot in U.S. Congress,

House, Select Committee on Narcotics Abuse and Control, *Drugs and Latin America: Economic and Political Impact and U.S. Policy Options*, Report of the Seminar held by the Congressional Research Service, 101st Cong., 1st Sess., April 26, 1989, p. 13.

36. Ron Sanders, "Narcotics, Corruption, and Development," p. 84.

37. Vincent Tulloch, "Terrorism/Drugs Combination Threatens Security," *Sunday Gleaner* (Jamaica), January 15, 1989, p. 10A; and Faye V. Harrison, "Jamaica and the International Drug Economy," *Transafrica Forum* 7 (Fall 1990): 55–56. Also see "Gang Wars: Drug Menace Rearing its Ugly Head," *Daily Nation* (Barbados), June 10, 1988; and "10 Arrested in Drugs Shootout [in St. Lucia]."

38. Louis Blom-Cooper, *Guns for Antigua: Report of the Commission of Inquiry into the Circumstances Surrounding the Shipment of Arms from Israel to Antigua and Transshipment on 24 April 1989 en Route to Colombia*, London: Duckworth, 1990, p. 2

39. U.S. Congress, Senate, Committee on Governmental Affairs, *Arms Trafficking, Mercenaries, and Drug Cartels*, Hearing, Permanent Subcommittee on Investigations, 102nd Cong., 1st Sess., February 27 and 28, 1991, pp. 127–130.

40. Blom-Cooper, pp. 47–52; 120–21.

41. Ibid. pp. 116, 117.

42. Ibid., p. 58.

43. Ibid., p. 131.

44. Sanders, "Narcotics, Corruption, and Development," p. 83.

45. "GAC Fined $1.2 U.S. for Transporting Ganaja," *Guyana Chronicle*, January 29, 1992, p. 3.

46. U.S. Congress, *Drugs and Latin America*, pp. 12–13; and Janice A. Cumberbatch and Neville C. Duncan, "Illegal Drugs, USA Policies, and Caribbean Responses: The Road to Disaster," *Caribbean Affairs* 3 (October-December 1990): 166–68.

47. *Drugs and Latin America*, pp. 12–13; Cumberbatch and Duncan, p. 168; and "U.S. Customs."

48. *Summary Report*, p. 73; and *Bahamas Narcotics Control Report 1991*, p. 12.

49. U.S. Congress, Senate, Committee on Foreign Relations, *International Narcotics Control and Foreign Assistance Certification: Requirements, Procedures, Timetables, and Guidelines*, Report prepared by the Congressional Research Service, 100th Cong., 2nd Sess., March 1988, pp. 1–2.

50. *Drugs and Latin America*, p. 129.

51. See, for example, "Trinidad Senator Advocates Hanging for Traffickers," *Stabroek News*, August 29, 1991, p. 9; and "Charles Says No to Drugs: Hang Them," *New York Carib News*, July 28, 1992, p. 3.

52. See "Court Refuses Bail to Nine-Month Pregnant Accused," *Stabroek News* March 3, 1992, p. 16; and "Drugs Accused Sentenced to Jail in Her Absence," *Stabroek News*, April 14, 1992, p. 16.

53. Government of Jamaica, Ministry of Justice, *Crime and Justice in the Caribbean (Keynote address by the Honorable R. Carl Rattray, Q.C., Minister of Justice and Attorney General of Jamaica)*, May 10, 1991, p. 7.

54. Government of Jamaica, Parliament, *Sectoral Debate Presentation of the Honorable K.D. Knight, Minister of National Security*, July 3, 1991, pp. 72–74;

"U.S. Customs, Air Jamaica Sign Anti-Drug Pact," *Jamaican Weekly Gleaner*, December 23, 1991, p. 5; and *International Narcotics Report*, 1992, p. 210.

55. Joseph B. Treaster, "On Tiny Isle of 300 Banks, Enter Scotland Yard," *New York Times*, July 27, 1989, p. A4; "Montserrat: Stormy Weather," *Economist*, December 9, 1989, p. 41; "Oh, My Brass Plate in the Sun," *Economist*, March 16, 1991, p. 84; and John Evans, "Montserrat, in a Cleanup, Pulls Licenses of 300 Banks," *American Banker*, March 28, 1991, p. 21.

56. See CARICOM Secretariat, *Report of the Third Meeting of the High Level Ad Hoc Group on the Regional Drug Program*, REP. 90/3/34 RDP, October 3, 1990.

57. Government of Jamaica, *Memorandum Submitted by the Government of Jamaica on the Establishment of Regional Training Center for Drug Law Enforcement Officers in Jamaica*, Kingston, Jamaica, 1991, p. 4.

58. See *Memorandum*, pp. 2–4; and *Sectoral Debate Presentation*, pp. 64–83.

59. *International Narcotics Report*, 1991, p. 133; "T&T, Venezuela Consider Joint Air Operations," *Trinidad Express*, July 24, 1991, p. 2; *Bahamas Narcotics Control Report 1991*, p. 5; "Venezuela, Guyana Agreed on Joint Anti-Drug Plan," *Stabroek News*, April 13, 1992, p. 1; and "U.S. Worried About Guyana Coke Trafficking," *Stabroek News*, August 15, 1992, p. 1.

60. James E. Meason, "War at Sea: Drug Interdiction in the Caribbean," *Journal of Defense and Diplomacy* 6 (No. 6 1988): 8.

61. See Sanders, "The Drug Problem," p. 22.

62. See Linda Greenhouse, "High Court Backs Seizing Foreigner for Trial in U.S.," *New York Times*, June 16, 1992, pp. A1, A8; and Nathaniel C. Nash, "U.S. Anti-Drug Moves Irk Bolivians," *New York Times*, September 20, 1992, p. L16.

63. Cited in Maingot, "Laundering the Gains," p. 171.

10 SECURITY SAFEGUARDS IN THE 1990s

> The making of national security policy requires choices about both the objectives of policy (ends), and the techniques, resources, instruments, and actions which will be used to implement it (means). Even if one assumes that neither political nor perceptual problems interfere with the process, these choices are not straightforward. . . . Complete security cannot be obtained in any anarchic system, and, therefore, to hold that goal as an aspiration is to condemn oneself to pursuit of an operationally impossible objective.
>
> —Barry Buzan

The turbulence and unpredictability of the post-Cold War era make the normal dangers of political predictions and prescriptions infinitely more hazardous. This chapter will, therefore, simply offer some general notions of safeguards Caribbean nations might adopt in the 1990s and beyond.

It is evident from the previous chapters that Caribbean states have been confronted with all the major problem areas facing small states—vulnerability, internal instability, intervention, and militarization—in varying degrees and at differing times over the years since independence. We saw how various nations attempted to deal with some of their challenges, at both individual and regional levels. It should also be fairly obvious that it is unrealistic to expect Caribbean countries to be able to address adequately all of the dilemmas they face.

Regional security is relational in that it is difficult to appreciate the national security dilemmas of one state without understanding the pattern of security interdependence in the area.[1] Security is also always relative—to problems, perceptions, capabilities, and geopolitics, among other things. Hence, all states exist with a certain margin of insecurity. Small states in the Caribbean and elsewhere have to accept an existence with a relatively wide margin of insecurity compared to, say, big powers, because of some of the factors mentioned above. Thus, there are aspects of Caribbean security circumstances that states in the region will simply have to live with because there are powerless to alter them. Included here are their military vulnerability and political penetrability because of geographical and capability limitations. It is, however, possible for Caribbean states to forestall intra-regional militarization, and prevent or resolve internal instability precipitated by political factionalism and illegitimate rule, for example. This suggestion does not, incidentally, derive from any sense of political fatalism; rather it springs from a certain political realism.

Caribbean leaders need to distinguish properly between the possible and the impossible. This would enable them to avoid pursuing security shadows and wasting precious time and scarce resources initiating or pursuing strategies with fairly obvious zero potential. In this respect it is useful to bear in mind the advice of one Indian diplomat-scholar:

> The political fortitude of Third World leaders to strike a balance between reasonable and exaggerated security needs must be imbued with a recognition of the penalties of social underdevelopment in their countries. Responsible governments, be they civilian or military, must weigh their competing socioeconomic and political responsibilities along with security considerations, . . . demand more objective assessments of external threats from their civil and military advisers, and must direct efforts towards diplomacy, thus seeking a balance between economic development and legitimate defense against likely (not hypothetically exaggerated) threats.[2]

Something common to all Caribbean societies is the friendly, trusting, and open nature of their peoples and institutions. This is a characteristic which, when transmitted to the security arena, may make these societies more politically and militarily penetrable, and susceptible to both internal and external threats. Trust and openness are partly due to the relative stability of the region, the absence of authoritarian politics, except once each in Grenada, Guyana, and Dominica, and the predominance of liberal democracy where a premium is placed on civil and political rights.

It is, therefore, relatively easy to gain access to many political leaders and security-sensitive facilities such as power stations, water supply systems, and communications networks. Greater security consciousness should be exercised to mitigate circumstances where Caribbean leaders and sensitive installations could become unnecessarily vulnerable. One intelligence official in the region was able to enter meetings of Caribbean leaders in CARICOM and OECS forums and take pictures at very close range. All this without being invited or challenged. He recalled seeing Nicaraguan "officials" lobbying Prime Ministers and other leaders at the May 1988 OECS Council of Ministers meeting in St. Vincent and the Grenadines, having gained the kind of easy access that could be dangerous to the safety of leaders and the confidentiality of some discussions.

Expanded security consciousness is especially important in a place like Guyana where the country's size (214,970 km^2) and population distribution—mostly along the coasts—leave vast areas of the country without effective security. It was this circumstance that allowed a group of Americans, Colombians, and Guyanese to build an illegal airstrip at Waranama, 400 miles from the capital, Georgetown. The Colombians and Americans were able to enter the country illegally and bring a generator, a water pump, two airplane engines, six transmitting sets, tool kits, arms and ammunition, and other supplies over a four-month period. The operations were to be part of an international drug processing and transshipment network involving Trinidad and Tobago, Miami, and Colombia. In January 1989 several of the conspirators were arrested and charged, and the equipment was confiscated.[3]

Abu Bakr and his Jamaat-al-Muslimeen came close to toppling the government of Trinidad and Tobago in July 1990. Without much difficulty, they overcame security officers around Parliament and elsewhere and held government officials hostage.[4] This again testifies to the need for expanded security consciousness in the entire Caribbean since the scenario could easily have been played out anyplace in the region. Further evidence of the need for expanded security consciousness and proof of its high dividends are found in the Jamaica arms transshipment case noted in the previous chapter. The arms traffickers had hoped that the Christmas festivities would bring the traditional laxity that could be exploited. But there was the kind of security consciousness that really should be the norm rather than the exception throughout the region. The Jamaican National Security Minister Errol

Anderson was quite right when he said: "[T]his incident once again illustrated the critical need for the highest vigilance on the part of our security systems . . ."[5] Thus, especially because of drugs, expanded security consciousness is needed in most places.

Accompanying this consciousness should be appropriate emphasis on training. It is recognized, both within and outside the Caribbean, that training is one of the major deficiencies of the region's security services. When I asked Lt. Commander Peter Tomlin of the RSS, former St. Lucia COP Cuthbert Phillips, Deputy OECS Director-General Augustus Compton, and Commander Dean Schopp of the United States Military Liaison Office in the Eastern Caribbean to name the main shortcomings of Caribbean security forces in general and that of the RSS in particular in the 1983 Grenada operations, they all placed poor training at the top of the list. More important, however, training should be appropriate to the Caribbean. In this regard, plans for the Jamaica-based Regional Drug Training Center are to be commended.

It makes little sense having training without the institutional networks and appropriate technology and facilities to use it, however. Two points should be made here. First, the technology and equipment should be appropriate or adaptable to the practices and circumstances of the region. Much of the transport equipment given to Eastern Caribbean countries by the United States after the 1983 Grenada intervention was written off due to accidents because (a) the vehicles were left-hand drive while Caribbean security forces use right-hand drive; and (b) they were too large for the narrow Eastern Caribbean roads. Thus the equipment had little net use-value, although adequate training could have reduced accidents due to (a).

The second point is that some Caribbean leaders should be more conscious of the value of functional security technology. For example, I was told by one security official in the region that while a security communications mechanism had been freely installed in RSS member-states by INTERPOL to network heads of government and security chiefs, for years it was not functional. This was because of the low priority accorded it by some leaders who had failed to adopt some internal measures to have the system activated. The resource constraints of these states often make choices about such technology and facilities both difficult and sensitive. Yet such choices are becoming ever more necessary.

The Commonwealth experts were correct in asserting: "[E]conomic progress could help substantially in reducing economic weakness and insecurity, especially to the extent that it produces economic resilience."[6] We saw in chapter two that the economic dimensions of the Caribbean's insecurity relate to low resilience, economic vulnerability, and operational deficiencies. While considerable disagreement exists among scholars and statesmen about measures best able to deal with these, there is general agreement that some set of alternative economic strategies is necessary. Strategies adopted should be cognizant of the geopolitical realities of the region, the region's actual and potential resources and deficiencies, and bilateral and multilateral economic and political mechanisms available.

The diversification of economic and trade links beyond the traditional European and North American contacts is both welcome and necessary. In this respect, Jamaica took the lead in 1991 by establishing an embassy in Japan, with a clear sense of Japan's importance in its own new international economic and trade outreach. The initiative taken at the 1991 Regional Economic Conference in Trinidad and Tobago to pursue a "politics of inclusion" in the search for economic security measures also should be consolidated.

The necessity for collaboration in the Caribbean derives from common regional problems, capability limitations by all states, the "community" orientation of Caribbean leaders, and a practical recognition that collaboration offers the best hope of dealing with the problems of any one nation. No single collaborative measure is sufficient for the Caribbean. Of greater importance though, Caribbean nations need a proactive approach to collaboration; not to be pulled along with the tide of events. In order to maximize the benefits of security collaboration, they should adopt an affirmative approach, making full and efficient use of various opportunities that exist at several levels: the subregional; the regional; the hemispheric; and the international. Again, the Commonwealth experts were right: "It is our conviction that any satisfactory approach to tackling problems of small states' security requires a series of complementary measures relating to all the key aspects of security-building to be initiated at the national, regional, and international levels."[7]

The OECS and the RSS are the two institutions at the subregional level that can provide scope for security cooperation and conflict management. As noted in chapter six, the OECS was formed in June 1981 with a view to maximizing the use of the limited resources of member-states. The treaty under which it was established provides for collaboration and harmonization in economic and trade matters, defense and security, and foreign policy and diplomacy. The year 1986 saw the renewal of a campaign within the OECS for political unification in the Eastern Caribbean; to transform the OECS from a pluralistic community into an amalgamated one. But up to fall1992 the absence of political will to do this had frustrated much of the enthusiasm, slowing the momentum to translate ideals into reality. The plan for integration of all OECS states has been revised to one of limited unity—of four of the seven countries: Dominica, Grenada, St. Lucia, and St. Vincent and the Grenadines.[8]

While there are security advantages of political integration, two observations are in order. First, an amalgamated security community in the Eastern Caribbean will not alter the geopolitical and other vulnerability of the subregion, or of the region, although it may create better scope for dealing with some of the economic problems. Second, it will not automatically remove the basis for internal security concerns, but may well exacerbate polarizations and strain the stability of the unitary state. Subregional leaders should, therefore, increase the operational efficiency of the present institutions to better provide for their security needs, while setting the stage for ultimate integration.

As regards the RSS, while there are serious limitations and shortcomings, as noted in chapter six, it should not be abandoned, but strengthened, as suggested in our RSS discussion. Emphasis on militarism is neither necessary nor desirable, but the RSS can be a useful halfway house with an ability to aid in intelligence, drug interdiction, SAR, and coastal patrol. The Deputy Prime Minister of Barbados, Phillip Greaves, announced in July 1992 that the RSS's Memorandum of Understanding was being revised. It is hoped that the matters raised here and in chapter six are among those dealt with in the new agreement. There are no region-wide military bodies within the Caribbean. We saw earlier that proposals for a Caribbean Defense Force foundered because of political disfavor and cost considerations. I do not support a region-wide standing army. Such is not needed.

Come July 1993, CARICOM will be twenty years old. Thus, in spite of many problems, Caribbean countries have an institutional mechanism on which to build, and to pursue deeper and wider cooperation to bolster economic, political, and military security. The "Three-way Plan," announced by Prime Minister Patrick Manning in May 1992, to create a Barbados-Guyana-Trinidad and Tobago economic union as a precursor to a political one, certainly deserves consideration, since it is likely to enhance the area's economic and political, if not military, security.[9] Chapter three showed Caribbean involvement in several hemispheric organizations and agreements, including the OAS and SELA. While Caribbean states attest to the importance of these in the political and economic areas, the OAS is not in the mainstream of Caribbean security and conflict management. This is unlikely to change in the near future, even with the 1991 admission to membership of Belize and Guyana. Moreover, the OAS has a mixed dispute resolution record that reinforces the low confidence in it that exists in parts of the region.[10]

As noted in chapter seven, several middle powers have strategic interests in the Caribbean and can act in ways beneficial or detrimental to its security. These include Brazil, Colombia, Cuba, Mexico, and Venezuela. Caribbean states should utilize the bilateral and multilateral contacts with these states to their maximum advantage. Some Caribbean specialists are highly optimistic about mutually beneficial connections between CARICOM and these middle powers. Indeed, some writers even recommend that Caribbean countries make the development of relations with Latin America a cornerstone of their pursuits.[11] The West Indian Commission went even further. It called for the creation of an Association of Caribbean States (ACS) to be "anchored on CARICOM and promoted by CARICOM." According to the Commission, the ACS would be a true "Caribbean Commonwealth," bringing together all independent island states in the Caribbean Sea and those Central and South American countries whose shores are washed by the Caribbean Sea.[12]

In a wider hemispheric context there is every reason to use the special bonds developed with Canada for security purposes, especially in the economic area. While Canada refrains from giving direct military security assistance, some of its development aid is used for this purpose. There is little doubt that the Caribbean and the United States need each other for both economic and military security, if not political security. The mutual interests in dealing with drugs dramatize this. However, a military or political alliance of the subordinate Caribbean with the dominant United States is inadvisable. Stanley Hoffman reminds us:

> The great power does not really have to ask whether it ought to mortgage its independence; the alliance it negotiates may well restrict its freedom of action, but does not force it into dependence. A small power, when it establishes a hierarchy of the risks it must minimize, must choose between security and independence whenever it cannot simultaneously curtail the rights that threaten both.[13]

The geopolitical reality of American dominance cannot be wished away; and it unlikely to change in the foreseeable future, in spite of the prognostications of Paul Kennedy's *Rise and Fall of the Great Powers*. It is a reality that the Caribbean must live with. Caribbean decision makers should, therefore, fashion practical relationships that permit them to benefit from America's economic and military strength while minimizing reliance on the United States for maintaining its political stability. The United States argued that its militarization of the Caribbean was partly intended to provide security for the region. Caribbean leaders should, therefore, provide for their own limited regional security.

As we saw in the geopolitics discussion, Britain, France, and the Netherlands are among extra-regional powers with strategic stakes in the region. Caribbean states should continue to utilize linkages with these nations. Maximum use should also continue to be made of support and training from the London-based Commonwealth Secretariat, and of the Commonwealth consultative network. I support the position that "membership in the United Nations itself . . . provides some element of deterrence against the possibility of total obliteration by a predatory neighbor."[14] But even in the face of the Guatemalan and Venezuelan claims, no Caribbean state faces total obliteration. The aim should therefore not be so much to utilize the United Nations to prevent total obliteration, but to use it practically to maintain security in the course of sovereign pursuits.

Guyana's diplomacy, and to a lesser extent Belize's, over the hostile territorial pursuits against them testifies to the benefit of the United Nations. It could be used to alert the international community to vulnerability and specific threats, and to gain international support and sympathy. The United Nations also has mechanisms, under Articles 33, and 52 through 54, to prevent or minimize the violation of sovereignty, and to aid in conflict resolution.[15] For all this though, it must be remembered that in the absence of decisive collective security action, the United Nations is a mechanism with considerable limitations in cases of direct military aggression.

Because of domestic, regional, and international changes, the security challenges into the next century will be different than those in the 1970s and the 1980s. Economic and environmental security issues are likely to take a place of prominence, with political and military concerns commanding relatively less attention than they did before.[16] These changes will require adaptations by both scholars and statesmen; theoretical and conceptual ones by scholars and practical ones by statesmen. What Theodore Sorensen said leaders in the United States need to better recognize is all the more true for leaders in the Caribbean whose nations are smaller, with significant capability limitations: That nonmilitary developments can pose genuine threats to long-term security and citizens' quality of life; that traditional concepts of national sovereignty are unable to cope with torrential transborder flows of money, drugs, arms, AIDS and other diseases, and immigration; that no single country can combat these threats alone; and that new regional and international rules and institutions will be necessary to dealt with the nonmilitary threats.[17]

There is a tall order for Caribbean peoples, governments, and nations to sustain their achievements since independence and advance through the forthcoming decades, relatively secure in political, military, and economic terms. Caribbean leaders are fully conscious of the danger of the region becoming a backwater in the century ahead. There is every expectation that they will act to prevent this. In this regard, the work of the West Indian Commission, formed in 1989 to "Prepare the People of the West Indies for the Twenty-First Century," should help set the intellectual context and political framework for the fulfillment of the quest for security in the Caribbean.[18]

Notes

1. For an examination of security as a relational phenonemon, see Barry Buzan, *People, States, and Fear*, 2d ed. Boulder, CO: Lynne Rienner, 1991, especially chapters 2, 4, 5, and 10..

2. Jagat Mehta, ed., *Third World Militarization: A Challenge to Third World Diplomacy*, Austin, TX: LBJ School of Public Affairs, 1985, p. 18.

3. See "The Illegal Airstrip Case: Three Colombians, One Guyanese Charged," *Guyana Chronicle*, January 25, 1989, pp. 1, 4.

4. See Selwyn Ryan, *The Muslimeen Grab For Power*, Port of Spain, Trini-

dad: Imprint Caribbean, 1991, especially chapters 5 and 6. For a discussion of the delinquency of the security services, see pp. 157–80. At a July 1, 1992 press conference in Trinidad following the release of Abu Bakr and his associates, Attorney General Keith Sobion attributed Bakr's success to a "security lapse." See Ria Taitt, "Sobion: We Have Nothing to Fear," *Daily Express* (Trinidad and Tobago) July 2, 1992, p. 1.

5. See "Text of Statement Made at a Press Conference at Up Park Yesterday by Minister of National Security Errol Anderson," *Sunday Gleaner*, January 8, 1989, p. 16B. See also "Arms Shipment: Traffickers, Terrorists Involved," *Sunday Gleaner*, January 8, 1989, pp. 1, 13B.

6. Commonwealth Study Group (hereinafter CSG), *Vulnerability: Small States in the Global Society*, London: Commonwealth Secretariat, 1985, p. 55.

7. Ibid. p. 39.

8. See OECS Secretariat, *Forms of Political Union*, Castries, St. Lucia: OECS, 1988; "Season for Decision," in *Reaching for the Future—A Timely Trilogy*, Occasional Paper No. 2, West Indian Commission, 1991; W. Marvin Will, "A Nation Divided: The Quest for Caribbean Integration," *Latin American Research Review* 26 (No. 2, 1991): 3–37, esp. pp. 29–33; "RCA Session Opens," *New York Carib News*, September 10, 1991, p. 15; and "Federal System Favored by Windwards Assembly," *Stabroek News* (Guyana), November 3, 1991, pp. 12, 13.

9. See Tony Best, "New Political Union on the Cards?" *New York Carib News*, May 26, 1992, p. 3.

10. See, for example, Alsem Francis, "The Organization of American States and the Small States of the English-Speaking Caribbean: Legal Implications," in Anthony T. Bryan, ed., *The OAS and the Commonwealth Caribbean: Perspectives on Security, Crisis, and Reform*, Monograph Series 1, Institute of International Relations, St. Augustine, Trinidad, 1986; and Frank Clarke, "The Pacific Settlement of Disputes in the OAS," in Bryan, *The OAS and the Commonwealth Caribbean*.

11. See J. Braveboy-Wagner, "Caribbean Foreign Policy: An Examination of its Limitations and Needs," *Caribbean Affairs* 1 (July-September 1988): 77–89; Anthony T. Bryan, "The Geopolitical Environment: Latin America," in Anthony T. Bryan, J. Edward Greene, and Timothy M. Shaw, eds., *Peace, Development, and Security in the Caribbean*, New York: St. Martin's Press, 1990; and Andrés Serbín, "The CARICOM States and the Group of Three: A New Partnership between Latin-American and the Non-Hispanic Caribbean?" *Journal of Interamerican Studies and World Affairs* 33 (Summer 1991): 53–80.

12. West Indian Commission, *Time For Action: The Report of the West Indian Commission*, Black Rock, Barbados, 1992, pp. 426–35.

13. Stanley Hoffman, *The State of War*, New York: Praeger, 1968, p. 138.

14. CSG, *Vulnerability*, p. 70.

15. For example, both the 1966 Geneva Agreement and the 1970 Protocol of Port of Spain signed by Britain, Guyana, and Venezuela over settlement of the dispute based on the Venezuela claim contemplate the use of Article 33 options.

16. For a better exploration of this subject, see Anthony Bryan, "International Relations of the Caribbean Towards the Year 2000," *Caribbean Affairs* 3 (October-December 1990): 13–34; and Ivelaw L. Griffith, "Caribbean Security: An Agenda for the 1990s," Paper for delivery at the XVIIIth Conference of the Caribbean Studies Association, Jamaica, May 1993.

17. Theodore C. Sorensen, "America's First Post-Cold War President," *Foreign Affairs* 71 (Fall 1992): 29.

18. See *Time For Action*. For a useful analysis of the workings of the Commission and its potential benefits, see Howard A. Fergus, "Let All Ideas Contend: The Consultative Strategy of the West Indian Commission," *Caribbean Affairs* 4 (October-December 1991): 42–55.

APPENDIX 1

MEMORANDUM OF UNDERSTANDING RELATING TO SECURITY AND MILITARY COOPERATION

Between:

The Government of Antigua and Barbuda, hereinafter referred to as the "Antigua Government,"

The Government of Barbados, hereinafter referred to as the "Barbados Government,"

The Government of the Commonwealth of Dominica, hereinafter referred to as the "Dominica Government,"

The Government of St. Lucia, hereinafter referred to as the "St. Lucia Government,"

And

The Government of St. Vincent and the Grenadines, hereinafter referred to as the "St. Vincent Government;"

collectively referred to in this Memorandum as the "parties hereto."

The Antigua Government, the Barbados Government, the Dominica Government, the St. Lucia Government, and the St. Vincent Government being parties hereto have reached an understanding relating to Security and Military Cooperation as follows:

This is the original (1982) version of the Memorandum done for and agreed to by the governments of Antigua-Barbuda, Barbados, Dominica, St. Lucia, and St. Vincent and the Grenadines. The text, therefore, does not refer to the governments of Grenada and St. Kitts-Nevis, which became parties to the Memorandum after 1982.

Definitions

1. For the purposes of this Memorandum of Understanding "Force Commanders" mean the Commander, Antigua and Barbuda Defense Force, the Commissioner of Police, Antigua and Barbuda Police Force, the Chief-of-Staff, Barbados Defense Force, the Commissioner of Police, Royal Barbados Police Force, the Commissioner of Police, Commonwealth of Dominica Police Force, the Commissioner of Police, St. Lucia Police Force, and the Commissioner of Police, Royal St. Vincent Police Force;

"Participating country" means Antigua and Barbuda, Barbados, the Commonwealth of Dominica, St. Lucia, or St. Vincent and the Grenadines;

"Service personnel" means personnel belonging to or connected with

- (a)   the Antigua and Barbuda Defense Force and the Antigua and Barbuda Police Force,
- (b)   the Barbados Defense Force and the Royal Barbados Police Force,
- (c)   the Commonwealth of Dominica Police Force,
- (d)   the St. Lucia Police Force, or
- (e)   the Royal St. Vincent Police Force.

Areas of Cooperation

2. The parties hereto agree to prepare contingency plans and assist one another on request in national emergencies, prevention of smuggling, search and rescue, immigration control, fishery protection, customs and excise control, maritime policing duties, protection of off-shore installations, pollution control, natural and other disasters, and threats to national security.

3. With regard to paragraph 2, the interests of one participating country are the interests of the others; and accordingly the participating countries shall have the right of "hot-pursuit" within each other's territorial waters.

Council of Ministers

4. The Ministers responsible for Defense in the participating countries shall be the Council of Ministers, which shall be the central policy-making body.

5. The Council of Ministers may appoint advisory Committees comprising such persons from the participating countries as might be necessary.

6. The Council of Ministers shall meet at least once a year.

Central Liaison Office

7. There shall be a Central Liaison Office, which shall be responsible to the Council of Ministers for coordinating the objectives of the Memorandum of Understanding.

8. There shall be a Regional Security Coordinator, who shall be the chief officer of the Central Liaison Office; and there shall be such other staff as the Council of Ministers shall determine.

9. The Regional Security Coordinator shall be appointed by the Council of Ministers.

10. Staff, other than the Regional Security Coordinator, shall be appointed by the Council of Ministers on the recommendation of the Regional Security Coordinator after consultation with the Force Commanders.

11. The Regional Security Coordinator shall also be adviser to the Council of Ministers in matters relating to regional security and shall be authorized to negotiate with extra-regional agencies on behalf of the parties hereto; but any negotiation conducted by the Regional Security Coordinator does not bind the Government of any participating country unless ratified in writing by the Government of that participating country.

12. The salaries of the staff of the Central Liaison Office shall be fixed from time to time by the Council of Ministers.

Central Fund

13. There shall be a Central Fund, forty-nine percent of which shall be contributed by the Barbados Government and the remaining fifty-one percent shall be contributed in equal amounts by the governments of other participating countries; but if circumstances change the percentage contributed by Barbados and the other participating countries shall be subject to renegotiation.

14. The Central Fund shall be administered by the Central Liaison Office and shall be used for

(a) paying the salaries of the staff and any other expenses of the Central Liaison Office,

(b) coordinating the objectives of this Memorandum of Understanding, and

(c) paying to the Barbados Government the cost of insuring the spares and documentation mentioned in paragraph 35.

15. The Central Fund shall not be used for operational purposes in a participating country; but where one participating country requests assistance from one or more of the other participating countries, in this Memorandum of Understanding referred to as the "requesting country" and the "sending country" respectively, supplies held by the Central Liaison Office may be used for the purposes of the operation and any supplies so used shall be replaced by the requesting country.

16. (1) The Regional Security Coordinator shall prepare and submit, for the approval of the Council of Ministers, estimates on a triennial basis, but where circumstances change during any triennium for which estimates were submitted the Regional Security Coordinator shall prepare and submit supplementary estimates.

(2) The Regional Security Coordinator shall, every three months, submit accounts to the Ministers of Defense of the participating countries showing, *inter alia*, the amount due by each participating country to the Central Fund, and any such amount shall be paid within thirty days after the receipt of the accounts by the Ministers.

(3) The Regional Security Coordinator shall submit any information or prepare any document requested by the Council of Ministers, and any other information relating to the functions of the Central Liaison Office that the Regional Security Coordinator considers the Council of Ministers ought to be informed about.

Planning and Operations

17. There shall be a Joint Coordinating and Planning Committee comprising Force Commanders.

18. Combined operations shall be coordinated through the operations room at the Barbados Defense Force Headquarters, St. Ann's Fort, Barbados or such suitable place as may be agreed between Force Commanders.

19. The manning of the operations room shall be agreed between the Force Commanders.

Command and Discipline

20. For the purposes of this Memorandum of Understanding,

(a)   the requesting country shall retain operational control over all troops participating in operations in that country;

(b)   the senior officer of the sending country shall exercise tactical command over his troops;

(c)   commanding officers shall be responsible for the conduct and discipline of their subordinate service personnel.

Jurisdiction

21. When service personnel of one participating country are within the jurisdiction of another participating country, they shall respect the laws, customs and traditions of that other participating country.

22. (1) The Service Authorities of one participating country shall have, within another participating country or on board any vessel or aircraft of that other country, the right to exercise all such criminal and disciplinary jurisdiction over its service personnel, as are conferred on the Service Authorities by the laws of their own country, including the right to repatriate personnel to their own country for trial and sentencing.

(2) The Courts of one participating country shall have jurisdiction over service personnel of another participating country with respect to offenses that are committed by service personnel of that other participating country within the first-mentioned participating country and punishable by the law of the first-mentioned participating country.

(3) Where the Courts of one participating country and the Service Authorities of another participating country have the right to exercise jurisdiction in respect of an offense, the Service Authorities of that other participating country shall have the primary right to exercise jurisdiction if

(i)   the offense is committed by a member of the service personnel of that other participating country against the property or security of that other participating country, or against the property or person of another member of the service personnel, or

(ii)   the offense arises out of an act or omission arising in the course of official duty by a member of the service personnel of that other participating country.

(4) In any case other that those mentioned in sub-paragraphs (1), (2) and (3) the participating country within which the offense is committed shall have the primary right to exercise jurisdiction; but where the country with the primary right decides not to exercise jurisdiction, it shall notify the appropriate authorities of the other country as soon as practicable.

Claims

23. The government of each of the participating countries shall insure its service personnel against any claims for damage or injury, including injury resulting in death, caused by acts or omissions of its service personnel in the course of their duties.

24. In the case of an omission by a participating country to insure its service personnel, or where for any other reason service personnel of a participating country are not covered by insurance, that participating country shall deal with and settle at its own cost any claim brought by any person in respect of damage or injury arising out of the course of official duty.

25. If the law of one participating country does not preserve, save and keep free a member of the service personnel of another participating country against damages for a claim to which paragraph 23 or 24 relates, the first-mentioned participating country undertakes to preserve, save and keep him free from any such damage.

26. The participating country within whose jurisdiction any damage or injury occurs shall settle any claim brought in respect thereof, and where the damage was done or the injury caused by the personnel of any other participating country, that other country shall reimburse the first mentioned country.

Training

27. Service personnel of the participating countries shall undergo training in any of the participating countries on agreement between the Force Commanders of the participating countries involved in the training exercise.

28. In training operations the Coast Guard units shall be permitted to enter each other's territorial waters on agreement between the Force Commanders of the countries participating in the training operations.

29. Where necessary, exchange billets shall be by mutual agreement between the Force Commanders of the units participating in the exchange.

Maintenance

30. Coast Guard vessels shall, when necessary, undergo maintenance work at HMBS Willoughby Fort in accordance with builders' specifications and recommendations.

31. Emergency repair facilities for Coast Guard vessels shall also be provided at HMBS Willoughby Fort.

32. For the purposes of paragraphs 30 and 31, the Commander of the Coast Guard of a participating country is authorized to liaise with the Base Engineer HMBS Willoughby Fort.

33. The Base Engineer HMBS Willoughby Fort shall, before commencing any maintenance or emergency repair pursuant to paragraphs 30 and 31, as the case may be, submit an estimate of costs to the Chief of Staff, Barbados Defense Force, who shall transmit the estimate to the Force Commander of the country whose vessel it is and await the Commander's decision.

34. By agreement between the Force Commanders, spares and documentation shall be kept at HMBS Willoughby Fort.

35. The Barbados Government shall insure the spares and documentation mentioned in paragraph 34 against loss or damage and recover the cost of insurance from the Central Fund.

Procurement

36. By agreement between the Force Commanders, arms, ammunition, uniforms, equipment, and stores may be procured under a joint procurement program.

37. Arms, ammunition, uniforms, equipment, and stores procured under the joint procurement program mentioned in paragraph 36 shall be transferred among the participating countries by agreement between the Force Commanders.

Operational Expenses

38. For the purposes of this Memorandum of Understanding
   (a)   the requesting country shall pay
      (i) the expenses incurred in accommodating and victualling the troops of the sending country, and
      (ii) the medical expenses of any troops of the sending country who need medical attention in the requesting country;
   (b)   each participating country shall meet its own fuel costs;
   (c)   each participating country shall meet the costs of materials used in training its service personnel; and
   (d)   each participating country shall meet the costs of materials and labor used in maintaining its vessels.

Limited Assistance

39. A participating country may request assistance from one or more of the other participating countries and where such a request is made
   (a)   the Ministers responsible for Defense in those participating countries, and
   (b)   the Force Commanders of those participating countries, constitute, respectively, the Council of Ministers and the Force Commanders for that limited purpose only; and this Memorandum of Understanding shall be read and construed accordingly.

Territorial Waters, Exclusive Economic Zone and Visiting Forces

40. The Governments of the participating countries shall review and update their laws

(a)   relating to their territorial waters and their exclusive economic zones, and

(b)   relating to armed forces visiting the participating countries.

Commencement and Termination

41. This Memorandum shall come into force, in respect of a participating country, on the day it becomes a signatory to this Memorandum; and the Memorandum shall remain in force in respect of that participating country until terminated in respect of that country on a day specified by notice in writing to each of the other participating countries given to them at least three months before the day specified in the notice.

42. In the event of the termination of this Memorandum of Understanding, either in relation to all of the participating countries or in relation to any participating country, any provision relating to any matter of the criminal jurisdiction of any country, the treatment of claims by any country and the financial obligations of any country shall remain in force until the matter is finally disposed of.

Done originally at Roseau, Dominica, October 29, 1982.

APPENDIX 2

Military, Paramilitary, and Police Forces in the Caribbean

COUNTRY	SECURITY SERVICE	HEAD OF SERVICE	TITLE
Antigua-Barbuda	Antigua & Barbuda Defense Force	Major Trevor Alistaire Thomas	Chief of Staff
	Royal Antigua & Barbuda Police Force	Edric Potter	Commissioner of Police
Bahamas	Royal Bahamas Defense Force	Commodore Leon Smith	Commander
	Royal Bahamas Police Force	Bernard K. Bonamy	Commissioner of Police
Barbados	Barbados Defense Force	Brigadier Rudyard Lewis	Chief of Staff
	Royal Barbados Police Force	Orville Durant	Commissioner of Police
Belize	Belize Defense Force	Lt. Col. Earl Arthurs	Chief of Staff
	Belize Police Force	Bernard Bevans	Commissioner of Police
Cayman Islands	Royal Cayman Islands Police	Allan B. Ratcliffe	Commissioner of Police

Appendix 2 continued

COUNTRY	SECURITY SERVICE	HEAD OF SERVICE	TITLE
Dominica	Commonwealth of Dominica Police Force	Desmond Blanchard	Commissioner of Police
Grenada	Royal Grenada Police Force	Lt. Col. Nestor Ogilvie	Commissioner of Police
Guyana	Guyana Defense Force	Brigadier Joseph Singh	Chief of Staff
	Guyana People's Militia	Colonel Godwin McPherson	Commandant
	Guyana National Service	Colonel Cecil S. Austin	Director-General
	Guyana Police Force	Laurie Lewis	Commissioner of Police
Jamaica	Jamaica Defense Force	Commodore Peter Brady	Chief of Staff
	Jamaica Constabulary Force	Roy E. Thompson	Commissioner of Police
	Island Special Constable Force	John Mock-Yen	Commandant
	Special District Constables	-----	Reports to Area Superintendent
	Police Mobile Reserve Division	Joseph R. Evering	Assistant Commissioner
	Port Security Corp	Bruce Bartley	Managing Director

Appendix 2 continued

COUNTRY	SECURITY SERVICE	HEAD OF SERVICE	TITLE
St. Kitts-Nevis	Royal St. Kitts & Nevis Police Force	Stanley Franks	Commissioner of Police
St. Lucia	Royal St. Lucia Police Force	Algernon W.F. Hemmingway	Commissioner of Police
St. Vincent & the Grenadines	Royal St. Vincent & the Grenadines Police Force	Randolph Toussaint	Commissioner of Police
Trinidad & Tobago	Trinidad & Tobago Defense Force	Brigadier Ralph Brown	Chief of Staff
	Trinidad & Tobago Police Service	Jules Bernard	Commissioner of Police
Eastern Caribbean	Regional Security System	Brigadier Rudyard Lewis	Coordinator

APPENDIX 3

ACRONYMS AND ABBREVIATIONS

ABDF	Antigua and Barbuda Defense Force
BDF	Barbados Defense Force/Belize Defense Force
CARICOM	Caribbean Community and Common Market
CDB	Caribbean Development Bank
CDPF	Commonwealth of Dominica Police Force
CDU	Caribbean Democratic Union
CLO	Central Liaison Office
COP	Commissioner of Police
CPF	Caribbean Peacekeeping Force
DDF	Dominica Defense Force
ESF	Economic Support Fund
FMF	Foreign Military Financing
GDF	Guyana Defense Force
GNS	Guyana National Service
GPF	Guyana Police Force
GPM	Guyana People's Militia
IADB	Inter-American Development Bank
IMET	International Military Education and Training
IMF	International Monetary Fund
INCB	International Narcotics Control Board
INM	(U.S.) Bureau of International Narcotics Matters
INTERPOL	International Criminal Police Organization
ISCF	Island Special Constabulary Force
ISER	Institute of Social and Economic Research
JCF	Jamaica Constabulary Force
JDF	Jamaica Defense Force
JLP	Jamaica Labor Party
MAP	Military Assistance Program
MAS	Mutual Assistance Scheme
MOU	Memorandum of Understanding
NAM	Non-Aligned Movement
NJM	New Jewel Movement
OAS	Organization of American States
OECS	Organization of Eastern Caribbean States

OPBAT	Operation Bahamas and the Turks and Caicos
PMRD	Police Mobile Reserve Division
PNC	People's National Congress
PNP	People's National Party
PPP	People's Progressive Party
PRA	People's Revolutionary Army
PRG	People's Revolutionary Government
PSC	Parish Special Constable/Port Security Corps
RABPF	Royal Antigua and Barbuda Police Force
RBDF	Royal Bahamas Defense Force
RBPF	Royal Bahamas Police Force
RBPF	Royal Barbados Police Force
RCMP	Royal Canadian Mounted Police
RGPF	Royal Grenada Police Force
RSC	Regional Security Coordinator
RSKNPF	Royal St. Kitts-Nevis Police Force
RSLPF	Royal St. Lucia Police Force
RSVGPF	Royal St. Vincent and the Grenadines Police Force
RSS	Regional Security System
SAR	Search And Rescue
SCMFA	Standing Committee of Ministers of Foreign Affairs
SELA	Latin American Economic System
SKNDF	St. Kitts-Nevis Defense Force
SSU	Special Service Unit
TTDF	Trinidad and Tobago Defense Force
TTPS	Trinidad and Tobago Police Service
UG	University of Guyana
UWI	University of the West Indies
UNDCP	United Nations Drug Control Program
USAID	United States Agency for International Development
WIR	West Indies Regiment

SELECTED BIBLIOGRAPHY

Articles and Books

Adkin, Mark. 1989. *Urgent Fury: The Battle for Grenada*. Lexington, MA: Lexington Books.

Alexis, Francis. 1984. "British Intervention in St. Kitts,"*New York University Journal of International Law and Politics* 16 (Spring): 581–600.

Anderson, Thomas D. 1984. *Geopolitics of the Caribbean*. New York: Praeger.

Ashby, Timothy. 1987. *The Bear in the Backyard: Moscow's Caribbean Strategy*. Lexington, MA: Lexington Books.

Benn, Denis. 1987. *Ideology and Political Development*. Kingston, Jamaica: Inst. of Social and Economic Research.

Black, George. 1985. "MARE NOSTRUM: U.S. Security Policy in the English-Speaking Caribbean," *NACLA Report on the Americas* 19 (July-August): 13–48.

Boulding, Elise, ed. 1992. *New Agendas for Peace Research: Conflict and Security Reexamined*. Boulder, CO: Lynne Rienner.

Braveboy-Wagner, Jacqueline. 1989. *The Caribbean in World Affairs*. Boulder, CO: Westview Press.

———. 1984. *The Venezuela-Guyana Border Dispute*. Boulder, CO: Westview Press.

Bryan, Anthony T., ed. 1986. *The OAS and the Commonwealth Caribbean: Perspectives on Security, Crisis, and Reform*. Monograph Series No. 1. St. Augustine, Trinidad: Institute of International Relations.

Bryan, Anthony T., J. Edward Greene, and Timothy M. Shaw, eds. 1990. *Peace, Development, and Security in the Caribbean*. New York: St. Martin's Press.

Buzan, Barry. 1991. *People, States, and Fear*. 2d edition. Boulder, CO: Lynne Rienner.

Campbell, John. 1987. *History of Policing in Guyana*. Georgetown, Guyana: Guyana Police Force.

Caribbean Conference of Churches. 1982. *Peace: A Challenge to the Caribbean*. Bridgetown, Barbados: Caribbean Conference of Churches.

Child, Jack. 1985. *Geopolitics and Conflict in South America*. New York: Praeger.

Clarke, Colin, and Tony Payne, eds. 1987. *Politics, Security, and Development in Small States*. London: Allen and Unwin.

Commonwealth Study Group. 1985. *Vulnerability: Small States in the Global Society*. London: Commonwealth Secretariat.

Cumberbatch, Janice A., and Neville C. Duncan. 1990. "Illegal Drugs, USA Policies, and Caribbean Responses: The Road to Disaster," *Caribbean Affairs* 3 (October-December):150–81

Danns, George K. 1982. *Domination and Power in Guyana*. New Brunswick, NJ: Transaction Books.

Domínguez, Jorge. 1984. "Cuba's Relations with Caribbean and Central American Countries." In Alan Adelman and Reid Reiding, eds., *Confrontation in the Caribbean Basin*. Pittsburgh: University of Pittsburgh Press.

Duncan, Neville C. 1991. "Political Violence in the Caribbean." In Griffith, *Strategy and Security in the Caribbean*. New York: Praeger.

Duncan, W. Raymond. 1985. *The Soviet Union and Cuba: Interests and Influences*. New York: Praeger.

Edwards, Stewart Hylton. 1982. *Lengthening Shadows: Birth and Revolt of the Trinidad Army*. Port of Spain, Trinidad: Imprint Caribbean.

English, Adrian. 1988. *Regional Defense Profile No. 1: Latin America*. London: Jane's Publishing Company.

Fauriol, Georges, ed. 1989. *Security in the Americas*. Washington, D.C.: National Defense University Press.

Francis, Anselm. 1992. "The Current Phase of the Belize/Guatemala Dispute," *Caribbean Affairs* 5 (January-March): 71–85.

———. 1990. "The Gulf of Paria: Area of Conflict" *Caribbean Affairs* 3 (January-March): 26–37.

Fursdon, Edward. 1988. "The British, the Caribbean, and Belize," *Journal of Defense and Diplomacy* 39 (No. 6): 39–41.

García Muñiz, Humberto. 1991. "Decolonization, Demilitarization, and Denuclearization in the Caribbean." In Griffith, *Strategy and Security in the Caribbean*. New York: Praeger.

———. 1989. "Defense Policy and Planning in the Caribbean: An Assessment of the Case of Jamaica on its 25th Independence Anniversary," *Journal of Commonwealth and Comparative Politics* 27 (March): 74–102.

———. 1988. *La Estrategia de Estados Unidos y La Militarización del Caribe*. Río Piedras, Puerto Rico: Institute of Caribbean Studies, University of Puerto Rico.

———. 1986. *Boots, Boots, Boots: Intervention, Regional Security, and Militarization in the Caribbean 1979–1986*. Río Piedras, Puerto Rico: Caribbean Project for Justice and Peace.

García Muñiz, Humberto, and Betsaida Vélez Natal. 1992. *Bibliografía Militar del Caribe*. Río Piedras, Puerto Rico: Center for Historical Investigation, University of Puerto Rico.

Gill, Henry. 1976. "Conflict in Trinidad and Tobago's Relations with Venezuela." In Leslie Manigat, ed., *The Caribbean Yearbook of International Relations 1975*. St. Augustine, Trinidad: Institute of International Relations.

González, Edward. 1982. *A Strategy for Dealing with Cuba*. Rand Corporation, R–2954-DOS/AF, September.

Granger, David A. 1985. *Defend and Develop: A Short History of the Defense Forces of Guyana*. Georgetown, Guyana: Guyana Defense Force.

————. 1975. *The New Road: A Short History of the Guyana Defense Force.* Georgetown, Guyana: Guyana Defense Force.

Griffith, Ivelaw L. 1993a. "Drugs and Security in the Commonwealth Caribbean," *Journal of Commonwealth and Comparative Politics* 31 (July).

————. 1993b. "Some Security Implications of Commonwealth Caribbean Narcotics Operations," *Conflict Quarterly* 13 (Spring).

————. 1993c. "Los Militares y los Cambios Políticos en Guyana." In Jorge Rodríguez Beruff and Humberto García Muñiz, eds., *Paz y Conflictos en el Caribe.* Río Piedras, Puerto Rico: University of Puerto Rico/Caracas, Venezuela: Nueva Sociedad.

————. 1993d. "Caribbean Security: An Agenda for the 1990s," Paper for delivery at the XVIIIth Conference of the Caribbean Studies Association, Jamaica, May 1993.

————. 1993e. "Security for Development: Caribbean—Asia Pacific Regional Mechanisms." In Jacqueline Braveboy-Wagner, W. Marvin Will, Dennis Gayle, and Ivelaw L. Griffith, *The Caribbean in the Pacific Century.* Boulder, CO: Lynne Rienner.

————. 1992a. "The RSS—A Decade of Caribbean Collective Security," *Caribbean Affairs* 5 (July-September): 179–91.

————. 1992b. "The Regional Security System—A Decade of Collective Security in the Caribbean," *The Round Table* 324 (October): 465–75.

————, ed. 1991a. *Strategy and Security in the Caribbean.* New York: Praeger.

————. 1991b. "The Military and the Politics of Change in Guyana," *Journal of Interamerican Studies and World Affairs* 33 (Summer): 141–173.

————. 1990. "The Quest for Security in the English-Speaking Caribbean," *Caribbean Affairs* 3 (April-June): 68–76.

Heine, Jorge, ed. 1991. *A Revolution Aborted: The Lessons of Grenada.* Pittsburgh: University of Pittsburgh Press.

Heine, Jorge, and Leslie Manigat, eds. 1988. *The Caribbean and World Politics.* New York: Holmes and Meier.

Henry, Paget, and Carl Stone, eds. 1983. *The Newer Caribbean: Decolonization, Democracy, and Development.* Philadelphia: Institute for the Study of Human Issues.

Holsti, Kalevi J. 1991. *Peace and War: Armed Conflicts and International Order 1648–1989.* Cambridge: Cambridge University Press.

Honychurch, Lennox. 1984. *The Dominica Story.* 2d edition. Roseau, Dominica: The Dominica Institute.

Hudson, Rex A. 1989. "Strategic and Regional Security Perspectives." In Meditz and Hanratty, eds., *Islands in the Commonwealth Caribbean.* Washington, D.C.: Library of Congress.

Jackson, Rashleigh. 1980. *The International Question.* Georgetown, Guyana: People's National Congress.

Kaufman, Michael. 1985. *Jamaica under Michael Manley.* London: Zed Books.

Kent, Mary Day. 1991. "Panama: Protecting the United States' Backyard." In Joseph Gerson and Bruce Birchard, eds., *The Sun Never Sets.* Boston: South End Press.

Lacey, Terry. 1977. *Violence and Politics in Jamaica: 1960–1970.* London: Frank Cass.

Lewis, Gary. 1986. "Prospects for a Regional Security System in the Eastern Caribbean," *Millennium: Journal of International Studies* 15 (No. 1): 73–90.

Lewis, Gordon K. 1985. "Some Reflections on the Leading Intellectual Currents That Have Shaped the Caribbean Experience: 1950–1984," *Cimarrón* 1 (Spring): 23–40.

Lewis, Vaughan A. 1991. "Small States, Eastern Caribbean Security, and the Grenada Intervention." In Heine, *A Revolution Aborted: The Lessons of Grenada.* Pittsburgh: University of Pittsburgh Press.

Levitt, Kari. 1988. "Canada and the Caribbean: An Assessment." In Heine and Manigat, *The Caribbean and World Politics.* New York: Holmes and Meier.

Lijphart, Arend. 1991. "Size, Pluralism, and the Westminster Model of Democracy: Implications for the Eastern Caribbean." In Heine, *A Revolution Aborted: The Lessons of Grenada.* Pittsburgh: University of Pittsburgh Press.

MacDonald, Scott D. 1988. *Dancing on a Volcano: The Latin-American Drug Trade.* New York: Praeger.

MacFarlane, Neil. 1989. "Intervention and Regional Security." *Adelphi Papers No. 196.* London: International Institute for Strategic Studies.

Maingot, Anthony. 1988. "Laundering the Gains of the Drug Trade: Miami and Caribbean Tax Havens," *Journal of Inter-american Studies and World Affairs* 30 (Summer-Fall): 167–187.

———. 1985. "Security Perspectives of Governing Elites in the English-Speaking Caribbean." *Essays on Strategy and Diplomacy No. 4.* Riverside, CA: Keck Center for International Strategic Studies.

———. 1983. "Cuba and the Commonwealth Caribbean: Playing the Cuba Card." In Barry Levine, ed., *The New Cuban Presence in the Caribbean.* Boulder, CO: Westview Press.

Manderson-Jones, R.B. 1990. *Jamaican Foreign Policy in the Caribbean 1962–1988.* Kingston, Jamaica: Caricom Publishers.

Manigat, Leslie. 1988. "The Setting: Crisis, Ideology, and Geopolitics." In Heine and Manigat, *The Caribbean and World Politics.* New York: Holmes and Meier.

Manigat, Mirlande. 1988. "Brazil and the Caribbean." In Heine and Manigat, *The Caribbean and World Politics.* New York: Holmes and Meier.

Maniruzzerman, Talukder. 1982. "The Security of Small States in the Third World." *Canberra Papers on Strategy and Defense No. 25.* Canberra, Australia: Strategic and Defense Studies Center.

Mars, Perry. 1992. "Foreign Influence and Political Conflict in the Post-Colonial Caribbean." *Working Paper No. 133.* New York: Center for Studies of Social Change, New School for Social Research, March.

———. 1985. "Political Mobilization and Class Struggle in the English-Speaking Caribbean," *Contemporary Marxism* 10: 128–47.

———. 1983. "Destabilization, Foreign Intervention, and Socialist Transformation in the Caribbean," *Transition* 7: 33–54.

Meason, James E. 1988. "War at Sea: Drug Interdiction in the Caribbean," *Journal of Defense and Diplomacy* 6 (No. 6): 7–13.

Meditz, Sandra W., and Dennis M. Hanratty, eds. 1989. *Islands of the Commonwealth Caribbean.* Washington, D.C.: Library of Congress.

Moore, John Norton. 1984. "Grenada and the International Double Standard," *American Journal of International Law* 78 (January): 145–168.

Moorer, Thomas H., and Georges A. Fauriol. 1984 "Caribbean Basin Security." *The Washington Papers/104* Vol. XI.

Nordlinger, Eric. 1977. *Soldiers in Politics.* Englewood Cliffs, NJ: Prentice Hall.

Pantin, Raoul. 1990. "Black Power on the Road: Portrait of a Revolution," *Caribbean Affairs* 3 (January-March): 171–185.

Payne, Anthony. 1991. "The Foreign Policy of the People's Revolutionary Government." In Heine, *A Revolution Aborted: The Lessons of Grenada.* Pittsburgh: University of Pittsburgh Press.

Perry, William and Peter Wehner, eds. 1985. *The Latin American Policies of U.S. Allies.* New York: Praeger.

Peters, Donald C. 1992. *The Democratic System in the Eastern Caribbean.* Westport, CT: Greenwood Press.

Phillips, Dion E. 1991. "Terrorism and Security in the Caribbean: The 1976 Cubana Disaster off Barbados," *Terrorism* 14 (No. 4): 209–19.

———. 1988. "The Creation, Structure and Training of the Barbados Defense Force," *Caribbean Studies* 21 (January-June): 124–157.

———. 1985. "Caribbean Militarization: A Response to the Crisis," *Contemporary Marxism* 10: 92–109.

Phillips, Fred. 1985. *West Indian Constitutions: Post-Independence Reforms.* New York: Oceana Publishers.

Pollard, Duke. 1987. *The Problem of Drug Abuse in Commonwealth Caribbean Countries.* Georgetown: Caricom Secretariat.

———. 1977. "The Guyana-Surinam Boundary Dispute in International Law." In Leslie Manigat, ed., *The Caribbean Yearbook of International Relations 1976.* St. Augustine, Trinidad: Institute of International Relations.

Rodríguez Beruff, Jorge. 1989. "U.S. Caribbean Policy and Regional Militarization." In Augusto Varas, ed., *Hemispheric Security and U.S. Policy in Latin America.* Boulder, CO: Westview Press.

———. 1985. "Puerto Rico and the Militarization of the Caribbean, 1979–1984," *Contemporary Marxism* 10: 68–91.

Rodríguez Beruff, Jorge, J. Peter Figueroa, and J. Edward Greene, eds., 1991. *Conflict, Peace, and Development in the Caribbean.* London: Macmillan.

Rolle, Ena Mae. 1990. "The Royal Bahamas Defense Force: The Formative Years," *Royal Bahamas Defense Force Magazine* (Tenth Anniversary Special Issue): 14–22.

Ronfeldt, David. 1983. *Geopolitics, Security, and U.S. Strategy in the Caribbean Basin.* Rand Corporation, R–2997-AF/FC, November.

Rothstein, Robert L. 1986. "The Security Dilemma and the 'Poverty Trap' in the Third World," *Jerusalem Journal of International Relations* 8 (No. 4): 1–38.

RSS Staff. 1986. "The Roles of the Regional Security System in the East Caribbean," *Bulletin of Eastern Caribbean Affairs* 11 (January-February): 5–7.

Ryan, Selwyn. 1991. *The Muslimeen Grab for Power: Race, Religion, and Revolution in Trinidad and Tobago.* Port of Spain, Trinidad: Imprint Caribbean.

Sanders, Ronald. 1990a. "Narcotics, Corruption, and Development: The Problems in the Smaller Islands," *Caribbean Affairs* 3 (January-March): 79–92.

———. 1990b. "The Drug Problem: Social and Economic Effects—Policy Options for the Caribbean," *Caribbean Affairs* 3 (July-September): 18–28.

Sayigh, Yezid. 1990. "Confronting the 1990s: Security in the Developing Countries."

Adelphi Papers No. 251. London: International Institute for Strategic Studies.

Schoultz, Lars. 1987. *National Security and United States Policy towards Latin America*. Princeton: Princeton University Press.

Searwar, Lloyd. 1992. "The Caribbean Conundrum." In Thomas G. Weiss and James G. Blight, eds., *The Suffering Grass: Superpowers and Regional Conflict in Southern Africa and the Caribbean*. Boulder, CO: Lynne Rienner.

———. 1987. *"Peace, Development, and Security in the Caribbean Basin: Perspectives to the Year 2000."* Report No. 4, Canadian Institute for International Peace and Security.

Sedoc-Dahlberg, Betty. 1986. "Interest Groups and the Military in Surinam." In Young and Phillips, *Militarization in the Non-Hispanic Caribbean*. Boulder, CO: Lynne Rienner.

Serbín, Andrés. 1991. "The Caricom States and the Group of Three: A New Partnership between Latin-American and the Non-Hispanic Caribbean?" *Journal of Interamerican Studies and World Affairs* 33 (Summer): 53–80.

———. 1990. *Caribbean Geopolitics: Toward Security through Peace?* Boulder, CO: Lynne Rienner.

———. 1989. "Race and Politics: Relations Between the English-speaking Caribbean and Latin America," *Caribbean Affairs* 2 (April-June): 146–71.

Shah, Rafique. 1971. "The Military Crisis in Trinidad and Tobago during 1970." In Trevor Munroe and Rupert Lewis, eds., *Readings in Government and Politics in the West Indies*. Kingston, Jamaica: University of the West Indies.

Simmons, David. 1985. "Militarization in the Caribbean: Concerns for National and Regional Security," *International Journal* 40 (Spring): 348–76.

Stone, Carl. 1991. "Whither Caribbean Socialism? Grenada, Jamaica, and Guyana in Perspective." In Heine, *A Revolution Aborted: The Lessons of Grenada*. Pittsburgh: University of Pittsburgh Press.

———. 1986. *Power in the Caribbean Basin*. Philadelphia, PA: Institute for the Study of Human Issues.

Sutton, Paul, ed. 1991. *Europe and the Caribbean*. London: Macmillan.

Tow, William T. 1990. *Subregional Security Cooperation in the Third World*. Boulder, CO: Lynne Rienner.

Vayrynen, Raimo. 1984. "Regional Conflict Formation: An Intractable Problem of International Relations," *Journal of Peace Research* 21 (No. 4): 337–59.

Watson, Hilbourne. 1991. "Coalition Security Development: Military Industrial Restructuring in the U.S. and Military Electronics Production in the Caribbean," *Caribbean Studies* 24 (January-June): 223–47.

Will, W. Marvin. 1991. "A Nation Divided: The Quest for Caribbean Integration," *Latin American Research Review* 26 (No. 2): 3–37.

Young, Alma H. 1991. "The Territorial Dimension of Caribbean Security: The Case of Belize." In Griffith, *Strategy and Security in the Caribbean*. New York: Praeger.

Young, Alma H., and Dion E. Phillips, eds. 1986. *Militarization in the Non-Hispanic Caribbean*. Boulder, CO: Lynne Rienner.

Government and Other Documents

Blom-Cooper, Louis. 1990. *Guns for Antigua: Report of the Commission of In-*

quiry into the Circumstances Surrounding the Shipment of Arms from Israel to Antigua and Trans-shipment on 24 April 1989 en route to Colombia. London: Duckworth.

Caribbean Development Bank. 1992. *Annual Report 1991.* Bridgetown, Barbados, May.

CARICOM Secretariat. 1991. *Final Communiqué—Twelfth Meeting of the Conference of Heads of Government of the Caribbean Community.* Basseterre, St. Kitts-Nevis, 2–4 July, CARICOM Press Release No. 54/1991.

———. 1990. *Report of the Third Meeting of the High Level Ad Hoc Group on the Regional Drug Program.* REP. 90/3/34 RDP, October 3.

Government Of Barbados. 1991. *Remarks by the Right Honorable L. Erskine Sandiford, M.P., Prime Minister, to a Meeting of Chiefs of Staff of Member States of the Caribbean Community.* St. Anns' Fort, Barbados, June 4.

Government of the Bahamas. Ministry of Foreign Affairs. 1992. *Bahamas Narcotics Control Report.* Nassau, the Bahamas, March.

———. Ministry of National Security. 1991. *Summary Report on the Traffic in Narcotic Drugs Affecting the Bahamas in 1990.* Nassau, the Bahamas, March.

———. 1990. *Summary Report on the Traffic in Narcotic Drugs Affecting the Bahamas in 1989.* Nassau, the Bahamas.

———. 1984. *Report of the Commission of Inquiry into the Illegal Use of The Bahamas for the Transshipment of Dangerous Drugs Destined for the United States.* Nassau, the Bahamas, December.

Government of Guyana. Ministry of Foreign Affairs. 1981a. *Documents on the Territorial Integrity of Guyana.* Georgetown, Guyana.

———. Ministry of Foreign Affairs. 1981b. *Memorandum on the Guyana/Venezuela Boundary.* Georgetown, Guyana.

———. Ministry of External Affairs. 1969. *Friendship with Integrity.* Georgetown, Guyana.

Government of Jamaica. Parliament. 1992. *Presentation by the Honorable K.D. Knight, Minister of National Security and Justice, Parliamentary Sectoral Debate,* June 10.

———. Ministry of Justice. 1991a. *Crime and Justice in the Caribbean: Keynote Address by the Honorable R. Carl Rattray, Q.C., Minister of Justice and Attorney General.* Kingston, Jamaica, May 10.

———. 1991b. *Memorandum Submitted by the Government of Jamaica on the Establishment of Regional Training Center for Drug Law Enforcement Officers in Jamaica.* Kingston, Jamaica.

Government of Trinidad and Tobago. 1991. *Address by the Honorable A.N.R. Robinson, Regional Conference on Security, Subversion, and National Security.* Port of Spain, Trinidad, May 31.

———. Parliament. 1990. *Speaking Notes for Dr. the Honorable Sahadeo Basdeo, Minister of External Affairs and International Trade on the Trinidad and Tobago-Venezuela Maritime Boundary Agreement.* Trinidad and Tobago House of Assembly, June 18.

———. 1974. *Report of the Caribbean Task Force.* Port of Spain, Trinidad, February.

Government of Venezuela. Ministry of Foreign Relations. 1981. *Summary of the Boundary Question with British Guiana, now Guyana.* Caracas, Venezuela.

United Nations. General Assembly. 1990. *Political Declaration*, XVIIth Special Assembly, Doc. A/RES/S–17/2, March 15.

U.S. Congress. House. Select Committee on Narcotics Abuse and Control. 1989. *Drugs and Latin America: Economic and Political Impact and U.S. Policy Options.* Report of the Seminar held by the Congressional Research Service, 101st Congress, 1st Session, April 26.

————. Committee on Merchant Marine and Fisheries. 1989. *Strategic Importance of the Panama Canal.* Hearing, Subcommittee on Panama Canal/Outer Continental Shelf, 101st Congress, 1st Session, November 2.

————. Committee on Foreign Affairs. 1985. *Soviet Posture in the Western Hemisphere.* Hearings, Subcommittee on Western Hemisphere Affairs, 99th Congress, 1st Session, February.

————. Committee on Foreign Affairs. 1985. *The English-Speaking Caribbean: Current Conditions and Implications for U.S. Policy.* Report by the Congressional Research Service for the Subcommittee on Western Hemisphere Affairs, 99th Congress, 1st Session, September 13.

U.S. Congress. Senate. Committee on Governmental Affairs. 1991 *Arms Trafficking, Mercenaries, and Drug Cartels.* Hearing. Permanent Subcommittee on Investigations, 101st Congress, 1st Session, February 27 and 28.

————. Committee on the Judiciary and the Caucus on International Narcotics Control. 1991. *U.S. International Drug Policy—Multilateral Strike Forces—Drug Policy in the Andean Nations.* Joint Hearings, 101st Congress, 1st and 2nd Sessions, November 6 (1989), January 18, and March 27 (1990).

————. Committee on Foreign Relations. 1989. *Drug Money Laundering, Banks, and Foreign Policy.* Report by the Subcommittee on Narcotics, Terrorism, and International Operations, 101st Congress, 2nd Session, September 27, October 4, and November 1.

————. Committee on Foreign Relations. 1988. *International Narcotics Control and Foreign Assistance Certification: Requirements, Procedures, Timetables, and Guidelines.* Report Prepared by the Congressional Research Service, 101st Congress, 2nd Session, March.

U.S. Defense Security Assistance Agency. 1988. *Foreign Military Sales, Foreign Military Construction Sales, and Military Assistance Facts as of September 30, 1990.* Washington, D.C.

U.S. Department of Defense. 1991. *Office of the Secretary of Defense, Defense Agencies, and DOD Field Activities Organizations and Functions Handbook.* Washington. D.C., April.

U.S. Department of State. 1992. *International Narcotics Control Strategy Report.* Washington, D.C.: March.

U.S. Department of State and Defense Security Assistance Agency. 1991. *Congressional Presentation for Security Assistance, Fiscal Year 1992.* Washington, D.C.

U.S. Drug Enforcement Administration. 1989. *Drugs of Abuse.* Washington, D.C.: Government Printing Office.

West Indian Commission. 1992. *Time For Action: The Report of the West Indian Commission.* Black Rock, Barbados.

———— 1991. *Reaching for the Future—A Timely Trilogy.* Occasional Paper No. 2. St. James, Barbados.

————. 1990. *Let All Ideas Contend.* St. James, Barbados.

Journals and Newspapers

American Banker (USA)
American Journal of International Law (USA)
Army Quarterly and Defense Journal (UK)
Belizean Studies (Belize)
Bulletin of Eastern Caribbean Affairs (Barbados)
Caribbean Affairs (Trinidad & Tobago)
Caribbean and West Indian Chronicle (UK)
Caribbean Contact (Barbados)
Caribbean Insight (UK)
Caribbean Issues (Trinidad & Tobago)
Caribbean Studies (Puerto Rico)
Caribbean Update (USA)
Caricom Bulletin (Guyana)
Caricom Perspective (Guyana)
Cimarrón (USA)
Contemporary Marxism (USA)
Conflict Studies (UK)
Courier (Belgium)
Current History (USA)
Daily Express (Trinidad and Tobago)
Daily Gleaner (Jamaica)
Daily Nation (Barbados)
Daily News (United States Virgin Islands)
Defense (USA)
EC [Eastern Caribbean] News (Barbados)
Economist (UK)
Facts on File (USA)
Financial Times (UK)
Foreign Affairs (USA)
Green Beret (Guyana)
Grenada Tribune (Grenada)
Guyana Chronicle (Guyana)
International Interactions (USA)
International Journal (UK)
International Security (USA)
International Studies Quarterly (USA)
Jamaican Weekly Gleaner (Jamaica)
Jane's Defense Weekly (UK)
Jerusalem Journal of International Relations (Israel)
Journal of Defense and Diplomacy (USA)
Journal of Interamerican Studies and World Affairs (USA)
Journal of Peace Research (UK)
Latin American Research Review (USA)
Latin American Weekly Report (UK)
Latin Finance (USA)
Millennium: Journal of International Studies (UK)

NACLA Report on the Americas (USA)
New Nation (Guyana)
New York Carib News (USA)
New York Times (USA)
New York University Journal of International Law and Politics (USA)
Political Science Quarterly (USA)
PS: Political Science and Politics (USA)
Review of International Studies (UK)
Roraima (Guyana)
Royal Bahamas Defense Force Magazine (Bahamas)
SAIS Review (USA)
San Juan Star (Puerto Rico)
Scarlet Beret (Guyana)
Stabroek News (Guyana)
Sunday Advocate (Barbados)
Sunday Chronicle (Guyana)
Sunday Gleaner (Jamaica)
Sunday Guardian (Trinidad and Tobago)
Sunday Sun (Barbados)
Survival (UK)
Transafrica Forum (USA)
Transition (Guyana)
Trinidad Express (Trinidad and Tobago)
Trinidad Guardian (Trinidad and Tobago)
Voice (St. Lucia)
World Development (UK)

NAME INDEX

SUBJECT INDEX

ABOUT THE AUTHOR

Ivelaw L. Griffith teaches Political Science at Lehman College of The City University of New York. His major research interests are security and foreign policy problems of developing countries, especially those in the Caribbean. He has contributed to several volumes, including *Strategy and Security in the Caribbean,* which he edited, *The Caribbean in the Pacific Century,* and *Paz y Conflictos en el Caribe.* He also has published in *Caribbean Affairs, Conflict Quarterly, Journal of Commonwealth and Comparative Politics, Journal of Interamerican Studies and World Affairs,* and *The Round Table.*